FR. VICTOR

THE STORY OF JUNG'S

'WHITE RAVEN'

FR. VICTOR WHITE, O.P.
THE STORY OF
JUNG'S
'WHITE RAVEN'

Clodagh Weldon

University of Scranton Press
Scranton and London

Library of Congress Cataloging-in-Publication Data
(Has been applied for but is not available at time of publication.)

Distribution:
The University of Scranton Press
Chicago Distribution Center
11030 S. Langley
Chicago, IL 60628

PRINTED IN THE UNITED STATES OF AMERICA

Dedication

ceol mo bheatha

Contents

Acknowledgements

I am grateful to the late Victor White O.P. who, as a theologian, opened up for me the riches of the Dominican intellectual tradition engaged in dialogue with fields of secular knowledge. I would like to thank Charles Brock, who introduced me to the work of C.G. Jung; my godfather, the late Fr. Peter Allen, who first sent me copies of Victor White's books; and Paul Parvis, formerly of the Order of Preachers, who suggested to me that more work needed to be done on Victor White. To those who have made significant contributions to the study of Victor White and C.G. Jung—in particular James Arraj, Adrian Cunningham, John P. Dourley, Ann Lammers, Aidan Nichols O.P. and Murray Stein—I extend my warm appreciation.

A debt of gratitude is owed to The English Province of the Order of Preachers. In particular, I am grateful to Dermot Morrin, O.P., who first introduced me to the Dominicans at Oxford, and encouraged me to study at Blackfriars Hall; to Fergus Kerr O.P., Philip Kennedy, O.P., and Brian Davies O.P. who read earlier drafts of this work; to Martin Robindra Ganeri O.P. for his help in the archives; to Bede Bailey O.P., Archivist of the English Province of the Order of Preachers, who allowed me unrestricted access to the Victor White material in the Archives of the English Province of the Order of Preachers in Edinburgh, and who, during many visits to the archives, gave freely of his time to assist me in my research; and to Allan White, O.P., Provincial for the English Province of the Order of Preachers, who granted permission to use archival materials, including unpublished documents and photographs.

To those in the Order who knew Victor White and took the time to engage in private written correspondence with me, I extend my sincere gratitude. In particular, I would like to thank: Fr. Bede Bailey, O. P., the late Fr. Adrian Dowling, O. P., Fr. Edmund Hill, O. P., the late Fr. Gerard Meath, O. P, and the late Fr. Stanislaus Parker, O. P. Several Dominicans spoke with me at length about

White, and I am especially appreciative of the time, memories, and insights of Fr. Bede Bailey, O.P., the late Br. Kevin Lloyd, O. P, the late Herbert McCabe, O. P., the late Fr. Matthew Rigney, O. P., and Fr. Columba Ryan, O. P. I am also grateful to Timothy McDermott, formerly of the Order of Preachers, who spent time in conversation with me; and to John Giannini, formerly of the Order of Preachers (now at C. G. Jung Institute, Chicago) who shared with me his memories of White in the mid-1950s at St. Albert's House of Studies in Oakland, CA.

Keith Ward, Regius Professor of Divinity Emeritus at the University of Oxford, offered significant guidance and many rigorous critiques of earlier drafts of this work. I am grateful to have had the privilege of studying with such a brilliant theologian, and remain indebted to him as a teacher and advisor. I am also grateful to Oxford Jungian analyst Petrina Morris who helped me to consider Jung's views on alchemy, and to two distant relatives of White, Douglas W. Smith and David White, who engaged in private written correspondence and provided significant genealogical and biographical details of Victor White.

The generosity of Dominican University in awarding a research grant for the summer of 2005, allowed me to return, once again, to the Archives of the English Dominican Province in Edinburgh. In addition, I am grateful to Jeffrey Carlson, Dean of the Rosary College of Arts & Sciences, for granting me a one course release in the Fall of 2005 to work on this book, and to my colleagues in the department of Theology. Kitty Rhoades and Molly Beestrum of the Rebecca Crown Library at Dominican University, and Tania Mann, student worker for the Department of Theology and Pastoral Ministry, offered invaluable assistance with the bibliography.

Jeff Gainey, Patricia Mecadon, and the staff at the University of Scranton Press far exceeded my expectations in their enthusiasm for and dedication to this project. I am especially grateful to my reviewer, David Burrell C.S.C. of the University of Notre Dame and my copyeditor John Hunckler.

Finally, I would like to thank my parents, who nurtured in me a love of God and a love of learning; and my husband, Tim, whose love helped me to complete this work.

Introduction

This book is about the English Dominican theologian Fr. Victor White, O. P. (1902–1960). In particular, it is a study of the impact of analytical psychology on his life and theology. As a young theologian thoroughly grounded in Aquinas, and living in the milieu of neo-scholastic Blackfriars Oxford, White fell under the influence of the analytical psychology of the Swiss psychiatrist C. G. Jung (1875–1961). The impact was life altering. Spurred by a passionate personal interest, White became very well versed in Jung's psychology—so well versed, in fact, that prominent analytical psychologists applauded his work as superior to that of many psychologists.[1] Jung recognized this, hailing White as the "only" theologian to truly understand him, and pinning great hopes on him for the transformation of the Western God image.[2] As a relationship developed, Jung appointed White as a founding member of the C. G. Jung Institute in Zurich, and in a manner akin to Freud's "crowning" of Jung as prince of the psychoanalytic movement, Jung expressed the hope that Victor White would be his successor. Although their relationship ultimately foundered over a dispute about evil and its transference onto God, White's was one of the first attempts from a Catholic perspective to consider the impact of Jung on theology. Like Aquinas in his day, White was open to new ideas, re-casting Thomism in the terms of contemporary thought and assimilating what he found of truth into his theology.[3] In these pages, I hope to provide an exposition and an interpretation of the main features of White's theology in what is—to the best of my knowledge—the first sustained account of his life and work.

He has been described as "a theologian of considerable power,"[4] and was extolled in 1960 as "an important factor in contemporary English theology."[5] But the paucity of scholarly literature on Victor White is astounding. The first published scholarly interest in White— to exceed a cursory paragraph or a footnote—was an article written

1

in 1981 by Adrian Cunningham, "Victor White and C. G. Jung: The Fateful Encounter of the White Raven and the Gnostic."[6] The article gave a preliminary exploration of White's theological interests and focused in particular on the question of evil which dominated and eventually devastated the Jung–White discussion in the late 1940s and early 50s. White's response to Jung's *Answer to Job* received several pages of attention in Edward Edinger's *The Creation of Consciousness* (bibliog. 1.1, 1984), and two books by Murray Stein—*Jung's Treatment of Christianity* (bibliog. 1.1, 1986) and *Jung on Christianity* (bibliog. 1.1, 1995)—also devoted several pages to the Jung–White relationship.[7] James Arraj's 1988 "Jungian Spirituality: The Question of Victor White" presented an overview of the problems which bedeviled White and Jung, and suggested that a spirituality which distinguished between faith and individuation would resolve White's either/or tension and allow an individual to be both Jungian and Catholic.[8]

A less optimistic approach is seen in a 1990 article, "A Dialogue between Psychology and Theology: The Correspondence of C. G. Jung and Victor White, O. P." by F. X. Charet. In it, he summarized Jung's key works on evil and God, focusing on Jung's side of the correspondence, and concluded that the failure of the Jung–White dialogue leads to a rejection of traditional Catholicism as a potential partner in Jungian–Christian dialogue.[9] This theme was also espoused in several of John Dourley's articles on Jung, White, and Martin Buber. Dourley's argument is that the Jung–White dialogue was an "exercise in futility," because White was committed to a theology of transcendence which, from Jung's perspective, is precisely that which "uproots" a human being from "the divine vitalities of its depths," precluding any experience of the "God within" which is so necessary to healing.[10] Also appearing in 1992, Adrian Cunningham's article, "Victor White, John Layard, and C. G. Jung," offered some further insight into the complex relationships between White, White's analyst, and Jung.[11]

The first book-length work to deal with White, at least in a partial way, was Ann Conrad Lammers' *In God's Shadow: The Collaboration of Victor White and C. G. Jung* (bibliog. 1.1). The book's focus is collaboration, and it is primarily (though not exclusively) concerned with the questions of evil and God. Consequently, little attention was given to the vast array of White's publications, not to mention a significant body of unpublished work. Deirdre Bair's recent biography of Jung, *Jung: A Biography* (bibliog. 1.1), devoted five pages to the relationship between White and Jung, also focusing on the dispute regarding evil and God.[12] More recently, two pamphlets published by The Guild of Pastoral Psychology have continued to probe the Jung–White relationship: Murray Stein's "The Rôle of Victor White In C. G. Jung's Writings" (bibliog. 1.1, 2004) argued that Jung saw White as "a symbol of the western malaise" and that this was the catalyst that led to Jung's *Answer to Job*; and Ann Lammers explored the feminine and evil in "The Missing Fourth in the Jung–White Letters" (bibliog. 1.1, 2005).

Finally, Aidan Nichols' *Dominican Gallery: Portrait of a Culture* (bibliog. 1.1, 1997) was the first and only work to address White as a significant twentieth-century Dominican theologian distinct from Jung. For Nichols, White—one sketch in his gallery of seven great Dominican theologians—is significant in himself, yet part of a common culture.[13] Essentially, the chapter on White is a brief outline of his life and a summary of his better-known works.

Although there has been some scholarly interest in Victor White, with the exception of Nichols' work, the interest has been primarily on his relationship and collaboration with Jung and not on White's theology *per se*. This book, therefore, addresses the neglect and intends to fill that void by providing the first sustained work on the life and theology of Victor White. Many of the sources for this book receive their first attention here, in this work. In addition to White's books *God and the Unconscious* (bibliog. 1.4, 1952), *God the Unknown* (bibliog. 1.4, 1956) and *Soul and Psyche: An Enquiry Into The Relationship of Psychiatry and Religion* (bibliog. 1.4, 1960), I have discovered a multitude of book reviews and over eighty published articles from which I have compiled the first comprehensive bibliography of Victor White. Furthermore, the research for this book took me to the *Archives of the English Province of the Order of Preachers* in Edinburgh where the Provincial Archivist, Fr. Bede Bailey, O. P., allowed me unrestricted access to the Victor White material. In the course of my research, I produced a catalogue of some ten boxes of unpublished lectures, manuscripts, letters, photographs, diaries, and dream journals of

Victor White. Included in this are copies of the unpublished letters of Victor White to C. G. Jung, (which are currently being edited by Adrian Cunningham and Ann Lammers). This book is the first work to take into account this vast wealth of unpublished material and, therefore, offers the most complete study to date of Victor White's life and theology. Finally, I gleaned valuable biographical information from two of White's distant cousins, and interviewed and engaged in correspondence with a dozen Dominicans and former Dominicans who were either contemporaries or students of Victor White.[14] This information provided me with an invaluable entry into the life of the Dominican Order and allowed me to capture something of the history and milieu of White's day in a way that library and archival research alone could not.

As White's theology is so intricately bound up with the situation of his day and the events of his life, I have deliberately chosen to explore the impact of Jung on White's theology within the structure of the narrative of his life. In the first chapter, therefore, I offer an overview of the more significant stages of White's hitherto undocumented early life, and try to recapture something of the religious (and particularly Dominican) climate in which he found himself and which influenced his theological interests in the 1930s. Such a preliminary chapter is important because it further facilitates an understanding of the dramatic nature of the impact of Jung's psychology—in such a climate—on White's theology.

Chapter Two deals with White's awakening to the ideas of Jung, his fascination with these ideas, and his early consideration of how Jung might be read, assimilated, and recast in relation to Thomistic theology. I attempt to show how White's own theology arose in response to, and was shaped by, the impact of some of the central tenets of Jung's psychology. In addition, I highlight some potentially problematic issues which Jung's psychology immediately raised for White's Thomistic theology—especially, transcendence and immanence and the distinctly religious nature of Jung's language.

Chapter Three traces the development of Jung's impact on White which, by 1945, prompted White to initiate a written correspondence with Jung (bibliog. 1.3 and bibliog. 2.2). I explore Jung's hope that White would be instrumental in the transformation of the Western God image, and the impact that such a hope had on the young

Victor White. Further, I probe the plausibility of such a hope in relation to Jung's methodology, and examine White's attempts to read Aquinas *through* Jung by looking at some of the following theological issues: revelation, faith and knowledge, transcendence and immanence, analysis and confession, and worship. In highlighting some of the deficiencies of Jung's psychology—a significant element of Jung's impact on White—I show a more definite methodology of "supplementation" in relation to Jung which further exposes key aspects of White's theology.

In Chapter Four I consider the impact on White of Jung's understanding of evil; Chapter Five is an exploration of the theological and personal issues raised for White by Jung's inclusion of evil in the God image. Other issues discussed include White's attempt to critically appropriate Jungian ideas into his theology, and to synthesize the universal with the particular as evidenced in his work on the doctrines of Mary and on the dying God.

Chapter Six explores the continuing impact of Jung on White following their split over Jung's *Answer to Job* (bibliog. 1.2). It evinces the formulation of a more explicit method in White's theology, namely his appropriation of the discoveries of C. G. Jung in relation to what they disclose about the needs of the psyche, and the articulation of Catholicism as the answer to those needs. By the late 1950s, White's theology (both dogmatic and sacramental) is characterized by this predominant theme of the healing power of God's revelation through the Catholic Church.

The concluding chapter offers a brief summary of the impact of analytical psychology as it manifested itself during the different stages of White's life, followed by an analysis of the neo-scholastic climate and the basic theological presuppositions of White as they relate to the scope of Jung's impact. Finally, this chapter critically assesses White's contributions to the history of twentieth-century English theology.

Thomas Gilby, O. P., once summed up White's life and theology in the words of St. Augustine, "Deum et animam scire cupio": I desire to know God and the soul.[15] This was White's passion, his quest, his life. My hope is that—in bringing to light his theology and, in particular, the impact of Jung's psychology on his theology—I have done justice to this remarkable man.

ONE
1902–1940

1902–1922

Gordon Henry White was born in South Croydon on October 21, 1902.[1] His father, John Henry, had married Beatrice Mary at St. Peter's on June 4, 1901, and, when Gordon was born, they moved to 39 Avondale Road. Like the man who would later have such an impact on his life, Carl Gustav Jung, White also came from a family of clergymen. Jung's father was a minister of the Swiss Reformed tradition, White's a high church Anglican vicar.[2] "At St. Augustine's in South Croydon the very ritualistic John [sic] White in 1908 and 1909 was severely criticized by several of his congregation for, amongst other things, introducing a cope into church, wearing a biretta, having a Sanctus bell and holding views favourable to intercessory prayers."[3] Imbued with ritual and symbol from an early age, White was prepared to be receptive to Jung's work long before he encountered it. This receptivity can also be seen in his fascination, as a boy, with the stories of pagan and Christian mysteries—and with the similarities between them. As with Jung, such stories did not promote his skepticism (as they had with Freud), but rather, impressed upon White a deep sense that human beings are by nature religious:

> . . . I remember when, as a boy, I read one of those books published by the Rationalist Press, it had just the opposite effect on me to that intended. The Christian Scriptures and the Catholic rites to which I was accustomed, without losing their wonted sense, gained a quality and a sense of which my pastors and catechisms had told me nothing: a sense of solidarity with creation, with the processes of nature, with the cycles of the seasons. Dramatisations of the processes of

vegetation they might be, but had not Christ himself drawn the analogy between the Christian self-sacrifice and the grain of wheat which must die if it is to bear fruit? Moreover, these books gave me a new sense of solidarity with humanity as a whole; whatever else I was doing when I attended Mass, or followed the Church's calendar of fast and feast, I was doing something not entirely different from what men and women of every creed and colour seemed to have been doing since the world began.[4]

As a boy White could scarcely appreciate how his awareness of the existence of universal patterns would, with the impact of Jung's concept of archetypal ideas, dominate his life and thought as a man.

Beyond this, little is known about White's early life. He attended the Limes School in Croydon, by which time his family had relocated to the Vicarage in St. Augustine's Avenue. It was here that his two younger brothers, John Francis Christopher and Basil Philip Dawson, were born,[5] and from here that White went to All Saints' School in Bloxham. Toward the end of his teenage years, White was received into the Catholic Church, and at the age of 19, he left England to train for the priesthood at the English College in Valladolid, Spain.[6] But Valladolid was not meant to be, and a year later, in September 1923, White joined the Dominicans.

The Dominicans

The Order of Preachers (*Ordo Praedicatorum*) offered a life of preaching suffused with study that attracted the young White. It would be a life in community, teaching theology, expounding the faith. Initially he went to Woodchester where he was immersed in the chants and the divine office, and began to study the history of the Order, the lives of the saints, and scripture. It was here that he was clothed as a novice and given the name Victor, and where, on September 30, 1924, he made his profession in the Order (that is, he took simple vows).[7]

Following his profession, White was sent to Staffordshire, to the Priory at Hawkesyard, where he conducted his basic studies under Hugh Pope, O. P., and Luke Walker, O. P., receiving a basic grounding in logic, metaphysics, natural theology, and moral philosophy.[8]

Pope had been a casualty of the anti-modernist regime—in 1913 he was banished from the Angelicum in Rome for a controversial article that he had written on theology and scripture.[9] His treatment was typical of the climate in which White found himself. In 1903, for example, Alfred Loisy's work was put on the Index; in 1906 professors were removed from Italian seminaries over suspicions regarding their orthodoxy; and in 1907 Pius X condemned rebels in the Church in an *Allocutio* to new cardinals.[10] In the same year, the decree *Lamentabili*[11] and the encyclical *Pascendi*[12] appeared, in which Pius X condemned the "doctrine of the modernists." In 1909 came the indictment that Genesis must be read literally,[13] and in 1910, Pius X's anti-modernist oath, by which teachers of theology and philosophy had to swear their loyalty.[14]

It is important to read White against the background of a Church fortifying itself against modernist infiltration. For the modernists, faith seemed to stress experience "at the expense of voluntary intellectual assent" to Church doctrine,[15] and modernists were suspected of holding that religion developed from the need for God in the soul. This meant that the truths of religion changed to meet humanity's changing consciousness.[16] One can see why the impact of Jung on White some years later would rouse anti-modernist suspicions. Jung believed that the God image of the Western psyche, the God within, was moribund and needed to be transformed to include both the shadow side and the feminine—the truths of religion changing to meet humanity's changing consciousness.

Aside from condemnation, the Church also responded with a series of defensive measures. In June 1914, Pius X endorsed Leo XIII's 1879 directive *Aeterni Patris*,[17] decreeing that students were to remain faithful to the doctrines of Thomas Aquinas. Leo XIII had hoped that in reviving the philosophy of Thomas, the Church would have a solid basis "for the refutation of errors,"[18] in particular, the errors of modernism. In reinforcing this, Pius X warned that all teachers of philosophy and sacred theology who "deviated as much as a step" from the teachings of Aquinas "exposed themselves to great risk."[19] Teachers in seminaries were carefully screened, and they were commanded to use the *Summa Theologiae* as *the* text. A month later, in July 1914, the Vatican's Sacred Congregation for Studies put out *Twenty-Four Theses*,[20] which were designed as a summary of Thomas' teachings to which all theologians were required to assent. With the promulgation of The Code of Canon Law in 1917, Pope Benedict XV reinforced that theology and philosophy should be taught in all universities and seminaries according to the thought of Aquinas. This soon degenerated into scholastic manuals, which were the staple diet of many seminaries in Europe.[21] By 1923, Pius XI had declared St. Thomas Aquinas to be the universal doctor of the Church, his philosophy adopted by the Church as her own.[22] And so, in reaffirming Aquinas, for whom faith was not a religious sense but intellectual assent to truth revealed by God, the antidote to the modernists was provided.

Accordingly, it was while at Hawkesyard that White began to work his way systematically through the *Summa* of St. Thomas, just as the directives of canon law required.[23] Bemoaning the malaise in intellectual formation, Columba Ryan, O. P., wrote: "A land of intellectual dust Hawkesyard truly was."[24] After four years there, White was ordained a priest on June 2, 1928, at St. Mary's Oscott.[25] White spent the next year studying for the Licentiate in Sacred Theology (STL) at the Dominican House of Studies at Louvain in northern Belgium, the site of an old Catholic University founded in 1432.[26] It was at Louvain that Leo XIII had, in 1882, established the *Institut Superieur de Philosophie*[27] as a center for the study of the teachings of Thomas Aquinas, with Cardinal Mercier as its president. What is significant about the Louvain school is that they attempted to bring the thought of Aquinas into the modern world. Thomism was considered to be as relevant to the modern world as it was to Thomas' generation, the *philosophia perennis* that should be adapted to counter any philosophy or theology that sought to appropriate modern philosophy.[28] Thus, one can see why Victor White, in appropriating some of the ideas of Carl Gustav Jung, would find himself at odds with the neo-scholastics[29] at Blackfriars Oxford.

Although there were professors there, such as Stanislas Martin Gillet who did read modern psychology,[30] White was dismayed that the only course of study at Louvain was a systematic reading of Aquinas and the commentaries that elucidated it. He was deeply frustrated that Thomas was abstracted from a historical context, and that his concepts were not related to the modern world. To reinterpret Thomas in relation to modern streams of thought would prove to be a major challenge for White, especially with the rear guard of neo-scholastics at Blackfriars Oxford.

Fortunately, his Provincial, Bede Jarrett, O. P., whose vision the Oxford house was, had ideas that corresponded with White's aspirations to dialogue with the modern world. Jarrett had founded the Dominican House of Studies in Oxford on August 15, 1921, exactly seven hundred years after the Dominicans had first arrived in Oxford. His great hope was that it would be a part of the university.[31] On May 4, 1929, the house became a priory, and the community, which included Victor White, moved there on May 29, 1929. Jarrett, eager to bring the philosophical and theological tradition of Aquinas to the concerns of the day, wanted the Dominican community to engage with contemporary scholarship at the university. Accordingly, he appointed lectors who believed that Aquinas was not to be taught by manuals, but rooted in history, art, philosophy, psychology, literature, and culture. Victor White was one of those lectors.

After receiving his Licentiate in Sacred Theology,[32] White began, in 1930, to teach as professor of dogmatic theology; he also found himself teaching moral theology and ecclesiastical history. As a teacher, he was, as his students recall, so very different from most lectors during that highly scholastic period at Hawkesyard:[33]

> And I look back on him now because he rescued us from a kind of dogmatic Thomism—oh which was rife—in the Church and in the Order. And it more or less implied with a very strong implication that nobody had ever written anything about theology before St. Thomas and nobody had ever written anything about theology since—which is rubbish [laughs]. And Victor saved us from all that.[34]

> He kind of shielded us from the dangers of dogmatic Thomism.[35]

> The late Victor White gave me (and indeed the whole English Dominican Province) the reality of Aquinas stripped of the scholastic obfuscations of so much modern Thomism.[36]

> We owe him a great debt because he opened our minds to a living theology that was not easy to find in those days.[37]

> I was taught dogmatic theology by Victor White for two years . . . all I can say about him is how I found him as a lecturer on St. Thomas. And what was so astonishing is that he wasn't deadly boring . . . somehow it was immensely stimulating, an intellectual feast.[38]

However, a rear guard of neo-scholastics remained, suspicious of those—like Victor White—who countenanced a change in the way that Aquinas was studied. Their prevailing fear was that Thomas would be watered down by an encounter with the fields of secular knowledge, a fear that was exacerbated by modernism. As Ryan noted, "The regime from which Victor and others suffered came in on the wave of anti-modernism and you had to be pure full-blooded Thomists without asking any modern-style questions."[39] Any challenge to the received neo-scholasticism was perceived as modernism, as White would later realize. Indeed, the very term "Modernism" was, as Gabriel Daly remarked, "invoked as an incantation" against any interchange with the modern world.[40] Before long, a conservative brand of Thomism was enforced in the Dominican Order, and Blackfriars "was then taken over by the rear guard whose only view was that their gift to the University of Oxford was that they'd teach some true scholastic philosophy."[41] In reality, it meant that there was very little contact with the university, although students had already been forbidden, prior to ordination, to have any participation in secular universities. Students even needed the approval of the student master to read anything other than Aquinas.

The visit of the Master General of the Order, Stanislas Martin Gillet, in 1932, created further problems. He disapproved of the pattern of studies in Oxford, writing to the Provincial Chapter, "In place of the general formation, identical for all our students, provided and laid down in the *Ratio Studiorum*, common to all our *Studia Generalia*, they have prematurely adopted an adaptation of these same studies to the supposed needs of England and the characteristics of the national temperament."[42] Gillet perceived Oxford to be a perilous place, promoting permissiveness of thought among Dominicans. It was, therefore, his desire that the Dominican students would conduct their studies in the sheltered setting of Hawkesyard, away from the nefarious environs of Oxford academe.[43] But it was Bede Jarrett's vision that prevailed, and White remained in Oxford, able to engage with the fields of secular knowledge.

White and the Vision of Thomas

White's first publication in 1932, a pamphlet for the Catholic Truth Society, "Scholasticism," reflected his reaction to the rear guard, and to this climate in which he found himself. Tracing the history of scholasticism, White feared the "tragedy" that the Thomism of his day had "failed sadly to keep pace with, or even in touch with, the progress of secular knowledge."[44] And yet, he argued, it was Aquinas who had shown *all* truth, whether it be found in science or philosophy or revelation, had the same source—the God from whom all truth comes.[45] Within such a framework, White, like Aquinas before him, was open to truth "wherever it presented itself."[46] Indeed White saw it as his own task to build on Aquinas' achievement, suggesting that "it is the aim of the modern Thomist to integrate all modern discoveries and scientific achievements, all that is truly valuable and permanent in post medieval thought, into the Thomistic synthesis, for the good of man and the glory of God: in short to do for our own age what St. Thomas did for his, building on the foundations he laid."[47] In so conceiving his "immense task," White was preparing the framework for his discussion with Jung. White would learn from Jung how religion functioned in the psyche, appropriating what he found to be true, and supplementing it with his theology when he found Jung's thinking deficient. White thought that, if all is from God, then the ideas of the modern world should enrich religion, and religion should enrich modern scholarship.[48] But it would be another ten years before White's encounter with Jung. White's abiding theological interests lay elsewhere in the 1930s.

Ecumenism

It was the subject of ecumenism—promoting dialogue with the Anglican Church into which he had been baptized, and with the Christian East—that dominated White's writings and activities in the 1930s. He was, as Donald MacKinnon noted, "a considerable oecumenist."[49] A strong advocate of the octave of prayer for Christian unity, White was heavily involved in the "Laxton Conversations"—discussions between the Dominicans who ran a school at Laxton, and the Anglican Fathers of the Society of the Sacred Mission. They met regularly to discuss such things as revelation, infallibility, and the development of dogma.[50] From Laxton to Le Saulchoir, the French House of Studies, White represented the English Dominicans for a meeting with Yves Congar and separated Christians in 1938. In fact, it was Victor White who translated Congar's *Chrétiens désunis* (1937) into English—*Divided Christendom* (bibliog. 1.4, 1939).[51]

Socio-political Responsibility

The approaching war marked a shift in White's interests. He became very concerned with the socio-political responsibility of Catholics and in 1940 he wrote several letters to *The Catholic Herald* on this topic.[52] In these letters, White urged all Catholics to put pressure on the government to end the war, and bid them not to co-operate in the direct killing of civilians. True to his character, White was not afraid to speak publicly on these contentious matters.[53] The war deeply troubled him and was to mark the beginning of a difficult stage in White's life.

TWO
1940–1945

The Awakening to C. G. Jung

For Victor White, the 1940s were markedly different from the 1930s. As I showed in Chapter One, White's published concerns in the 1930s were ecumenism, the socio-political responsibility of Catholics (particularly in relation to the ongoing war), and the teachings of Thomas Aquinas.[1] But, after the prolific publishing of this earlier period, something happened to White to curtail his output in the years between 1939 and 1941. Moreover, while his affinity for Thomas continued into the 1940s, it was during this period that a new interest was developing. White was being awakened to the thought of the analytical psychologist Carl Gustav Jung.

What exactly it was that drew a Thomist in neo-scholastic Blackfriars Oxford to this "terrible creature,"[2] the suspiciously viewed Jung—particularly in a climate none too receptive to such thought—remains to be seen. Jung had, in fact, been in Oxford two years before to preside over the International Medical Congress for Psychotherapy, and to receive an honorary doctorate in science from the University, the first ever to be given to a psychologist.[3] But it was not until 1940 that White was actually drawn to Jung's ideas, as he revealed in a letter to John Layard of No. 1 Northmoor Road, Oxford on September 19, 1940. He began: "I am a Catholic priest who has become badly 'stuck.' It is the writings of Dr. Jung that has given me some inkling of what it is I am up against."[4] The philosopher theologian Donald MacKinnon had suggested to White that he meet with Layard[5] who was an anthropologist—and a Jungian analyst,[6] trained by Jung himself. Layard was not a Catholic, though the subsequent correspondence with White would suggest he was well immersed in, and familiar with, the Christian tradition. He and his wife Doris later became Catholics through their association with Fr. Victor.[7]

Further illumination as to White's initial interest in Jung comes from the first of a series of lectures that White gave at the Dominican House of Studies, St. Albert's, in Oakland, California, in 1954. He introduced himself:

> I am by profession a theologian. But I am a theologian to whom, some fourteen years ago, something happened. Suddenly, or perhaps not so suddenly, theology ceased to have any meaning to me at all: I could not get my mind into it, or anything to do with it, except with horror, boredom and loathing. You may imagine that that was quite a serious thing to happen to a theologian. Other theologians and pastors did not seem able at all to help me out of my difficulties. And so I was forced to turn to the psychologists. I had not been particularly interested in psychology up [un]til then, but I had read a certain amount of Freud and Jung, and I did have a hunch that the method and approach of Jung might have something that spoke to my condition.[8]

For Jung, God was a living mystery experienced wholly in the psyche. For White and, indeed, for Jung's father—"how hopelessly he was entrapped by the Church and its theological thinking"[9]— God was utterly transcendent, revealed through Scripture, the tradition of the Church, and reason. As Jung put it, ". . . [my father] believed in God as the Bible prescribed and his fathers had taught him. But he did not know the immediate living God," the God who was "above His Bible and His Church."[10] As a boy Jung was "shaken and outraged" to witness his father tormented by faith and its "arch sin"—that "it forestalled experience" of the God within.[11] Indeed he would later refer to his father's failure to experience "the immediate living God" as the "tragedy of [his] youth."[12] It is significant, therefore, that White's theology was similar to that of Jung's father. In particular it was a theology grounded in Aquinas whose Aristotelian intellectualism was seen by Jung as "more lifeless than desert,"[13] language which resonates with Columba Ryan's assessment of Hawkesyard—the place of White's formation—as "a land of intellectual dust."[14] As Jung saw it, it was precisely this dry intellectualism which was responsible for, and which compounded, "the prejudice that the deity is *outside* man."[15] Jung wrote, "They want to prove a belief to themselves, whereas actually it is a matter of experience."[16] White himself was fully aware of the effects of such an arid intellectualism, writing to Jung in 1945, "Hawkesyard is the place where I received the earlier part of my Dominican training, and doubtless developed many of the 'complications' from which analysis from John Layard, T. Sussman—and a good deal of subsequent attempts at self-analysis—have (I hope) pretty thoroughly delivered me."[17] Some years before he had become "badly 'stuck,'" and long before his encounter with Jung, White had written, "[Religion] must grip and transform the whole individual or it is worthless."[18] Aware of this need to be "gripped" it should be apparent why White, as one for whom theology had lost meaning, had a "hunch" that Jung's psychology spoke to his "condition."

To his analyst, John Layard, White revealed more of his "condition" as a man in turmoil, particularly in relation to his vocation as a Catholic priest and Dominican. He considered leaving the Catholic Church, and, shortly after his first letter to Layard, White did leave Blackfriars for a while,[19] staying with friends near Tatsworth. His Provincial, who at that time was Bernard Delany, O. P.,[20] suggested he go as an escort to South Africa or Australia with evacuees. Both ideas were attractive to White.[21] He also thought about returning to the Anglican Church in which he had been raised, and becoming a priest like his father and his younger brother, John Francis.[22]

But a more plausible option for White revolved around Dom Bede Winslow, O.S.B., of whom White spoke frequently to Layard.[23] Winslow was from St. Augustine's Abbey in Ramsgate, and he sought to establish a new ecumenical order based on the Belgian Benedictine model, Chevetogne, at Amay-sur-Mense. His hope was that Victor White and two Benedictine monks from St. Michael's Abbey in Farnborough would join him. The community would work for the reunion of the Eastern Orthodox and Catholic Churches in a life of prayer and work. They would edit the *Eastern Churches Quarterly*, a journal that Winslow had founded in 1936—and be a model of (and study center for) ecumenism.[24] White considered this very seriously, and Layard encouraged him to make inquiries.[25] This he obviously did, for, by January 1941, White talked of an impending meeting to discuss the Winslow community with the Provincial of the Dominican Order. Anxious about Delany's reaction and about the outcome, White expressed to Layard his great concern before the "fatal interview."[26] In the end, Winslow's proposal came to nothing—but caused great upset, especially at Farnborough.[27] The effect on White and his ongoing turmoil is unclear, though, in a letter he wrote to Layard on February 14, 1941, he was clearly suffering from depression. He viewed his vocation and indeed his life in the often repeated phrase, "of little use to humanity." Victor White had had a nervous breakdown.[28]

So, initially it was White's personal turmoil that drew him to Layard, and, through Layard, to his own experience of Jung's psychology. White had yet to begin a correspondence with Jung himself, but, from the correspondence with Layard during this period, there are signs of White's growing interest in Jungian psychology. Throughout these years of turmoil, he sent his dreams to Layard, and Layard subjected them to Jungian analysis.[29] From the correspondence, it is clear that White engaged with Layard in a capacity that was more than that of a patient or a client. Addressing him as "the Guru," he saw Layard as one from whom he learned and with whom he engaged on matters of psychology and religion. For example, he told Layard of his friend Richard Kehoe, O. P.,[30] a scripture scholar, who was interested in scripture and symbolism, suggesting to Layard that there were remarkable affinities between Jung's technique of dream interpretation and traditional canons of exegesis.[31] He was beginning to consider the impact of Jung's ideas. Furthermore, in a highly significant letter two months later, he wrote to Layard with his dreams of November 4, 5–6, and 7, 1940: "I do believe that my theological studies may yet be of interest and perhaps of some use to you, if only because *the resolution of my own case* [emphasis mine] may yet help to reveal to what extent Jung can be fitted into orthodox R[oman] C[atholic] theology without falling into the heresies of symolismus, immancatismus and the rest which pronounces anathema."[32] Without doubt it can be concluded that it was White's breakdown, and his association with Layard, that led him to the psychology of Jung. As he said in his own words some years later, he was "a dabbler in psychology by fate."[33] By the end of the year, his letters to Layard indicated that White was immersing himself in Jungian literature, and that he was reading Jung's *Golden Flower*.[34] It was a critical turning point in White's life, which made him a pioneer of the frontiers between analytical psychology and Catholic theology.

Potential Rocks Ahead

However, White's initial interest in Jungian psychology was far from the naive embrace some commentators have suggested.[35] The unpublished correspondence with Layard reveals that White was deeply aware of, and anticipated "the difficulties a Jungian must contend with sooner or later in his dealings with R[oman] C[atholic]s."[36] He knew that Christian suspicions of Jung needed to be allayed if there were to be any collaboration with Catholic theology.[37] Furthermore, White was also aware of the "rocks ahead" in relation to the restrictions upon him as a Catholic professor of theology—concerning two issues in particular. The first of these was authority, more specifically "the 'fascist' and 'authoritarian' conception of ecclesiastical authority" which White said he had "been so much up against."[38] Jung had also criticized what he saw as the "totalitarian truth claims" of the Catholic Church, arguing that *each interior experience* of the God image had validity. Consequently, the imposition of claims of absolute truth by an external authority was anathema.[39] Indeed, it was because of this issue of authority that White found it so difficult to go back to Blackfriars to work as a priest and theologian, although he was perplexed as to an alternative. He wrote: "I find myself little inclined to be in a position in which I must hide the light of Jung under a bushel. I feel rather, already, as the cured lepers etc. in the Gospel must have felt when they were charged to tell no man what had been done for them!"[40]

But the Catholic Church did not share White's enthusiasm for Jung, for his psychology looked like the agnosticism of the modernists which they so feared. Like the modernists, Jung also seemed

to stress experience while neglecting voluntary intellectual assent to
Church doctrine, and to hold that religion developed from the need
for God in the human soul. If this were indeed the case, it would
mean that the truths of religion change to meet man's changing consciousness. Thus, one can see why Victor White's interest in
Jung—who looked liked a modernist—would have the potential to
create problems for White regarding ecclesiastical authority. The
subjectivity of one's personal truth, and, with it, the "evolution of
dogmas,"[41] lay in contradiction to the Catholic faith—which holds
that the faith is handed down from the apostles and mediated,
unchanging, by the Church. As Pius X noted, the Church is not a
creature of human consciousness or a product of human effort
destined for progress toward perfection.[42] Furthermore, such
subjectivity—as expressed by the modernists and by Jung—makes
commitment to a religion of authority unpredictable. As a Catholic,
White was committed to the authority of the Church, but he also
appreciated the *emotional* importance of Jung's psychology. His
objection was not to the Church's authority per se but to the political
means by which religious truths were being enforced.

The anti-modernist oath,[43] the second concern that White
expressed to Layard, is such an example of the "fascist" conception
of authority that White was lamenting. White was particularly
disturbed by the stipulation that "one must assent under oath to the
proposition that faith is in no way what it calls an *eruptio subconsci-
entia*,"[44] that it was "not a blind religious sense welling up from the
recesses of the subconscious under the impulse of the heart."[45] This
was the view of the modernists, that man's religious sense is the origin of revelation. For Aquinas, on the other hand, whose position
White espoused, faith was an intellectual assent to a Truth revealed
by God. Although White knew that modernists who saw personal
experience as revelation had to be condemned,[46] his concern was that
the psychic origins of religious experience were being totally neglected. White appreciated that in Catholic theology the immanence
of God had, to a large degree, been neglected, and the transcendence of God exalted (because of the pervading fear of modernism).
But he disagreed with the *overemphasis* on the transcendence of God
stressed by the neo-scholastics as a response to the immanence of
the modernists. Rather, White thought that what was actually

needed was a recovery and an apologetic of immanence. He thought that Jung had something important to contribute here, and this is why he was so concerned about the anti-modernist oath.

White's concerns about his dealings with Jung did not come just from the repressive climate of the Catholic Church. He was equally aware that, theologically, Catholics would have difficulties with some of Jung's ideas. As early as December 1940, White expressed concern that "Jungians, by going beyond their empirical data and making metaphysical and metapsychological affirmations which are not necessarily decided by those data, may lay the foundations for a religion or ersatz religion which, so far from complementing Christianity, may contradict it radically."[47]

As I will show, C. G. Jung was deeply committed to an "empirical" standpoint, by which he meant that he was concerned only with that which could be perceived by the senses or could be traced back to physical causes.[48] What is unusual about Jung's claim to be an empiricist (certainly in the philosophical sense), and perhaps a good reason he should more accurately be called a phenomenologist, is that Jung included such things as patients' dreams as empirical data. In his *Psychology and Religion*, for example, Jung insisted, "I am an empiricist and adhere to the phenomenological standpoint." Jung went on to describe his methodological standpoint as being "exclusively phenomenological," by which he meant it was "concerned with occurrences, events, experiences, in a word, facts."[49] Committed to such a standpoint, Jung was not in a position to make assertions about God—other than as an observable psychological phenomenon.

White was one of the first theologians to acknowledge Jung's empirical standpoint, something Jung considered "very meritorious."[50] Indeed, it was the mutual recognition of their respective boundaries as empiricist and metaphysician (which I will consider more fully in the next chapter) that allowed their discussion to flourish for some ten years. However, it is not without significance that, as early as 1940, White was concerned that the psychologist stay within the bounds of his science—an almost prophetic concern when we consider that it was precisely Jung's transgression of the empirical data (even though he denied it) in his *Answer to Job*, that would lead to the breakdown of their discussion in 1955.

The Work

White's first *published* interest in Jung came in 1941, in a review of R. Scott Frayn's *Revelation and the Unconscious*.[51] Locating Frayn's work in "largely unchartered" territory, White admitted that "very few theologians have yet ventured into the vast and dark continent which the psychology of the collective unconscious has opened up." In his review, White portrayed Frayn as a "venturesome pioneer" and saw his work to be "of capital importance if only it blazes a trail where others may follow."[52] White himself would be at the forefront of those on this trail, and it seems no coincidence that he would have a chapter entitled "Revelation and the Unconscious" in his book *God and the Unconscious* (bibliog. 1.4, 1952).

Essentially, Frayn's book offered a basic introduction to the subject, considering what impact Jung's notion that revelation is located in the depths of the psyche has for Christianity. Jung believed that the origin of gods and demons, of myths and revelations, is the "concretization" of autonomous psychic contents. But White was quite clear that, on the contrary, revelation is not a purely psychic process. For the theologian—for whom the source and content of revelation is transcendental or supernatural—their positions seem mutually exclusive. This was an issue that White would address further in his first public lecture on Jung the following year.

The Frontiers of Theology and Psychology

This lecture, which White gave to the Oxford branch of the Guild of Pastoral Psychology (chaired by John Layard), "The Frontiers of Theology and Psychology,"[53] was well received in psychological circles—though less warmly by some of his brethren in theology, who viewed Jung as suspect.[54] Reflecting his private correspondence with Layard,[55] White's lecture was an attempt to allay suspicions of Jung and to clarify misconceptions about Jung's psychology. "There is a good deal of misunderstanding to clear up before analytical psychologists and Christian theologians can really get to grips."[56] White was concerned that Jung would be misunderstood if it was not made clear that Jung was concerned not with theology but with psychology. However, this would not be an easy task because, as White noted, "The fact remains that Jungian theory and technique are apt to cause the deepest misgivings by reason of the very religious aura which they assume."[57]

White was right to express concern about Jung's talk about God. It is important to note, however, that when Jung talked about God, he was talking about the God who existed solely in the realm of psychological truth. He was talking about the intra-psychic experience of the archetype of the Self by the conscious ego, particularly the Self of the collective unconscious, in which the ego is transformed or "made whole"—a process Jung called individuation. Jung talked about this experience in explicitly religious terms, asserting that the God image is synonymous with the collective Self.[58] In religious terms, as John Dourley noted, the Self as God image is in dialogue with the conscious ego. The conscious ego is required for the "redemption" of God (it must be "crucified"), and this occurs when the God of the unconscious is "incarnated" into consciousness.[59] God then "redeems" or "makes whole" the individual, who comes to self-realization—this is called individuation.[60] As Dourley aptly expressed it, God and humanity are involved in a process of "mutual redemption."[61]

In light of this, it is clear why White was concerned that theologians reading Jung's work would have the "deepest misgivings"! First of all, it seemed Jung was positing a wholly immanent God, and was thus guilty of psychologism, the theory that reduces God to a merely psychological phenomenon.[62] Second, it looked like Jung repudiated divine transcendence. Third, it appeared Jung "proved" Christianity and thus made faith (in place of knowledge) redundant. And fourth, although White did not mention this, it looked like Jung had inverted traditional Christian doctrines of redemption and incarnation, promoting a gnostic doctrine of self-salvation.

Turning to the first point, that Jung was guilty of psychologism, it is ironic that Jung had written some five years earlier, "Anyone who dares to establish a connection between the psyche and the idea of God is immediately accused of 'psychologism.'"[63] Jung defended himself against the charge: psychologism was a metaphysical theory that psychology could neither prove nor disprove.[64] White supported Jung on this point, arguing that Jung was concerned not with the nature of God, but with *images* of God and, as such, he did not invalidate the reality of God at all, for the Christian God transcended every image used for Him.[65] But, although White defended Jung on this point, he *did* believe that Jung had "apparently fail[ed] to understand at all" the Christian experience of God and accused him of repudiating divine transcendence.[66] His accusation is not without foundation, for Jung had earlier expressed that it is "psychologically unthinkable" for God to be "'wholly other,' for a 'wholly other' could never be one of the soul's deepest and closest intimacies—which is precisely what God is."[67]

For Jung, as White saw it, a transcendent God is no more than an interior psychological process capable of "endopsychic" explanation. If God could be described as transcendent in Jung's schema, it is *only* in the sense that the archetypes of the unconscious transcend the conscious ego and are in dialogue with the ego out of this transcendence.[68] Jung called this the "transcendent function," even though its dialogue with the ego takes place wholly within the psyche. In any case, Jung would later (in their correspondence) object to White's accusation that he repudiated the traditional Christian notion of divine transcendence, writing that he didn't exclude the *possibility* of a transcendent God, but that it was out of the realm of his field to talk in such terms. Jung was, in fact, open to "the possibility of divine grace allowing glimpses into the transcendental order of things," but maintained that psychology could not give a rational account of these, nor could it prove them.[69] White would later argue that theology was capable of this task, and he would propose a model of collaboration in which theology could "supplement" the findings of analytical psychology.

To the third point, by showing the existence of the God image, it looked like Jung had "proved" Christianity. Jung was not interested in whether religion was true, however, for he recognized the limitations of the kind of truth that could be yielded by empirical science. But psychologically, he had shown that it "worked." Some years before his encounter with Jungian thought, White had written an article on faith in which he affirmed the traditional Christian view: we believe not because it "works" but because God has spoken and it requires assent.[70] Jung, on the other hand, did not require faith in God but knowledge of the Self as God image, a view which led to the accusation that he was essentially a gnostic.[71] As we shall see in the next chapter, White would address the issue of the gnostic Jung more fully in 1949. But, in 1940, White voiced the concern of theologians with the following question: "Does it not seem that Jung would disprove Christianity by proving it?"[72] Again, Jung had, in part, replied to this in 1937 in *The Terry Lectures* at Yale University, where he had made it clear that it would be "a regrettable mistake" to take his observations as a kind of proof for the existence of God, declaring, "They prove only the existence of an archetypal god image, which to my mind is the most we can assert about God psychologically."[73]

White's task, then, in allaying the deep suspicion surrounding Jung's psychology, was to communicate to fellow theologians that there was a distinction between God and the God image. Defending Jung, he wrote, "The empirical psychologist *as such* is unconcerned with the affirmation or negation of a metaphysical God; he is concerned only with the 'God-image' and its observable functioning in the psyche."[74] If we fail to make this qualification, that Jung was talking about *psychological* truth—it is psychologically true in as much as it exists—then certainly it would have *appeared* that Jung was making a metaphysical assertion, that the God within was the same as the God of Judaeo-Christian revelation. White would later suggest that only a religion which is true—or, at least, is apprehended as true—could "work," that its very "working" is dependent upon its truth.[75] Furthermore, he thought that, even if truth concerning God Godself did not fall within the scope of psychology, the longing for that truth—the *naturale desiderium*—is a basic element of the human psyche which psychology could not ignore.[76] In fact, this notion is expressed in Jung's undifferentiated libido.

Finally, to the fourth point, to the theologian it looked like Jung was saying that one could save oneself—and God—in a process of "mutual redemption."[77] In Dourley's articulation of Jung's thought, consciousness is required "to redeem the hidden God of the unconscious" which, in turn, brings about the redemption (or making whole) of the individual.[78] On the contrary, a Thomist like White was committed to a God who does not "need" human beings and who redeems human beings from beyond the psyche.[79] Superficially, one can see why Jung's position, clothed as it is in the language of the theologian, would look attractive: it means that God is intimately involved with human beings and their suffering. However, the attraction is rather deceptive when one considers, as I have, what Jung actually meant. It is surprising, therefore, that White did not envision that theologians would have misgivings about this aspect of Jung's thought. This may have been due, in part, to White's initial acceptance of the distinctions that Jung made between God and God image.

It is clear, then, that White did have concerns about Jung's psychology from the beginning and that he was unafraid to criticize Jung's "speculations" into theology as "often distinctly amateurish."[80] His insistence on the distinction of the roles of metaphysician and empiricist, grounded in Aquinas' insistence that "every science must be met on its own ground and understood only in the light of its own premises and observations,"[81] would prove crucial to future discussion. Problems would arise, however, because although Jung, as an empirical psychologist, was unconcerned with the affirmation or negation of a metaphysical God, he was deeply interested in this question *personally*. Consequently, Jung's distinctions between God and God image often lacked clarity and "proved one of the most considerable tangles which confront the theologically minded student of Jung."[82] As I will show, this would prove detrimental to dialogue—and to any hopes Victor White may have had of assimilating the truths of Jung's psychology into his theology.

Recapturing Immanence: Thomism and Affective Knowledge

Of particular interest in this period are three articles that White wrote on "Thomism and Affective Knowledge."[83] Although he nowhere mentioned Jung in these articles, they are an important preface to key issues that would arise in White's conversations with Jung, especially in relation to the question of how we know God. As I have shown, their positions seemed to be diametrically opposed—White, committed to a transcendent God, and Jung, to a God who functioned solely within the psyche. Indeed, some scholars have suggested that theologies such as Victor White's are ultimately incompatible with Jungian theory because they are based on Aquinas' "dry logic wholly divested of an affective dimension."[84] But White showed that this was not the case for Aquinas, and in recapturing Aquinas' notion of affective knowledge—by which he meant non-sensory cognitive perception—offered some hope that two seemingly mutually exclusive positions might indeed have a point of contact. For Aquinas, according to White, we know God in two ways: by cognition (*per modum cognitionis*) and by inclination (*per modum inclinationis*).[85] Quoting Aquinas, he wrote, "'Knowledge which is possessed thanks to grace is twofold: one sort is purely speculative . . . the other affective.'"[86]

White reiterated Aquinas' two-fold approach to knowledge in a lecture that he gave to the Aquinas Society of London, showing how it correlates to Jungian thought: "Correct judgement may be attained," he wrote, "not only by study and rational process, but also by 'inclination' or 'connaturality.' Or, as we might express it today in terms of Jung's psychological functions, there are not only intellectual judgements but also feeling judgements."[87] White was referring to the four functions that Jung had posited of the psyche: thinking, feeling, sensation, and intuition. Sensation and intuition depend on an act of perception, they are not evaluative, and so Jung described them as irrational. Thinking and feeling, on the other hand, evaluate experience; they are cognitive—as is the knowledge by study or by affect that we see in Aquinas.

White showed how Aquinas contrasted the intellectual habits that are acquired by study with those habits that are acquired affectively (which are a gift of God). On the one hand, he said that we know (God) cognitively within the bounds of human limitations through study (*per usum rationis*). To illustrate this point, consider a person who does not have the virtue of chastity, but who has studied ethics and so, with an informed conscience, is able to make good judgments. She makes good choices by virtue of reason.[88] On the other hand, White (echoing Aquinas) said that to know (God) by inclination is a gift of the Holy Spirit. To further illustrate, consider a person who has the habit of virtue and judges rightly not by reason but because of an inclination toward it. Possessing the virtue, she judges "by connaturality." Echoing Aquinas, White concluded that when wisdom comes from a judgment it is "an intellectual *virtus*," but when it comes from Divine instinct "it is a gift."[89] God's knowledge "is not discursive or argumentative but absolute and simple," and thus knowledge, which is a *gift* of the Holy Spirit, is similar to it.[90]

However, White thought that the current exposition of the Thomistic account of knowledge of God was one-sided—his neo-scholastic brethren focusing solely on knowledge *per modum cognitionis*.[91] White argued that this was an incomplete rendering of Thomas' understanding of knowledge of God because it lacked any appreciation of "knowledge by 'connaturality,' 'by inclination' or *affectiva*."[92] Contrary to neo-scholastic exponents, White argued that Aquinas did, in fact, allow for "such experiential and affective knowledge, at least of a supernatural and mystical character."[93] He wrote: "St. Thomas was quite alive to the existence of an 'affective,' 'connatural' or 'experiential' knowledge distinct from the purely rational process." [94] In affirming the validity of affective knowledge for Aquinas, White was saying that it *is* possible to have direct experience of God which is cognitive but not sensual. We *can* know God by direct experience of the soul. This is significant, because Jung believed that we could *only* know God by a turn inward, by the direct experience of the psyche. He believed that if human beings were to be made whole, they needed to rediscover the immediate internal experience of the divine. Furthermore, he was convinced that an overemphasis of transcendence in theology—the belief that "the deity is *outside* man,"[95]—was "pathological," because as Dourley has noted, it "uproots" a human being from "the divine vitalities of its depths."[96] In other words, Victor White came out of a tradition which in Jung's view precluded experience of "the immediate living God."[97]

So, in relation to Jung, White's appreciation of affective knowledge offered real hope for bridging the gap between the transcendentalist White and the immanentist Jung—for both believed that we could know God by direct experience of the soul. Although White would affirm other ways of knowing God, and Jung would confine knowledge of God to the psyche, affective knowledge represented common ground. This is probably why White was so committed to redressing the one-sided exposition of knowledge of God, namely the "frigidly rational" and "rigidly scientific"[98] that he saw in contemporary Thomism. "It is probable," he wrote, "that the most serious obstacle in the way of a *rapprochement* between Thomism and much 'modern thought' is the widespread misgiving that Thomism ignores or rejects 'value perception' and 'value experience.'"[99]

There are two reasons for this neglect of "affective knowledge," though White was explicit only about the first of these. He suggested that the crux of the problem, and, in a sense, a reason for the neglect of "affective knowledge" in Thomas, was the separation of reason and experience. This is slightly misleading and needs to be qualified, because Thomists do not neglect experience, as such, but only neglect immediate non-sensory experience. Clearly, then, White must have meant religious experience. Historically, White blamed this split on the "Romanticist revolt" from reason, after which, he argued (drawing on Baron Friedrich von Hügel), there was a series of pendulum swings between "intuitive emotionalism" and "clear transparent thought."[100] This is interesting in relation to Jung, because Jung believed that human beings in the West in the twentieth century could no longer experience God because the psyche had been reduced to reason. They had lost what he termed the "mythopoeic imagination," the myth-making ability of the primitives that was also characteristic of the unconscious.[101] Jung's position also gives us some insight into why White's neo-scholastic contemporaries—who exalted the rational dimension of knowledge and neglected the affective (pathologically, as Jung saw it)—would be suspicious of White's contact with Jung.

This brings us to a second reason for the divorce of reason and experience, and one about which White was much more subtle—namely the *fear* of modernism both within the Dominican Order and the Catholic Church. The modernist emphasis on experience (which was shared by Jung) was seen as pure subjectivism and, as such, seemed very threatening. White himself supported this in *Soul and Psyche* (bibliog. 1.4, 1960), arguing: "The claims made for inner religious experience by the Modernists, have tended to make the very word suspect to many theologians. The Modernists exalted the 'religious sense' (concerning which they had their own unorthodox theories) at the expense of voluntary intellectual assent, and were condemned by Pope Pius X for identifying faith with this kind of experience."[102] The modernists "exalted the 'religious sense'" in that they substituted direct experience for propositionally revealed doctrine. White, on the other hand, was quite clear that the spiritual life could not be led without propositionally revealed creeds. He saw the dangers that an overemphasis on experience could bring, particularly, the "departmentaliz[ation]" of the spiritual life, and "escapism"—escape from hard thinking.[103] Furthermore, while White agreed that experience is a part of knowledge, he would certainly distance himself from the modernists, for experience is not knowledge in itself, and it does not convey truth unless it is reflected on by the mind.[104] Knowledge seeks the truth, or as Aquinas expressed it, "the conformity of thought and thing." This does not mean that to possess a thought which is conformed to a thing is to possess *truth* about a thing, because, said White, "I must also know that my thought is conformed to a thing if I am to *know* truth." In other words, direct perception alone is not enough because, as White wrote, "there is no true knowledge unless there be affirmation or negation."[105]

Essentially, White said that the knowing mind must be active in knowledge, in addition to passive experience. Here is a point at which I think White could potentially make a very serious contribution to psychology. Jung believed that we know (God) by direct experience and, in that we experience the manifestations of the soul, God exists. The God image is "psychologically true."[106] With this expression or—as White would later term it—"linguistic idiosyncrasy,"[107] Jung did two things: first, as Wolfgang Giegerich has argued, he created his own private species of truth;[108] second, he neglected the need for the soul to be formulated rationally—*exactly* the opposite problem of the neo-scholastics. This is why, within the boundaries of his "psychological truth," Jung could only say that the Self is an *image* of God rather than that the Self *is* God. Jung could not make such a metaphysical statement without transgressing the boundaries of empiricism that he had set for himself. It is a deficiency in Jung, as White later pointed out, because to say that something is true on the basis that it exists psychologically is problematic when it is quite clearly false.[109] Perhaps here White's commitment to knowledge by affect *and* knowledge by reason could supplement "psychological truth." Jung's phenomenological approach only allowed him to consider the fact of God—that is, the Self as God image is true because it exists. White's metaphysics, however, allowed him to consider, as well, whether such an idea was true or false in any other sense.

White was deeply concerned that, as a result of the "divorce" of experience and reason, rational knowledge and affective knowledge were seen in opposition to each other. Consequently, he feared that they would be seen as two separate fields of knowledge and thus two different fields of reality, rather than two different *approaches* to the same reality. Ultimately his fear was that this "epistemological dualism" could only lead to two gods: "the God of Thought, First Mover, Metaphysical Absolute" and "the God of 'religious experience.'"[110] White had, in fact, identified what would be a source of conflict with Jung, for Jung believed that God could *only* be known by direct experience of the psyche.

In view of this, it was crucial for White to relocate affective knowledge not in opposition to rational knowledge (this was the error of the modernists) but as *another aspect* of knowledge. He wrote: "An intellectualist philosophy which is content to ignore or make light of affective experience is not only doomed to impermanence, it must forfeit the claim to be either truly intellectualist or truly philosophical."[111] He continued:

> If intelligence is to be arbiter it is self condemned if it must confess itself unable to account for the most vital and intimate forms of personal experience. If philosophy is by definition a system of universal applicability, if it is to explain to us the ultimate reasons of all things to the extent that these are discoverable by human powers, it follows that a system which must exclude affective knowledge from its purview can make no valid claim to be strictly philosophical.[112]

White considered it of the utmost importance that the modern mind takes account of value perception, it being a human being's most immediate experience. Furthermore, as White argued in his article, "Tasks for Thomists," Thomism *must* be in touch with the needs of the modern world:

> For must it not be admitted that we thomists are sometimes apt to forget our responsibilities to the world and to the age in which we find ourselves, to live and work in academic isolation, too little heedful of

the crying spiritual and intellectual needs of others and of our own obligation to impart to them the heritage entrusted to us—forgetful even of the opening words of the *Summa* itself and of the whole purpose for which it was written?[113]

White was critical of those who misused the *Summa*, studying scholastic manuals "instead of God and his world,"[114] seeing them as an "insurmountable barrier" to the mind of Thomas.[115] Yet White defended Thomism against the cry that it was out of touch with the modern world by showing that Aquinas' approach to the nature of knowledge is much more phenomenological than is often supposed. But White realized that the notion of affective knowledge would be problematic for philosophy—especially Thomistic philosophy which was to be conducted "on purely scientific logical lines (*utrum haec scientia sit argumentative*),"[116] for this surely excluded the affective process. It is, said White, "as definitely excluded from 'argumentative' Theology as it must be from mathematics—though it must be considered *by* it."[117] However, White thought that theology was different because:

> Unlike the object of mathematics, the Object of divinity is *lovable*. God should be approached affectively. The disclosing of the Godhead made to man in Christ is not to be accepted by a "dead faith," nor to be contemplated merely by a loveless syllogising. The Son of God is indeed the Divine Logos. He is nevertheless no sterile Concept of the Divine Mind, but the Logos who breathes forth love in the Person of the Holy Ghost.[118]

Christian wisdom is, then, different from the wisdom of the pagans. The philosophers acquire knowledge by study, by speculation. But Christian wisdom also has a contemplative aspect. We know God by direct experience of the soul and this is brought about by love. White developed this idea in relation to Jung, in October 1944, in a paper that he gave to the Oxford University Psychology and Religion Society on Walter Hilton.[119] In this paper, White showed how, for Hilton, there are three parts of contemplation: thinking, feeling, and "that from the centre . . . which masters and uses both."[120] In other words, we know God by reason, by affect, and, most perfectly, by cognition *and* affection—in knowing and loving God. This third part White compared to Jung's transcendent function, for it is in this part, in knowing and loving God, that the soul is "reformed by grace" to the image of Jesus. It is the mystical union of God and the soul.

White described this process in very Jungian language, urging the contemplative to take "the way of introversion; of 'inward turning.'"[121] White said that when we look within, we realize that we must face the Shadow, which, for Jung, represents the dark side of an individual's personality—and, for the Christian, is the symbol of our need to acknowledge our sin. Although in this life the Shadow is always present, if it is recognized and conscious, it is harmless, indeed it is the way to what Hilton calls "The Ladder of Perfection" or what Jung calls "the way to integration."[122] For Jung, the Shadow "block[s] the way" to the soul image—the *anima* or *animus*, an archetype that can represent the whole of the unconscious.[123] The soul image is essentially the personification of the feminine nature of a man's unconscious and the masculine nature of a woman's—the *anima* taking the nature of eros for a man, the animus taking the nature of logos for a woman. According to Jung, in terms of outer attitude (*persona*), men think and women feel, but in inner attitude (*anima/animus*) it is the woman who reflects and the man who feels.[124] At face value, contemporary feminists might take issue with Jung, women once again reduced to irrational and intuitive. However, such a reading could also show that intuition has been devalued as female in philosophical accounts of rationality. So Jung has, in fact, given us an important reminder of its significant role in human reasoning.

White showed that, for Jung, the way to the soul image is blocked by the Shadow, and he saw a counterpart to this in mystical writing, using Hilton as an example:

> We remember that when Hilton's contemplative first looked into his home he found both "stinking smoke" *and* "a chiding wife." No wonder she was chiding, poor woman, suffocated and obscured in the stinking smoke of the unassimilated Shadow. When the Shadow is made conscious and so rendered powerless and clearly seen, smoke dissipates, the "other side" appears in all her beauty, and the way is ready for happy and tranquil union with her.[125]

White argued that this union of the "masculine rationality" and "feminine sensuality," both within the psyche and outside of the psyche in relationships, is life-giving. It releases "life-renewing energies" of the unconscious into consciousness, and this, he said, is essential for "the full realisation of the Christ-image, the integration of the whole man in union with God."[126]

As is now apparent, it looked to White like there was real possibility for Jungian-Catholic dialogue on spirituality—not just any spirituality, but those spiritualities that involved a "conscious confrontation," that engaged in a "dialectical process" which made them similar to Jung's individuation.[127] It is unfortunate that, while White recognized early in the 1940s that any real hope for a synthesis of Catholic and Jungian ideas would be on the level of the human person,[128] Jung's impact on White's theology led to discussions about doctrines of God where the two would prove to be ultimately incompatible. Although White never completely developed his ideas on affective knowledge,[129] they offered to the Thomism of his day a much needed apologetic of immanence—and to Jung, an acknowledgement that direct experience of God by the soul was possible. Furthermore, White's ability to recapture something neglected in Aquinas provides a *point de départ* for further discussion between Thomists and Jungians in an area where such discussion has perhaps been considered by contemporary scholarship to be foreclosed.[130]

St. Thomas Aquinas and Jung's Psychology

Later in 1944, White turned his attention more directly to the interface of Catholic theology and Jungian psychology in his article, "St. Thomas Aquinas and Jung's Psychology,"[131] which he published as a tribute to Jung on his seventieth birthday. Essentially, the article is a highly critical review essay of Fr. Witcutt's book, *Catholic Thought and Modern Psychology*.[132] Witcutt had considered the psychologies of Freud, Adler, and Jung against a background of English literature and in the light of Catholic theology, particularly that of Aquinas. White was unimpressed,[133] but he acknowledged that the work was "desperately needed," for it had not been considered by either the theologians or the psychologists in any scholarly manner,[134]—largely due to the "religiousness" of Jung, which was of concern to theologian and psychologist alike. Elaborating earlier expressed concerns, White observed:

> A theoretical dichotomy between religion and practical psychotherapy, even at the cost of fostering schizophrenia, has seemed to the more timid preferable to the risks of admitting the psychotherapist into the holy precincts of religion itself, or to the still greater risk of luring the pastor of souls away from the security of his textbook lore to face the realities of the human psyche in the raw.[135]

Earlier in this chapter, I showed why theologians might have had misgivings about Jung's "religious" psychology and, indeed, why psychology would fear the intrusion of metaphysics. As a Thomist who believed that grace perfects nature, and that the body and soul are unitive, White considered the separation deeply un-Catholic. Furthermore, from a therapeutic standpoint he could see that such a separation was "disastrous."[136]

White thought that Jung offered a therapeutic approach that was different from Freud's historical causal approach—which had made any type of psychotherapy suspect to many Catholics. Thus, White could see how important it was to clarify Jung's position, once again revealing his desire to dispel any misconceptions about Jung's psychology. First of all, he emphasized that Jung's therapy was not suggestive of "a preconceived mould of alleged 'normality'" but rather, was helping people confront their Shadow and move toward integration.[137] Furthermore, White reaffirmed Jung's phenomenological standpoint, emphasizing that his psychology "is not primarily a θεωρία" but "a πρᾶξις"[138]: "Jung is, first and foremost, not a philosopher but a healer; a theorist only in so far as he generalises from his therapeutic experience."[139] White argued that the praxis orientation of Jung's psychology precluded the possibility of a preconditioned psychology: "[The fact that Jung] resolutely refused to disregard the facts which came under his observation in his 'immediate experience with human beings' when these did not happen to fit in with *a priori* pseudo-scientific theories of his time, enabled him to rediscover the perennial 'testimony of the soul'—the *anima naturaliter christiana* in Tertullian's sense."[140]

White was, in effect, aligning Jung with the *philosophia perennis*, showing that, in fact, his psychology was not so much "ultra-modern" (as Witcutt saw it) as it was a rediscovery of the wisdom of the ancients (which was deeply rooted in the Catholic tradition). Jung himself had made this discovery of the *philosophia perennis* in substituting the "undifferentiated libido" for Freud's "sexuality." He knew that his psychology was "less a new discovery than a rediscovery of ancient universal principles of spiritual and mental healing and hygiene; readapted, it is true, to the particular needs of modern 'civilized' Western man."[141] In 1934, in his *Archetypes of the Collective Unconscious* (CW 9i: 3–41), Jung had traced the articulation of the idea of archetypes—primordial images—to the writings of Plato, Irenaeus, Dionysius the Areopagite, and Augustine.[142] Irenaeus, for example, said that the creator of the world did not fashion things directly from himself, "but copied them from archetypes outside himself."[143] Augustine had spoken of "*ideae principales*," which are not themselves formed, but are contained in the divine understanding. Jung could see that Greeks and the Church Fathers were "gripped by the psyche" as it manifests in archetypal ideas.[144] White thought this highly significant, for if Jung's thought had correspondence with the *philosophia perennis*, and the *philosophia perennis* was "enshrined" in Aquinas' thought, then there was great hope for dialogue with Jung.[145] He wrote:

If we would compare and coordinate the work of St. Thomas and that of Jung, it is essential that at the outset we differentiate clearly between the several pre-occupations and methods of the two men. Both, of course, start with the same data—the only available data, the actual workings of the human psyche. Both undoubtedly (however much the fact may be obscured in the conventional manuals of "Thomistic Psychology") are keen and fearless observers of brute psychological fact. But in their treatment of the facts they, more often than not, differ widely. St. Thomas is a philosopher; perceiving facts he argues to their causes, observing acts he infers potencies—he infers the psyche, the soul, itself. As a philosopher, his concern is with explanation of the phenomena. Such is not Jung's role; he has repeatedly and rightly disclaimed it. For him, quite rightly within the limits of his empirical methodology, the psyche itself is not an established conclusion but a postulate. Observing the same phenomena, his primary concern is not with rational explanation, but with the practical problems of sickness and health; with coordination and balance of the parts with a view to the health of the whole. We shall misread him entirely if we read into his writings a philosophical answer to such problems as that of the origin of ideas—or even of the origin of the "archetypes" (concerning which, indeed, he has expressly confessed his ignorance).[146]

White saw that Jung's treatment of the psyche was based upon purely empirical observation, and that Catholic theology could offer to Jungian psychology rational justification for its observations. As an example of his proposed method, White used Aquinas' "amor" and suggested that it complements Jung's "undiffereniated libido" by providing "a rational justification and analysis" of Jung's empirical observations.

> [Aquinas] can do more than establish Jung's metapsychological postulates as rational conclusions; for in so doing he reveals their deeper implications which, in their turn, are of immense importance for the psychotherapist in his work. Thus this amor, or libido, is found to imply a "natural desire" for the possession of God—a conclusion which Jung's own empirical work constantly suggests and confirms, but is unable to establish.[147]

Aquinas can complement Jung, "because his treatment of the human psyche transcends, though it is based upon, purely empirical observation."[148] White suggested several other areas for possible collaboration. He thought that rational justification for Jung's ego and *anima-animus* can be found in Aristotle's distinction between the irrational and rational parts of the soul.[149] But perhaps even greater possibilities lie in ethics, precisely because Jung's psychology is praxis and not theory. For example, Aristotle and Jung were both teleologically orientated toward the "foursquare man."[150] The way to the goal, though expressed in different language, is essentially the same for both: for Jung it is the way of "conscious acceptance and integration of the unconscious"; for Aristotle it is "the making of the ἀλόγον to participate in the λόγος."[151] For both, White argued that the way is "effortless and spontaneous."[152] Furthermore, Jung thought that instincts are not "predetermined to their objects" (as was the case for Freud), but that they are "*meant* to be transformed," and this brings about integration. In Jungian terms, "the serpent of temptation in the garden becomes the instrument of health and life in the desert."[153] White thought that a parallel could be found in Aristotle's *Nicomachean Ethics* (which is taken up by Aquinas), in particular the idea that the virtues of the sensitive appetite participate "in right reason."[154] Finally, according to White, neither Jung nor Aristotle could give a "coherent picture" of the ultimate goal. For Aristotle, the Absolute Good is not attainable by human beings in this life, just as the Self is unattainable but remains a symbol to which one is drawn.

So, four years after the initial impact of Jungian psychology, White could see that, despite concerns, there were a number of areas where Jungians and Catholics might find agreement. Furthermore, not only had White found Jung's thought personally beneficial, but he could see that Catholic theology also had much to offer Jung by way of supplementing his empiricism. In setting forth the idea of supplementation as a model for his own theological synthesis, White was also beginning to define his task in relation to Jung.

Psychotherapy and Ethics

White continued to lecture on topics relating to Jung and, in August 1945, gave a paper, "Psychotherapy and Ethics," to The Newman Association.[155] At that time, he himself was training to be an analytical psychologist, as a letter from psychologist Gerhard Adler indicates.[156] Up until 1945, very little attention had been given to the moral dimensions of psychotherapy, but White saw the "practical urgency" as "too acute" just to wait for an "ethicopsychotherapeutical synthesis."[157] Echoing the fears of Rome he wrote:

> Do we not, in doing so, risk the undermining of our moral principles, perhaps of our religion and our faith? Rumours have reached us, perhaps, of alleged psychotherapists who, after long and costly weeks of treatment, prescribe some such homely palliatives as a dose of fornication, divorce, cutting loose from hearth and home, or some other form of uncleanness, injustice or impiety. We have heard vaguely that one whole and important school of psychological analysis regards the elimination of God and conscience, thinly disguised as superego, as the chief desideratum in any successful analysis. Ugly rumours have reached us too of dark doings in the treatment itself: of conditioning to certain patterns of behaviour under compulsions induced by hypnosis or drugs; of confessions of dark secrets and immoral abreactions compelled by drugs or shock; of analysts who conceive it to be their

first task to induce their patients to fall in love with them and whose whole treatment consists in holding morbid and pornographic conversations. Even if we do not credit such rumours, there remains a fundamental misgiving not lightly to be set aside. Are we not in any case, in submitting to psychological treatment, subjecting our minds to the direction, perhaps to the domination, of another mind, and one whose moral and religious standards may be fundamentally unsound and are in any case fallible? Even if we could be assured on that, must it not inevitably be that the whole end and aim of any psychologist who knows his business is to fashion the mind of his patient to his own standard of "normality," and must not the "normal" inevitably be in accordance with the standard of the majority of men, i.e., in accordance with the standard of conformity to this wicked world? Will he not inevitably filch from us our religion and whatever ethical standards we may have which are not those of the world around us?[158]

White's comments offer a flavor of the attitude toward psychotherapy in the 1940s, and they give us some indication as to why his association with Jung brought him under suspicion from the Order and from Rome. White was determined to address some of the misgivings about psychotherapy, and proposed that Catholics turn to Jung's psychology—for Jung had distanced himself from the "predetermining causality" of Freud and thereby liberated psychotherapy.[159] This, in part, addressed Catholic misgivings because "the psyche and its phenomenal manifestations are no longer to be conceived purely or primarily in terms of determined cause and effect, but as a relatively closed self regulating system possessing its own potentialities of recovery and renewal through the interplay of simultaneous coefficient functions."[160]

In a postscript to this article, and drawing on the work of J. C. Flugel, White further highlighted his preference for Jung over Freud. If for Freud the image of God as Father is an illusion created by the child which comes from dissatisfaction with the earthly father, for Jung the earthly father is "the unsatisfactory bearer of the image which the adult will find realised through his image of the Father God."[161] In other words, whereas Freud had dismissed religion as a projection of the repressed contents of the unconscious, Jung did not dismiss religion because he did not limit the unconscious to an individual's repressed contents, but also allowed for the collective unconscious, the source of religious symbols.[162] We can see why Jung's approach was more attractive to White—and potentially more compatible with Catholic theology—than was Freud's.

A Task "Gigantic Indeed"

White's initial encounter with analytical psychology came from a personal experience of the healing power of Jung's psychology, and his desire to integrate Jung's thought into his theology was subsequent to this. White believed that Jung had something to offer to Catholics, for his method encouraged a direct experience of God that brought healing, which he thought was neglected by a religion of assent to propositionally revealed doctrines: "Can we honestly say . . . that Christian doctrine is commonly presented among us in all its psychological relevance as the *Verbum salutis*, the Divine message and pattern of integral human health and wholeness?"[163]

As I have shown, White himself had only appreciated the psychological relevance of the divine message following the impact of Jung's psychology in his life. Consequently, this impact had implications for his own theology. It had, for example, forced a re-evaluation of Thomistic approaches to the direct experience of God, which led to the recovery for Catholic theology of an apologetic of immanence, and the reconsideration of spiritualities of "conscious confrontation" which were similar to individuation. On another level, the admitted impact of Jung on his life, and White's attempt to embrace some of Jung's concepts and incorporate them into his own synthesis, had brought White under suspicion in the Order as a modernist.

White was not, however, naively embracing all of Jung's psychology. On the contrary, he was deeply aware that there were problems—particularly in relation to doctrines of God. Thus, he wisely distanced himself somewhat from Jung, unable "to give unqualified assent to every word that Jung himself has written."[164] But he believed—in this period 1940–45 at least—that if important qualifications were made between psychology and theology, between God image and God, that there was much potential for fruitful dialogue. With such distinctions in place, White was confident that the work of Jung provided "sound foundations on which to build."[165] His model and his task would be to supplement the empirical foundations laid by Jung—by providing the rational justification for what Jung's psychology suggested, but which his phenomenological methodology could not confirm. White was aware that the task he had set for himself and others was "gigantic indeed."[166]

THREE
1945–1948

Jung's Attraction to White's Catholicism

Fascinated by the stirrings of the divine in the unconscious that he had discovered through Jungian analysis in the early 1940s, the forty-two-year-old White wrote the first of some eighty letters to Jung, acknowledging the "immense debt of gratitude" that he owed to the man who was twenty-eight years his senior.[1] With his letter of August 3, 1945, White also enclosed some of his own writings concerning Jung's psychology, seeking affirmation that the disciple had understood the master.[2] Jung's reply of September 26 would mark the beginning of a remarkable relationship:

> I'm highly interested in the point of view which the Church takes with reference to my work . . . I must say that I never would have expected so much appreciation and real understanding from the theological quarter.[3] Owing to rather obvious reasons Protestant theologians are rather reticent and they don't know yet whether I should be condemned as a heretic or depreciated as a mystic. As you know, mysticism and hereticism enjoy about the same bad reputation in Protestantism. So there is not much hope for me from that side.[4]

Jung had dared to establish a connection between God and the psyche, and he was fully aware that this idea of the "God within" would lead to accusations of "morbid mysticism."[5] He also knew that he would be condemned by many as a heretic because the God within was incompatible with traditional Christian notions of a God who was utterly transcendent. But the fear of and reticence toward Jung was hardly unique to Protestant theologians, and although Catholic theologians were more appreciative of the mystical tradition, they too defended the notion of a transcendent God, and were, for the most part, deeply concerned about what they perceived as Jung's heretical modernist tendencies. A closer consideration of Jung's writings gives further insight into the "obvious reasons" why he saw little potential for dialogue with specifically Protestant theologians. Jung thought that, at the Reformation, an "alarming poverty of symbols . . . came about," when Protestants, in acts of "chronic iconoclasm," cast out their images, statues and rituals.[6] As a result, the "sacred images" that had, up until that point, expressed "important unconscious factors," were lost,[7] and the Protestant soul was "cast out into a state of defencelessness that might well make the natural man shudder."[8] Jung believed that, prior to the Reformation, symbols had protected human beings from a direct experience of the divine, and ritual had provided "a safe way of dealing with" the unpredictable forces of the unconscious.[9] For Jung, it was a matter of great regret that Protestantism had lost contact with the unconscious and its symbolic expressions because it meant that God was no longer experienced in the psyche. The inevitable consequence of this, as Jung saw it, was that Protestant theology of his day had become overly rational—having "succumbed to a species of rationalistic historicism and [having] lost any understanding of the Holy Ghost who works in the hidden places of the soul. It can neither understand nor admit a further revelation of the divine drama."[10]

However, this contact with the "sacred images" or symbols that were "expressive of important unconscious factors" was still very much a part of the rituals of Catholicism (even if unconsciously!),[11] and so, Jung saw that there was more potential for dialogue with the Roman Catholic tradition than with the Protestant tradition in which he had been raised.[12] Further explanation of Jung's attraction to Catholicism over Protestantism may be given in a letter of October 1, 1945, in which Jung expressed to White his belief that the *sola fide* of the Protestants had lost too much of the tradition of doctrine. Jung's use of theological terminology is slightly misleading because it is the *sola scriptura* that has the tradition of doctrine as its counter position, not the *sola fide,* and the *sola fide* finds its counter position in faith and works. What Jung means by this term *sola fide* is that the Protestant is left to God alone, a point well illustrated in *The Terry Lectures,* which Jung had delivered at Yale in 1937. There he said: "The Protestant is left to God alone. There is no confession, no absolution, no possibility of any kind of an atoning *opus divinum.* He has to digest his sins alone and he is not too sure of divine grace, which has become unattainable through lack of suitable ritual."[13] Jung was simply reiterating to White his view that, because Protestants discarded symbols, ritual, and dogma at the Reformation, they *only* have faith in a transcendent God *rather than* knowledge of the God within. Jung did, however believe that if Protestants survived this loss they had "the unique spiritual chance of immediate religious experience."[14]

For the Catholic, faith is similarly a voluntary assent to that which has been revealed by God, but it is also the case that the experience of the unconscious—of which Jung wrote, and which he saw as essential for healing—finds expression in the symbols, rituals, and dogmas of Catholicism. In *The Terry Lectures,* for example, Jung compared dogma to other phenomena of the unconscious: "Dogma is like a dream, reflecting the spontaneous and autonomous activity of the objective psyche, the unconscious."[15] And later, in the letter of October 1, 1945, Jung expressed to White his interest in what the theologian had to say about dogma, "namely that *the dogma is the hitherto most perfect answer to and formulation of the most relevant items in the objective psyche* [emphasis mine] and that God has worked all these things in man's soul. The scientist however cannot prove such an assertion; he can only try his best in his limited sphere."[16]

In fact, Jung went further than this, suggesting that, in matters of psychological truth, the dogma was more valuable than science— because, whereas theory "expresses and formulates the conscious mind," dogma "represents the soul more completely" in that it expresses the irrational through image.[17] At first glance, this seems an unusual claim from one who calls himself a scientist. But upon closer examination, it is clear that Jung was exalting dogma as a more complete representation of the soul—for it expresses both the unconscious and the conscious. The dogma represents the experience of the unconscious *and* the attempt by the Church to (consciously) formulate that experience over the years, what Jung called the "codified form" of the original religious experience.[18] In *The Terry*

Lectures, for example, Jung suggested that the dogma "expresses aptly the living processes of the unconscious in the form of the drama of repentance, sacrifice and redemption."[19] That which Catholics believe is revealed by God in scripture, and the tradition of the Church, also finds expression in Jung's living archetypes of the unconscious. Further examples include the suffering god man—which Jung traced back five thousand years in myths and pagan religions[20]—the death of the old man and the spiritual rebirth of a new one,[21] and the virgin mother.[22]

It should, I hope, be clear why Jung was deeply attracted to Catholicism from a psychological viewpoint. From White's point of view, his personal experience of the healing power of Jung's psychology had shown him that there is a correlation between revelation and the unconscious—though for White revelation is not just something that happens within the "relatively closed system of the psyche"—it is also outside the psyche, i.e., it is transcendental. Jung's attachment to his self-defined empiricism would not allow any metaphysical assertion about the nature of a transcendental God who reveals Godself in history. But as a theologian, White was not so constrained, so his proposed model of supplementation offered great potential for theoretical coordination.

Jung's "White Raven"

Jung certainly shared this hope for collaboration, expressing in this same and "exceptionally long" letter of October 1, 1945 his appreciation of White's "conscientious and far sighted work."[23] Acknowledging that he had read the three articles that White had sent to him, Jung responded in a highly favorable manner. "My first reaction was: what a pity that you live in England and that I don't have you at my elbow when I am blundering in the wide field of theological knowledge." He continued:

> Excuse the irreverential pun: you are to me a white raven inasmuch as you are the only theologian I know of who has really understood something of what the problem of psychology in our present world means. You have seen its enormous implications. I cannot tell you

how glad I am that I know a man, a theologian, who is conscientious enough to weigh my opinions on the basis of a careful study of my writings.[24]

Just as ravens are not usually white, the oxymoron employed here is clear: theologians do not usually understand psychology. But Victor White was different. He did understand Jung's psychology because he himself had *experienced* its healing power and its ability to revitalize a theology which, for him, had been bereft of meaning. As such, Jung saw White as one like the ravens sent by God to feed the prophet Elijah in the wilderness as he fled from Ahab to Cherith.[25] It is not insignificant that Jung elsewhere identified *himself* with the prophet Elijah (as an archetypal figure who appeared to him as an inner guiding figure), for the implication would be that this is how Jung saw White—as a raven to Elijah.[26] If Jung is drawing on the Old Testament reference, he is saying that White is to him a savior figure: one who is sent by God—like the raven[27]—who not only understands psychology but also "feeds" the prophet Jung.

A second interpretation of Jung's appellation "white raven" for Victor White is more psychological. Ravens usually being black, and aside from the pun (White's name), Jung was making a subtle reference to the image of the shadow in the psyche—negating the shadow by saying it is white rather than black.[28]

While these interpretations are possible, I would like to suggest a third—from a reading in alchemy—which I think has been overlooked by scholars. If my reading is correct, then Jung, in calling Fr. Victor a "white raven" was, in fact, referring to the Western God image which he saw as moribund, and the great *potential* that he saw in White for its transformation. As Jung had just published *Psychologie ünd Alchemie* (1944) and had been working on his *Mysterium Coniunctionis* for four years at the time of writing to Fr. Victor (and would continue to do so until 1954), this third interpretation seems highly plausible. This view requires some background and explanation.

Jung had begun to read alchemy in 1928,[29] and, upon his first encounter, considered it "blatant nonsense,"[30] an experience that would later resonate for White.[31] But as he began to study and understand the symbolism, Jung soon realized that in alchemy he could find many parallels with the processes of the unconscious. It was, he said, "a momentous discovery":

> The experiences of the alchemists were, in a sense, my experiences, and their world was my world. This was, of course, a momentous discovery: I had stumbled upon the historical counterpart of the psychology of the unconscious. The possibility of a comparison with alchemy, and the uninterrupted intellectual chain back to gnosticism, gave substance to my psychology.[32]

White appreciated Jung's discovery. He too could see that the alchemists were "Jung's prize witnesses to the collective unconscious."[33] For Jung, the experiences of the alchemists established the historical foundations for his psychology,[34] without which his psychological observations would remain "suspended in air, a mere curiosity."[35] Jung believed he had shown that the processes of the unconscious mind work with the same images throughout history: in the myths of the ancients, the texts of the gnostics, the practices of the alchemists, the dogma of Christianity, the dreams of modern woman and man. All shared the same intention: the transformation of imperfect matter into gold, into "the second Adam, the glorified incorruptible body of resurrection."[36]

Jung was convinced that the God image in the Western psyche needed to be transformed, and alchemy had provided some historical grounding for this process of transformation. At the beginning of the alchemical process, or the *opus*, one is involved in the struggle to find the *prima materia*, also referred to as the chaos. This primal matter is placed in a vessel and subjected to a process of transformation. In this process, the chemical compound is subjected to fire, and as it begins to burn, one encounters the blackness or the devil—this is called *nigredo* by the alchemists. It is the experience of death which, though painful, is necessary for rebirth. Significantly, the common term for *nigredo* in alchemy is *caput corvi,* the head of the raven,[37] so named because of its blackness and its symbolism of death. For Jung, this was a cause for celebration: "When you see your matter going black, rejoice, for that is the beginning of the work."[38] This encounter, like the encounter with the shadow, leads to suffering—a suffering from the confrontation of the opposites. Matter "suffers" until the blackness is transformed and *the black raven becomes white.*[39] I would argue that in calling White his "white raven," Jung saw in him this great potential for transformation.

Once the black raven has become white, this state of whiteness—known as *albedo* or daybreak to the alchemists—represents the ideal state. As one cannot really live in this ideal state, blood is needed to bring life, and this is represented by the red or the *rubedo*, also known as the sunrise. Jung wrote:

> Only the total experience of being can transform this ideal state of the *albedo* (or the white) into a fully human mode of existence. Blood alone can reanimate a glorious state of consciousness in which the last trace of blackness is dissolved, in which the devil no longer has autonomous existence but rejoins the profound unity of the psyche. Then the *opus magnum* is finished: the human soul is completely integrated.[40]

Jung's interest in alchemy had very little to do with chemistry and everything to do with the parallels he saw with the individuation process. For Jung, what happened in the alchemical vessel was really a projection of what was happening in the inner world of the alchemist, i.e. the process of transformation known as individuation. It was a process that Jung saw as essential to healing, and a process which, in his *Answer to Job*, he saw in God.

Therefore, I think that in calling Fr. Victor his "white raven," Jung was indicating that he saw in White this great potential in relation to the transformation of the Western God image.[41] The old God image must die in order that the shadow can be integrated, and, of course, the God image would have to also include the feminine. In subsequent chapters, I will consider the impact that Jung's understanding of a God image that includes the Shadow and the feminine would have on White's understanding of a wholly good God, perfect and immutable,—Father, Son, and Spirit.

Although White's attitude toward alchemy was at times somewhat ambivalent, I think that this third interpretation—that the white raven refers to the great potential that Jung saw in White in relation to the transformation of the Western God image—is what Jung was really getting at. White spoke, for example, of "the seeming gibberish of the old alchemists,"[42] and "the oddities of alchemy,"[43] yet he was clearly fascinated by it. He found Jung's *Psychologie ünd*

Alchemie "a tremendous experience . . . enormously illuminating,"[44] and in a hardly disinterested review of the book, White talked of his own "alchemical propensities," which the two later discussed in Zurich in August 1946.[45] Following Jung's request for the Church's ordinances against alchemy, White pursued the topic in their correspondence,[46] and among White's lecture notes and private papers is a folder of alchemical writings which he kept. It is, therefore, highly probable that White would have understood the reference to the white raven as alchemical, and thus as a reference to the transformation of the Western God image.[47]

This reading is given further support when one considers that, at the end of White's life, Jung would refer to his own work as the *opus magnum*—and to the "apparently vain hope" that White would continue it. In alchemy, the whole process of integration (or individuation, as Jung called it) was called the *magnum opus*. Jung was essentially saying that he had found in Victor White a rare theologian—rare because he understood that the Western God image needed to be transformed—and that he could communicate this to other theologians. With this understanding, and with these expectations laid upon him by Jung, the impact of analytical psychology upon White's theology was clearly enormous. Unfortunately, as I will show, Jung's hope was in vain. Because, although White thought his psychology emotionally orthodox, it ultimately clashed with traditional Christian doctrines about God, to which White, as a Catholic, was committed.

Jung's So-called Empiricism

In the same letter of October 1, 1945, a letter which "staggered" White,[48] Jung addressed the issue of what Murray Stein has called "his so-called empirical stance,"[49] and Victor White's real appreciation of this "empirical" method. As I showed in the previous chapter, Jung had established "empirical" boundaries within which to do his psychology which were, strictly speaking, phenomenological. Jung had derived this methodology from Kant, whom he found greatly illuminating,[50] "the greatest of all sages ever born on German soil."[51] Victor White was also very aware of the influence that Kant had

had upon the early Jung.[52] One idea in particular made a profound impression upon Jung. Briefly stated, it was Kant's idea that things-in-themselves (*noumena*) are totally inaccessible and, therefore one must restrict oneself to things as they appear (*phenomena*). Somewhat uncritically, Jung accepted this distinction between *noumena* and *phenomena*, believing that Kant had thereby "erected a barrier across the mental world."[53] Furthermore, he thought that this distinction between *noumena* and *phenomena* "made it impossible for even the boldest flight of speculation to penetrate into the object."[54] Kant had, for Jung at least, defined the limits of knowledge.[55] Embracing Kant as the basis for his "empirical" approach to the psyche—what Jung himself called "Kantian epistemology expressed in everyday psychological language"[56]—Jung could not comment on the thing in itself but only on the thing as it appears. In the dialogue with White, this meant that Jung could not comment on God, but only on the God image.[57] In other words, by choosing Kant as the basis of his self-defined empiricism, Jung precluded any possibility of talk about a transcendent God. He had no choice but to restrict himself to "a purely empirical point of view," and "refrain from any application of metaphysical or philosophical considerations."[58]

Jung was impressed that, unlike other theologians, Victor White had understood his approach, and particularly the framework he had established for his psychology:

> You have rendered justice to my empirical and practical standpoint throughout. I consider this as a very meritorious act, since most of my philosophically or theologically minded readers overlook my empiricism completely. I never allow myself to make statements about the divine entity, since that would be a transgression beyond the limit of science. It would therefore be unfair to criticize my opinions as if it were a philosophical system.[59]

Most of Jung's "theologically minded readers" overlooked Jung's empiricism because, as I showed in the previous chapter, his psychology was clothed in the language of theology. Jung himself was aware that talk of the Self as God image within sounded more like theology than psychology. In *The Terry Lectures*, delivered at Yale in 1937, he said:

I know such formulations remind one fatally of wild metaphysical speculations. I am sorry, but it is exactly what the human mind produces and has always produced. A psychology which assumes that it could do without such facts must artificially exclude them. I should call this a philosophic prejudice, inadmissible from the empirical standpoint. I should emphasize, perhaps, that we do not establish a metaphysical truth through such formulations. It is merely a statement that the mind functions in such a way.[60]

Unlike other theologians, White was able to articulate (and, at least in the beginning, believe) that when Jung talked about God, he was talking about psychological truth, and not the nature of God. In other words, Jung thought that the Self as God image (Jung's "God") is true *inasmuch as it exists*.[61] Without this important distinction, it would indeed look like Jung was making a metaphysical assertion, that the God within was the same as the God of Judaeo-Christian revelation (and therefore incompatible with traditional notions of a transcendent deity). Thus it is also clear why Jung relentlessly asserted himself as an empiricist, albeit in the qualified sense of one who adhered to the phenomenological standpoint.[62] He emphatically desired "to give a wide berth to anything dogmatic or metaphysical, since it is not the scientist's task to preach the gospel."[63] Jung attempted to assure both the theologians and the scientists, often characterizing himself as the misunderstood prophet:

It is a common and totally unjustified misunderstanding on the part of scientifically trained people to say that I regard the psychic background as something "metaphysical," while on the other hand the theologians accuse me of "psychologising" metaphysics. Both are wide of the mark: I am an empiricist, who keeps within the boundaries set for him by the theory of knowledge."[64]

In view of such misunderstandings, Jung was impressed that he had found in White a theologian who seemed to appreciate his empirical standpoint, who seemed to have grasped that when Jung talked of God he meant the God who existed solely in the realm of psychological truth. Jung set a high value on White's attempt to really understand him and represent his psychology accurately.[65] In his second letter to Jung, for example, keen to address the "intellectual misgivings" of English Catholics toward Jung, White wrote: "It would truly be a very great help to know whether I do not misrepresent your position in the matter of the relation of your psychology to 'Religion'—or, more precisely to 'God.'"[66]

At least in the early years of their correspondence, White thought that Jung was careful to distinguish psychological statements from theological statements. He thought that Jung's concern was with *images* of God rather than the nature of God. And he had every reason to believe that this was the case. A good example can be seen in Jung's letter of October 1, 1945, when he corrected White for accusing him of repudiating divine transcendence. Drawing on what seemed to be a clear distinction between God and God image, Jung qualified his position:

> *I merely omit, since I am unable to prove it.* I don't preach, I try to establish psychological facts. I can confirm and prove the interrelation of the God-image with other parts of the psyche, but I cannot go further without committing the error of a metaphysical assertion, which is far beyond my scope. *I am not a theologian and I have nothing to say about the nature of God.* There is no place for subjective confessions in science. Whatever I say about "God" is said about the image *expressis verbis.* And the image is relative, as you yourself have stated [emphases mine].[67]

Jung did not repudiate divine transcendence, reassuring White that it was simply out of the realm of empirical psychology to talk about the nature of God. White later expressed that he "fully realized" that this was the case, and that, although he thought Jung's work unclear on this point in places, he was "truly penitent."[68] What is clear from this is that White initially accepted Jung's often-repeated assertion that his Kantian and self-defined empiricism precluded any metaphysical assertions as beyond the boundaries of his discipline. As Stein aptly put it, "[Jung's] so called empirical stance . . . included an interpretive method that was mortally infected by a neo-Kantian dismissal of metaphysics."[69]

Aside from this preclusion, there are other reasons that Jung wanted to distance himself from metaphysics. He wanted to assure the psychologist that, although his psychology sounded metaphysical (indeed, it is arguable that Jung *grounds* metaphysics in the psyche), he did indeed give "wide berth" to that for which there is no scientific evidence. Dourley has suggested that Jung also wanted to distance himself from what he saw as "the tragedy" of his youth: the metaphysics which had oppressed his father.[70] I think Dourley is correct on this point, for, as I showed in the previous chapter, Jung was deeply frustrated by the utterly transcendent God of metaphysics— which he believed was responsible for his father's and humanity's loss of the experience of God in the psyche. Accordingly, it made sense for Jung to distance himself from metaphysics and align himself with the experiential, with his (self-defined) empirical viewpoint. Furthermore, it seems that Jung thought that distancing himself from metaphysics would shield him from the criticism of and rejection by both psychological and theological academe.

However, although Jung distanced himself from talk about the nature of God (or claimed to), he was not disinterested in what the theologian had to say. Jung did indeed have his own theological opinions about his psychological findings. In an astounding passage in this same letter to White, he made the admission that his "secret purpose" was *profoundly* bound up with metaphysics: "My personal view in this matter is that man's vital energy or libido is the divine pneuma all right and it was this conviction which it was my secret purpose to bring into the vicinity of my colleagues' understanding."[71] Far from restricting himself to "the observation of phenomena" and "refrain[ing] from any metaphysical or philosophical considerations,"[72] Jung admitted to White, whom he had been trying to assure of his strictly empirical and non-metaphysical standpoint, that this experience of the Self as God image (that is, of wholeness) really *is* the experience of the Holy Spirit.

Publicly, Jung wanted to make his attachment to empiricism very clear. Publicly, he talked about the Self as God image but insisted that his commitment to empiricism would not allow him to assert that it is God Godself. Publicly, at least, I think Jung used his "so-called empirical stance"[73]—which was not strictly empirical in the philosophical sense—to shield himself from criticism of his own methodology, and to take a pre-emptive strike at two critical views in particular: first, the belief among psychologists that his psychology was indulgently metaphysical (for which there was no scientific evidence); and second, the belief among theologians that his psychology was metaphysical reductionism. Although White was singled out and commended by Jung for appreciating his "empiricism," White would grow increasingly skeptical,[74] writing in an unpublished manuscript, "Jung is an empiricist—or claims to be."[75] Qualifications aside, the point is that Jung defended his "empirical" standpoint with a passion, and invoked it as a shield against criticism. Perhaps Jung thought that it would indeed reassure scientists that he was not indulging in metaphysics, and theologians that he was not a metaphysical reductionist. At the same time, it meant that Jung could freely observe the God image as an "empirical" fact without having to deal with any metaphysical implications.

But privately (and he did say that this is his *personal* opinion) Jung had admitted to what can, on the basis of the empirical standpoint he invokes, only be "unscientific intuition,"[76] namely, that the God image is, in fact, the experience of the divine. Jung's neo-Kantian (and self defined) empirical method simply did not allow for the kind of metaphysical claims he wanted to make for it. Furthermore, Jung contradicted an earlier assertion that he had made in the same letter to White, namely, that he never allowed himself to make statements about the divine entity, that being a transgression of science. Jung had conveyed to White that he was open to *the possibility* that the God image is God but that he omitted such conclusions as he could not prove them. Elsewhere Jung had stressed that the *image* of the Holy Spirit is a living psychological reality.[77] What is noteworthy in this letter is that Jung was *not* saying, as he had earlier enunciated, that his intuition was that the God image is God—but he can't prove it or make a metaphysical assertion. Rather, Jung stated that he thought the God image *is* God, *and* it is his "secret purpose" to bring this to his colleagues. Indeed, it seems he reiterated this admission elsewhere, saying of the Holy Spirit, "He is a transcendental fact which presents itself to us under the guise of an archetypal image."[78]

Is this not a metaphysical statement of the type Jung persistently denied making? Although Jung never denied the existence of the metaphysical, he repeatedly insisted that his "empirical" method did not allow him to make metaphysical statements. It seems, however, that his "unscientific intuition" did. Colin Wilson put it well when he said that "the scientific psychologist was a public image and, to some extent, a public deception."[79] If this is the case, and Jung as an "empiricist" had asserted the unfairness of criticizing his opinions as if they were a philosophical system, it is surely necessary to reassess Jung's attempt to protect himself from such criticism. Furthermore, in assessing Jung's impact on White, it is important to acknowledge that Jung seemed to make claims that his methodology precluded, and to consider the role this played in an increasingly complex dialogue with Victor White.

Spreading the Good News

If Jung really did believe, as he had privately confessed to White, that the experience of the God image in the psyche was the experience of God, and that this was attainable through his psychology, it is plausible that he also had an unspoken hope for the Jungianization of Christianity. After all, he had also confessed to White that it was his "secret purpose" to bring this belief to the vicinity of his colleagues. Jung had known since his childhood (indeed it was his "secret") that, from the viewpoint of immediate experience, Christianity was dead. Because Victor White had *experienced* the power of Jung's psychology to be the revitalizing force for Catholic Christianity, I think that Jung knew he could use him, not unlike one healed in the gospels, who then spreads the good news of his salvation.[80] Furthermore, Jung was confident that White had really understood him.[81] White would be Jung's emissary to Catholic Christendom just as Jung had been Freud's emissary to the Gentiles. Although Jung always denied that he had any intention of founding a new religion,[82] he did see himself as addressing "those many people for whom the light has gone out, the mystery has faded, and God is dead."[83] He clearly hoped that Christianity would be revitalized (and, indeed, transformed) by embracing his notion that direct experience of God in the psyche was necessary for healing. The Catholic Church, however, did not share the perception that it needed revitalizing, and certainly did not see the necessity of enlisting Jung's help! Victor White, on the other hand, on the basis of his own experience, had informed Jung that he agreed "entirely" with his point of view.[84] Knowing this to be the case, Jung could write with some confidence:

. . . you feel as I do, that the theologian ought to learn a new language.
. . . Understanding begins with the individual mind and this means
psychology. It is a gigantic task indeed to create a new approach to an
old truth. More than once I have put the question to my theological
friends: what about new wine in old skins? The old way of interpreting
has itself to be interpreted, this time with the help of science.[85]

Expounding on what appears to be his method of evangelization,
Jung suggested to White that to speak to human beings about God,
one must use the language of psychology. "You cannot," wrote
Jung, "preach to a man who does not understand the language."[86]
To talk to educated people about God "means nothing," because
ideas about God have either been "dismissed . . . as nebulous fantasies,"[87] or considered conceptually rather than experienced "as a
thing living in the human soul."[88] This would have resonated with
White's experience in the early 1940s (which I depicted in the previous chapter) of the meaninglessness of the God-talk of theologians.
Fortunately for White, he had been "pretty thoroughly delivered"
from this experience (or lack of experience!) with the aid of his
psychiatrist, John Layard, who had also been a Jungian analyst.[89]
In such analysis, the patient begins to discover what Jung called the
"strange language" of the unconscious, which "tells him of eternal
truths."[90] Significantly, the patient will realize that he has heard
these truths before: in the dogma and creeds of religion.[91] It was
Jung's belief that dogma formulated the contents of the collective
unconscious.[92] While Jung's "empirical" methodology restricted
him from drawing any metaphysical conclusions about this, White's
metaphysics allowed him to articulate the "enormous implications"
of Jung's psychology, and Jung was definitely interested in what the
theologian had to say. "I envy you," he wrote, "and all those
enjoying full possession of Scholastic philosophy, and *I would surely
be among the first to welcome an explicit attempt to integrate the
findings of psychology into the ecclesiastical doctrine* [emphasis
mine]. I am sure I should draw the greatest benefit from it."[93]

Certainly, it was in Jung's interests to encourage White to integrate psychology into ecclesiastical doctrine, for, in theory, it could
only aid the Jungianization of Christianity. And from White's perspective, it meant that the implications of Jung's psychology, which
Jung's self-defined methodology would not allow him to articulate,
could indeed be articulated. But there is no question whatsoever

that ecclesiastical doctrine would not be so embracing of Jung, his God within, and his healed disciples. Even though there would be no official statement on psychology from the Vatican until 1953, Jung looked like a modernist, and, as I showed in the previous chapter, this alone would have been enough to rouse the suspicions of Rome. White would have looked like he was appropriating the errors of modern philosophy. But as White saw it, as long as important distinctions were made between psychology and theology, between God image and God, he did believe that some theoretical coordination with Jung was possible. Whenever those distinctions lacked clarity, however, White must have questioned whether Jung's psychology could be integrated into ecclesiastical doctrine, whether new wine could be poured into old wineskins.[94] How, for example, could Jung's God within be integrated into a doctrine of a transcendent God? Or how could Jung's quaternity (which included evil) be integrated into a doctrine of God as perfect and Trinitarian? *Even if* Jung's distinction between God and God image were accepted, integration into ecclesiastical doctrine looked unworkable, and this is an issue I will consider more fully in subsequent chapters.

It is of some significance that Jung's use of the biblical image of wineskins to envision the integration of his psychology into ecclesiastical doctrine was in fact a *misreading* of Matthew's gospel, for Matthew wrote, "People do *not* put new wine in old wineskins. Otherwise the skins burst, the wine spills out, and the skins are ruined. Rather, they pour new wine into fresh wineskins, and both are preserved"[emphasis mine].[95] Jung's psychology could not be contained within the limits of ecclesiastical doctrine, and White was, I think, becoming more aware that Jung's psychology would pose a challenge to traditional teaching about God. First, because he often stressed not the doctrinal but the *emotional* orthodoxy of Jung's psychology, and second, because he consistently proposed a model other than the integration of Jung's psychology into ecclesiastical doctrine: complementing and supplementing. White showed how Jung's psychology and Thomistic theology could be seen to complement each other, and further, he supplemented the empirical foundations, laid by Jung, with metaphysics.

Reading Aquinas Through Jung

To this end, White gave himself to the task of reading Aquinas *through* Jung. Writing again to Jung on October 9, 1945, he told of "a very considerable and growing interest among Catholics" in England in Jung's psychology, mentioning that he had been asked to give a series of lectures in London on Jung and Aquinas.[96] The impact of Jung on White's theology was clearly considerable, and White knew himself to be indebted to Jung.[97] Writing to Jung on October 23, 1945, White confessed, "Since reading your books, and still more since my own analysis, I have found myself more and more compelled to expound the *Summa* of St. Thomas Aquinas in psychological terms and with constant reference to its vast psychological relevance and implications."[98]

Having begun to consider the impact of Jung's work, White developed a reputation as a Dominican who, like Aquinas, was bold enough to see that psychology was not the enemy but that it works toward friendship with theology.[99] But White was concerned that some of his contemporaries in the Order had neglected Aquinas' "magnificent conception" that *all* truth—whether it be found in science or philosophy or revelation—came from God: "The relative autonomy of the various sciences, each differentiated by its particular methods and *'rationes cognoscibiles'* seems to be largely forgotten in our day."[100] The results of this amnesia were, said White, "quite deplorable." Although White applauded the work of fellow Dominicans, like Richard Kehoe and Gerald Vann, who shared his vision (and that of Thomas),[101] this was a scathing comment on the neo-scholastic rear guard at Blackfriars. At the same time, it was a defense of White's view that Thomism must be engaged with fields of secular knowledge—including the work of Jung—with different approaches to the Truth. White gave one example of this approach in the letter, drawing once again on the affective dimension of Aquinas' theory of knowledge of God, which allows for some discussion with Jung—particularly on the experience of God in the soul—which exclusively transcendent theologies precluded. White showed that, for Aquinas, that to which everyone gives the name *God* is rational and affective, transcendent and immanent:

For him, "quod omnes dicunt Deum", while remaining super- (or, if you prefer, extra-) rational is necessarily implied (Summa I.ii.3) and immanent (I.viii) in "quod sensu constat", besides being expressible only in symbol (I.i.8) and analogy (I.xiii), and being actual (though not necessarily conscious) object of all Love and Desire.[102]

We know God by reason and by affect, and, most perfectly, by cognition and affection—that is, in knowing and loving God. Having recaptured this affective aspect of Thomas for a generation that had lost it in the wake of modernism, White could, from a Jungian standpoint, legitimately speak of the therapeutic value of Aquinas. By emphasizing an affective dimension, White had connected Aquinas with Jung's notion of the healing which is brought about by an immediate experience of the God of the unconscious.

Jung was immensely grateful for this information on St. Thomas, as his reply, on February 13, 1946, indicated. The letter began, "My dear Father White,"[103] and proceeded to tell White of the growing interest in Zurich of the way White read his psychology. Jung wrote: "Once I mentioned a parallel that you draw between St. Thomas' philosophy and my psychology, which remark met with great interest, they asked me to give them fuller details."[104] Jung's emphasis here is, I think, significant: *a parallel*. Jung knew that their *points de départ* were diametrically opposed: Thomas' psychology was metaphysical, his psychology was empirical. As such, the only real possibility of a discussion would be, as he would come to express it, "the *comparison* of certain Thomistic statements with the statements of empirical psychology."[105] Realistically, this was the most White and Jung could have hoped for, though as will become apparent, both men harbored much greater hopes for discussion.

Fueled by such hopes, White made plans, in April 1946, to make his first visit to see Jung in Switzerland.[106] In a letter dated April 13, 1946, Jung expressed his delight and suggested some time between August 12 and 27. White was invited to stay, not at his official residence, Küsnacht, but in his country house at Bollingen, on the upper part of Lake Zurich, indicating that their working relationship was developing into a friendship. After a fortnight together, enjoying Jung's cooking and sailing on the lake,[107] and discussing such topics as alchemy and evil,[108] White left Bollingen August 27, and traveled to Bellinzona and Porto Ronco. He rejoined Jung at Ascona on September 2 for the Eranos Tagung, an interdisciplinary conference that had begun in 1933, which explored links between Western and Eastern thinking.[109] The Eranos, a name chosen by Rudolf Otto from the Greek word ἑορτή meaning "feast," had became "a sort of unofficial picnic for the Zurich school of analytical psychology."[110] The following year, at the invitation of Jung, White himself would present a paper.

Caution: Rocks Ahead!

After visiting Jung, White wrote to him, on October 13, 1946, and told him of a dream in which he and Jung were sailing from Norway to England with Jung "the captain at the wheel."[111] In recalling the dream, White said that they were "scudding along . . . at considerable speed and amid perilous rocks" until the boat "mounted the shore" and then "sailed down the streets dexterously missing all the buildings and the traffic." However, although dangerous, White was not afraid, "because the <u>Wind</u> was taking care of us and would never wreck the pair of us." Jung was not surprised by the dream, as his reply of November 6, 1946 revealed: "I had all sorts of feelings or 'hunches' about you and about the risks you are running. We are indeed on an adventurous and dangerous journey! But the guiding principle is the 'wind', i.e., the *pneuma*. Norway is the northern country, i.e., the intuitive sector of the mandala."[112]

On December 11, 1946, using the same imagery, White expressed to Jung the hope that "the πνεῦμα will continue to blow and keep us both off the rocks." White knew subconsciously the risks he was running both on the personal level and within the Church. Personally, psychology and dogma would eventually pull him in opposite directions, requiring that he sacrifice either his life or his faith. It is interesting that after White's visit to Bollingen, Jung told a pastor friend:

> Last year I saw an English Dominican who spontaneously admitted that *everything* depended on whether the Church would go along with modern psychological developments or not. I was very surprised to hear that from a *Catholic* theologian. I wouldn't have gone so far.

But it does seem to me that it would be appropriate if theology at least knew about the existence of the unconscious. This would be facilitated by St. Augustine's "Noli foras ire, redi ad te ipsum, in interiore homine habitat veritas."[113]

Of course, "everything" depended on it—for Victor White at least. White had experienced this return into himself and had discovered the rich healing resources which dwelt there. But unfortunately for White, Jung's inner deity looked like the "religious sense" of the condemned modernists, and so it was unlikely that the Church would "go along with" modern psychological developments. This, in spite of the fact that the immanence of God did indeed have a place in the Church's tradition, not least in Augustine. But because the neo-scholastics wanted to distance themselves from the modernists, the immanence of God had been neglected and (overcompensating!) the transcendence of God exalted. White therefore found himself deeply torn between his psychological experience and his Church. This inner turmoil vis à vis Jung's psychology would eventually bring White to a breaking point, on which I will elaborate in the final chapter.

White knew the risks he was running within the Church and the Dominican Order. Yet, as his lecture notes reveal, White was undeterred, emphatic about the need for Catholics to dialogue with psychology for apologetic, pastoral, and interdisciplinary reasons. First of all, on the apologetic level, White believed it was important to show that psychology had not debunked theological truth. Jung himself had addressed this, drawing an analogy with physics: a physicist may explain how light functions, but it does not mean that there is no light. White often took up this apologetic concern, telling Jung, for example, of a lecture to undergraduates at Trinity College Oxford who "have formed the suspicion that you want to 'debunk God'! They have called me in to remove their doubts, which I trust I shall effectively do!"[114] Jung was no apologist for Christianity, but White thought that his claims for "empiricism" had effectively removed the main opposition to theology. Thus, as long as it was made clear that Jung was talking about the God image and not the nature of God, suspicions of debunking could be allayed.

The second reason that White thought Catholics should dialogue with psychologists was pastoral. If psychology was engaged in the healing of souls, White thought that Catholics had a pastoral responsibility to help souls who would not go to a psychologist. This would eventually lead to the establishment, in 1954, of The More Clinic, the aim of which was to meet the needs of patients in a Catholic atmosphere by modern psychological methods.[115]

Third, White thought that the psychology of the unconscious had the potential to throw light on Catholic truth itself, and that theology could likewise make an important contribution to psychology.[116] Some of the major themes of religion, such as birth, sacrifice, death, salvation, and resurrection, are played out in the unconscious, and this clearly provided ground for the mutual enrichment of faith and psychology. But there is little doubt that this was a risky endeavor for both men.

On December 18, 1946, a week after what would turn out to have been a prophetic dream, White received a handwritten letter from Jung, described by Adler and Jaffé as "the first of a long series of hand-written letters, often of many pages, showing his great personal interest in the correspondence with W[hite], who seemed to be able to give Jung what he felt he needed most: a man with whom he could discuss on equal terms matters of vital importance to him."[117]

Years before, Jung had expressed a desire for cooperation with a theologian, and as one also well grounded in psychology, White fulfilled that wish beyond his expectations.[118] Jung concluded the letter, "Please write again to me. You have a purity of purpose which is beneficial."[119]

A Medieval Approach to the Collective Unconscious

White wrote again, sending Jung a copy of an article entitled "St. Thomas' Conception of Revelation,"[120] in January 1947. The article was the first that White had written since the correspondence with Jung had begun, and it clearly reflected the thought of one pondering the impact of Jung on his theology. "I am convinced," wrote White, "that Aristotle and Aquinas have much to offer us for the organisation and interpretation of those new vistas which are being opened up again for many a modern man, especially thanks to analytical psychology."[121] This is certainly of interest, because Jung did not share White's optimism, thinking Aquinas' appropriation of Aristotle over Plato disastrous because it led to a "turning away from our psychic origins."[122] In fact, he had expressed to Hugo Rahner, S. J., that he found scholasticism pathologically unaware of the unconscious: "Scholastic language and its presuppositions are no longer appropriate for contemporary man if one wants to give him any understanding of the human psyche. I know this not *a priori* but from repeated experience."[123] Jung knew from experience, particularly that of his father, that scholastic language was in part responsible for humanity's "turning away" from the God of the unconscious, and that this had led to an overly intellectual approach to a God "*outside* man."[124] Jung saw this as pathological because it prevented human beings from "an immediate experience of divine grace"[125]—and thus it prevented healing. But White was more optimistic about scholasticism in relation to Jung, as his earlier ability to recapture an apologetic of immanence in Aquinas' notion of "affective knowledge" had shown. And now, in this article, in exploring Aquinas' concept of revelation and the processes that revelation involved in the psyche, White offered great insight into how Thomas had dealt with the problem of the collective unconscious. Furthermore, White did much to challenge the misconception among analytical psychologists that Aquinas neglected to consider rationally the "manifestations of unreason"—the irrational phenomena—of the psyche.[126]

In the article, White explored Aquinas' concept of revelation, beginning with the question: what happens when we say "God reveals"? In characteristically Thomistic fashion, White answered this question by saying what does not happen. To say "God reveals" is not to say that something happens in eternity. Nor does it say anything new about God. For if God has revealed Godself in the person of Jesus Christ, "there is no more for God to say." But because there is much for human beings to see, revelation must continue.[127] Thus, White explored revelation through the recipient of revelation—whom he called the prophet: ". . . what happens when we say that God reveals, is precisely *the psychological event in the prophet's mind*—the 'visio prophetica,' his awareness of what is commonly hidden from human perception [emphasis mine]."[128] For Aquinas, revelation is the prophetic vision. This is not Aquinas' only definition of revelation, but certainly it is that which was relevant to White and his discussions with Jung. After all, it is not God who is veiled in ignorance—what White calls "the unconsciousness"—but human beings. Jung essentially inverted this: *God* was unconscious and needed to be redeemed by the conscious ego. But for Aquinas, *human beings* were "unconscious" because human reason is finite and God can never be known by human reason. This point needs elaborating, because it is very relevant to dialogue with Jung (or preclusion of such dialogue, in that—from Jung's perspective—it causes human beings to "turn away" from the God within). For Aquinas, the world becomes intelligible when images are received by the senses in the passive intellect, and are illumined by the active intellect, allowing its essence to be abstracted. And since God is immaterial—God is not an object of sense experience— God is therefore unknowable in essence. God is, in other words, beyond our understanding. How, then, could a Thomist like Victor White find agreement with Jung who believed that God *could* be known (and *only* be known) by direct experience of the psyche? (As I have shown, Jung thought that theologies which saw God as an unknowable transcendent were pathological.)

For Aquinas, said White, it is revelation—the prophetic vision—that can and does remove some of these veils of ignorance.[129] As Aquinas expressed it, "Revelation is the very perception itself of divine things, by which prophecy is brought about, and by this very perception the veil of darkness and ignorance is taken away."[130]

White noted that this revelation, or prophetic vision, can occur both naturally and supernaturally. Revelation as natural prophecy is that which the love of God calls up in human beings (*donum sapientiae*).[131] It is a non-sensory cognitive perception of God, or what White had earlier called "affective knowledge." The natural prophet (and here White includes all baptized Christians) does not see eternity but receives revelation of "something *present* which is *significant* of the future."[132] Although White did not mention Jung, there is clearly a point of contact here, because, for Jung also, it is

God who takes the initiative in revelation, the numinous power of the archetype holding the ego in its grip. But, whereas the Christian mystic might talk of the experience of the Christ within, Jung would say that she is referring to the archetypal experience of wholeness (that is, the Self as God image).

Supernatural prophecy, on the other hand, consists in divine secrets being revealed to a human being (*sapientia dei*). The supernatural prophet sees "something *present* that is *significant* of eternity," as in the case of Jeremiah and the almond tree, or Amos and the basket of fruit.[133] It is the result of God's action on the human intellect wherein truths are impressed upon the mind of the prophet.

It is clear that in White's account of Aquinas' natural and supernatural prophecy, God "can never be directly known . . . by the finite intelligence." God is "the Eternal, Transcendent, Infinite Godhead."[134] Thus, for Aquinas, revelation is not something we grasp (*mathein*), but rather something we experience (*pathein*), something that happens to us.[135] It follows, then, that the vehicle of revelation "is not the rational concept but the concrete image."[136] And the images a prophet sees are symbols, which represent a reality that cannot be put into words, but are used, out of necessity, "for what wholly transcends sense perception or rational comprehension."[137]

If the prophet sees images, then the imagination is central to understanding Aquinas' notion of the prophetic vision.[138] For Aquinas, said White, the prophet must have a good imagination—even over and above good morals.[139] After all, a man could lack charity and yet have a very perceptive mind.[140] White recalled that it was Aristotle who said that it is not the best people who have the best dreams.[141] Jung was fascinated with this idea, writing to White, "I must say it gave me a new light on St. Thomas. His views are really astonishing. . . . I thank you very much that you let me have your paper. With your kind permission, I should like to quote something of it in my paper on the Trinity."[142] Jung wanted to quote the "excellent point" that revelation has more to do with good imagination than with good morals. He added, "I should even say that there is only a good prophet when the devil has caught hold of one of his legs."[143]

In both natural and supernatural revelation, the imagination is the vehicle of Divine Revelation. White noted that that which a person perceives by her external senses is ordinarily limited to what is present in space and time. But the inner sense faculty of *phantasia* "can and does produce images . . . of what is absent . . . from the external senses.[144] The imagination may be directed in several ways to produce *phantasia*—first, according to White, by the will, such as in "the conscious production of art." This is paralleled in Jung, who encouraged his patients to draw mandalas as a way of activating the unconscious mind.[145] Second, the imagination may be directed by the sense impressions which a person receives. Third, the imagination can produce images "of whose origin the subject is unconscious," for example, in the dream.[146] This would have resonated with Jung, for whom the dream was the primary medium of God's revelation to the individual. Prior to Jung, Aristotle had in fact questioned whether dreams might be divine in origin,[147] Aquinas had thought that some were,[148] and White also thought it possible. However, Jung differed from White in believing that revelation occurs wholly within the psyche: it is in the inner dialogue of ego and unconscious, of human and divine, that the individual receives revelation. Fourth, the imagination may be directed by biological or chemical factors (Aquinas' "humours," for example) to produce *phantasia*. Again this would have resonated with Jung, who believed that LSD allowed the archetypes to come into the field of consciousness. Finally, White said that Aquinas thought that angels were capable "of producing images in human consciousness."[149]

Aquinas' angels deserve closer attention because they afford insight into how Aquinas dealt with the problem of the unconscious. For Aquinas, angels are immaterial, or, in White's words, "separated intelligences of metaphysical speculation."[150] In the Bible they are message bearers, "mediating the unknown to consciousness."[151] White showed that, for Aquinas, the immediate causes of supernatural and natural *prophetia* are biological or physical. Images are produced by an "agitation" of bodily spirits and humors, for example, the excitation of neurons of the brain. For Aquinas, the angels are bound by the laws of nature and have to act "through the organs of the body," in accordance with the sense-experience of the receiver.[152] How then, within these constraints, do angels inform the human mind? In two ways, said White, drawing on Aquinas. First, by indirectly fashioning images in the imagination. And second, by a "strengthening" (*confortatio*) of the human understanding. Because angels do not have the capacity to form ideas in the human intellect, there will be no new images; but the capacity of the intellect to judge images will be greater.[153] In other words, angels increase the prophet's power of judgment.

What is clear here is that judgment is essential to the apprehension of Truth, without which it has no meaning (*significatio*).[154] It is just an image, absolutely useless in and of itself. White gave an example of what he meant: I may, like Pharaoh, have a vivid dream, but unless I can judge or interpret it, it is useless to me. After all, it was Joseph, the interpreter of dreams, and not Pharaoh, the dreamer, who was the prophet. For Aquinas, as mediated through White, Joseph was "the receiver of revelation."[155] Perhaps the most obvious parallel, which White did not make, but which Jung would have appreciated, is the way in which people go to their analysts for dream analysis. It is no small coincidence that Jung identified himself with the prophet.

White sent this article to Jung on March 8, 1947,[156] and Jung read it with "great interest."[157] Jung thought the angels in particular were "simply wonderful." He himself believed that angels were experienced by human beings as archetypes of the collective unconscious. But, unlike Aquinas, who thought that angels existed as spiritual realities, Jung could not say that they were more than images—his "empiricism" would not allow him to do this. But he did think they had profound symbolic value, and, as such, they could have a healing effect on the recipient, not unlike his image of God. Further, he thought that angels, when projected out of the unconscious, were embodied in the forces of light and goodness, and that our dark side was embodied in demons.

In his reply of March 27, 1947, and significant of their developing friendship, Jung addressed White as "Victor" and asked that Victor call him "C. G."[158] A month later, on April 23, 1947, Jung wrote to White and invited him to present his paper at the Eranos Tagung in Ascona. He wrote:

I have gone once more through your splendid essay "De Revelatione." I think, if you would give a short survey of The Psychology of

St. Thomas at the Eranos meeting, you would fulfil our expectations. You must realise that our public appreciates the demonstration of medieval psychology which is strange to our ears. We are not used to it as our colleagues are. Moreover a genius like St. Thomas, who takes into consideration the action of angels and demons, will be accepted with the greatest attention, because it gives us a chance to understand how a medieval mind tackled the modern problem of the collective unconscious. Thus a part of your essay on St. Thomas, if you arrange it a bit for the occasion, would do.[159]

White was truly thrilled by Jung's invitation,[160] and spent much of this time preparing for the lecture.[161] Once again, he took up the subject of a medieval approach to the unconscious, presenting his lecture, "St. Thomas' Conception of Revelation," and prefacing it with another lecture, "The Aristotelian Conception of the Psyche."[162] In the latter, White further attempted to dispel popular misconceptions about Aquinas, particularly the accusation that he was solely concerned with the intellectual faculties of the psyche.[163] This was absolutely crucial if there was to be any constructive dialogue with Jung, who, as I have shown, thought that the emphasis on the intellectual faculties was responsible for "the prejudice that the deity is *outside* man"[164] — a prejudice which Jung saw as the root cause of the spiritual crisis of humanity. Although White could agree with Jung that "the remedy for our modern ills is to be found in religion," he diverged from Jung in his belief that "religion will only help us if it assumes an intellectual character."[165] White saw it as his task to show that Aquinas was not only concerned with the intellectual, but very much alive to empirical observation and practical therapy.[166] Aquinas' *De Passionibus*, for example, includes such things as the principle of compensation[167] and the psychological function of weeping.[168]

But White was not suggesting that Aquinas had anything to offer psychology as an "empirical" science. Rather he thought that the Aristotelian-Thomistic account of the psyche might meet some of the deficiencies of a purely empirical approach to the psyche by offering a more integral metaphysical appreciation. White wrote: "Their contribution, as I see it, is to supplement and complement rather than supplant modern psychological findings and methods."[169] It was a model that had correspondence in his dream life.[170] White had received details of a dream from Jung on December 27, 1947, but had initially "not dare[d] to comment." However, he changed his mind after a vision of his own, in which, despite Jung's request, he had not offered the Catholic "Friday fish" to his Protestant friend Jung, thinking that, as a Protestant, Jung was under no such obligation to abstain. Jung, in return, had looked at him "reproachfully and disappointed and ill." As White saw it, the reproach meant that he should not have denied the man he had "come to know and love" the fish (the "ΙΧΘΥΣ"), for in so denying him that which was significantly symbolic of sacrament and salvation in Catholic theology, he was denying him what he truly believed.[171] The vision thus also reinforced White's proposed model of supplementation of Jung's thought with the healing message (*salus*) of Catholicism.

White was deeply aware of the limitations of Jung's "empirical" approach to the psyche, many of which Jung himself recognized. He knew that empirical psychology could not, for example, affirm or deny the transcendental validity of the psyche's own images and judgments. As I have shown, Jung repeatedly asserted the boundaries of his "empiricism," and saw metaphysics as logically excluded from the realm of scientific inquiry. But, heavily influenced by Aristotle, White was emphatic that the psyche could not be exclusively empirical. Immersed as he was in Aristotle's *De Anima*, White was convinced that the psyche was "incurably rationalist."[172] In fact, White thought the *De Anima* was far more important for psychology than Aristotle's specifically psychological works, such as *De Sensu et Sensato* or *De Memoria et Reminiscentia,* because it offered what White called "pure intellectual thinking *about* the psyche."[173] Aristotle wanted to present the psyche in rational terms, and I think that White's indebtedness to Aristotle on this point exposes a major deficiency in Jung's psychology—namely, that his methodology precluded any possibility of a rational formulation of the psyche. It is precisely this deficiency that allowed White to propose a model for doing theology that was based on supplementing and complementing Jung.

As I showed earlier in this chapter, Jung had constructed a methodology based on Kant which, as Jung saw it, separated the phenomenal and noumenal worlds, and thus, for Jung, the God image and God. Jung believed that this dependence on Kant gave him an "empirical"—in other words, a scientifically sound—psychology, while at the same time it justified his observation of the world of phenomena. This world was, in Jung's schema, the world of unconscious images. It was, in particular, the world of the God image. God was an image, a phenomenon, an "empirical" fact. But Jung's usage of Kant's "barrier" between the phenomenal and noumenal worlds absolutely prevented Jung from affirming or denying that the God image is God. Furthermore, Jung clearly saw his dependence on Kant's methodology as essential to the credibility he so craved as a scientist. Jung didn't *want* God to be formulated rationally (at least publicly) for fear of being regarded as indulging in metaphysics—as scientifically suspect. He knew that talk of a God image within sounded like metaphysics, and so he needed to "impose on [him]self every conceivable restriction in interpreting it" to protect him as a scientist.[174] Kant was the perfect choice. Even if Jung had wanted God to be formulated rationally, a Kant-based methodology absolutely precluded this.

However, Jung did not want to ignore the experience of phenomena like the God image, even though such images seemed inherently metaphysical. Essentially the choice of Kant as the basis of his "empiricism" allowed Jung to observe that which might otherwise have been dismissed as metaphysical nonsense.[175] He did not have to ignore phenomena such as the God image. Further, inasmuch as these phenomena were experienced, it allowed Jung to give them the status of empirical facts.[176] Essentially, this meant that Jung could talk about the experience of the God image within as "psychologically true," while at the same time protecting himself from the inherently metaphysical character of the God image.[177] Jung had the best of both worlds. As Wolfgang Giegerich has expressed it, "[Kant's] barrier, the way Jung used it, gave psychology licence to 'plunge into the world of the mysterious' *without* having to be *intellectually responsible* for these experiences."[178] Giegerich's point is that Jung's dependence on the Kantian "barrier" between the phenomenal and noumenal worlds, which Jung used as the framework of his distinction between God image and God, relieved Jung of thinking:

The Kantian barrier immunized psychology as a field against its own contents, against their speculative character, so that it could self-indulgently and innocently observe and imagine them (like we watch television), without itself having to undergo the alchemical decomposition-sublimation process that it liked to observe and talk about and that would have put psychology (if it had entered it) into a position where it could, and would have to, itself *think* speculatively, dialectically.[179]

By choosing Kant as the basis of his "empiricism," Jung had effectively precluded the kind of "pure intellectual thinking *about* the psyche" that Victor White so much admired in Aristotle. In fact, as White put it, Jung saw this desire for the soul to be formulated rationally as "an infantile regression to pre-Kantian naiveté."[180] With Kant's methodology in place, Jung did not have the logical means to say the God image is God, to "equate the image with 'the transcendental X' to which it points."[181] Furthermore, in choosing Kant, Jung ensured that the field of psychology and the contents of the psyche were, as Giegerich put it,

. . . neatly immunized against one another, neither one challenging, seducing, infecting, decomposing the other. No *coniunctio oppositorum*, no *mysterium coniunctionis*, no "psychology of transference" *in* the logical structure of psychology *itself*, namely between the knower and the known, logos and psyche, theory and phenomenon, but a right hand that does not have to know what the left hand is doing.[182]

The result of Jung's choice of Kant as the basis of his "empiricism" is, as his critics have rightly asserted, that the soul and its manifestations are reduced to the level of images. Ultimately, this meant that Jung could say that God was "psychologically true"—in other words, God was true within Jung's newly invented category of truth.[183] But God could not be "true" in any other sense, for Jung's methodology disallowed the possibility that God could be formulated rationally. Thus, in relation to Victor White, who, like Aristotle, saw the need for the soul to be formulated rationally, Jung's choice of Kant as the basis for his "empiricism" (which precluded this) would put the two men at odds. "It is true," White would later write, "that Aristotle can have little validity for us if we suppose the *Kritik* to be beyond criticism . . ."[184] This being said, from White's perspective, it *did* mean that a model of "supplementing and complementing" was appropriate; his metaphysics could supply some of the deficiencies created by Jung's choice of Kant. White could, for example, point to the deficiency of Jung's schema wherein, restricted by his methodology, human beings had fashioned gods in the likeness of his own psychic content. Victor White, on the other hand, with a less restrictive methodology, could make the metaphysical claim that revelation made it known that the psyche is made like God, and for God, and to partake in the eternal life of God. Psychology makes God in man's image (as a projection of the God image), revelation makes man in God's image. So, while not denying Jung's empirical claims about the God image, White could supplement with talk of God Godself.

New York, New York

In September 1947, White traveled to America for a sabbatical made possible by Mrs. Frances Leggetts, a millionairess friend at Ridgely Manor in Stone Ridge, New York, who had offered him a "sinecure chaplaincy."[185] While there, he continued to exchange ideas and dreams with Jung. He spent his time lecturing on the unconscious and God,[186] and working on his book *God and the Unconscious*, which, at least in its early stages, he envisioned would be "a fairly comprehensive treatise."[187] But White soon became disillusioned with the work and, by November 1947, writing to his friend, the novelist Antonia White, confessed, "C. G. Carus wrote the book I wanted to write 100 years ago." [188] Jung offered encouragement to White during this period and agreed to write a preface to the work. He was still deeply impressed with White's aptitude for understanding his psychology, and wrote to White in New York, inviting him to be a founding member of an "Institute of Analytical Psychology" in Zurich (now the C. G. Jung Institute). In a letter dated December 27, 1947, Jung wrote, "I have been asked to write to you whether you would be inclined to allow us to put your name on that list. You risk no further obligations. We only hope that you would add the moral authority of your name to the new enterprise . . . Your name would be in good society. Personally I would be much obliged to you if you could do us this pleasure."[189]

He continued, somewhat prophetically, "As I am getting on in age and as I am going to be gathered to my ancestors and avatars within a measurable time, the Institute is meant to carry on the work."[190]

Within a very short time, White had become highly respected, not only as a theologian, but also as an analytical psychologist—although it dismayed him that he was always seen as the theologian and not the analyst.[191] Further, it is clear that, even as early as 1947, Jung envisioned White's role in continuing his work for the transformation of the Western God image: he would be Jung's "white raven." White was honored by Jung's invitation—as Jung's letter of January 30, 1948 indicates—and although White's letter has not been preserved, it seems that White was also trying to raise interest in the institute with the hierarchy in Rome.[192] Hints of this emerge in Jung's expression of "many thanks for your personal willingness to contribute to our endeavours! I have not yet heard from Rome."[193]

Although there did seem to be some attempts by the English Province of the Order of Preachers to build bridges between Jung and Rome,[194] it was unlikely that Rome would be interested in an "Institute of Analytical Psychology." After all, its founding father seemed to have appropriated a series of what Rome perceived as heresies, including gnosticism, neo-Kantianism, and modernism. In a climate where "any truck with the modern world would have been deemed suspect,"[195] this would have roused Rome's suspicions of White and further alienated him from the neo-scholastic rear guard in the Dominican Order. Nonetheless, White himself was indeed a founding member of the C. G. Jung Institute of Zurich which was opened on April 24, 1948.[196]

White and the Gnostic Jung

While still in New York, White received a very warm welcome at the Analytical Psychology Club, where he gave a lecture on February 20, 1948.[197] Members of the club had been fascinated by a passage in Jung's *Modern Man In Search of a Soul*, and, at Jung's

recommendation, had called upon White to elucidate.[198] The
passage that intrigued them reads as follows:

> *I do not believe that I am going too far when I say that modern man, in
> contrast to his nineteenth century brother, turns his attention to the psyche
> with very great expectations; and that he does so without reference to
> any traditional creed, but rather in the Gnostic sense of religious experi-
> ence* [emphasis mine]. We should be wrong in seeing mere caricature or
> masquerade when the movements already mentioned try to give them-
> selves scientific airs; their doing so is rather an indication that they are
> actually pursuing "science" or knowledge instead of faith which is the
> essence of western religions. The modern man abhors dogmatic postu-
> lates taken on faith and the religions based upon them. He holds them
> valid only in so far as their knowledge-content seems to accord with
> his own experience of the deeps of psychic life.[199]

The members of the club looked to White to help them understand who these gnostics were, and what Jung meant by contrasting
faith and religious experience. White agreed to provide some illumination on both of these points, though he was "staggered at [his]
own effrontery," and admitted "some demon of the unconscious
has persuaded me to display to you, not the honest fruits of long toil
and deep research, but some amateurish prancings on a most
intractable hobby-horse."[200] Despite his self-deprecation, it is significant that Jung thought him a suitable expositor of his thought.

From the beginnings of his first encounter with Jungian ideas in
the early 1940s, White had been very much aware of Jung's affinity
with gnosticism.[201] Indeed, Jung's enthrallment with the gnostics
had a deep impact on White, provoking him to consider the sects
that had been condemned by his own Church, and thus question
"that there might be more to it than a bygone form of non-sensical,
fanatical superstition—of no interest to myself or to any modern
man."[202]

For White, gnosticism is defined as salvation through knowledge, in contrast to the Christian notion that salvation comes
through faith which manifests itself in love. Correcting Jung, whose
talk of "the gnosis" gives the impression that there was only one
sect, White was clear that there was no one coherent body of belief
and practice known as Gnosticism. Indeed, in his later works, Jung

was very careful to distinguish between *gnosticism* as it was known in its varied expressions in the second century and *gnosis*, which he sees as a special kind of knowledge, a distinction he had gleaned from Fr. White.[203]

White presented some of these gnostic systems: most notably, Valentinus[204] and the *Pistis Sophia*, whose doctrines he subjected to a "psychological diagnosis"[205]—as a way of exploring the similarities between gnosticism and analytical psychology. One such example is introversion. White suggested that the Greek philosophers, who preceded the gnostics, unintentionally elicited a reaction of introversion: "The psychological law of compensation teaches us that the hypertrophy of one set of functions and attitudes, and the consequent atrophy of their opposites, call forth the compulsive domination of those opposites. Thwarted in its centrifugal flow into an external world, which is unable to assimilate and integrate, the libido is forced to flow back, centripetally, to the interior world of the collective unconscious."[206] Expressed more simply, White was saying that gnosticism emerged following a period of predominantly rationalistic Greek philosophy, and as a compensation, gnosticism was more experiential in its approach to knowledge.

White identified a second example of diagnostic similarities between gnosticism and analytical psychology in the shadow side. As he saw it, the gnostics recognized that the shadow side was absent from the Christian worldview: "What is striking about gnostic systems is that they are based exclusively upon the manifestations of the unconscious, and that their moral teachings do not baulk at the shadow side of life."[207] Jung discovered in gnosticism what White calls "the repressed side" of the Protestantism in which he had been raised. For Jung, that tradition represented an overly rational approach to faith, like that of his father and the early Victor White, which repressed the knowledge of an inner experience. But the gnostics shared with Jung this sense of humanity's connectedness to the religious experience of the psyche.

White, was not, however, uncritical of Jung on the issue of the gnostics and the shadow side. Jung himself had said that the gnostics "do not baulk" at the shadow side of life, that the gnostics seemed very comfortable with "the dark and noxious powers of the unconscious."[208] But as White noted, the gnostics, "absorbed in [their] lightsome world of fantasy" had their *own* shadow side: "the world of fact."[209]

The *Pistis Sophia*, one of the few actual gnostic texts to be preserved, provided further psychological interest for White. Offering a detailed exposition of the text, he argued that in the *Pistis Sophia* we have, ironically, a salvation not by gnosis but by faith.[210] As White saw it, it represented "[the] struggles of a gnosticist who has felt and faced the tension of his gnostic vision with the counter-claims of Catholic and Evangelical Christianity."[211] In the final section of the lecture, White explored this tension, offering further insight into what Jung meant by contrasting faith and religious experience—a contrast that is most evident in the struggle between orthodox Christians and gnostics in the human psyche today. He concluded:

> I have already suggested that every analysant is in some measure a gnostic (I do not say a gnosticist): a Knowing One who has experienced some interior vision of the archetypal, collective psyche—or at least (like the outer fringe of the old gnostic's followers) is probably involved in transference on someone who has. And whether we profess orthodox Christianity or not, we are all in more or less conscious degree inheritors also of its distinctive values and attitudes.[212]

The tension between the gnostic vision and the claims of Christianity is perhaps most poignantly brought out in the respective positions of Jung and White. Jung was the gnostic, White the orthodox Christian. Jung had experience, White had faith. But the terrain is slightly more complex because, as a result of the impact of Jung's psychology on his life and thought, White also experienced and was subsequently subject to an inner tension between his *experience* of Jungian spirituality and his *belief* in orthodox Christianity. White was, as a Dominican, grounded in the tradition of Aquinas. As such, he saw faith as an infused virtue, a gift that allowed him to assent to a body of divinely revealed knowledge (such as, for example, God is three and one).[213] However, as White noted, "No dogma is just a proposition that requires a purely intellectual assent."[214] For White, belief in God required the discernment of reason, along with the dimension of grace.[215] Jung's view, on the other hand was quite different from this, as his response to White's "excellent lecture"[216] indicated. In fact it was White who provoked Jung to consider the question of faith:

> Your paper has made me think: *Have I faith or a faith or not?* I have always been unable to produce faith and I have tried so hard that I finally did not know any more what faith is or means. I owe it to your paper that I have now apparently an answer: faith or the equivalent of faith with me is what I would call respect. I have respect for the Christian Truth. Thus it seems to come down to an involuntary assumption in me that there is something to dogmatic truth, something *indefinable* to begin with. Yet I feel respect for it, although I don't really understand it. But I can say my life work is essentially an attempt to understand what others apparently can believe. There must be—so I conclude—a rather strong motive-power connected with the Christian truth, otherwise it would not be explicable why it influences me to such an extent. My respect is—mind you—involuntary; it is a "datum" of irrational nature. This is the nearest I can get to what appears to me as "faith."[217]

White was most gratified by Jung's appreciation of his paper. He was, however, perplexed at Jung's involuntary "respect" for Christianity because of his own experience: "What you say of faith interests me profoundly: indeed I think it is crucial."[218] The reason White thought it so crucial . . . it highlighted the difference of perspective between himself and Jung. White's assent to God was voluntary and rational, mediated by revealed doctrines. Jung's "faith" (respect), on the other hand, was involuntary and it came from experience, the experience of the unconscious—which also happened to find expression in many of the symbols and rituals of Christianity. But dogma did not always accord with the experience of psychic contents, and, subsequently, Jung thought that the Christian notion of faith—in a God "*outside* man"— had precipitated a "turning away from our psychic origins."[219] In fact, Christian faith had always been a stumbling block for Jung because, as Jung saw it, faith had crushed his father. In seeing faith as a virtue that enabled voluntary assent to revealed doctrines about God, White was, therefore, more closely aligned with Jung's father than with Jung—though Jung seemed oblivious to this, remarking that he could not "produce faith" no matter how hard he tried.[220] In fact, he had pondered whether believers were endowed with a special "receiving organ" which enabled them to "tune in" to faith.[221] Denied this "charisma of faith," Jung recalled how he had to fall back on "the experience of religious realities which I had to accept without regard to their truth."[222]

So for Jung, "faith" (respect) is involuntary and it comes from experience. It is that which is elicited in him when the archetype of the Self as God image—which he saw as living— "seizes and controls" him.[223] Thus whereas White's faith is a *voluntary* acceptance of divinely revealed knowledge, Jung's "faith" is that which allows him to cling to an *involuntary* and immediate experience (and thus, for Jung, knowledge) of "the God within."[224] Talk of such knowledge of a God within sounded deeply gnostic, an accusation most famously penned by Martin Buber.[225] Although Jung tried to defend his "empirical approach," such assertions that the experience of the archetype of the Self *is* the experience of the God within, seemed gnostic to the core.[226] In an unpublished manuscript, Victor White defended him: "Of course, Jung's psychology is not wholly a Gnostic one. Jung, too, was concerned with the preservation of the scientific method in his psychology of the unconscious."[227] Jung's "scientific method"—essentially his neo-Kantian "empiricism"— allowed Jung to experience phenomena which might otherwise have been dismissed as metaphysical nonsense. Thus inasmuch as archetype of the Self as God image "seizes and controls"—a numinous experience—it was, to Jung, an "empirical fact." But to the extent that this experience was identified with the experience of the God within, Jung is, as White came to realize, unquestionably a gnostic: "[Jung's] tragic dilemma is that his deepest, most profound, and most moving portraits of the deeper regions of the unconscious proceed out of a mode of thought which can without difficulty be termed 'Gnostic.'" [228]

Although not a gnostic in the ancient sense of the word, Jung was clearly, as White had depicted him, a "Knowing One." Jung himself acknowledged his gnosis in *The Symbolic Life* where he wrote: "I have gnosis so far as I have immediate experience. . . ."[229] The important point to note is that, for Jung, it was not because he had believed that he "knows" God, but because he had experienced. This position, and its divergence from orthodox Christian faith, was reiterated by Jung in an interview that is generally considered by scholars to be his "gnostic affirmation."[230] The year was 1959, the date October 22, and Jung was interviewed by John Freeman for the BBC.[231] Freeman had asked Jung about his religious upbringing, and Jung acknowledged his belief in God as a child. Freeman then asked, "Do you now believe in God?" Clearly surprised by this question, Jung responded: "Now? [*Pause*] Difficult to answer. I know. I don't need to believe, I know."[232] Jung knew that his response was controversial, as subsequent correspondence confirms, and so it is no surprise that he offered further clarification in an open letter to *The Listener*:

> I did not say in the broadcast "There is a God." I said "I do not need to believe in god; I *know*." Which does not mean: I do know a certain God (Zeus, Jahwe, Allah, the Trinitarian God, etc.) but rather: I do know that I am obviously confronted with a factor unknown in itself, which I call "god" *in consensu omnium* ("*quod semper, quod ubique, quod ab omnibus creditor*"). I remember him, I evoke him, whenever I use his name over-come by anger or fear, whenever I involuntarily say: "Oh God". . . .
>
> . . . Since I *know* of my collision with a superior will in my own-psychical system, *I know of god.*[233]

Jung thought that his own experience characterized the quest of human beings in search not of belief in God but of an experiential knowledge of God. Jung did not need to believe in God—a transcendent God beyond the psyche—because he knew of the existence of the God within. And he knew precisely because he had experienced God *as a phenomenon of the psyche*. So Jung was talking not about God Godself—for nothing can be known about God—but about the psychological function of the God image as it is experienced in the psyche.

Not only did Jung, as he saw it, not "need" to believe in God, but such belief was precluded by his methodology. Jung was an empiricist who adhered to the phenomenological standpoint, and was therefore committed to the position that belief in a transcendent God is not knowledge. Belief is not knowledge because the object of belief (God) is "something that transcends consciousness"—it is, by definition, unknowable.[234] Behind this assertion, that belief is not knowledge, lay Jung's dependence on Kant. Jung believed that

Kant had defined the limits of knowledge which, as I showed earlier in this chapter, only allowed him to talk of things as they appeared (that is, the God image), and not things in themselves (that is, God Godself). So Jung could talk about God only insofar as God was something which could be experienced as a psychological phenomenon and was, therefore, empirically verifiable. This position—that experience, and not belief, is knowledge—is well conveyed in a letter from Jung to his colleague, Bernhard Lang: "I am sorry to say that everything men assert about God is twaddle, for no man can know God. Knowing means seeing a thing in such a way that all can know it, and for me it means absolutely nothing if I profess a knowledge which I alone possess. Such people are found in the lunatic asylum. I therefore regard the proposition that belief is knowledge as absolutely misleading."[235] I could say that I believed, for example, that God is three and one, but the truth value of such an assertion cannot be determined by empirical methods (and so it *seems* meaningless, or "twaddle" as Jung put it). Jung's "knowledge" of God, however, came from the fact that he had *experienced* God (or, more accurately, the God image) as a psychological phenomenon. Thus, when Jung was asked "Do you regard yourself as a believing person?" he could *only* answer *no*:

> When you ask me if I am a believer I must answer "no." I am loyal to my inner experience and have *pistis* in the Pauline sense,[236] but I do not presume to believe in my subjective interpretation, which would seem to me highly obnoxious when I consider my human brothers. I "abhor" the belief that I or anybody else could be in possession of an absolute truth.[237]

Jung thought that those who did profess belief had been overpowered by an inner religious experience of which they were unconscious. Further, he thought that the believers' knowledge of God came not from the experience, but from a subsequently imposed interpretation by faith. So, for example, my belief that God is three and one comes not from experience, but because I have the gift of faith that enables me to assent to a body of revealed knowledge—that is, doctrine. This interpretation "seeks to represent the experienced content of a vision, for instance, as the visible manifestation of a transcendental Being, and it invariably does so in terms of a traditional system and then asserts that this representation is the absolute Truth."[238]

If I were true to my experience rather than my subsequently imposed interpretation, I might find, as Jung did, that God functions psychologically not as trinity but as quaternity (with a feminine and shadow side). One can see how, in assessing the impact of Jung on White, this would have created problems for Victor White who had experienced Jungian spirituality as something "emotionally orthodox" but who was committed to a Church which defined and taught religious truths. Jung was highly critical when the interpretation of faith was imposed as absolute truth because he thought that each interior experience of the God image had validity. As I showed in Chapter Two, White had also expressed his concerns about ecclesiastical authority. He was clearly sympathetic with Jung's view that (psychologically, at least) each experience of the God image had validity, but was ultimately committed to the authority not of the psyche, but of the Catholic Church.

So, for the believer (like White), faith is knowledge (or more accurately, acceptance of divinely revealed knowledge[239]); for the Jungian, experience is knowledge. For the believer, the object of faith is the God who is immanent and transcendent; for the Jungian, the God within. Jung's "knowledge" was the experience of the God within; White's "knowledge" was faith—which allowed assent to divinely revealed knowledge. As far as Jung was concerned, White's belief was not knowledge, it was metaphysics (that which was logically excluded by Jung's own methodology).

Now, we know that White had experienced Jungian spirituality as something "emotionally orthodox." It was as a result of the impact of Jung's psychology on his life and thought that White found himself torn between his *experience* of Jungian spirituality and his *belief* in orthodox Christianity. White had knowledge as a gnostic (to a certain and qualified degree), *and* as a believer: "While gnosticism has no room for faith, faith has room, indeed, need, for gnosis."[240] White tried to reconcile this tension by finding points of contact between the Jungian experience and the Catholic tradition. For example, in the previous chapter, I showed how White recaptured Aquinas' notion of "affective knowledge," which had been neglected in the context of a neo-scholastic Church defending itself against modernism. Furthermore, after White recaptured the importance of the immanent and experiential in the Catholic tradition, the tension—between White's experience of Jungian spirituality and his belief in orthodox Christianity—was clearly diminished.

However, the impact of Jung on White went beyond White's subsequent consideration of theology through Jungian eyes. For, although White accepted the emotional orthodoxy of Jung, and attempted to find points of contact in the Catholic tradition, he strongly held to the conviction that Jung alone was unsatisfactory. A fine example of this came in a lecture given by White at Cambridge where he questioned, "Shall we throw down Aquinas and take up Jung? No. We need rational inquiry about God also."[241] Experience is important, and White's recognition of this had led to his search to retrieve it from the tradition. But experience alone is incomplete. As I argued earlier in this chapter, for Victor White, like Aristotle, the soul must be formulated rationally. So the model White had proposed—of supplementing Jung's "empiricism," and its deficiencies, with metaphysics—once again came to the fore. Fellow Dominican Giles Hibbert aptly referred to it as the "'Catholicization' of Jung by Victor White," a trend that was becoming increasingly fashionable in Dominican theology of this period.[242] Indeed, according to one commentator, "It began to seem as if the English Congregation of the Order of Preachers had endorsed Jung in a corporate and quasi official manner."[243]

But the Catholic Church was not quite so enthusiastic about this trend. Simply put, Jung looked like a gnostic, and the gnostics had been condemned by the Church as heretics in the second century. According to White, the Church Fathers had seen gnosticism as a threat to orthodox Christianity for a number of reasons: gnosticism is exclusivist, whereas Christianity is for all; gnostic liberation is only for the pneuma (freed from the body and the psyche), whereas Christianity is Catholic—for the whole man; gnosticism is docetic, Christianity is incarnational; and finally, gnosticism "subject[s] mystery to the comprehension of the ego," whereas Christianity is "open to the fullness of mysteries."[244] In view of the condemnation of this sect as heretical, the impact (on White) of Jung (who, labeled as a "gnostic," seemed to embody this heretical position) was all the more far-reaching, placing White under the suspicions of the Order and of Rome.[245] Although Jung was not a gnostic in the second-century heretical sense, the label, and its connotations of heresy, were sufficient to influence Jung's impact on White, particularly in relation to White's perceived orthodoxy (or lack thereof). That is not to say that Jung was not a gnostic. In that he identified the numinous experience of the archetype of the Self on consciousness with the experience of the God within, he certainly was.[246] And this twentieth-century brand of gnosticism perturbed the Church, for, as I argued in the previous chapter, it looked like immanentism and the reduction of God to the psyche. Although White defended Jung's concerns as being with God image and not God, the suspicions surrounding Jung, and the impact this had on his associates (like White), cannot be underestimated.

Symbols of Transformation

White was undeterred, and persisted in his efforts to bring about an encounter between Jungian psychology and Catholic theology. He continued to lecture on "The Unconscious and God" at various colleges and institutions in Chicago and San Francisco.[247] It was during this time that White turned his attention to the psychological function of Catholic symbols and liturgical practices in relation to human *salus*. There is little doubt that Jung had influenced this consideration. After all, Jung had expressed in his writings, and to White personally, his belief that the experience of the unconscious found expression in the symbols, rituals, and dogmas of Catholicism. Further, Jung's whole psychology was focused on the importance of the symbol (and particularly the archetype of the Self as God image) for human wholeness. Showing where Jung's psychology and Catholic theology found correlation, White wrote "Modern Psychology and the Function of Symbolism" for *Orate Fratres* in April 1948.[248] The article provides us with a clear example of White's approach to the impact of Jung's psychology on his thought. First, it shows how Jung's ideas engendered a reconsideration of Catholic belief and practice, particularly in relation to worship. Psychology, White wrote, is "of great help to ourselves in realising the purpose of the rites and symbols which we perform unthinkingly and mechanically." [249] Second, it shows agreement, between psychologists and theologians, that human beings need religion and that religious rites and symbols have a function in human life and character. Finally, this article is an excellent example of White's proposed model of supplementing the deficiencies of analytical psychology with metaphysics:

> . . . the standpoint of the psychologist is more limited than that of the theologian—or even the simple Catholic. The psychologist as such cannot lay down what is the true and final purpose of human existence, in what ultimately human perfection and fulfilment consist. Such questions cannot be answered within the restricted framework of method or field of enquiry which the psychologist sets himself.[250]

In the article, White argued that religious rites and ceremonies are not for God's sake, but for our own—and for our healing. As I have shown, Jung, like White, acknowledged that human beings need religion, but Jung's was specifically an internal religion which brought healing through an immediate experience of the God within. Although talk of a God within was unacceptably gnostic for a Catholic theologian like White, one point on which they could agree was that human beings need religion for their *salus*. Theologically and psychologically, worship is about our human needs.

Theologically, the tradition of the Church, from St. Paul to Aquinas, had consistently held that we praise God for our own sake.[251] Articulating the reasoning behind this belief, White drew primarily on Aquinas. First, Aquinas argued that we do not worship God for God's sake. God is already full of glory and nothing can be added to that by a creature. Second, he argued that in honoring and praising God the human mind is put in subjection to God. Further, this subjection brings fulfillment, for, as Aquinas had argued, everything attains its fulfillment by being subject to that which is above it: "'As the body is alive only in subordination to the soul, and as the air is alight only in subordination to the sun, so are we only truly alive and alight in subjection to our God.'"[252] So, for Aquinas, to say that we worship God for our own sake—to meet our own needs—is to say that worship is essential for human flourishing. Worship is pleasing to God not in that God needs or vainly desires compliments, but "precisely because it is good for us and necessary for us; and our neglect to worship is bad for us."[253]

But is it not selfish to say that we worship for our sake and not God's? Not according to White. On the contrary, "it is a thoroughly humbling thought that we need religion, and that the all-perfect, all-glorious God does not." [254] Human beings need religion. As White saw it, God is aware of our needs, and God's command to worship him is an accommodation to those needs. This is not selfish. In fact, it is to love ourselves unselfishly, "to co-operate with God's love for our true selves as he would have them be."[255] It is because God loves his creatures and desires what is good for them that he commands them to worship. Jung's "empirical" method would not allow for such an assertion about the love of God and God's purposes for the existential fulfillment of his creatures. But he did see that, from a psychological point of view, religion functioned in the human psyche for the good. It is from this perspective that White wrote, ". . . we should be neither surprised nor resentful that modern psychotherapy has become increasingly occupied with the function of such rites and symbols in human life, and their effects on human character and conduct."[256]

Jung's fascination with the function of rites and symbols came from the analysis of his patients, where he noticed that even his non-religious patients had dreams and fantasies brimming with the ideas, symbols, rituals, and stories of religion. Jung's idea finds parallel in the writings of some of the Church fathers. Tertullian, for example, attempted to persuade the pagans with the suggestion that the soul was naturally Christian—the *anima naturaliter christiana.* In support of this, he pointed to the spontaneous manifestations of the soul—even the pagan soul—with its God, its devils, immortality, heaven, hell, sin, guilt and redemption.[257]

When these religious symbols, rituals, and stories emerged in the analytic process, Jung noticed that healing came through contact with them. He thought that particularly religious symbols emerged precisely because it was in these symbols that the patient found the revelation of a world "which transcends his understanding and control." Through the revelation of symbols and his connectedness to them, the patient "begins to find freedom from the prison house of his own sick conscious mind." [258] According to Jung, the symbol does two things: it expresses the inexpressible, and it brings about the transformation of the psyche. Both of these ideas would be used by Victor White in his fresh appreciation of the language of Aquinas.

As I showed earlier in this chapter, Jung thought that this experience of the unconscious found more conscious expression in public worship—in the symbols, rituals, and dogmas of Catholicism. Further, he thought that it fulfilled a similar function for the growth and health of the human soul. Although White approached the subject from a different point of view, his conclusions regarding the function of symbols were similar to those of Jung. Concerning the importance of symbol in expressing the inexpressible, White wrote: "A Thomist cannot read Jung's account . . . of the nature of a symbol without being reminded of St. Thomas' treatment of the need for symbolism in the first Question of the *Summa*." [259] In his introduction to the *Summa*, Aquinas questioned whether Holy Teaching should use symbol and imagery. Aquinas' answer was that the nature of human beings is such that we can only "attain to the spiritual . . . in and through corporeal creation," and therefore, it is necessary that the Holy Teaching should be presented "in and through corporeal figures." [260] So, unlike poetry, which uses metaphor for the sake of style or aesthetics, Holy Teaching uses metaphor "from necessity." Holy Teaching has to employ metaphor because God is utterly beyond human comprehension. [261]

However, the symbol cannot be limited to the cognitional, said White, concurring with Jung that the symbol also has power to transform the psyche, "in moulding human character, in constellating, dissipating and directing human attitudes." [262] Adding to Jung's observation, White suggested a correlation with Aquinas' understanding of the efficaciousness of sacraments and symbols: "The *ex opere operantis* efficaciousness of symbols lies in their power to move and change us, not indeed physically, but as objects which attract, unite and change our will and affection (*per modum causae finalis*). Of themselves they are unproductive of grace, but they induce us to respond to them in God-given grace-saving Faith in the truths which they represent." [263] As White noted, Aquinas argued that it is our response to the sacraments of the Church (the *opus operantis*), that makes them efficacious. Like Jung's symbols of transformation, the sacraments have this power "to move our hearts and wills," and to confer the grace of God upon us "by the very fact of their being performed (*ex opere operato*)."[264] This is divine love "in the service of human needs."[265]

The Analyst and the Confessor

White's more psychologically focused writings continued, and in July of that year, still in America, he wrote "The Analyst and the Confessor."[266] In it, White was much more forthright about his distance from analytical psychology, clearly articulating his dislike for any superficial comparison of theology and analysis.[267] Thus, while acknowledging the similarities between the sacrament of confession and psychological analysis, White challenged popular attempts to minimize the differences, attempts to see confession as a "naive, underdeveloped pre-scientific analysis," and analysis as "secularized confession".[268] There is little doubt that this blurring of the roles of analyst and confessor was in part due to the confusion that had arisen from Jung's calling one stage in the analytical process "confession." White's article, then, was very much aimed at allaying the fears of Catholics, and it is a fine example of his "great clarity" in distinguishing the role of the priest and that of the analyst[269]—a clarity which, as I have shown, was much applauded by Jung.

White's approach was largely apologetic. Despite the fact that analysis and confession look similar, his aim was to show that such similarities are often but a semblance. He observed, for example, that in the practice of confession the priest and confessor follow a pattern which has already been determined by the Church, a model that would be anathema to the psychological analyst.[270] There are a number of additional points where, as White saw it, confession and analysis prove "similar yet dissimilar."

First, it appears that both confession and analysis deal with alienation, but upon closer examination, it is clear that the cause of alienation in each is not the same.[271] Confession deals with the *malum culpae*—the evil that we (voluntarily) do and of which we are conscious. Analysis deals with the *malum poenae*—the evil that we (involuntarily) suffer and which belongs to the unconscious.[272] If the cause of alienation is dissimilar, so too is the manner with which it is dealt. Alienation as a result of deliberate sin *requires* not only confession, but also contrition and satisfaction. Confession in this case is clearly a recognition that an action is wrong. But alienation as a result of involuntary human compulsions cannot require the confession of sin, for one cannot confess the repressed things of which one is unconscious.[273] It is psychological analysis which takes the individual to the world of the unconscious to discover the psychological motivation behind these human compulsions. Thus, the causes of alienation, the *malum culpae* and the *malum poenae*, are essentially different—indeed, as voluntary and involuntary, they are opposites.[274]

Although this is the case, White followed the tradition in expounding a causal link between them. The *malum culpae* is the ultimate cause of *malum poenae*. That is not to be aligned with Job's so-called friends in the view that all suffering must be due to the sufferer's sin. Rather, said White, original sin is the [indirect] cause of all disorder, and this includes psychological disharmony.[275] If the theological model is correct, then the psychotherapist is faced with specifically religious issues. Jung was deeply aware of this long before his encounter with White. In 1932, he wrote: "Patients force the psychotherapist into the role of priest, and expect and demand that he shall free them from distress. That is why we psychotherapists must occupy ourselves with problems which strictly speaking belong to the Theologian." [276]

Individuals go either to confession or to psychological analysis as a way of dealing with alienation. Once the alienation (be it sin or the repressed human compulsions) has been "confessed," the manner with which the alienation is dealt differs considerably. The analyst, for example, would not make moral pronouncements in the way that the confessor judges the objective morality of actions. However, and here Jung's comment regarding the analyst's need to be aware of the theological issues comes to the fore, the analyst cannot but be aware of the moral values of the patient and their relation to mental health. Failure to deal with temptation and guilt, for example, is, as White notes, well documented as a cause of neurosis.

Subsequent to the confession of sin, the Catholic believes that the individual in sacramental confession is forgiven, and that this is "the efficacious sign of reconciliation with God."[277] White made little of the obvious transference at play which is so central to the analytical psychologist (and, indeed the psychoanalyst)—namely, that as the sin of the Israelites was dealt with in its transference to the lamb or the goat (the "scapegoat"), the sin of the Catholic has been transferred onto the priest who is acting *in persona Christi*.

However, two important differences relating to forgiveness and reconciliation are noted by White. First, in sacramental confession, that which is transferred is not an unconscious compulsion, but sin that has been committed by an act of the will. Second, to call that which is effected when some *imago* is transferred onto the analyst "a reconciliation" is somewhat spurious. Indeed, one could only legitimately talk of a reconciliation insofar as "the transference is resolved, the projection withdrawn and assimilated to the patient's own conscious ego."[278] Even in such a case, the reconciliation effected is, unlike in sacramental confession, wholly intra-psychic.

A response to White's article came several months later, on September 24, 1948. Jung apologized for his tardy response, explaining that he had felt "rather rotten" and this had prevented him from even opening White's letter. But when he did read it, his response was favorable: "I am very grateful to you that you took up the revenging sword in my favour."[279] Jung had been accused of usurping the role of the priest, though, in his defense, it should be noted that Jung would often send his Catholic patients to their priest before embarking on an analysis—precisely because he believed that the sacrament of confession put them in contact with the rich healing resources of the unconscious. Although White's article was not intended as a defense of Jung, at least not explicitly, Jung viewed it as a "revenging sword" precisely because White had, like Jung, demarcated the distinct roles of analyst and confessor. And this was a distinction which both men needed, to shield them from criticism in their respective fields.

Mission Impossible?

At the beginning of this chapter, I argued that Jung hoped that Victor White would be instrumental in the transformation of the

Western God image, which he saw as so necessary to mental health. Jung had laid great expectations upon White. But could these expectations really be met? As a Catholic committed to revealed doctrines about God that were not open to "transformation," it seemed as if White had been given a mission that he could *not* fulfill. But, as I have shown, White facilitated this mission with a careful distinction between metaphysics and empiricism, between God and God image. With such distinctions in place, talk of the "transformation" of the God image (and not of God Godself) allayed the suspicions of many—allowing White to succeed where others had failed.

Perhaps White's greatest contribution in the late 1940s was to show that the experience of Jung's God within and White's faith in a transcendent God were not mutually exclusive options—*at least not for White*. Although Jung's psychology was wholly intra-psychic and precluded faith in the Transcendent, White's methodology allowed him to appropriate what was valuable in Jung's psychology and supplement it where deficient. Insightful of this method in his approach to theology is his comment: "We must really understand what Jung's psychology lacks and needs, and show how our faith and philosophy can meet and so heal it." [280] So, for example, Jung's experience of the God within was, of itself, unsatisfactory (and indeed questionably heretical) to the traditional Catholic. However, such was its impact on White that it pressed him to recapture the immanent dimension of God that had been neglected in the wake of the modernist crisis. As a metaphysician, he was further in a position to meet the deficiencies of Jung's psychology, to "heal" it of its gnostic heresies by supplementing Jung's vision with belief in a transcendent God. Finally, although it was clear that Jung and White disagreed over major issues in this period—such as transcendence and immanence, faith and experience—White's model allowed for fruitful coordination between the two men.

It was a model which, for White, defined their relationship in the 1940s. It allowed White to benefit from the findings of analytical psychology, particularly in understanding the psychological relevance of the Catholic faith. It further afforded him the opportunity to complement the deficiencies of Jung's psychology with rational inquiry about God. Ultimately this approach warded off the inevitable confrontation between the authority of the psyche and the authority of the Church. But one issue in particular would change that. In the next chapter, I will show the inadequacies of such a model in sustaining their relationship, particularly as the two men began to discuss the issue that would eventually destroy their relationship—the question of evil.

FOUR
1948–1952

The American Revolution

As I have shown, Jung's impact on White's life and thought was considerable, and America afforded White a less restrictive environment to engage with Jungian material than had the confines of neo-scholastic Blackfriars Oxford (where his association with the heretical Jung was deemed suspicious by some of the brethren). Thus, it is no surprise to read in White's letter to Jung of June 1, 1948, "I confess that I am not relishing the idea either of leaving the USA or returning to England."[1] White returned in September 1948, breaking his journey with a week at Jung's Tower in Bollingen.[2]

New York to Blackfriars Oxford was, as he had anticipated, a difficult transition. In the months that followed, he did not write to Jung, later assigning his silence to the isolation he felt as priest and psychologist.[3] Jung sensed something was wrong, and, in December 1948, anxiously opined that White's journey to America had marked a turning point in their relationship: "The spirit prompts me to write to you. It is quite a while ago since I heard of you and very much longer since I have heard you really. I may be all wrong, but I confess to have a feeling as if when you were in America a door had been shut, softly but tightly."[4]

As I have suggested, Jung had hoped that White would be instrumental in the transformation of the Western God image. Still harboring such hopes, Jung continued: ". . . I take the liberty of knocking at your door. I suppose you are very busy. Don't feel pressed for an answer, please! I am looking for my own peace . . ."[5]

In a deeply cryptic conclusion, Jung wrote: "Light that wants to shine needs darkness."[6] Jung's comment is, I think, deliberately ambiguous.

On one level, it is *Jung* who is the one knocking at the door, identifying himself with the Light of the World, the light to the Gentiles who will come and sup with those who hear his voice and open the door.[7] This supports my view that Jung saw himself as an emissary to the Gentiles, a man with an unspoken hope for the Jungianization of Christianity. On another level, Jung is referring to *the* archetypal light—God—who in Jung's view also needs the darkness to shine.[8] Jung thought that if the God image were to be re-animated, it needed to be transformed to include the darkness, to include the shadow side. I would argue, therefore, that despite the effect of White's trip to America, Jung's language implies that he still saw him as very much in the fore of his vision for the transformation of the Western God image.

Further, in a letter of January 1949, Jung addressed White's anxieties, encouraging him in this very task:

> . . . England and our old world is your Rhodus, hic salta! One's anxiety always points out our task. If you escape it you have lost a piece of yourself, and a most problematic piece at that, with which the Creator of things was going to experiment in His unforeseeable ways. They are indeed apt to arouse anxiety. Particularly so, as long as one can't see below the surface. The independent mind in you is subject and object of the divine experiment . . .[9]

For Jung, this "divine experiment" had its source in the unconscious. White himself would later joke that the Creator of things "was up to some experiment" with him, though as a Catholic, White did not limit this to the God of the unconscious.[10] In any case, both men clearly saw America as an important part of this "experiment."

Adrian Cunningham has speculated that Jung's concerns regarding the effect of America on White were precipitated by the fact that it was his own journey to America, in 1909, which prepared the ground for *his* split with Freud. "Freud had seen in Jung his heir apparent, the Joshua who would enter the promised land after him."[11] Although the idea is undeveloped, I think that Cunningham was basically correct. To Freud, Jung was his "crown prince," the heir apparent of the psychoanalytic movement. Jung viewed White in like vein, the "white raven" who would "carry on the *opus magnum*."[12] America was significant to the Freud–Jung split because it was here that Jung came to the realization that Freud ultimately placed his own authority before truth.

Stated briefly, it was on their trip to America that the two men had analyzed each others' dreams, but the reticent Freud had refused to proffer significant personal details necessary for analysis, declaring, "But I cannot risk my authority!" It was for Jung a moment that foreshadowed the end: here was a man who put his personal authority over and above Truth.[13] I would suggest that it was also in America that Jung and White had a similar foreshadowing of the end which related to the tension between authority and truth. For White, as much as he resisted it, the source of authority was ultimately the Church; for Jung, authority came from the psyche. White thought that Jung placed the authority of the psyche before Truth; Jung thought that White placed the authority of the Church before Truth—at least psychological truth.

With such antithetical approaches, the basis for fear was well founded. In a letter to White on January 8, 1949, a letter written from his tower at Bollingen, Jung voiced this fear, saying, "I was afraid America had spirited you away altogether. . . . On my side it was an inner urge that prompted me to write. I felt a need to hear from you. The effect America had upon you looks exactly like something that went right through to the unconscious, whence it will appear again after a more or less prolonged incubation, in a new form."[14] If, for Jung, America did indeed represent the conflict between authority and truth, then his intuition regarding White's journey to America would ultimately prove fatefully accurate. White experienced the emotional orthodoxy of Jung's psychology, but when it came to Christian doctrine, he would ultimately place the authority of his Church over that of the psyche.

Reviewing the Self

A good example of this tension arose in October 1949. White had been invited to review the sixteenth Eranos, an interdisciplinary meeting for the Zurich school of analytical psychology, for *Dominican Studies*.[15] White's review focused mainly on Jung's paper "Über das Selbst," which would become chapter four of his work *Aion*.[16] Jung's hypothesis in this paper was that the archetypal image of wholeness, of the integrated human being, is the Self. As Jung saw it, it was an image that comprised "both conscious and unconscious, light and dark, acceptable and rejected elements."[17] Further, it was an image that Jung had encountered in dreams, art, myths, and religion, and which he saw functioning in the psyche's drive toward wholeness.

White was particularly interested in Jung's assertion that, for Western man, "the archetypal image of the Self . . . is embodied in the figure of Christ."[18] In fact, very often the archetype of the Self finds expression in god images. Although Jung saw Christian doctrine as "irrelevant, meaningless, and pointless,"[19]—something which White himself had experienced—Jung thought that the image of Christ continued to be the archetypal image of the Self. However, if the archetype of the Self comprises "both conscious and unconscious, light and dark, acceptable and rejected elements," then Christ does not immediately appear to be an appropriate image of the Self. White wrote: "This image . . . is of a God who is all Light, and 'in whom there is no darkness at all' . . . and of a man who is wholly sinless and faultless."[20]

Jung affirmed White's observation, offering a psychological perspective in "Christ, a Symbol of Self," a paper he seems to have given to White in manuscript form and which would appear in his 1951 publication *Aion*. Here he wrote: "The Christ symbol lacks wholeness in the modern psychological sense, since it does not include the dark side of things but specifically excludes it in the form of a Luciferian opponent."[21] As Jung would argue in *Answer to Job*, he believed that God excluded the dark side in the incarnation, specifically choosing to incarnate his good side alone. But ultimately Jung believed this to be psychologically harmful, for it meant that society is only presented—in the Christ figure—with half of the archetype. Further, he argued that if this "dark and unacceptable side" is neglected or repressed, it becomes unconscious, and then "manifests itself both in the individual and in society in negative and destructive—even totalitarian— forms."[22]

White did not disagree with Jung on this point, indeed he had experienced it—at least emotionally—to be orthodox. But in relation to the Christ, White was troubled, and could not concede that Christ had a shadow side. White could, however, affirm Jung's suggestion that the other half of the archetype appears in the Anti-Christ. White wrote: ". . . it is an integral part of the original doctrine of Christianity itself that the coming of Christ must result in the coming of the Anti-Christ, and even in his at least temporary triumph."[23] From a psychological viewpoint, Jung described the coming of the Anti-Christ as "an ineluctable psychological law."[24] In other words, Jung thought that the greater the Christ image was differentiated, the stronger its "unconscious and complementary opposite" would become.[25]

White was in agreement with this, applauding Jung's psychological theory and its impact in revitalizing theology: "[The Christian theologian] will be grateful for this impressive presentation of the relevance of Christianity to the individual and social conflicts of modern man, and perhaps also for this challenging recall to a fundamental Christian truth which has been too much neglected by theologians and preachers."[26] Ultimately, however, White would be unable to accept the second stage in Jung's theory—certainly as it applied to Christian doctrine. That is, that once the opposites are differentiated in consciousness, the Self works to unite them. This would mean good and evil included in Christ as an archetype of the Self. Further, White was, by his own admission "less compliant with the reason" Jung set forth to account for the neglect of the other half of the archetype of the Self—"the dark and unacceptable side of the human totality."[27] Indeed it was this very reason (to which I now turn) that began the debate that almost destroyed their friendship.

Neglecting Evil? Jung's Attack on the *Privatio Boni*

As Jung saw it, the reason for the neglect of the dark side of totality lay in the conception of evil as a *privatio boni*.[28] He wrote: "Through the doctrine of the *privatio boni* . . . evil was characterized as a mere diminution of good and thus deprived of Substance."[29] Jung believed that if evil is deprived of substance, it has no reality, and therefore will not be taken seriously. He thought that the articulation of evil as the *privatio boni* encouraged the neglect or repression of the dark side of totality. But before I consider Jung's attack on the *privatio boni*,[30] it is important to examine what the doctrine actually says.

The *privatio boni* had arisen in the writings of the early Church fathers[31] in response to the question *What is evil?*[32] That is, what is meant when people use the word evil? It is a question that deals with the essence or the substance of evil. Briefly stated, the *privatio boni* says that evil is not an essence, that it has no substance (οὐσία) of its own. Indeed it cannot have substance because, according to this view, God is the *Summum Bonum* who brings into being all that exists (has substance) and so all that exists is good. Being is identified with goodness; evil has no substance.[33] Now, to say that evil is insubstantial is not to say that evil is nothing (οὐκ ὄν) for if it were nothing it would be unreal and experience indicates that it is only too real.[34] Rather, it is non-being, a not-something (μὴ ὄν) which, as such, can only be defined in relation to its opposite, good. As Aquinas put it, "Like night from day, you learn about one opposite from the other. So you take good in order to grasp what evil means."[35] Unlike evil, which has no substance, good has substantial existence, it does exist on its own. Evil, therefore, when defined in relation to its opposite, is an absence of good.

However, as Aquinas notes, "It is not every absence of good that is called evil."[36] A man can lack the strength of a lion or wings to fly but that does not make him evil—it is not part of the essential nature of what it means to be a man that he should have the strength of a lion or the wings of an eagle. Therefore, according to Aquinas, "It is absence of the good in the privative sense which is called evil."[37] So, because it is an essential part of the nature of a lion to have strength, or an eagle to have wings, a lion in whom this strength is absent or an eagle without wings is lacking a good, and it is this lack that we call evil.[38] Similarly, when human beings commit injustices against each other they are acting in a manner that is less than human.

Herbert McCabe, O. P., who said that his knowledge of and love for Aquinas came from his teacher Victor White,[39] put it like this: "We call a person bad (or in this case sometimes, evil or wicked) just because he or she doesn't measure up to what we think we can expect of human beings. Cruelty, injustice, selfishness, are just dispositions or activities that don't measure up to our idea of what a proper human being should be like, they are not fitting to a human being."[40] In other words, the *privatio boni* says that evil is that which occurs when something fails to meet the expectations which God intended for that something. It should be clear that, in the privative view, *evil* is not restricted to the realm of morality.

Further intricacies of the *privatio boni* will be elucidated in the course of this chapter as I examine the unfolding dispute between White and Jung. For now, having briefly stated the doctrine of the *privatio boni*, it should, I hope, be clear why Jung thought that this doctrine was responsible for the neglect of the dark side of totality. His objection was primarily this: if evil is described as μὴ ὄν, then it is said to have no substance; and if no substance, then no reality; and if no reality, then the dark side of totality is neglected or repressed—with terrible consequences for humanity.

In Jung's analysis, the archetype which represented totality was the Self, and for Western humanity, this was embodied in God images and (especially) the Christ symbol. However, the archetypal image lacked wholeness because it did not include the dark side. In fact, it excluded it in the form of the Anti-Christ. Ultimately, Jung believed that the culprit for this exclusion was the doctrine of the *privatio boni*. This needs some explanation, and Augustine's account is most helpful here.

Briefly stated, Augustine's opponents, the Manichaeans, had accounted for the existence of evil by positing that there are two gods, one creating good and one creating evil (both substantial). But Augustine was not satisfied with this account because it conflicted with belief in one God as held in the Judaeo-Christian tradition. He sought to defend monotheism against the Manichaeans, but to do so he also had to deal with the question of the existence of evil.[41] In his response to the Manichaeans, Augustine essentially found himself with two options: either God is the *Summum Bonum* who brings all things into existence and, therefore, all things are good and evil has no substance (the *privatio boni*); or the quasi-Manichaean position that God is not the *Summum Bonum*—and evil is included in God. Augustine chose the former, excluding evil from the Godhead. Even the devil was created good and his evil represented as a privation.

Jung found this idea abhorrent and opted for the quasi-Manichaean view that evil is included in God. This allowed for a "whole" (that is, one that includes the shadow), rather than a perfect, Christ image. He would refer to Augustine's choice (which was, as I will show, also endorsed by Victor White) as a "desperate attempt to save the Christian faith from dualism."[42] Jung evidently recognized the connection between the *Summum Bonum* and the *privatio boni* and charged both as responsible for neglecting the dark side of totality: "The *Summum Bonum* . . . is the effective source of the concept of the *privatio boni* which nullifies the reality of evil."[43]

Although Jung was correct about the source of the *privatio boni*, proponents of the doctrine would disagree with Jung that it nullifies evil. As I will show, Victor White was, in the course of their discussion, at pains to stress that evil, though μὴ ὄν, is a real existing force. But Jung was not convinced. As he saw it, to speak of evil as "a mere diminution of good"—that has no substance—gives the impression that evil has no reality.[44] He wrote: "[Evil] is unfortunately only too real, which is why psychology must insist on the reality of evil and must reject any definition that regards it as insignificant or actually non existent. Psychology is an empirical science and deals with realities."[45]

Jung feared that a definition in which evil was insubstantial trivialized the very real force of evil that he saw and experienced in the world. He was convinced of this long before his discussion with Victor White. In 1932 Jung wrote: "When one sees how things develop in the world, one sees the devil is really in there, that there is an abysmal evil at work. One cannot explain the destructive tendency in the world as the mere absence of good or as a mistake made in something originally good."[46] Jung's problem is that to talk of a "destructive tendency" *sounds like* something positive, and so to express this tendency using the language of privation gives the impression that evil is utterly trivialized.

Although Jung was prepared to admit that the *privatio boni* "may be a metaphysical truth,"[47] his concern was with the negative impact that such an articulation can have in promoting the disregard for evil as a real force. "Evil can no longer be minimized by the euphemism of the *privatio boni*. Evil has become a determinant reality. It can no longer be dismissed from the world by circumlocution."[48] Expressed more simply, the language of privation does not do justice to the reality of evil as it is experienced. After the horrific evils perpetrated in the Second World War, Jung reflected more specifically on this idea in his work *Aion*, arguing: "One could hardly call the things that have happened, and still happen, in the concentration camps of the dictator states an 'accidental lack of perfection'—it would sound like a mockery."[49] As Jung saw it, the actions of someone like Hitler *look like* positive acts of evil and not the absence of some good that is expected to be there.

It is unclear whether Jung understood that according to the doctrine of the *privatio boni*, what made Hitler's atrocities evil was not the harm done to others but the harm done to Hitler. Herbert McCabe, O. P., put it like this, "There may well be those who think that what makes an action morally wrong is the harm it does to others, and they may be a little surprised that I say that what makes an action morally wrong is the harm it does to the perpetrator."[50] McCabe continued:

> An action may be morally wrong because it does harm to others, but what we mean by saying that it is morally wrong is that it damages the perpetrator. I can after all do a great deal of harm to others without doing morally wrong at all. I may bring with me to a foreign country some deadly infectious disease that I don't know about, so that in a few weeks people are dying in agony because of my arrival. If so, I have certainly harmed them by my arrival but I have not done anything morally wrong. If however I knew about it and went all the same, then you could well say that I was acting unjustly, that I was behaving in an irresponsible way in which no human being should behave, that I was defective in my humanity, that I was committing a moral evil. The moral evil would consist in the injustice and the way that I had diminished myself in acting like that.[51]

So, according to the doctrine of the *privatio boni*, the absence of some expected good lay in Hitler's failing to live up to the true nature that God intended. Hitler did not meet our expectations of a human being. Hitler's humanity was diminished by his actions. While this may well be the case, it is not difficult to see why Jung thought this a mockery: it appears to fail to do justice to the reality of evil and its victims. Jung thought that such a view was utterly offensive to human feeling. Thus he did not hesitate in rejecting the idea that evil is a privation of good, arguing that evil must be taken more seriously: "One must, however, take evil rather more substantially when one meets it on the plane of empirical psychology. There it is simply the opposite of good."[52]

Jung rejected a doctrine (or more accurately a *definition*) that had arisen in response to the question, "*What is evil* ?" To pose the question more explicitly, what is meant when people call something evil or bad? As Victor White correctly pointed out, this is not a question that Jung either asks or answers.[53] Indeed, Jung was bemused by the opinion that we know what is good and what is bad—he thought that what we know comes from our subjective judgment. He wrote, "People talk to me about evil, or about good, and presume that I know what it is. But I don't. When someone speaks of good or evil, it is of what he calls good or evil, what he feels as good or evil."[54] Jung did not consider good and evil as substances but rather as psychological judgments. He held the relativist position that what is good and what is evil is a human judgment. In other words, good and evil are principles of moral judgment that are relative to a particular person or situation. What is good for one man is evil for another;[55] what is virtue in some men is vice in others.[56] Jung wrote: "'Good' is what seems suitable, acceptable or valuable from a certain point of view; evil is its opposite."[57]

Curiously, however, Jung persistently denied that he relativized good and evil. At one point, for example, he qualified his position, writing "Because I take an empirical attitude it does not mean that I relativize good and evil as such. I see very clearly: this is evil, but the paradox is just that for this particular person in this particular situation at this particular stage of development it may be good."[58] Essentially, Jung said—in a less than precise way—that something can be intrinsically evil but instrumentally good. So, to give an example, abortion is an intrinsic evil but it could be an instrumental good—if, for example it saved the life of the mother. Or, to use an example which Jung himself gave: imagine a patient who knows that something is bad, does it anyway and then gets a bad conscience. Therapeutically, according to Jung, this may be very good.[59] With such an approach, the potential for conflict with Victor White is all too apparent. White stood in the tradition of Aquinas, who believed that one should never do evil that good might come. Thus, in the example cited, abortion could never be an instrumental good—it is always an intrinsic evil[60]—and one could never intentionally do wrong for "therapeutic" reasons.

Although Jung was unable to say what good and evil are in themselves, he was quite clear that, from the viewpoint of analytical psychology, evil cannot be defined as a *privatio boni*. His alternative, based on what he claimed we can know psychologically, was that good and evil are logically equivalent contraries.[61] That is to say that, for Jung, you cannot think of good without also thinking of evil.[62] Evil does not come from good, rather good and evil exist together as "coexistent halves" of moral judgment.[63] He wrote: "How can you speak of 'high' if there is no 'low,' or 'right' if there is no 'left,' or 'good' if there is no 'bad' and the one as real as the other?"[64]

This principle of opposites was central to Jung's understanding of the psyche and requires some explanation here. Jung's work as an analytical psychologist had led him to the conclusion that the psyche (the conscious, the personal unconscious, and the collective unconscious) was a "relatively closed system" characterized by a constant dynamic movement of psychic energy (*libido*).[65] This energy operates according to three observable principles: the principle of opposites (*enantiodromia*), the principle of equivalence, and the principle of entropy. The principle of opposites essentially says that everything will eventually run into its opposite. In psychological terms, this means that psychic energy involves "a dynamic oscillation" between "conflicting opposites" which in turn generates energy.[66] Of this, Jung was sure: "Whatever the intellectual definition and evaluation of evil may be, the conflict between them can never be eradicated, for no-one can forget it."[67]

The principles of equivalence and entropy are basic laws of thermodynamics—they deal with the way this energy is distributed in the psyche. The former says that "for a given amount of energy expended or consumed in bringing about a certain condition, an equal quantity of the same or another form of energy will appear elsewhere."[68] The latter says that "when two bodies of different temperatures come into contact, the flow of energy will always be from the hotter to the cooler," thus in the psyche energy flows from stronger to weaker "until an equilibrium is reached." [69] It is this framework which helps us understand that Jung could only conceive of good and evil as a pair of logically equivalent opposites.

The following quotations from Jung illustrate this view:

"To turn aside from good is nothing other than to be perfected in evil." [Origen]. This shows clearly that an increase in the one means a diminution of the other, so that good and evil represent equivalent halves of an opposition. [70]

Evil is the necessary opposite of good, without which there would be no good either. It is impossible to think evil out of existence. [71]

If, as adherents of the *privatio boni* argue, evil is insubstantial, then it is necessary, as Jung saw it, that good is also insubstantial. [72] It is clear that Jung did not think that they were insubstantial, though as a psychologist he disavowed himself of establishing them as metaphysical substances, preferring to speak of them as psychological judgments. But even Jung's very assertion that good and evil are logically equivalent opposites reveals that the so-called empiricist has given us a metaphysical statement. Further, it seems that even though Jung insisted that, as a psychologist, he could only approach good and evil empirically, [73] he was very much influenced by yet another philosopher—namely, Hegel.

Jung's notion—that the tension of opposites is a necessary part of the psyche's drive for wholeness—is clearly prefigured in Hegel's idea that contradiction is the source of development. Jung would have denied it—less than flattering, as he is, in his comments on Hegel's philosophy: "His impossible language . . . denotes that his philosophy is a highly rationalized and lavishly decorated confession of the unconscious." [74] As Jung saw it, Hegel's philosophy was not philosophy, but a disguise for the contents of his unconscious. Jung would later describe him as "that great psychologist in philosopher's garb." [75] Thus, he would deny that he was influenced by Hegel *qua* philosopher, asserting only that Hegel's work expressed the contents of the unconscious which unintentionally confirmed Jung's understanding of the tension of opposites in relation to individuation.

Two further points should be evident from the framework of the psyche just explained: first, if evil is excluded or repressed, then Jung's principle of equivalence indicates that it will manifest itself elsewhere in the individual and in society; and second, that once the opposites are differentiated, the Self, in its drive for wholeness, strives to unite them. In other words, Jung's God image includes both good and evil. White could accept the first point, but he would have serious problems with the second once it went beyond Jung's God image to Christian doctrines about God.

In summary, Jung's initial assault on the doctrine of the *privatio boni* was two-fold. First, he objected to the language of privation wherein evil is μὴ ὄν, fearing that if evil were described as insubstantial, it would not be taken seriously as a real existing force but would be neglected and repressed. Jung thought that this was deeply offensive to human feeling in the face of suffering. Second, Jung thought that the idea that evil is a privation of good contradicted his "empirical" theory which showed that good and evil are logically equivalent opposites—for if they are logically equivalent opposites it makes no sense to say that one was derived from the other.

White's "Correctio Fatuorum"

White did not hold back in his criticisms of Jung's position. Believing that Jung had totally misunderstood the doctrine, he accused Jung of a "brief and rather unhappy encounter with scholastic thought."[76] Brief and unhappy because it seems to me that Jung simply did not realize that, for White (as for Aquinas) the *privatio boni* is, as David Burrell has noted, "a grammatical elucidation" of a metaphysical truth.[77] White wrote:

> These somewhat confused and confusing pages might be dismissed as another infelicitous excursion of a great scientist outside his own orbit, were it not that the matter is one which is heavy in its consequences for psychology itself, and more especially for the understanding of the character of Christian warfare. It is regrettable indeed that, supported only by such naive philosophizing, the most pregnant movement in contemporary psychology should be burdened with an irrelevant association with gnostic dualism.[78]

White saw in Jung's "confused and confusing" pages a number of misunderstandings and at least two heresies. White thought that Jung's principal misunderstanding lay in his failure to appreciate that the definition of evil as a *privatio boni* was in answer to quite a different question than the one that Jung himself posed. "The *privatio boni* in St. Augustine and St. Thomas was not of course in answer to Dr. Jung's question (Is Evil a real existing force?—their answer to that of course was Yes) but to the question What is evil, i.e., Why is this called Bad?—a question Dr. Jung neither asks nor answers."[79]

White was correct in his analysis of Jung's approach. Jung was absolutely unconcerned with the verbal point that White seems to be making (that the *privatio boni* is a definition of what is meant when the word *evil* is used), and it is unclear whether Jung even realized that White's point was verbal—or more precisely a grammatical elucidation of a metaphysical truth. Jung, for his part, seems to have focused on the explicitly metaphysical question of whether evil is a real existing force, though he did not see it as such a question.

On the contrary, because for Jung evil is *experienced* as a real force, he would regard the statement "evil is a real existing force" as *empirical* rather than metaphysical (where *metaphysical* is roughly equated with Kant's noumenal world—that for which, from Jung's "empirical" perspective, there is no evidence).[80] So, when Jung said that the language of privation affords evil no reality, and that it minimizes evil in human consciousness and thus undermines its seriousness, White thought that Jung was blurring a metaphysical question (though one which Jung saw as empirical) with a grammatical point about a metaphysical truth. White therefore dismissed Jung's very valid criticism because it seemed to him irrelevant in relation to the question of what is meant when we use the word *evil*—which is the question that the *privatio boni* addressed.

As for Jung's heresies, White accused him of "neo-gnosticism"[81] and "quasi-Manichaean dualism."[82] It should be clear from the previous chapter that Jung's "neo-gnosticism" was apparent in his identification of the numinous experience of the archetype of the Self on consciousness with the experience of the God within.[83] Jung himself admitted his attraction to the gnostics in his work *Aion*, and, more specifically, to their approach to the question of evil. He wrote: "The intensive preoccupation of the Gnostics with the problem of evil stands out in startling contrast to the preemptory nullification of it by the Church fathers."[84] As is clear from his writings, Jung was drawn to the gnostic insistence that evil has a cause (bringing him indisputably into the realm of metaphysics): "The gnostics have the merit of having raised the question πόθεν τὸ κακόν; (*whence evil* ?). Valentinus as well as Basilides are in my view great theologians, who tried to cope with the problems raised by the inevitable influx of the collective unconscious."[85]

Jung was dissatisfied with the *Summum Bonum* not least because he thought that it implied that if God is the source of all perfection, God cannot be the cause of evil, and therefore all evil must come from man.[86] Jung thought that man isn't that bad and God isn't that good. His disagreement with the *Summum Bonum* essentially came from a psychological perspective, together with an anthropology-cum-cosmology of opposites. He argued that the unconscious drive for equilibrium implies that the *Summum Bonum* must have an opposite—which he called the *infinum malum*.[87] It is not difficult to see why the gnostic idea that there were two such opposing and eternal principles was attractive to Jung: it provided a counterpart to his psychoanalytic experience of the opposites as they manifested themselves in the archetype of the Self as God image.[88] At the same time, the gnostic idea of opposing principles also gave Jung a more satisfactory answer than the *privatio boni*—to the question *Whence evil* ?[89] So, from a Catholic perspective, White was absolutely right to see Jung as a neo-gnostic, and it seems that Jung would not contest such a charge.

Somewhat related to this is White's accusation that Jung had adopted a *quasi*-Manichaean dualism. White's qualification (quasi-Manichaean) is important because Jung is not positing two gods as did Mani and his followers. But, in that Jung located good and evil in God, one can see why White leveled the charge. Jung resisted it, and this is most evident in his work *Aion*, where he argued that early Christian writers such as Clement of Rome spoke of the left and the right hand of God without falling into dualism. Jung applauded their approach, writing:

[It] proves that the reality of evil does not necessarily lead to Manichaean dualism and so does not endanger the unity of the God-image. As a matter of fact, it guarantees that unity on a plane beyond the crucial difference between the Yahwistic and the Christian points of view. Yahweh is notoriously unjust, and injustice is not good. The God of Christianity, on the other hand is *only* good. There is no denying that Clement's theology helps us to get over this contradiction in a way that fits the psychological facts.[90]

In Clement's view, God needed both the left and the right hand to carry out his will: with his left hand he carried out evil and with his right hand good. This idea is well attested in the Old Testament, the Deuteronomist for example wrote: "I will kill and I will make live."[91] It is further seen in Luther's God, which, I think, is highly significant (in view of the religious tradition in which Jung was formed). For Luther, God is not Being (as Aquinas held) but Person in whom there is a conflict of Love and Wrath, Mercy and Justice. It is not difficult to see how the *privatio boni* would not even enter into this kind of schema. Privation is very much rooted in the idea of God as *Summum Bonum*: if God is good and good is being, then evil cannot be. It is not surprising, in view of this, that Jung found Clement more palatable than Augustine!

However, White was absolutely right that Jung was closer to a quasi-Manichean position than he was Clement's theology, because, psychologically speaking, Jung thought it necessary that good and evil were located in God as a complex of opposites. Jung would expand this idea in his *Answer to Job*, a book which led theologians to believe that Jung had "enthroned" evil in the Godhead forever.[92] Indeed it was White's response to this particular image of God in Job that curtailed their discussion in the mid-1950s—and almost destroyed their friendship. But it is significant, I think, that White had noticed strains of Manicheism in Jung as early as 1949.

In a stinging conclusion to his review, White suggested that a little basic reading on the subject would absolve Jung of his heresies:

An elementary study of (for instance) St. Thomas's sections in the Prima Pars On the Good, On the Goodness of God, On Evil, and On the Cause of Evil, should suffice to dispel Dr. Jung's misunderstandings and misgivings, and to supply a metaphysic which would account for the phenomena which concern him at least as satisfactorily as the quasi-Manichaean dualism which he propounds.[93]

This was, without a doubt, White's most mordant critique of Jung since their first encounter some years before.

Unconvinced: Jung's Response

Despite this, Jung's response some two months later was surprisingly good-natured. He began: "You have kept me busy for a while with your *correctio fatuorum* in *Dominican Studies*. I found it very interesting and illuminating."[94] In fact, he took White's advice regarding St. Thomas, though he admitted that he "did not feel refreshed afterwards!"[95] However, it did contribute to his further reflection upon the *privatio boni* and provoked him to voice three objections to it: first, Jung challenged the idea that all that exists is good because it is created by God, and, more particularly, the implication that all evil therefore comes from humans—a supposition which, Jung argued, has very dangerous consequences for humanity; second, he objected to the idea that evil is μὴ ὄν, and therefore, as he saw it, unreal; and third, he argued that the *privatio boni* is, psychologically speaking, illogical.

Turning to Jung's first objection—to the idea that God is the author of all that exists, and, therefore, all that exists is good—we see that Jung's target was, more specifically, the implications that he saw stemming from this view, namely, that evil, which is μὴ ὄν, comes from humans. Jung told White how this idea led him to the writings of Basil the Great (330–379AD), whom he accused of being "the perpetrator of *omne malum ab homine, omne bonum a Deo*."[96] Jung's claim is indeed supported in Basil's *De Spiritu Sancto*, where it is clear that the notion that all evil comes from man had its origin in his belief that God is good and thus cannot be the author of evil.

> It is . . . impious to say that evil has its origin from God, because the contrary cannot proceed from the contrary. Life does not engender death, darkness is not the origin of light, sickness is not the maker of health. . . . Now if evil is neither uncreated nor created by God, whence comes its nature? That evil exists, no-one living in the world will deny.

What shall we say, then? That evil is not a living and animated entity, but a condition [διάθεσις] of the soul opposed to virtue, proceeding from light-minded [ῥαθύμοις] persons on account of their falling away from good. . . . Each of us should acknowledge that he is the first author of wickedness in him.[97]

So, for Basil, evil is not a substance but a disposition of the soul to deviate from being fully in accordance with one's nature as God intended it. In other words, evil is a *privatio boni.* Jung informed White of his aversion to Basil's theology, disagreeing with the notion that all that exists is good because it is created by God, and more particularly the implication that all evil therefore comes from humans. Jung explains his reasons to White, three in all. In summary his three reasons are: human beings are good and evil, and this must reflect the Creator who is good and evil; empirically, if evil is a "mutilation of the soul" this is not a lack but a psychic reality; and, if the soul is originally created good, there must be a *cause* for its mutilation, and that cause is God.

Turning to the first reason, we see that Jung's alignment with the "impious" is clear. Arguing against Basil's *omne malum ab homine*, Jung suggested that if all evil comes from human beings and if human beings reflect the Creator, then the good and evil in humans reflects the good and evil in God. Indeed, in his earlier writings, Jung had expressed this same view when he asserted, for example, that "an inexplicable mood, a nervous disorder, or an uncontrollable vice" is in fact "a manifestation of God."[98] (Elsewhere Jung explained that he saw God—the God of the unconscious—as both the source of our fear of the "unspeakably terrible," and the source of the strength to withstand the terror.)[99] Jung's God within is good and evil. Perhaps the best example of this can be seen in Jung's own childhood realization "that God could be something terrible" which he described in his autobiography.[100]

Jung told of a vision—"the most momentous vision of my whole life"—that he had as a boy at the age of twelve. From his school courtyard, he could see Basel Cathedral, and above the cathedral God sat in splendor on his throne. As he watched, he became anxious, anticipating that something terrible was about to happen. Jung resisted the thought for three whole days until eventually, like Abraham, he mustered all his courage and let the thought come.

I saw before me the cathedral, the blue sky. God sits on his golden throne, high above the world—and from under the throne an enormous turd falls upon the sparkling new roof, shatters it, and breaks the walls of the cathedral asunder. So that was it! I felt an enormous, an indescribable sense of relief. Instead of the expected damnation, grace had come upon me, and with it an unutterable bliss such as I had ever known.[101]

When faced with this emotionally excessive situation (to use Jung's words), Jung believed that he had not invented this thought but that it had come from the will of God. Like Otto's *numinosum*, it was an overpowering and direct experience of God who willed the destruction of his Church. And yet, though it now seemed certain to Jung that God "could be something terrible," it was enormously illuminating. It said to Jung: experience dictates that the will of God is not the same as the God traditionally defined in the creeds of the Church. Rather, the God experienced in the psyche is a God of good and evil. Further, Jung believed that the experience of this God within—good *and evil*—was essential for wholeness. He wrote, "[God] wants reflecting human beings who are at the same time capable of surrendering themselves to the primordial creative darkness of his will, unafraid of the consequences."[102]

Jung was very much aware that the idea that the dark side is a manifestation of God to which humans should surrender fills many people with horror. In response, therefore, Jung urged his readers to imagine an experience of the power and intensity of evil. Then he argued that to think that all that evil comes out of human beings would be a considerable negative inflation. He expressed this in a letter to Victor White:

This *privatio boni* business is odious to me on account of its dangerous consequences: it causes a negative inflation of man, who can't help imagining himself, if not as a source of the [Evil], at least as a great destroyer, capable of devastating God's beautiful creation. This doctrine produces Luciferian vanity and it is also responsible for the fatal understanding of the human soul being the original abode of Evil.[103]

Jung was concerned about what he saw as the "deleterious effects" of the language of privation on humanity. He believed that the *privatio boni* had essentially cast off evil from God who had then become the *Summum Bonum*. As a result, psychologically speaking, evil was left to operate on its own with no relation to wholeness, balefully bedeviling human beings. Furthermore, when faced with the question of the origin of this evil, the *privatio boni* implied that if God is all good, then this evil must come from humans. Jung found this idea abhorrent. This is clear not only in his letter to White, but also in *Aion*, where he wrote: "If this paramount power of evil is imputed to the soul, the result can only be a negative inflation—i.e., a daemonic claim to power on the part of the unconscious which makes it all the more formidable."[104]

It is for these two reasons—the danger of negative inflation, and his belief that humanity reflects the good and evil in the Creator—that Jung expressed to White that he was very much opposed to the idea that the psyche is the "the original abode of Evil."[105] Rather, Jung's psychological experience suggested that evil comes from man *and God*.

Jung's second objection to Basil's idea that man is the source of all evil is empirical. He suggested that, if evil is a mutilation of the soul and evil is privation, then its existence is a lack, and evil is trivialized. As he expressed it in *Aion*, evil becomes "a mere negligence," "a byproduct of psychological oversight."[106] Jung's problem with this was that when something—evil, for example—is traced back to a psychic condition or fact (such as a mutilation of the soul), it is definitely not reduced to nothing (psychologically speaking) but is a psychic reality. Jung was appealing to his self-defined empiricism against Basil.

Finally, Jung's third argument against Basil's *omne malum ab homine* focused on a more theologically vexing question: *who put the serpent in the garden*? In raising this question, Jung was making the point that evil was in the world before man and therefore man could not be the sole cause of it. Indeed, Jung made the same point in a slightly different way in *Aion*. If the soul was originally created good, and if evil is a mutilation of the soul, then the soul has *really* been corrupted and *by something* real. Furthermore, if that "something" is the devil, then that leaves us with yet another question—who is responsible for the devil's mutilated soul? According to Jung, we must hold a real cause responsible and that cause is God. Once again, Jung was less than clear as to whether he thought that this cause is the God of the collective unconscious or God Godself. What is clear, as the three points above indicate, is Jung's rejection of Basil's idea that humans are the cause of all evil.

Launching into his second major argument against the *privatio boni*, Jung protested that if evil is described as μὴ ὄν, it will continue to be trivialized. It seems that Jung thought that White had not been convinced of this point as his letter reads as a reiteration of his arguments in *Aion,* a work that White had critiqued. Jung wrote: "As long as evil is μὴ ὄν, *nobody will take his shadow seriously.* Hitler and Stalin go on representing a mere 'accidental lack of perfection.' *The future of mankind very much depends upon the recognition of the shadow.*"[107]

As the letter continued, Jung expressed the view that evil should not be diminished. He wrote, "Evil is—psychologically speaking— *terribly real.* It is a fatal mistake to diminish its power *even merely metaphysically* [emphasis mine]."[108] Although Jung had earlier expressed the view that the *privatio boni* may be true metaphysically (by which he seems to have meant "in objective reality"), it is clear in this letter that he thought the *language* of this metaphysic of evil—White's "grammatical elucidation"—was both offensive and dangerous. "Evil verily does not decrease by being hushed up as a non reality or a negligence of man."[109]

White had not tried to convince Jung that evil as a *privatio boni* was real—at least not in the written correspondence. Rather, he had merely stated that the *privatio boni* was not intended to answer the question of whether evil was a real existing force—but added that Augustine and Aquinas thought that it was.[110] Indeed, if Jung had read Aquinas—refreshed or not—he would have seen that defining evil as a *privatio boni* did not mean for Aquinas that evil is unreal. The point was well made by White's student, Herbert McCabe, O. P., and McCabe's student, Brian Davies, O. P., in their exposition of Aquinas. They wrote:

> Badness is just a lack, but a particular lack. Now does this mean that badness is unreal? Certainly not. Things really are bad sometimes and this is because the absence of what is to be expected is just as real as a presence. If I have a hole in my sock, the hole is not anything at all, it is just an absence of wool or cotton or whatever, but it is a perfectly real hole in my sock. It would be absurd to say that holes in socks are

unreal and illusory just because the hole isn't made of anything and is purely an absence. Nothing in the wrong place can be just as real and just as important as something in the wrong place. If you inadvertently drive your car over a cliff you will have nothing to worry about; it is precisely the nothing that you will have to worry about. So badness is quite real.[111]

Someone boiling with envy and malice cannot just be described as lacking something. And bad moral qualities can be ascribed to people just like good ones. Fred might be described as just. But he might also be described as unjust. In this sense, so we may say, moral failure is a positive matter. But envy, malice, and comparable drives still involve failure in being as good as one could be. What worries us about them is the fact that they make people less than what they should be. What worries us about them is that those in their grip are settling for a lesser good.[112]

As I have shown, Jung was quite open to the possibility that evil as a *privatio boni* may be true metaphysically (by which he meant the opposite of empirically, that is, in a supra-sensory way). However, he was absolutely averse to the language of privation, fearing that articulation of evil as a privation entices humanity to regard evil as unreal. This, he argued, is potentially very dangerous, because it encourages its repression in the individual and in society. So, even if—metaphysically speaking—evil is real, linguistically speaking, the *privatio boni* promotes disregard for evil as a real force.

Jung's third and final objection to the *privatio boni* was that, from a psychological perspective, it is illogical nonsense. Expressing his disdain for metaphysics as that for which there is no empirical evidence, he told White, "The question of Good and Evil, so far as I am concerned with it, has nothing to do with metaphysics, it is only a concern of psychology."[113] As a concern of psychology, Jung's empirical method had indicated to him that good and evil were logically equivalent opposites. Therefore, it seemed "irrational illogical nonsense" to say, as adherents of the *privatio boni* said, that one was derived from the other. It seems to me that Jung's alternative is metaphysical in itself (and here I don't use metaphysical in Jung's peculiar sense!)—as it clearly seemed to Victor White, who had accused Jung of quasi-Manichaean dualism. Jung denied such charges emphatically, saying, "I make no metaphysical assertions and even in my heart I am no neo-Manichaean; on the contrary I am deeply convinced of the unity of the self, as demonstrated by the mandala symbolism."[114]

Jung could only deny that he was a neo-Manichaean on the grounds that he located the presence of evil not in God Godself ("Good and Evil . . . should not be projected upon a transcendent being"[115]), but in the God of the unconscious. Evil in the consciousness of humanity is, in Jung's opinion, a reflection of the good and evil in the creator—that is, the God of the unconscious who creates consciousness.[116] "Thus you avoid Manichaean dualism without *petitiones principii* and other subterfuges. I guess I am a heretic."[117] Although admitting his own heresy in regard to traditional Christian doctrine, Jung turned the accusation of Manichaean dualism on White, proclaiming, " . . . dualism is lurking in the shadows of the Christian doctrine: the devil will not be redeemed, nor shall eternal damnation come to an end. Origen's optimistically hoping or at least asking whether the devil might not be redeemed in the end was not exactly welcomed."[118]

Jung believed the *Christian* position to be dualistic because Christ and the devil, heaven and hell were eternally opposed. He applauded Origen's approach because it avoided such dualism. Further, he thought Origen's idea that the devil might be redeemed was closely aligned with his own (non-dualistic) view that psychological health required that the shadow must be brought back to the whole—evil must be assimilated.[119] Jung was unconvinced that a privative view of the devil—even the devil is good because created by God, and any corruption of the good comes from a perversion of the will opposed to God—avoided the problem of dualism. It simply made no (empirical) sense to him to say that everything that God did was good.

In summary, Jung's objections to the *privatio boni*, as they were articulated in this letter, are as follows: evil preceded humans in God "the creator of consciousness"[120] and, therefore, all evil cannot come from humans as the *privatio boni* suggests; it is dangerous to say that evil is a μὴ ὄν for it encourages a disregard for evil as a real force; and, psychologically speaking, the *privatio boni* is illogical. Jung concluded the letter: "I know you must criticize me. I am decidedly not on the winning side, but most unpopular right and left. I don't know whether I deserve to be included in your prayer."[121]

Dreaming of Privation: White's Response

White replied on February 10, 1950, evading the issue of the *privatio boni* in favor of more personal conversation—his preparation for an examination in Rome,[122] and his lectures for the Theology Faculty at the University of Oxford on "Theological Truth and the Psychology of the Unconscious."[123] White concluded with the promise that he would address the issue of the *privatio boni* in his next letter. But that letter of May 1950 began, "This is still no threatened essay on the *privatio boni*!"[124]

Although their conversation was once again postponed, White shared with Jung aspects of his unconscious life which are revealing of the two men's respective approaches to the *privatio boni*. White told of a dream in which he and Jung were sitting by the lake. Evening encroaches, and in the darkness White sees a light, like a meteor. Jung does not see it, but in the opposite direction he sees a low flying aircraft. Then, at ninety degrees, the meteor and the aircraft intersect, both men see a cross and darkness covers the land. White was convinced that the dream was about their disagreement regarding the *privatio boni*. He wrote: "You and CG are looking in opposite directions at something different. What you each see, you see—and argument will not help."[125]

Jung however disagreed with White's analysis of the situation, dismissing his appearance in the dream and suggesting that the "other character" was, in fact, White's personality number two, that is, the unconscious. Characteristically, Jung was trying to convince White by steering him to the truths of the unconscious. In other words, Jung was trying to convince White that his unconscious life offered a different perspective on evil—the Jungian perspective! White did not agree with Jung's analysis of his inner tension and instead reiterated his conviction that—on the question of the *privatio boni*—he and Jung were looking at different things. "The radical difference between you is not one of judgment or argument, but of perception: he does not see what you see in front of you and you do not see what he sees behind him [sic]."[126]

There are two levels on which I think White was absolutely right. First, White perceived the question of evil as a *privatio boni* as a grammatical elucidation, as it had been for Aquinas. Jung did not perceive this. He focused on a totally different question of the experience of evil as a real existing force. On a second level, when Jung talked about evil, he was talking within a moral framework; White on the other hand talked about evil within a teleological framework. Expressed more simply, Jung saw evil as a principle of moral judgment; White saw evil as that which occurs when something fails to meet the expectations which God intended for that something. According to Jung, being is morally neutral and moral judgments are subjective. According to White, however, being is goodness and human beings can be right or wrong in their moral judgments.

Furthermore, each of these approaches to evil reflects the different ways in which Jung and White viewed God. According to Jung, God is a God of good and evil (which he understood morally—or amorally, in *Answer to Job!*). According to White, on the other hand, God is the *Summum Bonum*, that is, God is *all* good. But White, like Aquinas, did not understand this in terms of moral goodness. Rather, he understood it teleologically: God is good (where good is defined as that which is in accordance with its nature) because God cannot be other than God is and therefore God is fully in accordance with God's nature. In other words, God is good for the very reason that God is perfect.[127] Thus, for White, Jung's suggestion that God could be evil was inconceivable because—in White's Thomistic schema—to be evil would be to fall away from God's true nature, and God cannot do that because God is immutable. Behind these perspectives (I would suggest) the *Protestant* Jung and the *Catholic* White are all too apparent— Jung's God as person (and therefore moral agent), and White's God as Being (not an agent who acts, but *actus purus*).[128] It is clear on these two points alone that both men approached the question of evil from very different perspectives. Thus, it is clear why White could attribute their disagreement to perception.

Having noted their differences of approach, White concluded the letter and, for the time being, concluded the discussion of the *privatio boni*:

> For the moment I do feel that that discussion [of the *privatio boni*] has reached deadlock. What is so perplexing to me is the fact that it is

precisely your psychology which has enabled me to experience evil as the *privatio boni*. For my part I can give no meaning at all to psychological terms like "positive negative," "integration disintegration" if evil is NOT *privatio boni*. Nor can I see any motive for "integrating the shadow"—or any meaning in it either—if the shadow is not a good deprived of a good![129]

The impact of Jung's psychology on White was such that he had experienced evil as the *privatio boni*. As White saw it, Jung's whole psychology was about moving toward wholeness, a move which he thought implied the notion that something was lacking. Jung himself had described unconsciousness as "one of the toughest roots of all evil"[130] and the integration of the shadow as supplying an absent good, namely consciousness. Although Jung was aware that his psychology gave the impression to White (and others) that evil was a *privatio boni*, this was, in the final analysis, an idea that Jung resisted. In *Aion*, for example, he wrote: "Looked at superficially, the shadow is cast by the conscious mind and is as much a privation of light as the physical shadow that follows the body. For this superficial view, therefore, the psychological shadow with its moral inferiority might also be regarded as a privation of good."[131]

But ultimately Jung thought that such a reading of his psychology failed to take into account "the full operation of the opposites":

On closer inspection, however, it proves to be a darkness that hides influential and autonomous factors which can be distinguished in their own right, namely *anima* and *animus*. When we observe them in full operation—as the devastating, blindly obstinate demon of opinionatedness in a woman, and the glamorous, possessive, moody and sentimental seductress in a man—we begin to doubt whether the unconscious can be merely the insubstantial comet's tail of consciousness and nothing but a privation of light and good.[132]

Once again it is clear that Jung's argument was that the language of the *privatio boni* fails to do justice to the reality of evil as it is experienced. Although White had experienced it as real in precisely this way, Jung's writings suggest that he saw White's reading as superficial. Perplexed by this, and unable to convince Jung that the *privatio boni* afforded evil any reality, White believed that the discussion had reached deadlock.

Jung replied to the letter almost immediately, focusing his response on their respective approaches as "empiricist" and meta-physician (as he understood this):

> Your metaphysical thinking "posits," mine doubts, i.e., it weighs mere names for insufficiently known οὐσίαι. That is presumably the reason why you are able to integrate a shadow μὴ ὄν, while I can only assimilate a substance, because for "positing" thinking "nonbeing" is just as much an ens or ὄν as "being," i.e., a conceptual existence. You are moving in the universe of the known, I am in the world of the unknown. That is, I suppose, the reason why the unconscious turns for you into a system of abstract conceptions.[133]

Following a Kant-based empiricism, Jung distinguished between phenomenon and noumenon, the known and the unknown, archetypal image and the archetype itself. As a metaphysician (in the neo-scholastic sense), White was not quite so restricted. He could, as Jung remarked, "posit" that evil was a μὴ ὄν. But as an empiricist, Jung could not say what evil is in and of itself. He operated in the world of the unknown. As such, from an empirical perspective, he argued that there was no evidence to suggest that evil was a *privatio boni* and, further, that such a definition conflicted with the empirical fact that evil is experienced as the logically equivalent opposite of good. It is from this perspective that Jung, unlike White, was unable to assimilate a shadow that was μὴ ὄν.

Although the difference of perspective regarding evil divided the two men, it did not diminish their affection for each other, and Jung concluded the letter with the hope that White would visit him in Switzerland that summer.[134]

Neglecting the Feminine? The Assumption of Mary

With the discussion of the neglected evil on hold, White turned his attention to the neglected feminine in an article on the "scandal" of the Assumption of Mary body and soul into heaven.[135] Coming seven months before Pius XII declared the Assumption to be a dogma of faith in the Apostolic Constitution *Munificentissimus Deus*,[136] the influence behind the article was clearly Jung's. As

I showed earlier in this chapter, Jung thought that the Self was the archetypal image of wholeness, of the integrated human being. Further, as an image of wholeness, the Self is dark as well as light, feminine as well as masculine, material as well as spiritual. Of particular interest to White was Jung's assertion that the archetypal image of the Self finds expression in God images.

As Jung saw it, the Western God image neglected not only the dark side but also the feminine and "terrestrial" sides.[137] Consequently, Jung was most taken by the archetype of the mother as it found expression in the Catholic Church, believing that it was a positive move toward supplying the missing feminine.[138] He noticed, for example, that the Church celebrated the feast of the Assumption every August 15 and had meditated upon it in the rosary for seven hundred years, since the time of St. Dominic. In 1948, he wrote: "The archetype of the mother is decidedly developing inside the Catholic Church, aided by remarkable miracles (Assisi and Fatima), also the attempts at bringing about the official recognition of the *conclusio* that Mary has been taken up into heaven together with her body."[139]

Jung was drawn to the popular but, as yet, not dogmatically formulated belief that Mary was assumed body and soul into heaven. Two aspects related to the belief particularly impressed him as an analytical psychologist. First, he thought it highly significant that attempts to declare the widely held belief in the Assumption a dogma had come from the "deep longing" of the Catholic laity. "The impelling motive behind it did not come from ecclesiastical authorities, who had given clear proof of their hesitation by postponing the declaration for nearly a hundred years, but from the Catholic masses, who have insisted more and more vehemently on this development. Their insistence is, at bottom, the urge of the archetype to realise itself."[140] As Jung saw it, this illustrated that the archetype of the mother was very much alive in the Catholic Church, "nourished by the popular psyche."[141] The laity desired that the belief in the Assumption be declared a dogma, and this in itself was powerful evidence of "the living archetype forcing its way into consciousness."[142] Furthermore, Jung believed their desire expressed a psychological need—the need to integrate the neglected feminine side.[143]

The second thing that impressed Jung was the great symbolic value of what he understood to be the addition of the feminine to the Christian conception of a trinitarian God. As he saw it, the Assumption anticipated the divinity of the *theotokos* as a "conclusio probabilis,"[144] and thus also anticipated the Quaternity. This he believed to be symbolized not only in the inclusion of the feminine, but also in the inclusion of the material. He argued that if woman, the "terrestrial element (virgo terra!),"[145] is included in the metaphysical realm, then so too is matter—and its corrupting principle, evil.[146] There is little doubt that Jung applauded what he perceived as a transformation of the Western God image from Trinity to Quaternity believing that this represented a step toward wholeness. Ultimately, Jung thought that the transformation of the Western God image will have been completed when Mary is pronounced co-redemptrix.[147]

Although White agreed with Jung on the first point and, on the second point, could appreciate the symbolic value of the Assumption, he disagreed with Jung on two points of doctrine. First, White disputed Jung's interpretation of the elevation of Mary into the Trinity. In his view, Mary is not, as Jung asserted, a goddess.[148] In addressing this point in the article, White focused on the distinction between Jesus and Mary. His argument was that while at the incarnation the three divine persons of the Trinity assumed "a created human nature . . . into hypostatic union with the Person of the Son," at the Assumption the three divine persons "'assume' a human person" into the glory of the Godhead.[149] Mary participates in the divine glory but remains human in nature, and as a creature, is "infinitely distinct" from the Godhead. She is not divine, but divinized, a view cautiously expressed by White in the tradition of the "theosis" of the Church Fathers (that is, that God became man that man might become God). For White, Mary was not, as Jung saw it, a goddess, but the first of the redeemed community, the prototype of a human being sharing in the divine life of God.[150]

The second point of doctrinal disagreement was, for White, to be found in Jung's idea that the Assumption symbolized that matter (including its corruptible principle, evil) is included in the Christian conception of God as Trinity. White's disagreement with this was twofold. First, if God is perfect, it is inconceivable that matter with its corruptible principle, evil, could be included in the Godhead. This would be to fall away from God's true nature—and God cannot do that because God is immutable. Second, if Mary was, as the Catholic Church taught, immaculately conceived, then she was untouched by the corruptible principle and, therefore, it would be incorrect to say that "corruptible matter" participates in the divine life. Ironically, Jung had remarked that Mary was "spiritually disinfected" by the dogma of the immaculate conception,[151] it having been God's "elaborate protective measures" against Satan's tricks.[152]

Although the two men disagreed regarding the doctrinal understanding of the Assumption, White could agree with Jung that as a belief it also had great symbolic value. White showed, for example, how the idea of the Assumption, particularly as an expression of the reunion of "Son and Mother, Father and Daughter, Spirit and Matter" is indeed a pattern in human nature, in art, in literature and in mythology.[153] To support this, White drew attention to the work of Fra Angelico and El Greco who portrayed Mary as a crowned virgin, "squar[ing] the awkward triangle of the Trinity."[154] White further agreed with Jung that the Assumption is not an exclusively Catholic idea,[155] but an expression of "a universal archetypal pattern" which appears in other religions, in alchemy, and literature.[156]

However, and this is where the impact of Jung's emphasis on the archetypal image ends, White moved beyond the Assumption as a universal pattern to "the σκάνδαλον" of the Assumption of a *particular* person. "What is disturbing and offensive is this insistence, not on universal symbolism, but on the particular matter of fact; that a matter of fact is a matter of faith; in the further insistence that this fact of faith is realised in precise units of space and time, and in a definite specimen of flesh and blood—*haec ossa, haec carnes.*"[157] The scandal, said White, is one of particularity. It is the scandal of "the earthly *embodiment* of the mystery," the "concretization" of the living processes of the unconscious in the life of a particular person.[158] "It particularizes it to *this* body (and body in general is a non existent abstraction), it accentuates the scandal of this fundamental article of our belief. . . . it is not any particular body, but the body of Mary that is revived and assumed."[159]

Turning to the Bible, White noticed that the praise for Mary in Luke 11:27 was, in particular, "praise of the *body* of Mary." In Luke's story, Jesus casts out a demon from a dumb man subsequent to which a woman in the crowd exclaimed, "Blessed is the womb that bore you." Like the praise for the body of Mary expressed in the belief in the Assumption, the proclamation came from the crowd—the ordinary people.[160]

But White was not concerned only with the particular and, in fact, challenged those who adhere to the physical aspects of Christian doctrines but fail to see, or are scandalized by, their wider significance. Jung's insistence on the universal and White's insistence on the universal *and the particular* provide yet another example of White's methodology in relation to Jung—"to supplement and complement." It is no surprise, then, that White insisted that the particular and the universal must be held together, arguing that the full depth of particular mysteries can only be grasped when connected to the universal. ". . . Mary is the Womb, the fertile, obedient Earth in which all is rooted and nourished; her body is the mater-materia from which the divine Spirit, in fashioning the Body of Christ, fashions the new cosmos."[161]

White explained a little more clearly what he meant by this by looking at the account of the Fall in the book of Genesis. It is there, he said, that the original harmony of the universe was destroyed. Man's disobedience to the Word of God left the earth and the human body cursed.[162] White suggested that the result of this is all too apparent in history's tensioning of the opposites "of human mind and matter, male and female . . . the spiritual and the carnal."[163] The language, if not the theology, is clearly Jung's. As White saw it, the "reconciliation of opposites" required God's giving of his Word and Mary's acceptance of it body and soul.[164]

> This remarriage of heaven and earth can take place only within man, who alone is part of maternal nature and yet made to God's image and likeness. It takes place in Mary's womb in the Incarnation: God and man become one single Person. It is consummated in his Resurrection and Ascension to the glory of his Father. But the ground for this new creation is formed and prepared by the Immaculate Conception, and finds its full effect in the Assumption. The rehabilitation of Nature and of Woman, and the *redemption of our body*, is completed, but also

pre-typified, in the taking of Mary, body and soul, into the glory of the divinity.[165]

Showing further evidence of the influence of Jung, White expressed the opinion that the dogma of the Assumption was much more than an article of faith. "No Christian dogma is just a proposition that requires a purely intellectual assent; nor is it even just a symbolic presentation of ultimate reality offered for purely theoretic contemplation."[166] There are two ways in which White saw this to be the case. First, it particularizes the universal abstract ideas of reintegrating matter, supplying the missing feminine principle, and redeeming our bodies.[167] Secondly, White argued that it should summon us to look at the evils in our society which are caused by "the secularisation of matter," and which have propelled an "unnatural" split of spirit and matter. Lamenting this split, he wrote: "It is not long since laboratory and oratory were synonymous, the dividing line between prayer and chemistry was hardly discernible, and temple and theatre were hardly distinguishable."[168] This idea that spirit and matter are severed would have resonated deeply with Jung. Indeed, it is a point which Jung stressed in his own writings on the Assumption: "The declaration of the dogma comes at a time when the achievements of science and technology, combined with a rationalistic and materialistic view of the world, threaten the spiritual and psychic heritage of man with instant annihilation."[169]

As Jung saw it, a shift to a scientific world view had led to a deification of matter, with the disastrous consequence that the spiritual world had been divested of its qualities.[170] Jung, therefore, applauded the Assumption of Mary into heaven as a "counter-stroke" or a compensating reaction to the materialism of the age, because it symbolized earthly matter "stripped of all its specific qualities" when it entered heaven. "Understood correctly, the Assumption is the absolute opposite of materialism."[171] Jung thought that the Catholic Church had truly understood this, and thus, had allowed the archetypal symbolism to develop over the centuries. He thought that, in doing this, the Church exhibited a maternal character which he saw in stark contrast to the paternalistic spirit of Protestantism.[172] In Jung's view, Protestantism was paternalistic because it succumbed to the predominantly rationalistic attitude of the Western world. The result of this was a lack of connectedness to the symbolic and its healing powers and thus a total ignorance of the spiritual problems of his time.[173]

> The Protestant standpoint has lost ground by not understanding the signs of the times and by ignoring the continued operation of the Holy Ghost. It is obviously out of touch with the tremendous archetypal happenings in the psyche of the individual and the masses, and with the symbols which are intended to compensate the truly apocalyptic world situation today. It seems to have succumbed to a species of rationalistic historicism and to have lost any understanding of the Holy Ghost who works in the hidden places of the soul.[174]

Although appreciating that the papal declaration was a "petra scandali" for the unpsychological mind,[175] Jung did not withhold his criticism: from a psychological perspective, the Protestant critique of the Assumption was misconstrued. He wrote: "The logical consistency of the papal declaration cannot be surpassed, and it leaves Protestantism with the odium of being nothing but a man's religion which allows no metaphysical representation of woman."[176] To Jung, the declaration had logical consistency—in analytical psychology, the living archetype, when nourished by the popular psyche, ultimately forces its way into consciousness.[177] Equally, to the Catholic Church the declaration had logical consistency, though for different reasons: the Church was formulating as dogma that which had always been held in the mind of the Church.[178] But for Protestantism, without the empiricism of Jung or the (Catholic) idea of the development of doctrine, the Assumption had no logical consistency, and thus it was dismissed as papal arbitrariness, another corruption of Rome.[179]

Jung read White's article "with the greatest attention and interest."[180] Unlike White's contemporaries, who criticized his assimilation of Jungian ideas,[181] Jung was deeply taken with it, and admitted that his dreams indicated that White had stirred up something in his unconscious.[182] White's attention to the universal aspect of the Assumption resonated with Jung's own theories on the archetypal. But White's insistence on the particularity of the Assumption left Jung less than convinced, declaring that it sounded ". . . rather like blatant materialism, which arouses the strongest objections."[183]

For Jung, the power of the Assumption lay in the fact that it was "a living spiritual experience." He continued, "If the A[ssumption] means anything, it means a spiritual fact which can be formulated as the integration of the female principle into the Christian conception of the Godhead. It is certainly the most important religious development for 400 years."[184]

In later works, Jung affirmed the declaration of the dogma of the Assumption "the most symbological event since the Reformation."[185] Thus, Jung ardently contested what he perceived as White's attempt to particularize the Assumption as a concrete historical fact, fearing that if the Assumption is essentially an historical fact, then it has been divested of the spiritual.[186] In *Mysterium Coniunctionis*, for example, Jung argued that the Assumption represents an important step "beyond the confines of historical Christianity," which, he suggested "is the strongest proof of the autonomy of archetypal images."[187] In other words, Jung was concerned not with the reality of the Assumption (what he perceived as White's "particular") but with the lay person's *belief* in the reality of the Assumption and therefore with the reality of the idea.[188] He wrote:

> If we designate the A[ssumption] as a fact in time and space we ought to add that it happens really in eternity and everywhere, and what we perceive of it through our senses is corruptible matter, i.e., we don't see it, but we infer or believe in the idea. The conclusion took not less than 1900 years to reach its finale. Under those conditions it seems to me preposterous to insist upon concrete historicity. But if you say: I believe that Mary endowed with her *corpus glorificationis* (i.e., characterised by almost 'corporeal' distinctiveness) has attained her place in the vicinity of the Deity, I can agree with you.[189]

Jung thought that, in insisting on the particular, White meant that the Assumption was primarily a historical fact, but it is clear from White's response of December 1950 that Jung had misunderstood him. White wrote: "I was in fact at some pains to avoid saying it was "historical"—plainly in almost any recognizable sense of that very ambiguous word it is not!"[190] For White, the Assumption is not primarily about history but about faith. By this he does not mean that as a matter of faith "it touches only on an eternal idea," but rather that "the matter of faith is also a matter of fact in space and time."[191] It is clear, then, that White and Jung were in closer agreement on the neglected feminine than Jung had originally perceived, and certainly in closer agreement than on the issue of the neglected dark side.

White's "Peculiar Heresies"

White's close friendship with a man who advocated the transformation of the Western God image to include evil and the feminine, even though Jung's ideas were not fully endorsed by White, roused suspicions in the Church and the Order. In October 1950, White was called to Rome for an exam where he was required, as a teacher of theology, to take the anti-modernist oath that he so dreaded.[192] White inhabited a world fearful of modernism, both in the Order and in the Catholic Church. The modernists, as I showed earlier, stressed experience while neglecting voluntary intellectual assent to revealed doctrines about God which thus implied that religion develops from the need for God in the soul, changing to meet the changing consciousness of humanity. Emphasizing experience over faith, and the need for the transformation of the Western God image, Jung certainly looked like a modernist and, therefore, White's association with him placed him under suspicion. It is not surprising, therefore, that he was less than enthusiastic about "this ridiculous examination"[193] that he was required to take. But, in fact, his apprehension was unnecessary, as he later informed Jung. "My peculiar 'heresies' which I did not disguise—are tolerable even there."[194]

Essentially White's "heresies" lay in reading Aquinas through Jung, not something particularly "heretical" when judged from a twenty-first century perspective. But in the context of his day—with the rear guard of neo-scholastics at Blackfriars Oxford and the anti-modernist atmosphere of 1950s Catholicism—White's collaboration with Jung was viewed with the greatest suspicion. Indeed, one reviewer commented that White was treading on dangerous ground—so close to the ground of modernism.[195] White was undeterred by those suspicious of his work and continued to engage with Jung's ideas, appropriating that which was valuable and criticizing that which, from a Catholic perspective, was problematic. His model in this was Aquinas:

> It is well known what extensive, though never uncritical, use St. Thomas made of the infidel Aristotle, of the Moslem Averroes and Avicenna; it is less well known that, in the very first article of the Summa, arguing not about some natural philosophy but for our need for Divine revelation itself, St. Thomas has appropriated the arguments, not of some Catholic Doctor, but of the Jewish Rabbi Maimonides. If what is said is true, it is a reflection of the first Truth, of the Divine Ideas, no matter if it is discovered by a pagan (IIaIIae q.177 art.1 ad 3).[196]

A good example of White's extensive, though not uncritical, use of Jung's psychology appeared in a sermon that he preached at Easter 1951.[197] It is a sermon which shows White's appropriation of Jung's notion of archetypes and at the same time his criticisms of the limitations of Jung's psychology. Although White did not use the word "archetype," his sermon is an exploration of the universal pattern of the idea of passing from death to life seen in the Christian Easter, the Jewish Passover, and the fertility rites of the pagans. Further, it is an exploration of the similarities in the way that this idea is articulated and celebrated, ritually, in these different traditions. One example is the extinguishing of the old fire and the kindling of the new in the pagan Rites of Spring. This is paralleled in the story of the death of Jesus: darkness covers the land but three days later Jesus rises with the rising of the sun. The liturgy of the Easter vigil offers yet another expression as the people in darkness outside the Church begin the service with the lighting of a fire.[198] A second example of similarities in "Easter" rituals is the universal pattern of the Treasure Hunt which expresses the search for "the new embodiment of life." Often, said White, this is the task of a woman because "she represents yearning nature which has been deprived of the living spirit, the life she had both wedded and begotten."[199] Examples include Ishtar, Isis, Aphrodite, and Mary Magdalen. The pattern is further expressed in the child's search for the Easter eggs and in the medieval practice of the hunt for the Blessed Sacrament on Easter Sunday.[200]

White was convinced that these similarities in ritual were not a coincidence, although his reasoning for this is somewhat reserved.

He wrote: "In the providence of God it could hardly be so, nor could it be so in the minds of the early Christians, whether they were Semitic, Greek or Roman, who must all have been familiar with these old pagan and Jewish rites."[201] White's reserve in this sermon is significant. Beyond the providence of God, White did not say how the early Christians must have been familiar with ancient rites of other cultures. Were they familiar with these rituals because they observed them celebrated in the first century? Or are they expressive of what Jung would call the archetypes of the collective unconscious? White's emphasis on universal patterns would suggest the latter.

However, as with the Assumption, White did not want to limit the Christian Easter to the symbolic, to a universal pattern. Thus, although the rituals of different traditions may appear to be similar, White argued that Christianity is different for two reasons. First, Jesus is not just, as with other archetypal images, "an embodiment of the life of nature," but "true God and true Man in one person."[202] Second, whereas the passing from death to life in the old rites was about survival, in the Christian tradition it is about immortality. For example, the liberation of the Israelites from the death of slavery to the life of freedom indicated the survival of the children of Israel. Similarly, in the old rites expounded in Frazer's *The Golden Bough* (bibliog. 1.1), the idea evolves that it is (annually) expedient that one man should die for the survival of the nation. But in the Christian tradition Christ died and rose once and for all. So, for White, the paschal sacrifice signifies the shift from survival to immortality, "a sharing in the changeless life of God."[203]

The Dying God

White's ideas on this matter were further developed in two radio broadcasts, the fourth and fifth of a series transmitted by the BBC, in November 1951, on the theme of the Dying God.[204] White's first broadcast focused largely on Frazer's work *The Golden Bough*, a book which tried to solve the mystery of "a priest who had plucked a golden bough, a priest who had murdered his predecessor" and was now awaiting his successor who would also be his murderer.[205]

While exploring the mystery, Frazer noticed a universal pattern of belief and practice in which the idea was expressed that it is expedient that one man should die that the nation might not perish. A pattern emerged of a divine figure—usually a priest or a king—whose death was somehow necessary for the survival of the people. White suggested that the pattern is apparent in Jesus' entry into Jerusalem when he was greeted with plucked branches, and also in the words of the high priest Caiaphas, "It is better for you that one man should die instead of the people, so that the whole nation may not perish."[206]

In the radio broadcast prior to White's, Professor Henry Frankfort had dismissed Frazer's explanation of a "universal pattern" as too simplistic, arguing that the differences were just as significant as the similarities. Frankfort had argued that symbols such as the divine child, the suffering mother, the dying god, and the totemic feast were not necessarily "universal patterns" but were symbols that were deemed significant simply because they recurred in Christianity. White disagreed with Frankfort in favor of a hypothesis of universal patterns, further supporting my point that White's reasoning for the familiarity of the early Christians with ancient rites was predominantly archetypal. To support his belief in universal—or Jung's "archetypal"—patterns, White once again considered the similarities between pagan and Christian rites, focusing in particular on the Rites of Spring and the liturgy of Holy Week.

Restating the examples of universal patterns articulated in his Easter sermon, White also added the symbol of the mating of the priest king and one who represented the goddess. White suggested further evidence of a universal pattern by drawing attention to the Easter liturgy of the Christian Church when the paschal candle—which represents Christ—"is plunged into the baptismal font" with prayers alluding to "sexual union and fertility."[207] The influence is clear: Jung had earlier spoken of the baptismal font as the womb of the Church and the Holy water as amniotic fluid fertilized by the phallic symbol of the Easter candle plunged into the font during the liturgy. Indeed, Jung thought that the ritual expression of these symbols of the unconscious was very beneficial to the Catholic—"mighty projections [that] enable the Catholic to experience large tracts of his collective unconscious in tangible reality."[208]

He had discovered that many of these symbols associated with the dying god appeared in dreams and were important in the quest for wholeness. One example of a healing symbol is the motif of sacrifice: "the dominant psychological function of the sick personality" must die that a new and revitalized person might emerge.[209] It is indicative of Jung's impact on White that, in his second BBC broadcast on this subject, White expressed his belief that the significance of the sacrifice of the God man as a Christian symbol had in fact been rediscovered through analytical psychology. It was in analysis that Jung had seen the importance of discovering the collective archetypal factors found behind the problems of his patients. Further, he believed that the experience of the symbol had the potential to bring about the transformation of personality. The symbol, according to Jung, is ". . . the very instrument which, just because it was polyvalent, transformed consciousness itself and thereby the sick personality."[210]

White had little disagreement with this, for, as I showed in the previous chapter, he had argued in his 1948 article, "Modern Psychology and the Function of Symbol," that the symbol not only expressed the inexpressible, but that it also had the power to transform the psyche. Here again White made the same point: "A symbol, as we say, 'does something to us,' it moves us, shifts our centre of awareness, changes our values. Whether it is just looked at or heard, acted out, painted out, written out or danced out, it arouses not only thought, but delight, fear, awe, horror and the rest."[211]

White's conviction that our response to the symbol moves and changes us for the better was clearly influenced by both Aquinas and Jung. According to Aquinas, for example, the efficacy of sacraments or rituals is wholly dependent on our response to the symbol (*ex opere operantis*). Similarly, according to Jung, the symbols, if neglected, had the potential to be destructive, but if recognized, could "transform" or bring about the healing of the psyche. Jung believed that this could only come about by sacrifice. Sacrifice, however, was impossible to the conscious ego. It could only be possible to a power which transcends the ego (a power which Jung calls "God"). So, as Dourley put it, the ego is sacrificed to the God of the unconscious that a rebirth can take place, and is then given back—transformed and transforming (in theological terms, "resurrected").[212] Thus, as White saw it, "psychology has strangely confirmed what theology has always maintained, that sacrifice can only be complete and perfect when it is the free and whole self-oblation of a dying man, who must also be the dying god."[213]

White himself had experienced this healing transformation as a result of his encounter with Jung's psychology and was thus convinced that the symbol of the dying god "is still very active and alive" in the unconscious. [214] For White, the symbol of the dying god was not limited to Jesus the Christ but was a universal pattern appearing in myths, pagan religions, and dreams. However, although White defended the universal which he had clearly come to appreciate through Jung, he was, as he had been in his article on the Assumption, also concerned with the particular. Therefore, this question of whether Jesus the Christ was one more dying god was the focus of White's second broadcast for the BBC, on November 16, 1951.[215]

According to Jung, the importance of Jesus the Christ is mythological. White, on the other hand, suggested that the death of Jesus the Christ is different from the recurring myth of the dying god in three ways: in the death of Jesus the Christ the recurring myth is realized in history; in the sacrificial death of Jesus a new element is introduced, namely, self-sacrifice; and the myth is fulfilled in the God man and is, therefore, final.

Turning to the first point—that the recurring myth of the dying god is realized as historical fact in the person of Jesus the Christ—White wrote:

> If Christ is the victim of a ritual murder, he is still more obviously the victim of commonplace human passions and vested interests, the jealousy of the clergy, the avarice of Judas, the punctilious conservatism of the Pharisees, the disappointed fury of the revolutionary mob, the apparent diplomacy of Pilate. If there is a sacrifice, it is now a sordid and secular execution; if there is a Labyrinth, it is now the actual winding streets used by the man-in-the-street—in a provincial capital; if there is a Search, the searcher is now no goddess, but a very woman called Mary of Magdala, setting about the very human task of embalming a dead human body.[216]

Essentially, White said that the myth, the dream, the experience of the unconscious, has now been translated into actual life. It is exactly the same point that White had made when he argued that the scandal of the Assumption lay in the "concretization" of the living processes of the unconscious in the life of a particular person. It is also a point which baffled Jung, for he feared that the particularization of the symbol emptied it of any spiritual significance. White feared the other extreme, that a totally symbolic approach made the historical events of Calvary irrelevant. "Has not science made Christ also obsolete and superfluous?—in particular, has not the psychology of the unconscious, with its study and application of psychic transformation through symbolism, outmoded also the dying God-Man of Calvary?"[217]

White's critique is sharp. According to Jung, the source of healing is not the *actual* death of the God-Man on the cross but the *symbolism* of this dying god. Stated more explicitly, for Jung, the source of healing is, as Dourley put it, the sacrificial death of Christ ("the ego") to God the Father ("the unconscious") who is then resurrected ("transformed") in the Spirit ("the individuated Self").[218] This is something that has to be undergone by *all* human beings to achieve wholeness. White's fear and fundamental disagreement with Jung on this point is well voiced: "Perhaps analytical psychology itself is doomed to degenerate into a regressive mythology, an esoteric sect of initiates, if it fails to recognise the Word made flesh, the Christian demand for the earthly realisation of the symbol."[219]

Jung did not respond to this point, but it is clear from his writings that as an analytical psychologist he had serious reservations about the earthly realization of the symbol. Jung's concern was that if the healing brought by the sacrificial death of Jesus was restricted to a historical or literal interpretation, then human beings would not experience the individual sacrifice necessary for wholeness (that is, the sacrifice of the ego to the God of the unconscious).[220]

White's second point is that the death of Jesus the Christ introduces a new element into the story: whereas, in the ancient myth the dying god was sacrificed by murder, Christ, though murdered, also offered himself willingly as a self-sacrifice. White suggested that the cycle of sacrificial murder is broken and the universal pattern of self-sacrifice has become particularized—the dying god who sacrifices "for each and for all."[221] Again, Jung objected to the Christian belief that the Christ suffered and died once and for all, arguing that the suffering and death of Christ is merely a symbol of that which must be experienced by all humans in the quest for wholeness. It is, in effect, a specific example of Jung's view that experience and not faith is that which connects us with the healing symbols of the unconscious.

White's third important difference between the old ritual of the dying god and Christ is that, in Christ, the myth of the dying god was fulfilled, and this offers some finality. In the old dying god ritual, the priest would kill the one who had killed his predecessor and then he himself would be killed by his successor. However, the death of Jesus the Christ—the death of God—is not the end of the Christian story. White went on to suggest that the resurrection, the triumph over death, marks the fulfillment of the myth of the dying god.

It is clear from these three points that, although White was heavily influenced by Jung's empirical observation that the symbols of the unconscious brought about healing, he was also deeply aware of the limitations of this view and of the empiricism from which it proceeded. White wrote:

> Psychology can tell us, in a new way, why such things would be so, and, within the limits of empirical observation, how, why and what the symbols work. But much more than that it cannot tell us: it cannot tell us if there be any such Lord (even though it finds it must postulate a 'superordiated personality'); it cannot assure us that such sacrifice really exists. As Jung puts it in the essay I have mentioned [The Transformation Symbolism of the Mass], "Psychology can deal with the matter only from the phenomenological standpoint. The truth or reality of religion lies beyond the competence of psychology."[222]

It was a point that White had realized from the very beginnings of his encounter with Jung, namely, that Jung's meticulously maintained methodology precluded any mention of the metaphysical. Jung could articulate the function of symbols in the psyche, and talk, for example, of the "psychological truth" of sacrifice. But, as I argued in the previous chapter, his methodology precluded that they be formulated rationally.

It is at this point that Victor White seized the opportunity to supplement the deficiencies of Jung's psychology with metaphysics: "The psyche's own deepest yearning, even for its own health and sanity, is for truth and reality, whatever may be the cost of abandoning agreeable make-believe. At this very point, however, the limitations of psychology's own empirical method compel it ever to confess its ignorance, and to point elsewhere for any answer there may be."[223] White appreciated, from his encounter with Jung, what he perceived as the neglected emphasis on the experiential within his own tradition. But, as an Aristotelian, he could not waiver from the rational, from "pure intellectual thinking about the psyche"[224] and its symbols.

Jung: Radical Challenge to Religion

White's awareness of the deficiencies of Jung's psychology was supplemented with an appreciation of the challenge that Jung's deeply religious psychology posed to religion. In January 1952, White gave voice to this concern in a series of programs for the BBC European Service.[225] Most relevant to this work is the second of these programs in which White focused on the challenge of "the outstanding" Jung.[226]

As White saw it, Jung's challenge to religion is "far more serious and radical"[227] than that of Freud because, unlike Freud—who dismissed religion as an obsessional neurosis, and considered symbols "sources of disguised information" about a patient's repressions—Jung thought that religion prevented neurosis, and that symbols transformed the sick personality. Indeed, Jung suggested that "the *absence* of religion" was the root cause of the sick personality. In 1932, for example, Jung wrote, "Among all my patients in the second half of life (that is to say, over thirty-five) there has not been one whose problem in the last resort was not that of finding a religious outlook on life. It is safe to say that every one of them fell ill because he had lost that which the living religions of every age have given to their followers."[228]

Jung thought that repressed or unconscious religion was at the root of all sickness in society and in the individual. If we exclude God, he argued, then an unconscious substitute takes its place: a phobia, an obsession, or other neurotic symptoms.[229] Echoing Jung, White wrote, "When God is not recognised, selfish desires develop, and out of this selfishness comes illness."[230] It is a close rendition of

Jung who, in his alchemical studies had written, "When the god is not acknowledged, egomania develops, and out of this mania comes sickness." [231] For Freud, the very acknowledgment of God is neurosis. But for Jung, the failure to acknowledge God is the cause of neurosis and the acknowledgment of God prevents neurosis.

Consequently, for Jung it was very important whether a psychic phenomenon was called god or mania. He wrote: "It is not a matter of indifference whether one calls something a 'mania' or 'god.' To serve a mania is detestable and undignified, but to serve god is full of meaning and promise because it is an act of submission to a higher, invisible and spiritual being."[232] Jung believed that the God must be acknowledged. But, as White pointed out, Jung's God, which is an image, and not God Godself, looked like a reduction of God to a psychological function. Jung denied such charges, retorting that it was simply beyond his competence as an empirical psychologist to affirm that the God image is God.

White's critique could, I think, be more forceful: if God is just the God image and not God Godself, is Jung *really* acknowledging God?[233] And could Jung, with such a constrictive methodology, really make a true acknowledgment of God? I am not suggesting that Jung could or should have made a faith-based acknowledgment of God; his methodology would not allow it. But I am suggesting that Jung's psychology could, in White's terms, be "healed" by some "pure intellectual thinking *about* the psyche."[234] As White saw it, Jung's "God" needed to be acknowledged experientially, but he considered Jung neglectful of the "thinking function," neglectful of the need for "God" to be formulated rationally.

In concluding the broadcast, White was adamant that although Jung saw the absence of religion as the cause of the sick personality, he was no apologist for religion. Indeed, it was a point that White had stressed some years before, in a lecture at the University of Leeds, when he said: "It would be a great mistake to suppose that we shall find in Jung a satisfactory apologetic for, let alone a substitute for, Christianity."[235]

But the very religious nature of Jung's psychology and the fact that he appeared to use the language of theology compounded the challenge that he posed. Jung was not concerned with theology but with psychology, and if this was not understood by theologians, it was certainly understood by White. Of Jung's treatment of beliefs, White wrote: "[They] will certainly be misread if it is not clearly understood that they are primarily concerned, not with their theology or their "objective truth," but with their psychological function." [236] Once it is understood that Jung's concern is psychological, his challenge lies in the conviction that consciously or unconsciously religion affects our lives. "If Jung's work, directly or indirectly, enables us to understand what is involved when we either affirm, deny or doubt the reality of God, his searching challenge will indeed be met."[237]

The Cross

Aware of the radical challenge that Jung posed to religion, White continued to try to show how Jung's psychology could enrich Catholic theology. In April 1952, for example, White wrote a meditation suffused with Jungian archetypes on the Stations of the Cross.[238] In it, he suggested that the Way of the Cross is not just a remembrance of the death of Jesus (White's "particular") but a symbol of human life, the way of life and death (the "universal").[239] As the participants meditate on the stations, they see a story of their "hero," the archetypal "tragic hero." As Jesus is condemned to death, so, too, humans are condemned from the womb. As Jesus is made to carry his cross, so, too, humans carry the burdens laid upon them. As Jesus falls, so do we, and out of this experience we muster the strength to take up the cross and continue on the journey.[240]

The second archetype emerges when Jesus meets his mother. "Consciously or unconsciously," according to White, the image of our mother is "part of us." White suggested that it is in times of trouble that we return to the mother, as Jesus, the archetypal hero meets his mother in the way of the cross. For some, it is not the actual mother whom we seek out but a symbol of the mother. "Perhaps we no longer seek 'mother' in our actual mother, but in some person or institution which we secretly demand shall take her place."[241] This "secret demand" is expressive of the need to be detached from the mother, a detachment that is necessary for the development of the individual. White noted how this tension of love for the mother and the need for detachment from the mother is expressed in the life of Jesus the archetypal hero: the finding in the temple, the wedding feast at Cana, and the story of the mother and brothers of Jesus.

White argued that, in a similar way, all human beings must leave the attachments of family, and that, in doing so, they will encounter strangers who will help them to carry the crosses which they bear. For Jesus, the stranger is Simon of Cyrene; for others, White envisioned these "helpful strangers" as doctors and teachers.[242] But the human being needs not only strangers but also intimate relations, modeled in Veronica's love for Jesus. It is, according to White, only this love and our response to it that "will show our *verum eikon*, our real likeness as others see it; what we are, and not what we would like to be. It is often hideous. It is often hard to face our own face."[243]

As he moved through the stations, White noted that Jesus falls and rises a second and third time, signifying that the "rhythm of dying and rising is not only at the end, but all through the Way."[244] Finally, Jesus is stripped, nailed to the cross and placed in the tomb. White concluded that death, for us as for Jesus, is just the beginning.

White had focused largely on the symbolic rather than the historic or literal, and Jung was impressed. Writing to White, in the spring of 1952, he remarked, "Your meditation about the way of the Cross contains nothing I could not subscribe to. It is psychologically 'correct.' This amounts to a sincere compliment."[245] White had essentially articulated what Jung saw as the living out of a myth that was so necessary for the healing of the psyche. According to Jung, the way of the cross is a symbol of the individual's quest for wholeness. The suffering of Jesus is a symbol of the conscious suffering of humanity torn by divine opposites that vie for "a one-sided grasp" of consciousness.[246] Humanity, like Job, is at the mercy of Jung's God. Jesus' suffering is followed by his death, a symbol of the death of the ego as it descends into "the tomb" of the unconscious. As the tomb is opened, consciousness penetrates the unconscious[247], "redeeming" the God of the unconscious which occurs when God is "incarnated" into consciousness.[248] As Dourley put it, God then works "the redemption" or making whole of the ego, a process which involves the reconciliation of opposites, and the individual "rise[s] again in the experience of the Spirit-Self."[249]

It seems that White accepted the emotional orthodoxy of this idea, though it is clear that he thought that a view of the cross that was *only* symbolic was seriously deficient. Jung, for his part, was baffled by White's insistence on a historical literal approach to the cross—and was concerned that, in fact, it *prevented* atonement, that it prevented the individual from reconnecting with the God of the unconscious.

An Unshakeable Bulwark?

White's model of supplementation continued to define his relationship with Jung in this period, but the discussion of evil (in particular) proved such a model to be untenable. It is interesting that Jung's model for White was not one of supplementation but of transformation. Indeed, I argued earlier in this book that Jung's designation of White as the "white raven" is highly significant precisely because it is indicative of Jung's hopes—that White would be instrumental in the transformation of the Western God image.

On a psychological level (on the level of *images* of wholeness), it is clear that White was willing to endorse, for example, the inclusion of the feminine and the shadow side. Jung's authority was the psyche, and, although White listened to the psyche, his ultimate authority was the Church. Thus, on a theological doctrinal level, there can be little doubt that White, committed to Aquinas' perfect and immutable God, and within the context of the Church's strong reaction to modernism, could not endorse any such notion of an evolving God which included the feminine and evil. It is for this very reason that White was absolutely insistent on the carefully drawn boundaries between psychology and theology, between talk of God image and of God Godself. However, White was becoming increasingly aware that "the boundaries between them may seem to be more perilously undefined."[250] This was in part due to the lack of clarity in some of Jung's writings and an often conveniently inadequate differentiation of the God image and God.

Somewhat paradoxically, White at the same time feared that Jung was overly dependent on a rigidly defined empiricism. In 1951, White wrote: "The tendency to absolutise limitations of method, and *to make dogmas of metapsychological opinions* [emphasis mine], undoubtedly exists, and threatens to transform a psychological school into a philosophical or quasi-religious sect. A Catholic author is right to put his readers on their guard."[251]

As I have argued, it was precisely Jung's "absolutized" method which shielded him from the criticism of scientists who thought him overly metaphysical, and theologians who thought him a reductionist. It was also this "absolutized" method which allowed Jung to observe unconscious phenomena with freedom. Some critics, however—and this included White—were deeply suspicious of this methodology, believing that it allowed Jung to "dogmatize" what were essentially "metapsychological" opinions. White's choice of language is strangely reminiscent of the moment that Jung's suspicions regarding Freud were confirmed: when, in 1910 Freud indicated that it was "essential" to "make a dogma" of the sexual theory, and thus make it "an unshakeable bulwark."[252] It was, for Jung, a moment that foreshadowed the end of his relationship with Freud.

White's experience was not quite so dramatic, though it evinced his unease at the "undoubtedly dubious tendencies in contemporary analytical psychology, and in the written works of Jung himself."[253] The end, however, was in sight. White and Jung were now entangled in a discussion on evil which had been put on hold for lack of resolution. It would not remain on hold, and in the next chapter I will show how White attempted—albeit unsuccessfully—to force a resolution on the issue, and how Jung, with his publication of *Answer to Job*, forced the issue onto God.

FIVE
1952–1955

Collecting the Victims: Jung and the *Summum Bonum*

White's disagreement with Jung regarding the *privatio boni* continued into the 1950s, but the dispute was about to become more serious as Jung shifted his attention to what he saw as "the effective source" of the doctrine of the *privatio boni*: the *Summum Bonum*.[1] As Jung grappled with this traditional Christian notion of God, he cast himself in the figure of savior, clearly believing that it was his mission to "use [his] own poor means" to "collect the victims of the *Summum Bonum*."[2] The result was *Answer to Job* (bibliog. 1.2), a book which would have an enormous impact on White and subsequently on his relationship with Jung. Initially White was "thrilled"[3] when, in October 1951, he received news that the work was going to print,[4] and, by March 1952, White had his own copy of the work. It is to this work, and in particular the view of God espoused by Jung in this work, which I now turn.

God on the Couch: *Answer to Job*

Answer to Job essentially articulated Jung's struggle with the eternal questions raised by the story of an upright man in the hands of a seemingly capricious God. It is a work which from a theological perspective put God in the image of man, or as Charet expressed it, put God on the couch.[5] According to Jung, the "solution" to the problem of God raised by the Biblical story of Job is to see God as Trinity as a symbol of the "process of unconscious maturation taking place within the individual."[6]

141

What Jung meant by this is that God as Trinity symbolizes the process of individuation. The three persons of the Trinity represent the three phases in the development of personality: unconscious, conscious, individuated.[7] In the first stage, Jung's unconscious God, God the Father is both good and evil and unconsciously fails to differentiate between the two. He wrote: "The father denotes the earlier stage of consciousness when one was still a child, still dependent on a definite, ready-made pattern of existence which is habitual and has the character of law. It is a passing, unreflective condition, a mere awareness of what is given, without intellectual or moral judgement."[8] Thus, in the book of Job, Yahweh is not conscious, he is unreflecting.

Jung argued that the reason for this is that Yahweh's wife, Sophia, has been replaced by a second wife, Israel. Yahweh's "anamnesis of Sophia" (or, in Jungian terms, the repression of his *anima*) results in the exclusion of *eros* and leaves humanity pining with Job for her love of mankind (Job 28:12).[9] "The paragon of all creation is not a man but a monster! Yahweh has no eros, no relationship to man, but only a purpose man must help him fulfill."[10] Yahweh's anamnesis of his first wife Sophia, his "friend and playmate from the beginning of the world,"[11] shifts the focus to the faithfulness of his bride Israel. As he observes the incessant unfaithfulness of the harlot Israel, Yahweh is consumed, "jealous and mistrustful like any other husband."[12] Consequently, when Satan insinuates that Job could be unfaithful, a mistrustful Yahweh listens to Satan and agrees to test his faithfulness by inflicting great suffering upon him.

Jung saw the problem very clearly: Christianity teaches that God is all good, the *Summum Bonum* (indeed, this is the persona that God presents to Job), and yet this seems to be contradicted in the God images of the Old Testament (and additionally, he would argue, in empirical psychology)[13] where God is also the infinum malum.[14] In Isaiah 45:7, for example, God declares "I form the light and create darkness. I make peace and create evil"; and, in Job, Yahweh and Satan are closely connected,[15] Satan a son of God and part of "the intimate entourage of Yahweh,"[16]—Behemoth "the beginning of the ways of God" in Job 40.

It is therefore with some confidence that Jung wrote: "We have plenty of evidence in the Old Testament that Yahweh is moral and immoral at the same time, and Rabbinic theology is fully aware of this fact. Yahweh behaves very much like an immoral being, though he is a guardian of law and order. He is unjust and unreliable according to the Old Testament."[17] Throughout Jung's vast corpus it is clear that he thought that the Bible itself attests to the fact that God is both good and evil (in Jungian terms, a "complex of opposites"): "God in the O[ld] T[estament] is a guardian of law and morality, yet is himself unjust. He is a moral paradox, unreflecting in an ethical sense."[18]

So, in *Answer to Job*, Jung's hypothesis is that when Yahweh inflicts suffering on Job, his actions are those of one who is unconscious, one who is unreflecting, one who "fails to consult his omniscience."[19] Jung admitted that "from a human point of view," the behavior of Yahweh "is so intolerable." He argued, ". . . it is the behaviour of an unconscious being who cannot be judged morally. Yahweh is a *phenomenon* and, as Job says, 'not a man.'"[20] Elsewhere, Jung maintained that God is unconscious and cannot be held morally accountable because, as such, God does not know the difference between right and wrong. "His consciousness seems to be not much more than a primitive 'awareness' which knows no reflection and no morality. One merely perceives and acts blindly, without conscious inclusion of the subject, whose individual existence raises no problems. Today we would call such a state psychologically 'unconscious,' and in the eyes of the law it would be described as *non compos mentis*."[21]

If the God of Job was, as Jung suggested, unconscious, what happened to bring about a change in God such that the God encountered in the New Testament is no longer, in psychological terms, an unconscious God who fails to consciously differentiate between good and evil? Jung proposed that two figures, Job and Sophia, are the key to Yahweh's consciousness. First, in standing firm against Yahweh's attempt to corrupt him,[22] Job has shown himself to be morally superior to his creator—a view Jung had expressed long before he wrote Job. "The victory of the vanquished and oppressed is obvious. Job stands morally higher than Yahweh. In this respect the creature has surpassed the creator. As always when an external event touches some unconscious knowledge, this knowledge can reach consciousness."[23] According to Jung, the steadfastness of Job has made Yahweh cognizant of his shadow side. Yahweh cannot dismiss Job's moral superiority and this leads to reflection, the source of which is his wife, Sophia.[24] It is she, says Jung, who "realizes God's thoughts by clothing them in material form."[25] Commenting on this realization, Jung wrote: "[Yahweh] raises himself above his earlier primitive level of consciousness by indirectly acknowledging that the man Job is morally superior to him and that therefore he has to catch up and become human himself."[26]

Viewed from this perspective, the Incarnation is not so much about redeeming man (other than *from* God[27]) but about redeeming God. If there is any atonement, it is God's atoning for his sins against Job, becoming man because he has wronged a man.[28] In his later writings, Jung would express this notion in the more theologically explicit language of *kenosis*, though reinterpreting it from a psychoanalytic perspective. He wrote: "[Yahweh] sees that incarnation is unavoidable because man's insight is a step ahead of him. He must 'empty himself of his Godhead and assume the shape of the *doulos* [cf. Philippians 2:6]' i.e., man in his lowest existence, in order to obtain the jewel which man possesses in his self reflection."[29]

For Jung, then, it is *man*—in the person of Job—who is instrumental in bringing about the Incarnation. Job does not succumb to the "divine paradox," the source of his suffering,[30] and this forces *Yahweh's* self-reflection—which ultimately leads Yahweh to a higher level of consciousness through incarnation. Jung remarked: "Yahweh's decision to become man is a symbol of the development that had to supervene when man becomes conscious of the sort of God image he is confronted with."[31] Jung's reading of the Incarnation was not (at least as he saw it) theological, but a purely psychological observation that the Incarnation represents "the differentiation of Yahweh's consciousness."[32] Jung wrote: "It is not the world that is to be changed; rather it is God who intends to change his own nature."[33] God's nature is changed in that, to bring about self-realization, God incarnates only his light side, casting off his dark side and becoming wholly good. According to Jung, "This was a decisive step, not only for man, but also for the Creator— Who, in the eyes of those who had been delivered from darkness, cast off his dark qualities and became the *Summum Bonum*."[34]

This, however, raised a question for Jung which, I would argue, is decisively theological. If God is now all good, why does evil continue to exist? It is a problem that Jung had earlier explored in his studies on Christ as an archetype of the Self in his work *Aion* (bibliog. 1.2), where he wrote: "The morally ambiguous Yahweh becomes an exclusively good God, while everything evil was united in the devil."[35] In *Answer to Job*, Jung argued that if God is now the *Summum Bonum*, then the continuing prowess of the devil must be accounted for.

> . . . the power of evil is supposedly overcome, and one can hardly believe that a loving father after the whole complicated arrangement of salvation in Christ, the atonement and declaration of love for mankind, would again let loose his evil watchdog on his children in complete disregard of all that had gone before. Why this wearisome forbearance towards Satan? Why this stubborn projection of evil to man, whom he has made so weak, so faltering, and so stupid that we are quite incapable of resisting his wicked sons? Why not pull up evil by the roots?[36]

Jung argued that the reason for the continued action of Satan is that, psychologically speaking, God got into "dissociation" at the Incarnation. That is to say that in becoming the *Summum Bonum*, evil in the person of the devil was differentiated from God. Indeed, Jung had earlier argued the same point in a slightly different way when he accused Christianity of "splitting off" one half of the opposites in the person of Satan.[37] What he meant by this, I think, is that in his becoming conscious, God just incarnated his good side and neglected his shadow side. This further implies that when Jung talked of God becoming conscious he was not talking about a process of self-reflection wherein evil is rooted out. Rather, Jung's point was, I think, that being conscious is about being able to *differentiate* such things as good and evil, it is about becoming moral.

The point was well made some years later in a letter to James Kirsch: "The purpose of the Christian reformation through Jesus was to eliminate the evil moral consequences that were caused by the amoral divine prototype."[38] However, as I have noted, Jung thought that this differentiation which he saw as so necessary had in fact led to dissociation in the Godhead. "In time it becomes obvious that the Incarnation has caused a loss among the supreme powers: the indispensable dark side has been left behind or stripped off, and the feminine aspect is missing."[39]

As Jung saw it, evil must be integrated because without the dark side God is not fully human. Jung's problem with this was that if the father of Christ is the *Summum Bonum* then "the darkness is missing and Christ has not become man, because man is afflicted with darkness."[40] Jung argued that evil is the logically equivalent opposite (and thus the necessary complement) of good, without which the symbol is incomplete. The Christ symbol lacks wholeness, and if God is to be whole, then evil must once again be included in God. He wrote: "A further act of incarnation becomes necessary. Through atheism, materialism and agnosticism, the powerful yet one-sided aspect of the *Summum Bonum* is weakened, so that it cannot keep out the dark side, and incidentally the feminine factor, any more. 'Anti Christ' and 'devil' gain in ascendancy: God asserts his power through the revelation of his darkness and destructiveness."[41]

In proposing that the Godhead be transformed to include evil, Jung was making the point that, psychologically, the Christian symbol of Trinity is incomplete because it lacks a fourth which is the symbol of wholeness. Jung had argued for the inclusion of evil, of the material, and of the feminine, in his 1942 work "A Psychological Approach to the Trinity." He suggested that their omission from traditional Christian doctrine resulted in images of God that were one-sidedly masculine, good, and spiritual. Consequently, Jung believed that in denying the fourth, the God image of the Western psyche was impoverished. So, for Jung, evil is integrated and God is (psychologically) made whole. "Finally, in what represents the third stage (individuation), the Holy Spirit is sent to continue this process in human beings—'the vessel for continuing incarnation'[42]—in whom the new and transformed God image is born."

In summary, it should now be clear that in *Answer to Job* Jung had, as he advocated, "revised religious formulas with the aid of psychological insight."[43] The insight was essentially that the human psyche is naturally destined to individuate or become whole in a process which involves a confrontation with the unconscious, particularly the shadow side, in an attempt to achieve psychic balance (or, in Jungian terms, "the reconciliation of opposites").

In other words, unconscious aspects of the psyche which have been repressed are integrated into consciousness. It was with the insight of this process, which Jung called individuation, that Jung "revised" religious formulas in *Job*, essentially by projecting this process onto the Godhead. (Jung of course would argue that God images, because they are symbols of wholeness, reflect the nature of the opposites, so a God image without a shadow side could not be a symbol of wholeness.)[44]

To state Jung's "revision" more explicitly, the God encountered in Job is unconscious of the dark side of his personality; Job forces that confrontation with the shadow side (which then becomes dissociated); and, finally, evil must again be included—integrated into the Godhead. The result is a transformation of personality, or in Jungian terms, individuation. It should, I hope, be clear why Jung thus saw the Trinity as a symbol of the (not yet completed) "process of unconscious maturation taking place within the individual."[45]

White's Initial Response

White read *Antwort auf Hiob* long before it appeared in its English translation—Jung had sent him a copy of the manuscript in German[46]—and the impact of the book on White was immense, as his response of April 5, 1952, indicated. "It is the most exciting and moving book I have read in years: and somehow it arouses tremendous bonds of sympathy between us, and lights up all sorts of dark places both in the Scriptures and in my own psyche."[47] Significantly, White did not at this stage raise the questions that one might expect of a Catholic immersed in the Dominican tradition in relation to Jung's approach to God in *Job*. How can evil be included in God who is the *Summum Bonum*? If God is good and good is being then how can evil be? How can development occur in God if God is *actus purus*? How can God's nature change if God is perfect and immutable?

White seemed unconcerned with such questions, effusively applauding the work. But three years and several virulent reviews later, White's applause had clearly abated, and the work which had stirred up such passion within him now looked set to terminate his relationship with Jung. Exactly why White did not enunciate his criticisms in 1952 is unclear. One view is that White did not see the work as an excursus in Biblical theology—but in God *images*—and was, therefore, unconcerned with the distinctly theological questions that the text raised. A second view, set forth by Stein, is that White thought that the text would not be published but would remain in the hands of a chosen few,—a "wishful thought," said Stein.[48] Yet another view is that White was fully aware of the problems that Job created for the theologian but, as the text was not yet available in English, chose to ignore them. In any case, beyond the initial adulation for *Job*, White made no further mention of it in his letter.

Resolving the Deadlock

White was troubled, however, by another issue which continued to plague his discussion with Jung. "I do wish we could somehow resolve this deadlock about the *privatio boni*."[49] It is clear from White's letter that what he had once viewed as a purely academic discussion—regarding the definition of evil as a *privatio boni*—had become crucial precisely because it was so bound up with other issues that he and Jung had discussed. White wrote: "One can not, I now think, dismiss the matter as a matter of metaphysics with no psychological relevance: for, after all, metaphysical facts must enormously affect a whole *Weltanschaung*."[50]

As I showed in the previous chapter, Jung had dismissed the *privatio boni* as a psychological truth but had conceded that it could be true metaphysically. In effect, this consigned the *privatio boni* to the metaphysical realm and—because of his methodological preclusion of metaphysics—this meant that Jung could legitimately dismiss it as irrelevant, a view that White considered flawed. White wrote: "At first I inclined to think the difference was unimportant and academic; but now it seems to me it must affect one's value-judgments on almost everything (alchemy, gnosticism, Christ and anti-Christ, the Second Coming, the whole orientation of psychotherapy) without there being any dispute about the facts."[51]

For example, a brief consideration of their respective views on the Anti-Christ shows that they were inextricably connected with their views on the *privatio boni*. White, as an adherent of the *privatio boni*, believed that the devil is not intrinsically evil, but is created good with his evil represented as a privation. Clearly this view stemmed directly from a belief in God as the *Summum Bonum*—for if God is all good and God brings all things into existence (including the devil) then evil cannot be. For Jung, on the other hand, the Anti-Christ is the darkside of God which has been cast off at the Incarnation and which must once again be included in the Godhead. Clearly this view stemmed from Jung's contention that God is not the *Summum Bonum* but equally the *Infinum Malum*, and evil is definitely not a privation but just as substantial as good.

Issues such as this led White to realize that the definition of evil as a *privatio boni* was far more crucial than he had originally thought. Engendered with an eagerness to resolve the deadlock in their dispute, White made two suggestions. First, that a careful distinction between "perception" and "conception" could provide the key to unraveling the dispute. He wrote: "Would it help to concede that evil cannot be perceived (sensed or intuited) nor necessarily felt as privatio while maintaining that it can be conceived otherwise?"[52] White's suggestion seems to have been an attempt to bridge Jung's "empirical" question regarding the experience of evil as a real force (which, as I have argued, is really a metaphysical question) and his own assertion that the *privatio boni* is simply a definition of what people mean when they use the word *evil*.

White's second suggestion probed the question of whether their disagreement could be due to a confusion between "absence" and "negation."[53] The question, I think, reveals White's suspicion that the word "privation" is being *misunderstood* by Jung as a "negation" rather than understood as an "absence." White did not develop this question, but his point is an important one, particularly in relation to Jung's accusation that the privative view of evil affords evil no reality. If evil as a privation is an absence, a μὴ ὄν, then Jung's accusation is flawed, for the absence of what is expected to be there is just as real as the presence of something. But if evil as a privation is seen as a negation or not being (οὐκ ὄν), this would imply that evil is nothing, and if it were nothing then it really would be unreal. As this is *precisely* Jung's charge against the *privatio boni* it seems highly probable that he understood (or *misunderstood*) privation as negation.[54]

Jung replied to White's suggestions on April 9, 1952, agreeing that the *privatio boni* "is of the greatest importance."⁵⁵ In this letter, Jung set forth his viewpoint explicitly but added nothing new to the discussion, simply restating one of his three main arguments against the *privatio boni*: empirically speaking, good and evil are logically equivalent contraries—so the notion that evil is a *privatio boni* contradicts the empirical evidence. Jung did, however, add what seems to be a point of concession—that although the *privatio boni* is not empirically true, it may be a "metaphysical" truth, because human beings are motivated by archetypal motifs to make "religious or metaphysical assertions." Here he seems to use the word "metaphysical" to mean the unconscious expression of the unconscious philosopher or theologian.⁵⁶ This would mean that, for Jung, the *Summum Bonum* "and its consequence the *privatio boni*" belong to the same category as the Trinity or the Virgin Birth, that is, they are religious assertions. In other words, the *privatio boni* is consigned to the status of a symbolic truth, and is therefore removed from the possibility of being defended rationally. Indeed, wrote Jung, it is "as logically impossible as the Trinity."⁵⁷

White was unconvinced and, unlike Jung, he *was* concerned about rationally defending the *privatio boni*. Disputing Jung's assertion that the *privatio boni* is moved by an archetypal motif, White wrote: "There is nothing religious or archetypal in my motivation, nor anything illogical or transcendental, when I call an egg 'bad' because it *lacks* what I think an egg ought to have."⁵⁸ Again, it is clear that White's disagreement with Jung on this point stemmed from the fact that White was concerned with a verbal point, with the meaning of the terms *evil* or *bad*. There was no unconscious metaphysic of evil bursting forth as Jung might have believed. On the contrary, White argued that a bad egg has nothing to do with religion or archetypes but *everything* to do with grammar and logic. Jung's rejoining missive on bad eggs would, of course, dispute this, and White anticipated this disagreement in his concluding remarks: "Perhaps this is a <u>philosophical</u> deadlock, and I am not out to convert you to quite different philosophical premises . . . We move in different circles, and our minds have been formed in different philosophical climates."⁵⁹

White was undoubtedly correct about this, and it is significant that Jung marked the letter. As a self-defined empiricist with a disdain for metaphysics, Jung was not about to convert to the grammar and logic of evil as espoused by Aquinas and mediated through White. Jung was formed in the tradition of Kant, and as I showed earlier in this work, was enormously influenced by Kant's idea that *noumena* are totally inaccessible and therefore one must restrict oneself to *phenomena*. With the limits of knowledge defined for Jung in this way, he was unable to delve into what he perceived as the metaphysics of evil, and thus confined himself to the way that evil is experienced, namely as a logically equivalent opposite of moral judgment. The frustration for White, it seems to me, was that he did not think that he was making a metaphysical statement about evil but rather a grammatical elucidation of a metaphysical truth.

Bad Eggs

When Jung replied on April 30, his focus was the bad egg that White had presented to him as an example of privation—an egg is called bad because it lacks what an egg ought to have to be a good egg. Jung pondered the idea with a Jesuit, Fr. Lotz, who subsequently exposed him to the idea that evil is a disintegration or decomposition of the good. Attracted to this view, Jung wrote: "If you hypostasize— as the Church does—the concept or idea of Good and give to it metaphysical substance (i.e., *bonum=esse* or having *esse*), then "decomposition" would indeed be a very suitable formula, also satisfactory from a psychological viewpoint."[60] But as Jung contemplated the good egg that becomes a bad egg by decomposition, he was dissatisfied that this was an example of privation. "A bad egg is not characterized by a mere decrease of goodness however, since it produces qualities of its own that did not belong to the good egg. It develops among other things H_2S, which is a particularly unpleasant substance in its own right. It derives very definitely from the complex albumen of the good egg and thus forms a most obvious evidence for the thesis: Evil derives from Good."[61]

Jung admitted, therefore, that the formula of "decomposition" is satisfactory inasmuch as it acknowledges the empirical view that Evil is just as substantial as Good—because, he says, H_2S (i.e., hydrogen sulfide,—or brimstone) is "tangibly real." He disputed, however,

White's suggestion that it is a model of privation because, according to Jung, the bad egg (evil) is far from being μὴ ὄν. Further, Jung suggested that, rather than supporting a privative view, the "decomposition" theory supports *his view* that ultimately God is the source of evil. He wrote: "The 'decomposition' theory would lead to the ultimate conclusion that the *Summum Bonum* can disintegrate and produce H_2S, the characteristic smell of Hell. Good then would be corruptible, i.e., it would possess an inherent possibility of decay. The possibility of corruption means nothing less than a tendency inherent in the Good to decay to change into evil. That obviously confirms my heretical views."[62]

According to Jung, the *Summum Bonum* creates good things that have a tendency to go wrong. This confirmed Jung's "heretical views" because, as he saw it, it implied that the corruption does not come from man but from God. (With this, Jung restated his third argument against the *privatio boni*, the first two having been briefly restated above, and in some detail in the previous chapter). Further, Jung argued that his "heresies"—that corruption comes from God—are biblically attested in the "*immoral behaviour*" of the "*morally dubious*" God of the Old Testament. With characteristic humor, he italicized the question to White, "*Does the doctrine of the Church admit Yahweh's moral defects?*"[63] Jung already knew the answer to this question. Furthermore, he thought that his psychology admitted *exactly* what the Church needed to admit if human beings were to experience "the immediate living God."[64] Indeed, for Jung, Church doctrine was the culprit—guilty of "turning away from our psychic origins"[65] and thus "forestall[ing]" such an experience—precisely because it articulated a transcendent and wholly good God.[66]

In the final part of the letter, Jung combined two of his principal arguments against the *privatio boni*—that if evil is a privation it won't be taken seriously; and that the notion of evil as a *privatio boni* contradicts the empirical evidence of good and evil as logically equivalent opposites. His reformulated point combining these is this: the privative view is a nonsense because it suggests that evil is a "small good," and if evil is a small good, then it is still good and not bad. The implication, of course, is that a "small good" will not be taken seriously as a real and destructive force in the world.

He wrote: "On the metaphysical plane you are free to declare that what we call 'substantially evil' is in metaphysical reality a small Good. But such a statement does not make much sense to me."[67]

The problem for Jung was that evil is experienced as a substantial reality but the definition of evil as a privation implies that there must be some good for evil to exist and so it looks like evil is a "small good." White disagreed with Jung, responding with an analogy: "I do not say that 'Evil is a minute good,' on the contrary I say it is not good at all—just as I do not say that blindness is 'minute sight,' but no sight at all, an absence of sight: sight which simply does not exist. But blind men do exist, and are really blind. A blind man is a Plus (as a man) with a Minus (with regard to his sight)."[68] In other words, according to White, evil is a not a small good, it is not any kind of good but, rather, an absence of good, or good which does not exist. For White, this was simply a grammatical elucidation of a metaphysical truth. For Jung, on the other hand, the question was "empirical"—it was about evil as it is experienced as a real force in the psyche (which, to further complicate matters, seems to me to be a metaphysical statement). It is clear therefore that the two were often talking at cross purposes about different things, and often did not realize this to be the case.

A Public Disagreement

The relatively private disagreement between the two men would become more public with the publication of White's first book, *God and the Unconscious* (bibliog. 1.4, 1952), for which Jung wrote the foreword in May 1952. In it Jung praised White's "intellectual understanding" and his "competent exposé,"[69] and expressed his delight at their collaboration. "I must acknowledge with gratitude that the cooperation I had so long wished and hoped for has now become a reality."[70] As Jung saw it, analytical psychology and theology both attended to "the psychically sick and suffering human being," and thus it was natural that he should turn to those concerned with the soul, namely the theologians. "Surely it would be valuable for the theologian to know what is happening in the psyche of the adult; and it must gradually be dawning on any responsible doctor what an incredibly important role the spiritual atmosphere plays in the psychic economy."[71]

Jung longed for sustained dialogue with theologians, but had had little success because his empirical approach left theologians with the impression that his idea of myth depreciates religious doctrines, reducing them to the level of psychological function. Jung therefore appreciated Victor White's ability to clearly define the boundaries between them, and thus avoid such confusions. To give just one of Jung's examples, hearing the word *God*, the theologian will assume that what is meant is "the metaphysical *Ens Absolutum*." The psychologist on the other hand will assume that *God* is "a mere statement, at most an archetypal motif."[72] Without this realization, the grounds for confusion were enormous. The fact that White understood that Jung proceeded from empirical facts,[73] and that his methodology precluded talk of God Godself, was therefore much applauded by Jung.

Further, Jung recognized that White was able to see the enormous implications of his work. He wrote: "Fr. White's book has the merit of being the first theological work from the Catholic side which deals as deeply with the far-reaching effects of the new empirical knowledge in the realm of *représentations collectives* and makes a serious attempt to integrate it." [74] For Jung, it was White's appreciation of his method in particular that allowed for the cooperation with a theologian he had "so long wished and hoped for." The result was "not only [that] two apparently incompatible spheres come into contact, but [that] they also mutually animate and fertilize each other."[75]

But the mutual animation and fertilization was tempered by the dissonance which also befell them. Illustrating this, Jung used the foreword not only to applaud White's endeavors, but "to avail [himself] of the right to free criticism" offered him by White.[76] His criticism focused on the clashes that occur when two different fields of knowledge encroach upon each other, and of which the *privatio boni* provided the perfect example. Before exploring this particular clash, Jung described his first encounter with the *privatio boni* in his work as a psychoanalyst:

> I should never have dreamt of coming up against so remote a problem as that of the *privatio boni* in my practical work. Fate would have it,

however, that I had to treat a patient, a scholarly man, who had become involved in all manner of dubious and morally questionable practices. He turned out to be a fervent adherent of the *privatio boni*, because it fitted admirably with his scheme: evil in itself is nothing, a mere shadow, a trifling and fleeting diminution of good, like a cloud passing over the sun. The man professed to be a believing Protestant and would therefore have had no reason to appeal to the *sententia communis* of the Catholic Church, had it not proved a welcome sedative for his peace of mind.[77]

It was this case, Jung explained, that initially led him to consider this view of evil and its psychological aspect. As he did so, he felt "compelled to contest the validity of the *privatio boni* as far as concerns the empirical realm."[78] It is important to stress that Jung's criticisms were strictly empirical. He wrote: "Criticism can only be applied to psychic phenomena, i.e., to ideas and concepts, but not to metaphysical entities. The latter can only be confronted with each other. *Hence my criticism is valid only within the empirical realm.*"[79] Jung's carefully defined empiricism would not allow him to consider the metaphysical question of the substance of evil, and although he admitted that metaphysically "good can be a substance and evil a μὴ ὄν," he could not support this empirically.[80] For Jung, the definition of evil as a *privatio boni* is a metaphysical statement about the nature of evil, and it is therefore methodologically precluded from his purview. In addition it is clear that Jung thought that he was criticizing a metaphysical statement, believing that his psychological method permitted and encouraged the criticism of metaphysical statements thought to be "psychologically inadequate."[81]

A brief summary of Jung's empirical objections to the *privatio boni* will spare any unnecessary repetition, and my repeated reference to them will serve to highlight the narrative of the deadlock of "assertion and counter-assertion."[82] Here are Jung's arguments. First, from an empirical perspective, good and evil are not derived one from another but are logically equivalent halves of moral judgment. Thus, evil as μὴ ὄν is nonsensical because, if good is substantial, then, empirically speaking, so too is its opposite, evil. Second, if evil is defined as a μὴ ὄν it will not be taken seriously, but will be seen as "an accidental lack of perfection"[83] with dangerous psychological consequences. Third, in removing evil from God, the *privatio boni* has human beings as the source of evil—again, dangerous psychologically because it deprives human beings of doing anything good and gives them "the seductive power of doing evil"—that is, a negative inflation.[84]

Jung's critique was that of an empiricist, yet he expressed an awareness of the perspective of the metaphysician, Victor White, for whom his "empirical concepts would be a logical monster."[85] He was aware that, as a "philosopher and speculating heretic," he was "easy prey."[86] This was clearly part of the problem in the clash over the *privatio boni*, and not even the mutual insistence on carefully defined boundaries between empiricism and metaphysics could prevent it.

Jung's claim to operate solely within the empirical realm (and his use of this claim as an incantation against criticism) cannot go unquestioned. What, for example, are the statements "evil is a real existing force" or "good and evil are logically equivalent contraries" if they are not metaphysical statements? Certainly, Jung thought they were empirical statements because they were a statement of the *experience* of evil as "real" or "logically equivalent." For him they were *not* metaphysical statements—at least as Jung understood the word *metaphysical*—that is, as roughly equated with Kant's noumenal, or that for which there is no evidence. Thus the statement "evil is a real force" is a metaphysical statement only from the perspective of Victor White (that is, in the neo-scholastic sense), or Kant (that is, as necessary and universal truths about reality) or in the general sense of what constitutes ultimate reality—but not from Jung's perspective.

White, from his side, was not without similar encroachments of the empirical realm, claiming for example that empirical psychology allowed him to experience evil as a *privatio boni*. But Jung's encroachment was decidedly more problematic than White's because his methodology precluded metaphysics. White was not quite so constrained, however—even referring to himself as "an amateur psychologist"[87] in a way that Jung would not (and indeed could not) refer to himself as a theologian.

God and the Unconscious

White was "delight[ed]" with Jung's foreword to *God and the Unconscious* as his "*opus imperfectum*" of June 25 reveals. White's own preface to the book very closely mirrored Jung's foreword. Like Jung, he stressed the importance of understanding the language of the other, thereby eliminating some of the grounds for confusion. "The worker on the borderlands of religion and psychology must be bilingual."[88] This meant understanding, as Jung had emphasized in his foreword, that when the theologian uses the word *God* she is referring to God Godself, whereas when the psychologist uses the word *God* she is referring to an archetypal image.

The importance of being "bilingual" was clear, and critics certainly thought that this ability to speak and understand both "languages" was one of White's greatest strengths. Alan Keenan, for example, described White as "probably [Jung's] best interpreter in Europe. He is in addition a fine theologian and metaphysician."[89] Michael Fordham, the editor of the Journal of Analytical Psychology expressed the view that White's psychology was so good that trained psychologists had difficulty competing with him.[90] Applauding White's response to an "over cerebralised" Christianity, the Professor of Moral and Pastoral Theology at Oxford, V. A. Demant, described *God and the Unconscious* as the best confrontation of theology and analytical psychology to date.[91] Psychiatrist Philip Mairet called it a "brilliant treatise."[92] Writing in The Trident, theologian Laurence Bright, O. P. applauded White's "pioneer work" and—presenting him as one who "inherited something of St. Thomas' boldness"—highlighted his ability to remove suspicions that Jung was "the enemy."[93] While "far from uncritically accepting all views of Jung,"[94] he presented White like Thomas—as a theologian who wanted to use that "broad vision" and "assimilative capacity" to bring into his own synthesis that which he found of truth in Jung's vision.[95]

As I showed earlier, Jung himself set a very high value on White's ability to understand him, which was clearly a consequence of White's being bilingual. This was confirmed by Adrian Dowling, O. P., a student in the Order at the time: "He went and stayed with Jung—several times. We were told that Jung had said, 'You understand me.'"[96] Similarly, Columba Ryan, O. P., also a student in the Order at that time, implied that White was successful in negotiating the terrain in both fields: "Very few people bridge these two disciplines. And that's where [White] would've been very innovative." [97]

Despite his competency, White was aware of the difficulty of his task: "There is a difference, not easy to bridge, between the world of the empirical psychologist, accustomed to scientific training and method, and the trained theologian or philosopher whose mental processes, though no less disciplined, operate in quite different fashion." [98] Like Jung, White was only too aware of the clashes that occur when two different fields of knowledge encroach upon each other, especially clashes which stem from misunderstanding. On the philosophical and theological side, for example, White wrote: "The philosopher or theologian tends to read 'explanation' into the provisional postulates and working hypotheses of the empirical scientist, entities into his categories of classification, even moral codes into his statistically established 'laws,' unwarrantable trespasses into his own domain in the scientist's generalized 'theories.'" [99] Jung was dismissed by many theologians as a heretic, and White thought that this was, in part, due to the fact that they failed to understand that when Jung talked about God he was talking about the archetype of the Self as God image and not the nature of God. Further, Jung always insisted that his archetypes were a hypothesis for the recurrence of images in dreams, myths, and religions, and not explanations.

Unfortunately, the fact that Jung's language appeared to be the language of theology led to many accusations that Jung was guilty of metaphysical reductionism. But White did not exonerate the empirical psychologists either, and, leveling similar criticisms, he wrote: "Nor are scientific workers always so self critical as to be wholly guiltless of provoking such interpretations. They, on their side, tend to be impatient with meticulous linguistic analyses, sustaining conclusions far more remote from direct observation, which cannot be verified by methods to which they are accustomed, and which nevertheless amazingly lay claim to permanent and universal validity." [100] White's comments, though not specific, reveal something of his own frustration in his personal encounter with Jung. First, it is clear that White thought that Jung, in part, provoked misunderstanding by an often conveniently inadequate differentiation of God image and God. Second, in his unsubtle remark about the impatience of psychologists with "meticulous linguistic analyses," he was, without a doubt, referring to Jung's resistance to the grammar and logic of the *privatio boni.*

His conclusion, however, was deeply appreciative of Jung as both friend and collaborator: "What I owe to his personal friendship, our frank discussions, my direct acquaintance with his kindness, his genuineness and—above all—his astonishing humility, can never be expressed. My expressions of disagreement or misgivings about some of his views and approaches in no way reduce my indebtedness and gratitude." [101]

Turning to the book itself, White admitted that this was not the book he wanted to write, discovering in the course of writing the first two chapters that Albert Beguin, Hans Schaer, and Josef Goldbrunner had already done what he had intended.[102] Realizing that his "elaborate plans" for a comprehensive treatise were "too ambitious,"[103] White abandoned the project. Therefore, with the exception of the first two chapters, the ideas in the book had appeared in article form in preceding years[104] (and have already been discussed in this book).

His first chapter, "The Twilight of the Gods," deals with the question of the death of God. White noted how in previous generations the death of god was usually a prelude to transformation or displacement by a newer god, but was never seen as final and definitive.[105] Consequently, as the ancient gods died and rose, images of god were constantly being broken and transformed. White wrote: "For the fixed image evokes the fixed stare, the fixed loyalty which may blind man's vision to the claims of further and wider loyalties, and so paralyse the human spirit and crush its inherent will to advance and venture."[106] As a result, according to White, humanity was faced with an "evolving elusive Deity." This image, of course, is "an outrage" for the metaphysician—"an illogical monstrosity"— because change and decay cannot be attributed to the Transcendent and Absolute.[107] Although White shared this view, he argued that human images of God must be recognized as psychological fact. In other words, while God is immutable, every human image of God "must dissolve and elude man's grasp" if man is not to be made into the likeness of his own idols.[108]

Turning to his own age, White witnessed another "twilight of the gods," but, whereas in earlier generations gods died to be transformed or displaced by a new god, the Western God is really dead.[109] This he illustrated from the perspective of several disciplines: science has usurped the need for God; philosophy destroyed all reason for God; and psychology showed God to be an illusion, a projection of the unconscious. But, "myths die hard" and humanity now faces "the experiment in godlessness to which the mass of Western man is now committed."[110]

It is to this "experiment" that White turned his attention in the second chapter, "The Gods Go A-Begging," questioning whether the gods are really dead after all. Drawing heavily on Jung's psychology, White argued that the psychic energy that was once channeled into religion has not disappeared but has been repressed in the unconscious, and therefore continues to exert its influence on human behavior. For example, consider what happens to the omnipotence of a deity if that deity is no longer acknowledged. He suggested that this value, omnipotence, is projected onto the state or a leader. He was drawing on Jung, who wrote: "Whenever the Spirit of God is excluded from human consideration, an unconscious substitute takes its place."[111] White gave further examples of what happens when human beings cast out their gods and demons: "Gods and demons, heavens and hells, are ineradicable from the nooks and crannies of the human mind, and . . . if the human mind is deprived of its heaven above and its hell beneath, then it must make its heaven and corresponding hell on earth."[112] This is evidenced, according to White, in the use of religious language politics, particularly in the demonization of the opponent, and, similarly, in the deification of human beings as idols to be worshipped. These are all "symptoms of repressed religion" and a clear indication that although the gods are dead to Western consciousness, "they will not lie down."[113] God is a powerful force of the unconscious, an activity of the soul, which goes "a-begging" for our attention. While White does not believe this "God" is only an intra-psychic phenomenon—which should be acknowledged in the interests of healing—he is prepared to embrace Jung's ideas on the God of the Unconscious, and supplement them with theology.

The publication of *God and the Unconscious* established White as an authority on psychology and theology, and not just a Dominican who was an authority on Aquinas (which indeed he was,

Fr. Victor White O.P.

Fr. Victor White O.P.

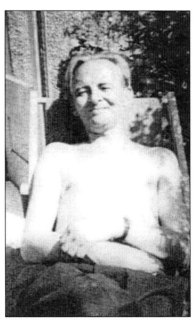

All photos of
Fr. Victor White O.P.

All photos of Fr. Victor White O.P. at the Seventh Catholic
International Congress of Psychotherapists and Clinical Psychology,
Madrid, September 1957.

All photos are Victor White's
parents, Rev. John Henry and
Beatrice Mary White.

Gordon Henry White

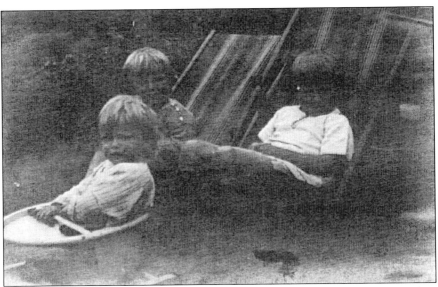

Gordon Henry White with his brothers John Francis Christopher and
Basil Phillip Dawson.

C.G. Jung and Victor White O.P. at Bollingen.

Jung and White, driving in Zurich.

C.G. Jung and Victor White, boating on Lake Zurich.

C.G. Jung, from White's personal collection.

Both photos of Victor White O.P. and Ambrose Farrell O.P., Rome.

Victor White O.P. &
Fr. James Weisheipl O.P.,
U.S.A

Mrs Frances Leggetts, Stone Ridge, NY.

BLACKFRIARS,
OXFORD.

3.0

19. 9. 40.

Dear Dr. Laird,

Our mutual friend, Donald Mackinnon,
promised to arrange for me to meet you some weeks
ago, but nothing seems to have come of it. As I am
expecting to have to leave Oxford any day, & as I am
extremely anxious to have a chat with you with you
before I go, I am venturing to write to you direct to
ask if it would be possible. I am rather badly tied
up at the moment, but afternoons between 2.30 & 4.30
are easiest for me.

The fact of the matter is that I am a
Catholic priest who has become badly "stuck". It is the
writings of Dr. Jung that have given me some inkling
of what it is I am up against. The necessity of
my leaving Oxford makes it impossible for me to
become a 'patient' even if you wanted to have me &
I had the means for the purpose, but there are one
or two immediate & practical problems on which I
should very much like your advice — at least as to
what not to do.

I hope you will forgive this rather
bold self-introduction. Even if you would prefer not

Copy of Letter from Victor White O.P. to John Layard, 19th September 1940.

BLACKFRIARS
OXFORD.
TELEPHONE 3607

3rd August 1945.

Dear Professor Jung,

Although I have never had the honour to meet you (outside of my dreams!), I am taking the very great liberty of sending to you some of my writings concerning your psychology, written from a Catholic point of view. I doubt, of course, whether you will have time or inclination to read them, let alone to comment upon them; but should you ever do so, it would be a great help to me & any future work I am able to do if I could be shown any points on which I have positively misunderstood you.

I might mention that there is great & growing interest in this country among Catholics (as well as many others) in the theory & practice of Analytical Psychology; & that I personally am one of very many who owe to you & your disciples in England an immense debt of gratitude.

May I be permitted to convey my belated congratulations on your recent birthday, & express my thankfulness for your recovery.

Yours very obediently & gratefully,

J. Victor White O.P.

P.S. I have also just finished a short criticism of your article "Zur Psychologie der Trinität" in Eranos Jahrb., Annals, + S.? — I will also take the liberty of ——

Copy of note card from Victor White O.P. to C.G. Jung, 3rd August 1945.

Prof. Dr. C. G. Jung

Küsnacht-Zürich Oct. 1. 1945.
Seestrasse 228

My dear Father White,

In the meantime I have finished reading the pamphlets you kindly leave sent to me. My first reaction was: what a pity, that you live in England and that I have you not at my elbow, when I am blundering in the wide field of theological knowledge. You must grant me though attenuating circumstances: beside all the other things I had to learn I arrived only very late at the treasure house of patristic wisdom, so late in fact, that my limited powers didn't suffice any more to acquire all which would be needed to elucidate and explain the perplexities of modern psychological experience. Excuse the irreverential pun: You are to me a white raven inasmuch as you are the only theologian I know of who has really understood something of what the problem of psychology in our present world means. You have seen its enormous implications. I cannot tell you how glad I am that I know a man, a theologian, who is conscientious enough to weigh my opinions on the basis of a careful study of my writings! This is a really rare occasion. ~~Prof Emil Brunner living with me in the same town is typical for the other kind of theologian who in the manner of the grand inquisitor imposes me off the slate. Whoever cannot acknowledge the truth of "gratia" in perfectis naturam" proves by this attitude, that he never experienced it. That is the kind of theologian which I always knew and there is one of the reasons, why I prefer experience to belief.~~ || My temperamental empiricism has its reasons. I began my career with repudiating everything that ~~smelt~~ smelt of belief. That explains my critical attitude...

UNIVERSITY OF BIRMINGHAM

SESSION 1958-59

The Edward Cadbury Lectures

SOUL AND PSYCHE

EIGHT PUBLIC LECTURES

by

THE REVEREND VICTOR WHITE, O.P., S.T.L.

Jan. 16. THE COMMON GROUND OF RELIGION AND PSYCHO-LOGY. The case for the identity of the "soul" of religion and the "psyche" of psychology, viewed from both the theological and the psychological standpoints.

Jan. 23. THE JUNGIAN APPROACH TO RELIGION. Why Jung's psychology calls for our special attention; some merits and difficulties in Jung's method in treating of religion.

Jan. 30. SYMBOL, DOGMA AND FAITH. The need for correlating Christian beliefs, images and practices with the findings of depth-psychology.

Feb. 6 TRINITY AND QUATERNITY. The universality and significance of quaternary symbols; the psychological function of the doctrine of the Trinity; the problem of the "missing fourth."

Feb. 13. THE "MISSING FEMININE." The feminine image in depth-psychology, the Bible and the Church.

Feb. 20. THE "INTEGRATION OF EVIL." The psychological and social results of the "repression of the shadow"; an analysis of the notions of the "acceptance" and "integration" of evil.

Feb. 27. HEALTH AND HOLINESS. The correlation of sanctity and sanity; the meaning of mental health and sickness; the compatibility of psychological disorders with holiness in this life.

March 6. RELIGION AND MENTAL HEALTH. The classical conception of religion and its relevance to psychological integration; the contemporary "failure of religion" in the light of depth-psychology.

FRIDAYS at 5.30 p.m.

at the

MASON THEATRE, THE UNIVERSITY
EDMUND STREET, BIRMINGHAM 3

Admission Free without Ticket

Copy of Poster advertising The Edward Cadbury Lectures by
Victor White O.P., 1958-59

SUPREMA SACRA CONGREGAZIONE
DEL
SANTO OFFIZIO

Prot. N. 339/57/i
(Nella risposta si prega citare questo numero)

Reverendissimo Padre,

Interesso la Paternità Vostra Rev.ma a voler dare informazioni sul conto del P. Victor White, O.P., professore nel Collegio di Blackfriars (Oxford) in Inghilterra.

In particolare, la P.V. si compiaccia dare notizie sulla dottrina del P. White e mandare un elenco, per quanto possibile completo, degli scritti pubblicati dal medesimo Padre.

In attesa di un Suo cortese riscontro, mi valgo dell'occasione per confermarmi con sensi di religioso ossequio

della Paternità Vostra Rev.ma

dev.mo

[firma] 1957

[annotazioni manoscritte]
scritto al P. Provinciale
per informazione
8. Jan. 1958

Reverendissimo Padre
P. MICHELE BROWNE, O.P.
Maestro Generale dei
Frati Predicatori
R O M A

Copy of a Request from Rome for information on Victor White O.P.,
10th December 1957.

Sketch of Victor White in his
coffin by Charles Lutyens.

Postcard from Victor White O.P.
to Mrs. Ginsberg.

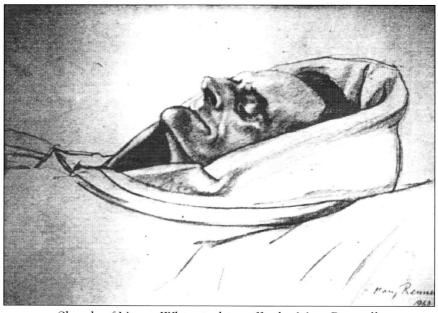

Sketch of Victor White in his coffin by Mary Rennell.

and by all accounts a very fine one). He gave many lectures and talks on such topics as "Analytical Psychology and Religion" in Oxford during Trinity term of 1951, "The Occult" to the London Wiseman Society in 1952, and "The Rites of Spring" and "Faith and Creeds" to the Guild of Pastoral Psychology in Cambridge in September 1952. His renown took him to Vallejo, where he lectured on another Jungian theme—"Man's Need for Religion."

White's other area of interest in this period was comparative religion[114] which, I would argue, was also heavily influenced by his contact with Jung, who had written extensively on the appearance of Eastern ideas in the Western psyche, and for whom Christianity was not the only expression of the unconscious. For Jung, the idea of an Absolute was anathema—at least from an "empirical" perspective. And, if White embraced this point of view entirely, it would certainly appear that he was at odds with the teachings of the Catholic Church. White believed that he was shielded from such a reality as long as images of God and God Godself were kept separate and uncontaminated. But, hovering ominously in the background was another contamination of an even more serious nature that would bring White into further discussion with Jung on evil.

Contaminating Good and Being

In the same letter that White had expressed his "delight" with Jung's foreword to *God and the Unconscious*, White expressed his desire to continue discussing "many matters about Bad Eggs, Jahwe's morals, Job and Elihu, you and Buber" during his upcoming visit to Zurich in July 1952.[115] Before that visit, however, Jung responded to White's desire with a letter on the *privatio boni*. In the letter, dated June 30, 1952, Jung began with the question of whether the *privatio boni* is a dogma of the Catholic faith[116] and then proceeded to suggest yet another key to unraveling the dispute. Jung wrote: "The crux seems to lie in the contamination of two incongruous notions of Good and of Being. . . . There is not the faintest evidence for the identity of Good and Being." [117]

Jung thought that White was guilty of ascribing to a metaphysic which contaminated Good with Being. For White, evil could be nothing other than non-being because God is the *Summum Bonum* who brings into being all that exists. So, all that exists is good. Thus, Being is identified with goodness and evil has no substance. For Jung, this identification was problematic for several reasons. First, if you assume you can identify Good with Being, then even from an empirical perspective evil can be nothing other than non-Being (because good and evil are logically equivalent contraries). Jung disputed this because his empiricism indicated that evil was not experienced as non-being, and, therefore, it seemed to Jung that the identification of Good with Being should not be assumed.

A second reason that Jung was deeply dissatisfied with White's acceptance of the identification of Good with Being was this: if good is substantial, then as a logically equivalent contrary, so too is evil. Jung wrote: "Evil is as substantial as Good."[118] Jung's argument appears to contradict his first point that if good is identified with being then evil can be nothing other than non-being. However, on closer inspection his point is this: reject the identification of good with being because it implies that evil is non-being whereas evil is not *experienced* as non-being—and, therefore, the identification of good with being is an incongruous contamination. Empirically, good and evil are logically equivalent opposites, so if good is substantial, so too is evil; if evil is an illusion, so too is good. Of course, Jung was not interested in substances but in moral judgments.

In a third argument against the identification of Good with Being, Jung argued that if Good is identified with Being then Satan must also be good, unconsciously recognizing the Christian view that the devil as a creature of God was created good. ". . . inasmuch as Satan exists, he is nothing but good, because Being = Good."[119] Jung's problem with this was that it seems to imply that "evil is a minute good." Satan's disobedience might be described as being "a little bit good," the implications of which disturbed Jung greatly. He wrote: "For that small Good he is in hell. Why should good be thrown into Hell? And at what percentage of goodness are you liable to get condemned?"[120]

Jung was correct in his representation that inasmuch as the devil exists, he is good. However, Satan's disobedience is not "a little bit good." It is not good at all but an absence of good—good which does not exist. Jung, however, did not see it this way: "If I am condemned to hell I am still nothing but good, in spite of the fact that I have lost 99% of goodness because Evil is not."[121] In view of this, Jung suggested to White that denying the existence of evil is Christianity's attempt to get around the problem of dualism. "You do deny it by calling evil a decreasing Good. Absolute Evil is for you a merely neutral condition, in which there is nothing at all, a μὴ ὄν."[122]

Jung concluded the letter, imploring White to abandon the contaminated notions of Good and Being: "Things would be quite simple if you could only admit that Good and Evil are judgments, having nothing to do with the incommensurable concept of Being."[123] According to Jung, "Being" is not identified with good, and so, there is not a correct way that one "should" act in relation to the good. Being is morally neutral, and this is why Jung could say that moral judgments are subjective judgments. In contrast, White identified Good with Being, so *Good* is what really exists as it should. According to White, morality is objective, and a person can be right or wrong about judgments in relation to the Good.

Bad Eggs, Good Coffee

White disagreed with Jung and wrote to him on July 9 to try to persuade him of the evidence for identifying Good with Being. Appealing to Jung's empiricism, White argued that the identification is made daily when, for example, we say "the weather is good" or "the coffee is good." White questioned, "What are these if not identifications of something which IS with something GOOD? (Of course the abstract <u>meanings</u> of Good and Being are not identical, or such statements would be tautologies)."[124]

White then attempted to dissuade Jung from the notion that the identification of Evil with non-Being necessarily implies that evil is unreal. Sensitive to Jung's critique, White admitted that the idea of evil as having no existence in itself while being perfectly real does not always seem obvious and convincing. He continued: "We say, 'the weather . . . the coffee . . . Mr. X . . . is bad or evil.' When I say that, I do not mean there is NO coffee, weather or Mr. X, but I do mean that they have NOT got something they should have."[125]

According to White, then, the identification of Good with Being is a matter of grammar and logic. White was not, therefore, about to admit that good and evil are moral judgments with nothing to do with Being, as Jung had suggested. Indeed, White was adamant that *good* is not a moral judgment, but a term. Thus, when we say, for example, "hell is evil" or "this egg is good" we are not talking about the validity of a particular judgment but *the meaning of terms.*"[126]

White, therefore, would not admit "the obvious fact" that good and evil are judgments, and was "baffle[d]" at Jung's insistence that theology must do exactly that: "But how can I, when every dictionary or logic book in the world tells me a judgment cannot exist in a single noun, let alone an adjective, but must always contain a verb? I am wondering if this is the crux behind the crux—a contamination of <u>perception</u> and <u>judgment</u>, and intellectual judgment in particular."[127] White's point is both grammatical and logical: single nouns cannot be judgments. Further, White was absolutely convinced that Jung was confusing perceptions (that which is sensed or intuited) and judgments.

Jung's overriding concern was the *experience* of evil, which White understood to be a matter of perception. However, Jung *talked* about good and evil as judgments. The problem for White as a Thomist was that sensation and intuition are *only* perceptions— and any judgment about good and evil would be "equally pointless and inappropriate."[128] The discussion would be somewhat clarified with White's realization that Jung's emphasis was feeling, which in Jung's schema is a judgment function.[129] In addition, White offered a theological objection to the idea that good and evil are moral judgments: if good and evil are limited to moral judgments, then *God* would be bound by moral law and this would be problematic for a Thomist—in fact White calls it a blasphemy.[130]

Finally, White turned his attention to Jung's accusation that Christianity denies evil (by defining it as a small good) to escape dualism. Clearly insulted, White wrote: "My dear CG, I love you and owe you more than I can say. When you write like that it hurts— I feel it is terribly unworthy of you—and I wonder *what made you do it.*"[131] White denied that evil is a decreasing or a minute good, arguing that it is not good at all. Using the analogy of blindness, White argued that blindness is not a decreasing sight or a "minute sight" but "no sight at all." It is, in the language of privation, an absence of sight which ought to be there. To say that blindness is an absence is not to say that it does not exist; the blindness is—not least to the blind man—very real. White further rebutted Jung's assertion that "Absolute evil" is a neutral condition, arguing that, on the contrary, it is a "non existent abstraction" which might be compared to "Absolute Darkness" or "Absolute Buttercups."[132]

White stayed with Jung at Bollingen from July 17 to July 27, 1952, though it is clear, from the letters that followed, that the two men did not resolve the question of the *privatio boni*. Shortly after his return to England, White received a letter from Jung in which Jung appealed to the empirical, suggesting that White should contemplate the *privatio boni* from a feeling standpoint and not just an intellectual one.[133] There is no record of any correspondence from August 1952 to April 1953, but in a letter to a mutual friend, Jung expressed his frustration regarding his discussion with White on the *privatio boni*, describing it as "a very unsatisfactory experience." At the same time, he optimistically opined that "the flaw demonstrated in the doctrine of the *privatio boni* has become visible to Victor too."[134]

At Variance with Self

Despite the break in correspondence, White did visit Jung again in May of 1953.[135] A few months after this visit, he wrote to Jung from the Dominican Priory at Hawkesyard where he was directing a retreat. The letter, though brief, was deeply insightful of White's own awareness of the impact of Jung's psychology on his life and thought: "There are times when I wish I had never heard of psychology, or anyhow could barricade myself behind a receptionist and a brass plate."[136] The problem for White was that he had experienced Jung's psychology as emotionally orthodox but this often put him at variance with the Catholic Church, consequently spawning much personal turmoil. A vivid example of this is in a letter that White sent to Jung on November 8, 1953, in which he raised the suspicion that Christ is an inadequate symbol of the Self because he lacks the shadow necessary for wholeness. Dogmatically, White was perturbed at this thought—it created a tension between psychology and his faith: "Their god simply isn't my God any more: my very clerical clothes have become a lie."[137] Further expressive of this inner turmoil, White disclosed to Jung his nightmares and his inability to sleep. Deeply troubled by thoughts of leaving the Dominican Order to save his soul, he admitted that, at the age of fifty-one, such thoughts were terrifying.[138]

At Variance with Jung

In addition to the personal problems prompted by a shadowless Christ, it is clear that the larger topic of Good and Evil was "still occupying [White's] mind" and "had by no means been wholly solved to [his] satisfaction."[139] Further, he thought that the issue "deserve[d] more serious attention" from an empirical standpoint, and therefore challenged analytical psychologists not to discard the *privatio boni* as an issue of "philosophical speculations and semantic inquiry" because, he argued, conceptions of good and evil come from the psyche and, as such, they have a significant influence on the way the psyche functions.[140]

In fact, Jung had made a similar point in his work, *Aion*, where he had insisted that psychology cannot remain indifferent to the conception of evil as *privatio boni*, charging it as responsible for much social and political malaise. With this in mind, White gave a lecture to the Analytical Psychology Club in London on the topic of the *privatio boni*, seen particularly from the point of view of Jung's psychology.[141] He did not hide his now public disagreement with Jung, writing, "I find myself rather painfully at variance with Prof. Jung, and with some more recent trends in metapsychology. There were, after all, so many other subjects where we could find ourselves in complete agreement and harmony. You will presently see that I am still uncertain how far the disagreement is purely verbal, and how far it is real, and deep and far-reaching in its consequences."[142]

Nor did he hide the frustrations that he and Jung had experienced in a discussion that so often seemed to be deadlocked:

> I think I am betraying no confidences when I say to you that Dr. Jung and I have had many personal discussions on this subject, and always,

it seems, without making any progress whatever, even without either of us quite understanding what the other was talking about. Each seemed to the other to be talking in circles and begging the whole question at issue; and I think I may say that a point came when the nerves of both of us were getting somewhat frayed. I, at any rate, was sore perplexed to understand what it was that prevented us from getting to grips at all.[143]

Feeling Their Way Forward

A suggestion from Jung that White should consider the *privatio boni* from a feeling standpoint, and not just an intellectual one, looked set to put their discussion back on track.[144] It was a suggestion that clearly had an impact on White: "Of course I saw my mistake. Our discussion had been all of the head, about the <u>concepts</u> of good and evil. I had in these discussions disregarded the <u>feel</u>, the acute tensions of good and evil, the music, the rhythm and clash of their interplay to which Dr. Jung is so intensely alive. This did not answer the question of how we are to <u>think</u> of good and evil . . . but it put the question into its proper focus."[145] With such an approach, the potential for progress in the discussion finally looked possible.

Influenced by Jung, White now considered that feeling was much more helpful than perception in talking about the experience of evil: "To the perception-function of sensation and intuition, just because they are only perceptions, any judgement or statement about good or evil will be equally pointless and inappropriate."[146] Feeling is more helpful because, said White, "It is a rational function, a judgement function."[147] For Jung, feeling was defined as "a process that takes place between the ego and a given content which imparts to the content a definite value in the sense of acceptance or rejection ('like' or 'dislike')."[148] According to White, this is identical to Aquinas' "*iudicum per inclinationem*," judgment which is made by way of inclination, affinity, love, or hate.[149] In other words, for Aquinas and for Jung, feeling is different from an intellectual judgment because it is just concerned with a subjective like or dislike. But, unlike perception, it is a judgment function.

White saw a further point of contact between Jung's notion of "concretistic feeling" and Aquinas' *apprehensione animae* (apprehension of the psyche), and therefore a point on which White and Jung might potentially find agreement. According to Jung, an evil does not present itself to "concretistic feeling" as an absence of good "but precisely as a positive reality—the strict contrary rather than the privation of good."[150]

White then turned to Aquinas, who had pondered a similar question, namely whether the absence of good causes more distress than the presence of some evil: "If privations presented themselves in the apprehension of the psyche (*in apprehensione animae*) in the same way as they do in reality (*in ipsis rebus*), the question would be of no account."[151] The question would be of no account because says White, "the presence of evil would be the same as the absence of a good." However, White realized that in the apprehension of the psyche, evil is not felt as an absence.

Quoting Aquinas, White wrote: "A privation itself possesses the character of some sort of being (*habet rationem cuiusdam entis*), and hence it is termed a mental reality (*ens rationis*)."[152] Thus, in Aquinas' "*apprehensione animae*" and Jung's "concretistic feeling," evil is felt as a positive reality and not as a privation. Explaining why this is the case, White wrote: "Such apprehension, whether or not feeling-toned, is confined to particulars, and is incapable of objective, analytic reflection: in this case it is the concrete object which is felt to be evil. Only intelligence, the intellectual judgement, can cope either with evil in the abstract, or can ask or answer the objective question whether it is a privation or something else which makes it [something] to be [judged] evil."[153] He continued: "The object [of sense apprehension] is the concrete object which is deprived: <u>malum</u> in the sense of the evil thing, not <u>malum</u> in the sense of the abstract noun which constitutes the evilness of the thing."[154]

White argued, therefore, that Jung and Aquinas did in fact agree—at least on the level of direct feeling: "Evil (or more exactly an object to be judged evil) appears as a positive psychic reality: the positive contrary and not the privation of its opposed good."[155] However, White was critical of an approach to evil that is solely based on feeling because, he argued, it renders the question of what is good and evil totally meaningless. He wrote: "In the concrete the good would be simply what I like, evil what I dislike; I should only have purely subjective criterion."[156] Newly appreciative and yet not uncritical of Jung's position from the point of view of the feeling function, White continued:

> If feeling were all, the world could only be experienced as two equivalent halves: the things a subject likes and the things it dislikes, the agreeable and the disagreeable. But human experience of good and evil has never been limited to this: and it may even be asked if the feeling function itself could ever develop and become differentiated had its subjective estimates of likes and dislikes not been checked, balanced, and often opposed by the search of thought for objective good and evil.[157]

While admitting the importance of feeling, White expressed concern that empirical data which is solely based on feeling "puts us on a very slippery slope."[158] As an Aristotelian, White passionately believed that the psyche could not be exclusively empirical, but that it was "incurably rationalist."[159] He wrote: "Knowledge of good and evil, in the sense of the thoughtful, reflecting search for the 'really good and the really evil,' in the long run as well as in the short run, and beyond the subjective criteria of like and dislike, is, I would submit, the specific burden of humanity without which a man is hardly human at all."[160] White did not mean that every human being had to be "burden[ed]" with "the abstract metaphysical question of good and evil." Rather, what he meant was that it was essential to human flourishing that an individual be able to reflect upon and differentiate between good and evil.

White was really advocating what he said Aristotle called the search for the "ἀγαθὸν κατὰ λόγον," the good discovered by reflective reasoning.[161] According to White, then, the *privatio boni* is not contrary to human experience, provided that such experience is not restricted to perceptions and feelings but also includes reflection. Jung's reluctance on the level of reflection came from a methodology which precluded metaphysics. Just as Jung distanced himself from talk of the nature of God, just as Jung's God could not be formulated rationally, so too, he could not talk about the nature of evil nor formulate it rationally. The empirical/metaphysical framework was, I would argue, the same, and White's model of supplementation was as appropriate in this as it had been in other areas.

The Thinker's Question

Approaching evil from the perspective of feeling offered some hope in unraveling the dispute between the two men, but it did not resolve it. White was still concerned that the thinker's question, "what is to be our *conception* of evil, how are we to *think* of it?"[162] could not be neglected, and he persisted in defending the *privatio boni* as an answer to that question. Thus, he also used this paper to articulate his disagreement with the following arguments made by Jung against the *privatio boni*: that the *privatio boni* affords evil no reality; that if evil is unreal, this implies that it is nothing—and such a view encourages immorality; and that good and evil can only be defined in opposition to one another as two equally positive contraries.

Turning to the first point of disagreement, White resisted Jung's claim that privation makes evil unreal. It is, he said, a claim which would leave a Catholic theologian "genuinely baffled." He argued that, on the contrary, evil as a privation is very real:

> It is just not [my] experience that privations are unreal bagatelles: privation of food or shelter or sight or money or health or other worldly goods [I] find to be very real and serious matters; and at least no less so the privation of less tangible realities like freedom, friends, justice, truth, honesty, law, order, faith, hope, love, the grace of God. . . . It [is] highly paradoxical to assert, and in the name of a matter-of-fact empiricism, that to say that hunger or famine (for instance) consist in an absence of real food from real people is to make it unreal. Such, hardly, will be the experience of the really hungry or the really famished.[163]

White admitted that there may be other evils where the reality of a privation may not seem obvious, as is the case when the absence comes about by something positive. A cataract, for example, causes a privation of sight. Jung had been unconvinced of the reality of evil as a privation in previous discussions, and there is little reason to believe that White's reassertion was about to convince him otherwise.

For Jung, evil, as a *privatio boni*, is unreal, and this implied that it is nothing, a view which encourages immorality. This is the second point at which White found himself at variance with Jung. As I showed earlier, Jung's initial encounter with the *privatio boni* came through the analysis of a patient for whom evil was nothing, "a trifling and fleeting diminution of good" which allowed him to carry on with his morally dubious practices. White challenged Jung's view, shifting his attack from the accusation that Jung saw the *privatio boni* as a negation rather than an absence (and hence, that evil is nothing) to the argument that there are probably many doctrines that could be made a "rationalization" for dubious morals. White included in this those who adhere to Jung's psychology as a defense mechanism, an escape "from their personal problems and mis-behaviour" into "a blissful world of collective archetypes and other people's mythologies."[164]

White's point is clear: neurotic rationalizations do not say any-thing at all about the validity of either the *privatio boni* or Jung's psychology. But White was not totally dismissive of Jung's critique, acknowledging Jung's contention that this minimizing of evil which he attributed to the *privatio boni* was, in his experience, far from exceptional:

> The case which originally drew [Jung's] attention to the subject was no exceptional rarity but only one specimen of a widespread *malaise*; that the *p[rivatio] b[oni]* is psychologically false and harmful, intrinsically a defence mechanism against the acknowledgement of evil, its reality, its terrible devastating power, and so an obstacle to integration. For reality [he tells us] is both good and evil—he calls them two [parts] halves of reality—and if the reality of evil be ignored, total integration will be ruled out.[165]

For Jung, there was little doubt that the *privatio boni* is the root cause of "the agony of our times." Although White could agree with Jung's "*diagnosis*" that, based on the notion of *enantiodromia*, an overemphasis on good at the expense of evil means that the repressed evil will gain more potency precisely because it is repressed, a view which White said "*seems* completely convincing," and is certainly "inescapably challenging," he did not agree with Jung's claim that the etiology of this malaise is the *privatio boni*.[166]

A third point on which White found himself at variance with Jung was Jung's view that good and evil can only be defined in opposition to one another as two equally positive contraries. White's problem with this was threefold. First, he argued that not all opposites are positive contraries and, therefore, that this is a good reason to consider good and evil as different kinds of opposites. White charged analytical psychology with negligence in its attention to the classification of different kinds of opposites. In supporting his case, White considered four different types of opposites:

> ". . . a positive and its contradictory, such as, for example, being and non-being, real and unreal; opposites which say nothing about themselves but only their relation to another animal body, such as, for example left and right; opposites that are not equivalent and can be defined not by the other opposite but by some external factor, such as, for example hot and cold (defined by a thermometer); and privative opposites (that is, where one half of the opposites is positive, and the other is its privation), such as, for example, sight and blindness, light and darkness, good and evil."[167]

White's classification of different kinds of opposites is clearly an attempt to persuade Jung *in Jungian language* of the logic of a privative view of evil.

White's second objection was more specific, namely, that if good and evil are positive contraries, then it follows that, for Jung, God is not only good but also evil, a view which is in contradiction to the traditional Christian view of a wholly good God. This, said White, was "particularly embarrassing to a Catholic theologian, and especially one who has made it his business to try to correlate theological and psychological findings and to commend Jungian psychology to the serious attention of his colleagues." [168]

Finally, in his third point, White argued that everyday *experience* shows that evil is not a positive contrary of good but rather a *privation* of the good:

> I say that this milk is bad, and I say that it is bad because it tastes and smells of gasolene. Doubtless some gasolene has gotten into the milk jug, and I might be inclined to say this badness is certainly no privation: on the contrary it is an addition of very positive gasolene.

But on closer analysis I shall see that the gasolene is not the badness: it may for all I know or care be very good gasolene. It is not the gasolene which I call bad but the milk; and I pronounce the milk to be bad because the gasolene has <u>deprived</u> the milk of the qualities, utilities and delights which I expect of milk.[169]

Although bad milk is different from bad human acts, White's logic in articulating the badness is the same:

Similarly, if we ask ourselves *why* we pronounce concentration camps, slave labor, a rape, a theft, a murder, a tyranny, a blackmail, a drug-peddling to be bad or evil, we shall invariably find, I believe, that it is not on account of any positive realities [qualities of good] we might conceivably find in them, but precisely because of the absence which they entail of freedom, human rights, fairness, integrity, justice and such like things or qualities which we esteem (rightly or wrongly) to be good.[170]

White concluded, therefore, that good and evil are privative opposites wherein good is positive and evil is its privation, a position that kept him at variance with Jung's idea that good and evil are positive contraries.

An Empirical Case for the *Privatio Boni*

Despite their disagreements on these points, disagreements which White thought stemmed from the fact that the *privatio boni* dealt with the thinking function (that is, how we are to think of evil), White considered, in the final section of his paper, whether the *privatio boni* really is only a conscious construction. Jung had suggested that it may be archetypal, a suggestion that White had in their correspondence vehemently denied, arguing that, on the contrary, it was a matter of grammar and logic. However, here we see a slight shift in White's thought as he made a case for the empirical investigation into the archetypal origins and conditioning of the *privatio boni*. The case is built on language, dreams, and personal experience.

Turning first of all to language, White argued that archetypal factors in language structure can be seen in the fact that evils are enunciated by the addition of a prefix or suffix such as 'non,' 'un,' and 'less' to "a positive noun expressive of something or some quality considered to be good."[171]

In his second argument, White turned to dreams. He recounted the story of an agnostic woman who was unaware of the *privatio boni*, but for whom the phrase "struggle of good and evil" in her dreams becomes "an absolutely meaningless phrase."[172] White thought that the only explanation for this was that there is only goodness, to which the woman is drawn. As White saw it, this is "an explicit witness to the unconscious,"—and provides evidence that the *privatio boni* could be archetypal.

White's final argument was drawn from his own experience of Jung's psychology which allowed him to experience evil as a *privatio boni*:

> When first I came, some twelve years ago, into the world of analytical psychology, I had no idea of Dr. Jung's views on good and evil. Certainly I had not myself any strong attachment to the p[rivatio] b[oni]. I was, of course, well acquainted with the idea: it had seemed sound, logical commonsense, but my assent to it had been purely intellectual, or what Newman would call notional. It had never struck me as having any vital personal importance to myself and to my own problems. It was precisely my own experience of analysis—limited as I know it has been—that taught me otherwise. I have it on record that at my first analytical interview, I was told that the whole psyche was all right, and so were its several parts and functions, but my dreams showed (as indeed they did) that these parts and functions were disordered, unbalanced, disintegrated. Whether or not I understood my analyst correctly, the penny dropped: this was exactly what my theological mentors had told me was evil in fallen man—a disorder, a disintegration of the parts and function of the soul. The Fall had brought it about, not that there was anything wrong with them in themselves, but that they were deprived of harmony, order and integration. I at once jumped to the conclusion—evidently too hastily—that the old idea that the good of man was a positive integrity, his evil a privation of that good, was a governing principle in analytical psychology also: the basic pattern of the integration process.[173]

White's experience affirmed his Christian theology: the shadow is essentially good and any evils represent a falling away from the good, i.e. they are a *privatio boni*. As White understood it, a lack of consciousness or a lack of love—which he saw as examples of evil in the shadow—were privations. Thus for White integration of the shadow (which he saw as necessary for wholeness), was about supplying these privations. Theologically speaking this was, as White saw it, a redemption of evil, a transformation of evil into good. He wrote: "As the privation which is hunger can be remedied only by supplying food, the privation for darkness by switching on the light, so (however much harder a task it might be), the evils which I found in the shadow, the ego, the persona, the anima could only be remedied by supplying their needs, their wants, their privations."[174]

Consequently, White was perplexed at Jung's view that evil is a positive contrary, arguing that the presentation of evil as something substantial would make integration impossible: "How could the shadow be integrated if it is not fundamentally good and desirable, if its evil were a positive, irreducible, contrary something and not a privation which could be remedied? . . . If the underlying supposition of analytical psychology was not that integration is a good and desirable thing and disintegration is an evil and undesirable thing, I did not know—I still do not know—what it is all about."[175] White concluded that, based on his own experience, an empirical case can be made for the *privatio boni*, or that it is at least not incompatible with analytical psychology.

Christ and the Shadow: A Personal Crisis

Three days after White had presented this paper, Jung wrote to White in response to a letter that White had sent him. White's letter had detailed the personal crisis precipitated by his concern that if Christ had no shadow side he could not be a valid symbol of the Self. Jung's reply began, "Forget for once dogmatics and listen to what psychology has to say concerning your problem: Christ as a symbol is far from being invalid."[176] Restating arguments that he had made in *Aion* and *Answer to Job*, Jung turned White's attention away from the shadowless Christ of the Christian tradition to psychology. Jung reassured White that, psychologically, Christ as a symbol of the Self is valid, but that he is only one half of the Self, the other half being the devil. According to Jung, it was at the incarnation that God had cast off his dark shadow side in the person of the Anti-Christ and had become wholly good in the person of Christ. As a result, Christ lacked a shadow side, which, as Jung saw it, made the symbol incomplete rather than invalid: "Making the statement that Christ is not a complete symbol of the Self, I cannot make it complete by abolishing it. I must keep it therefore in order to build up the symbol of the perfect contradiction in God by adding this darkness to the *lumen de lumine*."[177]

Jung anticipated that God would eventually invalidate the Christ symbol when the shadow side of God is integrated. But this time of the transformation of the Western God image had not yet come, it is but "an anticipation of a faraway future." White seemed to share the vision, because it was the anticipation of such a future that conflicted with Catholic doctrine and left him pondering his future in the Church. Responding to this inner conflict, Jung wrote: "It does not matter whether the ecclesiastical powers-that-be approve of your vision or not."[178]

Indeed, it was Jung who encouraged White to stay in the Church, arguing that "those who foresee" must stay behind their vision "to help and to teach." Jung encouraged White: "Whatever your ultimate decision will be, you ought to realise beforehand that staying in the church makes sense as it is important to make people understand what the symbol of Christ means, and such understanding is indispensable to any further development."[179] This resonated deeply with White, and he was immensely grateful for the letter with which he found himself in complete agreement.[180] Some months later, however, White was still troubled that his psychology conflicted with the Christian belief that Christ was omniscient and could not therefore have a shadow:

> As a theologian I don't for the life of me see how this can be squared with Catholic doctrine: what I am supposed and am under oath to teach . . . according to Catholic doctrine he could have no shadow: Even with his human mind he knew everything! Truly this is not defined dogma; but it is *quod semper, ubique et ab omnibus*. It's Aquinas—which as a Dominican I'm obliged to teach (though I've managed to skip that bit for several years now!)[181]

On the issue of the omniscience of Christ, White found himself more closely aligned with Jung than with the Catholic Church: "Christ had a shadow AND didn't know it (though I do!) AND projected it."[182] White did not believe that Christ was omniscient but that he had a shadow which he projected onto the Pharisees. Consequently, White felt that he perjured himself by staying in the order, externally professing that which internally he did not believe: "I feel this question of 'Can I stay where I am?' as a *moral* issue; and not just one of suffering, loneliness and discomfort. Is it honest to go on wearing a persona with which my inner thoughts and much of my outer conduct is in such violent contradiction?"[183] Disclosing to Jung the things that particularly bothered him, White wrote: "Can I again take an oath . . . that I believe all the Nicene Creed, the Creed of Pius IV, the anti-modernist oath, . . . and not to teach otherwise than the SOLID doctrine of St. Thomas Aquinas and his school? Ugh."[184]

White had already expressed his divergence with Aquinas on the issue of the omniscience of Christ, though it is unclear whether there were other points of disagreement. Certainly he found repellent the whole notion of the anti-modernist oath which required that he deny that faith is an eruption of the subconscious.[185] Further, it is clear from a broadcast that he gave on "Religious Toleration" that he was deeply disturbed by the 1950 encyclical, *Humani Generis*, in which Pius XII criticized the errors in the *nouvelle théologie*, many of which corresponded to that which was taught at the Dominican House of Studies at Le Saulchoir.[186] In addition, the encyclical condemned evolutionism and existentialism, and argued that the Catholic truth is unchanging. Engaged as he was with Jung's vision for the transformation of the Western God image, White looked like he fell into the category of the condemned. And although he resisted such condemnation, White was deeply concerned about the Church's distrust of theologians, and feared "the idolatry of dogma" he perceived to be developing in the Church.[187] The broadcast was well received, one reviewer in *The Listener* commenting, "Father White is on my unwritten list of broadcasts-not-to-be missed . . ."[188]

Jung replied at great length on April 10, 1954, having now realized "what a fatal challenge [his] psychology is for a theologian . . ."[189]

and thus deeply appreciative of White's "confidence, frankness, courage and honesty." As far as Jung was concerned, White's problem lay in taking doctrine too literally.[190] He further suggested to White that he was confusing the human and the divine Christ, the divine Christ being omniscient and therefore knowing that he had cast off his shadow, Satan; the human Christ being conscious of his shadow, though not completely so, and consequently projecting it.

Jung also attended to White's moral problem—created by the tension of the psychology that he had experienced and the faith that he professed: "You are always and everywhere in a moral conflict unless you are blissfully unconscious."[191] Responding more specifically to what White felt he could neither do nor profess, and particularly the anti-modernist oath, Jung wrote: "You can swear to it in all innocence, as well as I could, if asked."[192] The oath required that the individual swear that faith is not a blind religious feeling which erupts from the subconscious. Jung argued that, in its *ecclesiastical* meaning, the assertion of the oath was correct: "faith" is not such an eruption, but an intellectual assent to revealed doctrines about God—so there was absolutely no reason why White could not swear the oath. In a similar vein, Jung wrote: "Also you can *teach*, if asked, the *solid* doctrine of St. Thomas Aquinas, as I could if I knew it. You can and will and must criticize it, yet with a certain discrimination, as there are people incapable of understanding your argument."[193]

Jung intended to dispel, for White, the notion that he was perjuring himself by staying in the Order, and helped him to see that, even though he found certain things repugnant, there really was no *moral* reason why he could not stay where he was. Offering further psychological advice, and identifying with White as an introverted thinker[194], Jung wrote: "I would advocate an analytical attitude, which is permissible as well as honest, viz., take the Church as your ailing employer and your colleagues as the unconscious inmates of a hospital."[195] Jung's advice was clearly instrumental in White's change of attitude, and it is no small irony that it was Jung who had encouraged him to stay with the Dominicans. White wrote: ". . . the practical upshot is that here I stay; and I hope that a new attitude and perspective is forming . . ."[196]

White's decision to stay was (unconsciously!) affirmed in June 1954 when he received the degree of *Sacrae Theologiae Magister*, the highest honor that the Dominican Order confers on brethren whom it deems outstanding in teaching, research, and writing. Issued from Rome on May 28, it was conferred upon White in Oxford in June,[197] and it was expected that White would soon replace Daniel Callus, O. P., as Regent of Studies at Blackfriars Oxford.[198]

The Scandal of Regent

However, in what is generally regarded as a scandal in the English Province of the Order of Preachers, White was not made Regent of Studies in July 1954. Although it seems possible that some in the order may have been aware of White's doubts concerning his vocation—and, thus, deemed him an unwise choice for Regent—this is not the consensus of those present in 1954. As Columba Ryan, O. P., remarked, "In 1954 he was made an STM, and should really have been appointed Regent of Studies; but the Provincial (Hilary Carpenter, just re-elected for a third term, if I remember rightly) didn't really approve of Victor; and so, at the same time, he arranged for Ambrose Farrell to be made an STM and appointed Regent (generally regarded as a scandalous maneuver)."[199]

It is clear from a letter White wrote to Jung that White himself expected to be appointed Regent of Studies.[200] It is further apparent from the *Archives of the English Province of the Order of Preachers* that the Master of the Order, Emmanuel Suarez, O. P., expected White to be made Regent, but Suarez was killed in a biking accident in 1954. According to archivist Bede Bailey, O. P., the Provincial at the time was Hilary Carpenter, O. P., and he seized upon the opportunity to change the plans for the Province. Columba Ryan O. P. put it like this:

> The old regime represented by Hilary Carpenter simply didn't trust these young men. They were innovative from their point of view and what we had was a Regent here where we did our philosophy—it was a four-year course—and a lector primarus in Hawkesyard and these two posts were held by the sort of solid constabulary of the old regime.

> . . . And Victor ought to have been made Regent but they did not trust
> him. . . . [Victor was] vaguely recognized by the older men but they
> wouldn't trust him in any position of authority.[201]

If White had been made Regent, he would have had great influence over the manner in which Aquinas was taught at Blackfriars. According to Columba Ryan, O. P., White was "rather in disgrace, only in the sense that the older people in the province . . . were dyed-in-the-wool scholastics, and didn't allow any kind of departure."[202] A rear guard of neo-scholastics thought that White was untrustworthy in this respect because he advocated engagement with the modern world, and particularly with Jung—who looked liked a modernist and a Kantian. And so it was not White but Ambrose Farrell who was made Regent of Studies.

Unimpressed by this choice, Ryan commented, "Now Victor ought to have been made Regent. Ambrose Farrell was a dry-in-the-dust, not very intelligent canonist. Nice enough man, but totally ungifted."[203] Indeed, it was generally thought that Farrell was unworthy of the STM and that it was only conferred upon him so that Carpenter could appoint him Regent. Although White was by far the most appropriate man for the position, Farrell was a safe choice, according to Bede Bailey, O. P., who described him as "sufficiently well trained as a canonist never to come to a conclusion."[204] White did not withhold his own feelings on the matter, divulging to Jung that he thought Farrell was "a complete incompetent."[205] In fact, Farrell proved to be so, and Daniel Callus, O. P., was brought out of retirement to relieve him of the office in 1958.

Disappointment at his non-appointment as Regent was to be compounded a month later when the decision was made by the Order to send White to the Dominican House of Studies in Oakland, California, for five months. White's sense of rejection by the English Province is well voiced in a letter to Jung: "I am no longer 'indispensable' at Oxford: indeed, it seems definitely 'not wanted.' I am still left guessing the reasons: there could be several. But in many ways it is of course a huge relief."[206] Indeed, White was so "indispensable" that he would never again be entrusted with the task of teaching theology at Blackfriars Oxford. White was deeply embarrassed, confessing to Jung, "All my fuss about the oath, the degree, and my beautiful self sacrifice *pro bono publico* has been a sort of sacrifice of Isaac—or maybe something a great deal more comic."[207]

White left Oxford on October 16, 1954, and headed for St. Albert's, the Dominican House of Studies in Oakland, California.[208] Though bereft of the Dominican community at Blackfriars Oxford, White was not alone. In the midst of White's private papers, in the *Archives of the English Province of the Order of Preachers*, are two quotations from Old Testament prophets written by White in calligraphy on a scrap of card. The first, replete with deliberate ambiguity, reads: "Et ego non sum turbatus, te pastorem sequens ~ Jeremias XVII:16." (I am not disturbed, following you my pastor). Affirming that "the pastor" could be Jung as well as Yahweh, the second quotation reads: "And He Himself shall carry them that are with Jung . . . ~ Isaias XL:II."

Still Frustrated by Evil

The ongoing dispute with Jung on evil continued to gnaw at White, even in California. Ever hopeful that he might convince Jung of the privative view, White sent him the following passage from Aquinas: "Evil is the privation of good; and privation is in reality nothing else than the lack of the contrary habit . . . And even a privation, as apprehended, has the aspect of a being, wherefore it is called a being of reason. And in this way evil, being a privation, is regarded as a contrary."[209] White had, in fact, already quoted this passage in a paper that he had delivered to the Analytical Psychology Club of London in November 1953, where he used it to support the view that although evil is a privation, it is apprehended in the psyche as a positive contrary, thus offering a point of contact with Jung's idea that evil is experienced as a positive psychic reality.

It is, however, unclear whether Jung had even seen this paper because he was totally baffled by the Aquinas quote, declaring that he found it "a marvellous puzzle." Jung wrote: "I have brooded over it for many hours and I cannot make head or tail of it unless it is an attempt to give Evil some substantiality in recognition of the fact that we experience it as just as 'substantial' as Good."[210] Jung could agree that evil is experienced as a positive contrary but his bafflement lay in the insistence that this experience is articulated in the language of privation—he argued that this was no more than a "petitio principii." Equally bewildered by Jung's inability to distinguish thinking and feeling, White made a final attempt to restate his position in a letter written mid-Atlantic and dated March 17, 1955: "Although 'malum' is thought to be a 'privatio' (i.e., it is at least a psychological fact that it frequently is!), it is sensed to be a positive contrary—again a psychological fact."[211]

This was in fact the final statement on the question of the *privatio boni* in their correspondence, but it was far from the final statement on its source, the *Summum Bonum*. Indeed White was becoming increasingly troubled about Jung's portrayal of God in *Answer to Job*. The book that he had initially found so exciting was now a major source of concern and he was "frankly relieved" that *Answer to Job* had not yet been published in English.[212] As the publication date drew nearer, Jung anticipated the problems that misunderstandings of the book could potentially cause for White: "I know you will have some difficulties when my *Answer to Job* becomes public. I am sorry." [213]

White's private notes attest that he was fully aware of the difficulties. He knew that *Answer to Job* would be dismissed by theologians as "progressive revelation," and that Jung's portrayal of "God's education by man" would be deemed "preposterous, upside down."[214] White had spent the last ten years attempting to convince theologians of the notion that when Jung used the term God he was not talking about God Godself, but about the archetype of the Self as God image. But Jung's *Answer to Job* left White less than confident that this was in fact the case—as a review that he wrote for *Blackfriars* in March of 1955 indicates. Warning Jung of the as yet unpublished review, White wrote prophetically, "I am very afraid that you will think it unforgivable."[215]

As White now saw it, *Answer to Job* represented a personal "outburst" by Jung, and he did not see what could be gained from its publication. In fact, White asserted that when he had first received the manuscript, he was under the impression that Jung was "emphatic[ally]" against its publication,[216] and now feared that his own efforts "to make analytical psychology acceptable to and respected by the Catholics and Christians who need it so badly"[217] would be hampered. White wrote: "A public parade of the splenetic shadow makes me very sad indeed: it is so unlike the real you. I am sorry—but that is how I feel about it, and very deeply. However perverse my feeling, I am sure you will understand it springs from my affection for you yourself, and my appreciation of the tremendous importance for humanity of the work you have been given to do."[218] Though unrelenting in his critique, White concluded contritely, "I am penitent that I have laid my criticisms on so thick."[219]

As Jung saw it, White had every need to be penitent: "Your criticism of my motive concerning *Job* is certainly unjust and you know it," attributing it to an expression of White's "mental torment."[220] Far from being a parade of the splenetic shadow, Jung defended *Answer to Job* as "a straightforward application of [his] psychological principles to certain central problems of our religion."[221] Viewing it thus, he was clearly riled by White's attempt to reduce his work to "a case of mere spleen," and, with a suggestion that White re-read his work, he returned the charge, questioning, "Could we not apply the same qualification to your own bad temper?"[222] Jung thought that White's "critical outburst" originated in the fact that he lacked the courage to accept the consequences of analytical psychology because, as one "fed by an institution for services rendered," he was afraid of risking his "social existence" in the Order of Preachers.[223]

The Unforgivable Review

Whatever its origin, White's "critical outburst" was public by the end of March 1955. Jung's *Answer to Job*, the book that White had, in 1952, described as the most exciting and moving book he had read in years, was now, some three years later, "destructive and childish,"[224] a book of "infantile quality."[225] Jung's grievance against God had initially stirred up all sorts of dark places in White's psyche, but, by 1955, he was of the opinion that "[Jung's] grievance is hardly adult."[226] So very far removed from his initial enthusiasm for *Answer to Job*, White questioned: "Why does [Jung] identify himself with such childish standpoints . . . ?"[227]

In support of his critique, White noted that psychiatric journals received *Answer to Job* with "discreet silence," and that Jung's friends feared for his repute. In what is arguably the most damning passage of the review White wrote: "Is [Jung], after the manner of his own 'Yahweh,' duped by some satanic trickster into purposely torturing his friends and devotees? Or is he, more rationally, purposely putting them to the test to discover how much they will stand rather than admit the fallibility of their master—or how many, Job like, will venture to observe that the emperor has appeared in public without his clothes?"[228] The review continued in like tone, charging Jung with taking the principle of private interpretation of Scripture to an extreme,[229] and of deliberately reading the Bible "through a pair of highly distorting spectacles,"[230] the spectacles of his own psyche. Further, according to White, Jung was guilty of "naive misunderstandings and misrepresentations of elementary doctrine,"[231] for example that God is perfect, triune, and self-sufficient. The charges were unfair, as White himself admitted, and could be refuted if one would accept Jung's methodology, in other words, *if* one accepted that when Jung talks about God "he is talking about endopsychic images considered as psychological phenomena and not as signs for what they merely represent."[232]

It is clear that White *did* accept Jung's methodology, and had often made the important distinction between God and God image in defense of Jung. In view of this, White's accusation that Jung had a naive understanding of doctrine is surprising, for it looks like he was criticizing Jung as if Jung really did think that God (rather than God image) is a quaternity and not a Trinity, evil as well as good. But White then dismissed these criticisms as unfair, thereby revealing that this simply a rhetorical device to portray the standard theological critique of Jung—that *Answer to Job* is an attack on God Godself. Dismissing this attack, White affirmed that, although Jung was critical of Christian doctrines about God, his critique that Christian doctrines about God are deficient stems from a psychological perspective. In other words, empirically speaking, Christian doctrines about God are incomplete. In upholding the distinction between empiricism and metaphysics, White affirmed his conviction that Jung was primarily concerned with images of God. He was, however, highly critical that these images were not Job's but Jung's.

Predictably, Jung was offended by the directness of White's criticism and, particularly, that it had been voiced so publicly.[233] Responding to the review, he wrote: "Since I am the cause of much discomfort to you, I am not sure whether you care to see me or not. Please put conventionality aside and do not feel under any obligation. I can understand your true situation and I would prefer not to add to its spikes and thorns. Please decide according to your judgement. Needless to say, you can count upon my friendship."[234]

Following a meeting of the General Chapter in Rome in April, to which White had been sent as a representative of the English Province, he was scheduled to lecture at the Institute in Zurich in May.[235] Despite White's review, Jung had extended an invitation to him to stay at his official residence in Küsnacht. Commentators regard this as "something of a rebuff," for White had always been invited to stay with Jung at the Tower in Böllingen.[236] Declining the invitation, White explained, from a hotel in Zurich, that he did not want a conventional visit.[237] White further explained himself four days later, indicating to Jung that he did not want to meet on the basis of a simple "misunderstanding." For, although White could appreciate *Job* as "a stimulant to consciousness," there could be no misunderstanding that he was "quite definitely in painful agreement" with both the theological and scientific criticisms of Jung.[238] And so, he did not meet with Jung, but he did express his profound apologies for disregarding Jung's feelings in his "Review of Job," an apology which Jung marked on the letter.

In addition, White attached to the letter a handwritten manuscript entitled "Problems Arising from *Answer to Job*." White's primary concern with *Job* had been that it was "a parade of the splenetic shadow," and Jung's shadow at that. Reiterating this concern with a little more tact, White began: "If [*Job*] is not merely a subjective personal autobiographical crisis, what does it have to say to the public?"[239] Although in his private notes White described *Job* as "an 'amateur excursion' in Biblical criticism and theology,"[240] it is clear that in this manuscript he viewed *Answer to Job* as practical psychology rather than theology or exegesis, and thus proceeded to explore the content of this psychology and its implications. For Jung, wrote White, "God (=not me) is unconscious, capricious, evil as well as good, an 'unchastened bastard.'"[241] God is unconscious of his evil and thus, "my only hope is to know this as God still does not."[242] For Jung it is this "gnosis" or knowledge that brings about the redemption of the individual—and of God.

White identified three psychological consequences of this view as espoused by Jung in *Job*: responsibility for evil lies with God; to say that God is responsible for evil implies that the shadow side has been projected onto the God within and this lets human beings off the hook; and if the God within is evil as well as good, then the "emotional ridiculing of a 'good' God" is apposite. As White saw it, these three points reveal that, in *Answer to Job*, "the collective unconscious has become an escape mechanism," and he raised several points in response.

First, he argued that the "myth/symbol/doctrine of the Dark/Evil God" has harmful societal consequences because human beings are no longer responsible for evil.[243] Second, White argued that the "myth/symbol/doctrine" of an Evil God is psychologically impossible, because, he wrote, "We can *only* know it as a projection, precisely *not* what we call God."[244] Finally, White suggested that *Job* creates "special difficulties" for the Christian, such as the confrontation of myth and belief. Stated more explicitly, the Christian may *experience* evil in the self but doctrinally it would be immensely difficult to accept—and worship—a God in whom there is evil. As White would later articulate this tension, Jung's psychology is "clinically correct" even if "theologically misinformed."[245] In what is clearly a deeply personal conclusion, White wrote: "It must be evident that any would-be-Christian, especially if he is unavoidable in the position of guiding others, may be faced with the 'agonising reappraisal' of his position vis-à-vis analytical psychology— whatever may be his personal feeling with regard to C. G. Jung."[246]

Still grappling with his own "agonising reappraisal," White wrote a second letter to Jung from his hotel in Zurich, this time to express his regret that his review of Jung's *Job* had been published "without any regard for your feelings or my own feelings for you."[247] Two days later he wrote to Jung again with the disappointing news he had received that the Order was sending him back to California.[248] He apologized for troubling Jung with his "problems" and for the "ruthless tactlessness" of his *Job* review. Comparing himself to Job's friends, "however stupid" they were, he reassured

Jung of his friendship, "wrongheaded and heartless though it sometimes is."[249] White was confident, however, of the Biblical rather than the Jungian ending of Job and of the *Summum Bonum* rather than the additional Infinum Malum. He had come to the realization, therefore, that this was "au revoir for the present."[250] He concluded: "Perhaps I may tell you how deeply I feel with you in this wrestle with the Divine Mysteries and with our Brother Death. I must leave the outcome trustingly to them and to your own fearless honesty and humility. . . . For myself, it seems that our ways must, at least to some extent, part. I shall never forget, and please God I shall never lose, what I owe to your friendship."[251] Having made his peace, and yet still frustrated by what he saw as Jung's inability to take criticism, White added a postscript telling of the "horrible impression" that came upon him while he was in Zurich— "that my dear C. G. has around him only sycophants & flatterers . . . I *hope* I am wrong . . ."[252]

With the publication of *Answer to Job*, the problem of evil had been forced onto God, and it was increasingly unclear whether the God in question was God or God image. If Jung meant God Godself, then his critique of the *empirical* inadequacy of a perfect and immutable God was problematic for a Catholic Dominican who had embraced Jungian psychology. Even if Jung meant God image, the myth of an evil God was hardly something that White could accept. Thus, White found himself torn between his friend and his faith, and he chose the latter.

The Parting of the Ways

Although White continued to embrace the challenge of Jung's psychology, he was increasingly aware of the need to defend the traditional doctrines of Christianity in response to Jung. In addition, White's biography cannot be neglected. After all, White's crisis of vocation, the perceived rejection by his Province and their mistrust of his theology, and his ultimate break with Jung, all testify to the tremendous impact that Jung had had on his personal life.

As I have shown, White had responded to the challenge of Jung in his book *God and the Unconscious*, assimilating the truths he found valuable in articulating the Catholic faith. It was a book that confirmed his growing reputation as the expositor of an integration of Jung and Catholic theology in Europe. Furthermore, White's determination to resolve the dispute with Jung concerning evil was indicative not only of his response to the challenge of Jung but also of his desire to defend traditional Catholic theology. Although there was still major disagreement on the question of evil, it seemed that some progress had been made in this time period which, I would argue, was facilitated by White's return to the model of supplementation that he had proposed earlier in their relationship, a model which advocated that Jung's empirical findings could be complemented and supplemented with metaphysics.

Jung insisted that evil was experienced as a positive psychic reality, the logically equivalent opposite of good. By 1953, White had more clearly articulated Aquinas' belief (and his own) that on the level of apprehension, evil does indeed appear as a positive psychic reality. Both men could agree that on the level of perception and feeling evil is experienced as a positive contrary. Although White believed that Jung's theory of opposites was neglectful of the different kinds of opposites, and that the experience of evil as a *privatio boni* was not contrary to empirical psychology, he could agree with Jung on some level that evil is often experienced as a positive contrary rather than as a privation. Beyond this the two men diverged, and it was often unclear exactly what they diverged about. Jung was concerned with the question of evil as a real existing force, and he perceived this to be an empirical question. White was concerned with what people mean when they use the word evil—a grammatical elucidation. At times, however, each clearly thought that the other was dealing with a metaphysical question (and to an extent, each was).

Part of the problem lay with Jung's adherence to Kant's distinction between *phenomena* and *noumena* which, from Jung's perspective, precluded any discussion beyond the intra-psychic experience of evil. However, it seems that this preclusion did not prevent Jung from criticizing the definition of the *privatio boni* (which he saw as a metaphysical concept) as an empiricist. Similarly, although Jung insisted that his interest was strictly empirical and his concern is with images of God, his assault on God in his *Answer to Job* seems to go beyond images to the God of Biblical revelation. On the one hand, this lack of clarity regarding the boundaries of empiricism and metaphysics—from which White himself was not immune—enhanced the enduring difficulties in resolving the question of evil. On the other hand, it seems that Jung truly believed that his psychological method permitted the critique of what he perceived to be the inadequacies of certain (metaphysical) doctrines.

Murray Stein has argued convincingly that Jung was in a "privileged position" to evaluate "the relative adequacy or incompleteness of statements about God" because all words (including *God* and *privatio boni*) have a subjective dimension and say something about the psyche.[253] From this perspective, therefore, Jung *could* maintain the boundaries between metaphysics and empiricism and at the same time legitimately criticize doctrines of God and evil as inadequate from an *empirical* viewpoint (as "psychologically inadequate"[254]). White, I think, understood this and was unafraid to challenge the "empirical" perspective, particularly, as I have shown, on the question of evil as a *privatio boni* which, in contrast to Jung, White believed was empirically verifiable.

However, with the issue of evil focused onto God, the difficulties in sustaining their relationship were compounded, and the challenge of seeing God as evil as well as good was more than White could embrace. His public reaction to Job—and his decision to part ways—thus brought to an end the remarkable correspondence between Victor White and C. G. Jung.

SIX
1955–1960

Reassessing the Task

Although White and Jung parted ways in May 1955, White's
piece in honor of Jung on his eightieth birthday in July 1955,
which he wrote from California, was a clear indication that
his split with Jung had been far less acrimonious than the
Freud–Jung split of 1912.[1] Freud's impact on Jung continued long
after their split, as did the impact of Jung and analytical psychology
on White's life and theology—until his death in 1960.[2] The impact,
however, was markedly different, because the latent obstacles which
had loomed over their discussion since its beginning had now been
brought to the fore, and White was forced to reassess his task
accordingly. He wrote: "It is true that some of Jung's later speculations have vastly hindered rather than helped . . . notably, on the
nature of evil, on the Trinity and Quaternity, on the *Answer to
Job*."[3]

These "speculations," which White had earlier referred to as
"metapsychological opinions"[4] troubled him greatly, not least
because they were embraced by Jung's followers as "a new dogmatic
orthodoxy."[5] One such example is Jung's addition of the "missing
fourth"—the feminine and the shadow—to the Christian doctrine
of the Trinity in order to make it a symbol of wholeness.[6] As White
saw it, Jung had deviated "from the narrow path of strictly psychological exposition."[7] Further, he attributed this tendency to
"metapsychologize" to the "profound influence" of Kant's *Kritik*
on Jung's methodology.[8] In addition, White was critical of the fact
that Kant had become *the* standard in Jung's interpretation of

empirical data, and was suspicious that Jung's Kant-based methodology precluded the consideration of other positions as psychological fact (such as, for example, the doctrine of the *privatio boni*).[9] Ultimately, Jung's over-dependence on Kant was a significant factor in hindering the discussion with White. As White put it, ". . . Kant's word is law, and his *erkenntnistheoretische Schwelle* a taboo on no account to be criticized."[10]

A second factor in hindering discussion, and one which stems from this over-dependence, is what White saw as "the troublesome Jungian habit of calling the God-imago or the God-complex 'God'—and vice versa."[11] Jung had consistently asserted that he was concerned with "a psychic experience which is understood to be and formulated as God," and not with the nature or reality of God Godself.[12] Indeed it was Kant's barrier between the phenomenal and noumenal worlds that had provided Jung with a methodology to distinguish between the God image and God. White believed, however, that Jung was increasingly guilty of "consistently confus[ing]" the distinction between God image and God,[13] and further accused Jungians of a "bland indifference" in their usage of *God image* and *God*.[14]

As White saw it, this confusion and indifference could be attributed to Jung's "empirical" method. For Jung, God could *only* be known as a phenomenon of the psyche, and not through any rational knowledge; indeed his methodology rendered it "downright impossible."[15] Articulating the implications of this, White wrote: "While the empirical psychologist can check his patient's father-imago or mother-complex against the 'real' (i.e., complex-free and empirically knowable and verifiable) father or mother, there is no 'real God' in any way knowable or verifiable to which the God-imago or God-complex can be compared. To the psychologist as such, there is no God independent of the imago or complex."[16]

Thus, although White was critical of the blurring of *God* and *God image*, he *did* understand a possible *reason* for the frequent synonymity of these terms in analytical psychology. From the perspective of the theologian, however, the blurring was a significant factor in hindering further "bridge building"[17] between theologians and psychologists. For this reason, White appealed to psychologists for a more precise use of language[18] and a "more rigorous and comprehensive application" of empirical methods.[19]

The Needs of Human Souls

Despite these hindering factors and a stance more critical toward Jung in the years following the split, White did not see his task as "attacking" Jung's psychology, nor as "defending" Catholicism against Jung.[20] Rather, he reasserted his task as concerned with the needs of the human soul: "The task should . . . [be] of direct encounter with the raw material and crying need of perplexed human souls. Only so can theology appear in its true role as primarily concerned with the *Verbum salutis* and the *salus animarum*."[21] In this encounter with the raw material—the primordial images or archetypes of which Jung spoke—White agreed with Jung that, as he stated in 1945, the task of collaboration is "to show 'how the dogma is the hitherto most perfect answer to, and formulation of, the most relevant items in the objective psyche' which psychology reveals, 'and that God has worked all these things in man's soul.'"[22] In other words, that the dogma, which Catholics believe has been revealed by God, also expresses the living archetypes of the collective unconscious.

In 1945, White had emphasized the importance of Jung's empirical research in disclosing the needs of the psyche, and suggested that Catholics might benefit from this. It was, after all, his experience of Jung's psychology that had revitalized his own theology in the early 1940s. Even after the split with Jung, White continued to reassert the importance of psychology in disclosing the relevance of dogma to the needs of the human soul.[23] He spoke in Madrid to the seventh Catholic International Congress of Psychotherapists and Clinical Psychology in September 1957, for example: "For my part, I cannot doubt that depth-psychology, and especially the work of C. G. Jung, can immensely aid and enrich a theologian's work by offering him a means whereby he may better understand, not indeed the intrinsic truth, authority or content of dogma, but its relevance to the needs of the human Soul."[24]

For White, Jung's greatest contribution was his acknowledgment of the fact that "religious factors . . . underlie the structure of the psyche," and that these factors play a pivotal role in mental health.[25] White believed that psychology could disclose the salutary or unsalutary effects of dogma on the human psyche:

> We cannot afford to condemn it on the grounds that it can tell us nothing of religious truth, but can concern itself only with how religion works, or fails to work. For religious truth is, after all, a truth that is supposed to work, and indeed to bring healing to the nations. If psychology can tell us anything of how it does so, or fails to do so, it has something to offer the modern religious preacher and teacher, and indeed the modern churchgoer generally, which he can ill afford to neglect.[26]

White was very clear, however, that psychology could add nothing to revelation.[27] In fact, White had—since the beginning of his encounter with Jung—asserted that it was *revelation* that could "supplement and complement" the deficiencies of Jung's psychology. It was in these "post-Jung" years that White's approach to Jung was stated even more explicitly—Catholicism *answers* the very needs which empirical psychology has disclosed.[28]

Catholicism: The Healing Power of Revelation

A good example of this more explicit approach can be found in an article that White wrote in 1956 on the subject of guilt and its resolution, as explored from theological and psychological perspectives.[29] Central to the discussion is White's agreement with Jung that the "epidemic guilt sense of our times" is due to the fact that human beings have lost contact with the healing resources of the collective unconscious, or—as White put it—"the 'living symbols' of the God in Christ reconciling the world to himself (2 Cor. 5:19)."[30] Indeed, White acknowledged the role of analytical psychology in reawakening the need for healing, particularly in its re-articulation of the Old Testament phenomenon of transference, which he also saw expressed in the sacraments of Confession and the Eucharist. On Confession, for example, White remarked: "The mature Christian, just because he fully acknowledges his guiltiness, is preserved from narcissism and the fascination of ego-idealization. He is also preserved from the liability to project his 'shadow' side, and he is made to understand that avoidance of this is also a condition of divine forgiveness."[31]

The influence of Jung is unmistakable and it reaffirmed White's insistence that analytical psychology is central to the revitalization of theology. Ultimately, however, White argued that it is not exclusively the revelation of God *in* human beings which brings about healing, but rather the revelation of God *to* human beings from outside of the psyche. This idea is further set forth in an article that White wrote on the sacrifice of the Mass in June of 1957.[32] Jung had argued extensively that healing involves the sacrificial death of the ego to the unconscious which is then transformed into the individuated self.[33] Confirming his belief that dogma is the most appropriate formulation of the contents of the collective unconscious, he argued that this process—individuation—was symbolically expressed in the Mass: "The mystery of the Eucharist transforms the soul of the empirical man, who is only part of himself, into his totality, symbolically expressed by Christ. In this sense, therefore, we can speak of the rite of the individuation process."[34] Stated more explicitly, the sacrificial death of Christ to God the Father and his resurrection in the Spirit is, according to Jung, a *symbol* of the sacrificial death of the ego to the unconscious—which is then transformed into the individuated self.[35]

White appreciated that analytical psychology illuminated the psychological relevance of the symbol of sacrifice in the quest for wholeness, particularly in highlighting the necessity and yet the impossibility of human sacrifice.[36] Ultimately, however, he argued that only the realization of the symbol in the *actual sacrifice of Christ* in the Mass could bring true healing.[37] Although Jung found the symbols of the Mass to be transforming, he certainly did not agree with White's view that Catholicism "answered" the needs of the psyche. On the contrary, Jung thought that White's insistence on revelation from a God *"outside* man"[38] *prevented* true healing ("atonement") because it led to a "turning away from our psychic origins,"[39] and dissuaded human beings from undergoing the *individual* sacrifice necessary for wholeness.

Under the Suspicion of Rome

By the 1950s, Rome, it seems, was more cognizant of the fact that psychological processes had an important function in the human soul and, therefore, that theology should not be opposed to psychology. Addressing the fifth International Catholic Congress of Psychotherapy and Clinical Psychology in Rome in 1953, for example, Pope Pius XII remarked, "It has been supposed that we should accentuate the opposition between metaphysics and psychology. This is quite wrong. The psychological [realm] itself belongs to the realm of the ontological and the metaphysical."[40] Lying in the tradition of Aquinas, for whom the soul is that which animates the body, White had little dispute with Pius, for his remark implied that the "psychic apparatus" could not lie outside of this source of vital activity.[41] In addition, White thought that Pope Pius' statement offered a point of contact with Jung—for whom the separation of soul and psyche was the root cause of the sickness of modern man.[42] But Pius certainly did not share White's enthusiasm for Jung. Aware of the suspicions surrounding his work, White joked with Jung, in August 1956, "Maybe I'll even get on the Index!"[43]

On December 10, 1957, White came one step closer to this when a letter requesting information on his teaching and publications was sent from Rome to Michael Browne, O. P., Master General of the Dominican Order.[44] Upon his return from California, White had been assigned to a non-teaching post at Blackfriars Cambridge in 1956,[45] so his publications were of more concern. Within months, White received a letter from Browne ordering the suspension of *God and the Unconscious*.[46] White had earlier expressed his outrage at the Church's silencing of theologians,[47] and had become increasingly concerned that theology and the Church's magisterium should be more clearly distinguished.[48] He was particularly troubled by Browne's letter because the work in question had in fact received an *imprimatur* in May 1952 from the Archdiocese of Birmingham. A letter from the French translator Augustin Léonard, O. P., may cast some light on the situation:

> J'ai moi-même traduit *God and the Unconsious*. Mais cette traduction française qui, j'espère, est très fidèle à votre texte vient de se voir

refuser l'imprimatur de l'évêché de Tournai en Belgique qui est
l'évêché de mon éditeur. . . . L'imprimatur a été refusé à Tournai, non
pas à cause de votre livre que le censeur déclare 'd'une parfaite ortho-
doxie,' ce dont j'étais bien persuadé, mais parce que ce censeur a été
réprimandé par Rome à cause de la traducion d'un ouvrage de Dodd
et est devenu à cause de cela d'une timidité extrème. Il objecte par
exemple à la préface de Jung.[49]

Léonard's words indicate that although White's book had an
imprimatur, the censorial proclivities and reprimands of Rome had
precipitated a certain timidity, and a book with a preface by Jung was
enough to rouse some suspicion. White, however, had no intention of
suspending the book—as he explained in a memo to the Provincial of
the English Dominican Province, Hilary Carpenter, O. P. As White
saw it, he had signed a contract with Collins USA that was "morally
binding" and, thus, Rome's suspension was meaningless.[50] Carpenter
was unimpressed with White's attitude, but he was soon to be succeeded as Provincial by Henry St. John, O. P. Affirming White's
indignation, St. John promised to back White "energetically."[51]

Hac Lacrymarum Valle

Although dismayed by the ecclesiastical opposition to Jung's psychology, the strained ecclesial relations which ensued, and the split
with Jung in 1955, White's enthusiasm for Jung remained strong. In
June 1958 he wrote to Jung, expressing deep regret over their split:
"I have no doubt that my feeling of estrangement (as distinct from
mere disagreement) was my own fault. . . . I often think of you dear
C. G., with great affection and gratitude; and I very much hope that
all goes as well as possible with you *in hac lacrymarum valle*."[52] The
two met in Zurich in July of that year,[53] but Jung's response to
White's doubts regarding their split was delayed until October 1959.
Jung wrote: "Concerning your doubts about your general attitude
I must mention in self defence that you expressed yourself publicly
in such a negative way about my work that I really did not know
what your real attitude would be."[54]

White's attitude was clear: despite their disagreement, Jung's
psychology was immensely valuable to the theologian in better

understanding dogma and its function in the human soul. "Although the Church has rightly insisted that dogmas were all a *verbum salutis*—message of health and wholeness—and heresies a destructive source of disintegration, it has not been her business to explain how and why it should be so."[55] It had, however, been the business of C. G. Jung who, much to his "astonish[ment]," found himself "concerned with such things."[56] Indeed it was he whom White credited with having "raised and expounded the question of the psychological function and relevance of dogma."[57] In his work, "A Psychological Approach to the Dogma of the Trinity," for example, Jung wrote: "The central symbol of Christianity must have, above all else, a psychological meaning, for without this it could not have acquired any universal meaning whatever."[58]

Astonished by Jung's insight, White wrote: "A theologian is amazed to find that he stumbles on many of the most recondite problems of the theology of dogma without having obtained it from theologians, but from his direct experience of psychic happenings."[59] But White should not have been surprised. Jung's insight was completely consistent with White's deep commitment to Aquinas' "magnificent conception" that *all* truth—whether it be found in science or philosophy or revelation—came from God, a commitment that he had espoused long before his encounter with Jung.[60] In addition, White had, in his 1958 "Holy Teaching," articulated a further point of contact between Jung and Aquinas in Aquinas' notion that the purpose of *sacra doctrina* is *salus humana*.[61] White wrote: "It should not, then, be a matter of surprise to the theologian, still less of pained resentment, that dogmas are found to be highly relevant to psychological health and sickness, and their manner of functioning in the psyche a matter of profound concern to the practical psychotherapist."[62]

But it is the articulation of Catholicism as *the answer* to the needs which empirical psychology has disclosed which became the prominent theme of White's post-split writings.[63] Most significant in this respect are the Edward Cadbury Lectures of 1959 which, at the invitation of Professor G. W. H. Lampe, White gave at the University of Birmingham.[64] These lectures were published in 1960, the year of White's death, as *Soul and Psyche: An Enquiry into the Relationship of Psychiatry and Religion* (bibliog. 1.4,

1960), a work which shows White "equally at home with Aquinas and with Jung,"[65] and for which his "unrivalled . . . familiarity with Jung's thought" and "enviable . . . theological scholarship"[66] were praised.

The Missing Fourth: The Feminine

Perhaps the most striking example of White's theme—that the healing power of revelation is to be found in Catholicism—can be found in *Soul and Psyche* in response to Jung's claim that the Christian doctrine of the Trinity is an inadequate symbol because it lacks the "missing fourth", the shadow and the anima.[67] Jung thought that the Trinity as a God image had lost its symbolic meaning because it had been uprooted from the inner archetypal experience of which it was a conscious expression.[68] Further, he thought that if the anima and the shadow were not integrated, they could become unconscious and potentially destructive. In other words, if the Western God image is to be a symbol of wholeness, then it needs to be transformed, and Jung hoped that Victor White would be instrumental in this transformation. White, however, could not fulfill these hopes because, although he himself had been transformed by Jung's psychology, he thought that Catholicism offered *the answer* (that is, healing) *without* such a transformation of God.

But White was taken by Jung's contention that the Christian doctrine of the Trinity does not include a concrete representation of the feminine. Certainly he could agree with Jung that, despite the emergence of Sophia, the God of the Old Testament is "unmistakably masculine."[69] Indeed, White thought that the same applied to the God of the New Testament, who "is still a Father and not a Mother, a Father with an only begotten Son—and not a daughter." [70] So, in *psychological* terms White argued that God is indeed presented as an "anima ridden male," one who is unconscious of the repressed feminine side of his personality.[71] As such, the male characteristics (termed "logos" by Jung) dominate, and the female characteristics (Jung's "eros") are neglected, often with harmful consequences. White commented: "Such a religion . . . may all too easily become an instrument of repression, and so of individual and social disintegration."[72]

White recognized the unconscious demand for the representation of the feminine in the quest for wholeness, and argued that, in order to be "whole," the male must be reconciled with its complementary opposite. For Jung, this meant that the male must identify with his feminine side (*anima*) and the female with her masculine side (*animus*).[73] If, therefore, the God image is an image of wholeness, it must include both masculine and feminine, opposites which the image reconciles.[74] Psychologically, then, White concurred with Jung that there *is* a need for the representation of the feminine in God. However—and here he diverged from Jung—White argued that the feminine *is* represented in the Catholic tradition *without* the need for the transformation of the Western God image. To illustrate this, White turned to four sources: the Bible; the Church fathers; Aquinas; and the Assumption of Mary. Turning to the first of these, White argued that the feminine is represented in Sophia,[75] in the metaphorical mothering of God in second Isaiah, in the image of creation, in the adamah which gives birth to Adam, in the people of God as his chosen bride, in Mary, in the Church.

From the second source, the Church Fathers, White argued that the feminine is represented in Eve, Mary, and *ecclesia*, and that these concepts were often used interchangeably: Mary, for example, is the new Eve brought forth from the side of the second Adam, and as the first of the redeemed community she is a symbol of the Church.[76] In addition, White argued that Jung's belief—that the veneration of a feminine figure is "a comparatively late and gradual compensation for the alleged inadequacies of the all-masculine Trinity"[77]—is proven to be false in the writings of the Fathers.

White's third source for the representation of the feminine was Aquinas. If, as Aquinas argued, all created perfections are contained in Divine Being, "it may be inferred those of motherhood no less than fatherhood."[78] Using another example, White argued that, although for Aquinas the divine essence cannot be separated from the divine persons, one might "consider and contemplate" the divine essence without the divine persons.[79] Although Aquinas' contributions do not meet the psychological need for a *concrete* feminine image of the divine, White suggested that they do indicate that Christianity is not closed to the feminine in God.

Finally, White turned his attention to Mary, and in particular her Assumption which, he argued, is a symbol of humanity's "participation in the Trinity."[80] Jung had recognized this, but he was disappointed that Catholics rejected the view that the Assumption made Mary a goddess or a fourth co-equal person of the Trinity. Jung's problem with this was twofold: first, if Mary is a creature it means that she is inferior to her son and so ultimately the image of God remains male; second, it implies that the feminine is inclined toward the male ideal with the consequence that "woman loses her power to compensate the masculine striving for perfection."[81] Jung wrote: "As long as a woman is content to be a *femme à homme*, she has no feminine individuality. She is empty and merely glitters—a welcome vessel for masculine projections. Woman as a personality, however, is a very different thing."[82] In other words, Jung thought that this doctrine could result in the inhibition of the development of the woman's own personality. Jung argued that, for a person to become whole, there must be a balance of male and female that can be achieved either within the psyche or "symbiotically" through marriage.[83]

From a psychological perspective, it is clear that there *is* a need for the representation of the feminine, and that, in relation to Mary, Jung thought that this demanded not creatureliness but equality with God. Although White recognized the psychological need for the representation of the feminine, he did not think that this required, as Jung believed, the transformation of the Western God image—it was *not* necessary that Mary be a goddess or that she be included in the Trinity. As White saw it, Mary was a creature and not a goddess, and all her glories had come from God. This did not, however, mean that White dismissed the psychological aspect of the doctrine. Rather, he *inverted* Jung's schema wherein the image corrects doctrine and used *doctrine* to correct "the false impressions" of the image.[84] Thus, in relation to Mary, he proposed that Mary is not an image of "the ideal attitude of woman towards man," but rather an image of human beings (male and female) inclined towards God.[85]

Ultimately, then, White disagreed with Jung's view of a Trinitarian "God within" who must integrate the "missing fourth" in the quest for wholeness. Indeed, he thought that Jung's God—essentially an immanent symbol—was psychologically dangerous precisely because it inevitably casts its shadow and God becomes "introjected and burdensome." In lecture notes, for example, White wrote:

> When the Trinity becomes a purely immanent symbol—a pattern for human behaviour for men in space and time—whose nature in persons are apprehended as something not uncreated, but as creatures; not as infinite and immeasurable entities but as measurable and comprehensible ones in space and time; not as eternal and timeless but as in time; not as omnipotent but as limited, complementary powers or function—this symbol is an inadequate and dangerous one.[86]

Jung inverted the traditional Christian doctrine of man in the image of God to God in the image of man. His "God" is in the image of man who integrates the missing fourth in the quest for wholeness. And it is a "God" which White rejects. Attacking Jung's confusion between God and God image, White suggested that, in the very concept of the transformation of the Western God image, the "transformation" applies to the wholeness of human beings and not to God Godself: "The Three in One is to be kept at a respectful, adorable distance: it is a transcendental mystery in no wise to be confused with the intrinsic completeness of the creature."[87] White therefore rejected Jung's notion that God as Trinity is a conscious expression of the process of individuation and subsequently his conviction that as a God image the Christian doctrine of God as Trinity has lost its symbolic meaning. As a child, Jung had been deeply frustrated with his father's inability to articulate the relevance of the doctrine of the Trinity, claiming that he did not understand it.[88] This experience encapsulates Jung's basic problem: faith in a transcendent Trinitarian God causes a "turning away from our psychic origins"[89] and thus from the inner archetypal experience of the Self as God image. Consequently, the doctrine loses its symbolic meaning and cannot be understood.[90]

Simply put, in the inner archetypal experience of the God image, the anima and the shadow are integrated and the trinity becomes a quaternity, whereas the transcendent God of faith remains Trinitarian. Although White disagreed with Jung, his argument was notably different from his earlier arguments regarding transcendence and immanence. In earlier discussion, White had argued that although a transcendent God potentially "forestall[s]" a direct experience of God in the psyche, this does not preclude direct experience if, in addition, a theology of immanence is recaptured in Aquinas' notion of affective knowledge. In this post-split context, however, the thrust of White's argument is different: the transcendence of God does not make the Trinity "psychologically irrelevant" because it is part of God's revelation *to* human beings for their *salus*.[91]

White further insisted on a God who is revealed *to* humans as Trinity and not *in* humans as quaternity, arguing that (theologically) this revelation must be relevant to his *salus* and should not therefore be "transformed." White wrote: ". . . the integrity of the images or symbols which dominate a man's soul are of the utmost importance to his own well-being. . . . if they were to distort the full significance of the symbol they will be hurtful or harmful to him."[92]

White made two further arguments to support his position that the Trinity does have symbolic value psychologically. First, he contested Jung's notion that psychological health is determined by quaternary shapes, suggesting that it could, for example, be determined by a person's values or their God.[93] Second, he argued that, psychologically speaking, Three in One and One in Three *is* relevant because the Unity "preserves the psyche from that dissociation" that occurs with polytheism. He continued: "The insistence of the dogma and of the liturgy that the Three are co-equal and inseparable, and to be 'worshipped and con-glorified together,' and not in isolation, should preserve the psyche from many one-sided religious aberrations."[94]

A third point that White could have made but didn't is articulated in the writings of Edward Edinger, namely, that Trinitarian symbols "express the 'dynamic' and 'developmental' aspect of individuation, whereas quaternity symbols express a static and completed goal."[95] The point is an important one, because Jung himself had often asserted that individuation was a process and its goal was often not realized—at least not by many.[96] In any case, it is clear that, on a psychological level, White concurred with Jung that there

is a need for the representation of the feminine in God. However—
and here he diverged from Jung—White argued that the feminine *is*
represented in the Catholic tradition *without* the need for the transformation of the Western God image. This further shows that
White's model was more dialectical than a simple-minded supplementation—his own Catholicism had been transformed by an
appropriation of Jung's psychology which included a reappraisal of
the feminine.

The Missing Fourth: Job's God Revisited

Even more contentious was Jung's insistence that the Western God
image must be transformed to include evil, a point most famously
penned in *Answer to Job*. The impact of this idea on White had been
enormous, from his experience of the emotional orthodoxy of integrating the shadow to his inability to see that this process was a
necessity for the Western God image. (I say "a necessity" because
without the inclusion of the shadow the God image could not be an
image of the Self, that is, an image of wholeness).[97]
    Ultimately the idea led to the Jung-White split. Several years on,
the idea continued to impel White's incredulity, producing two
further reviews of *Job* which, though critical, were less damning
than the first which had caused the split. Writing in the *National
Review* of Jung's "subjection of the Divine to psychological exploration," White commented: "The editors call it provocative but we
are uncertain what it is intended to provoke."[98] He continued:
"Were it not for the preface, we might read most of it as a straight
religious satire in the line of Voltaire . . . with no pretensions to be
'science.' . . . The preface may appease the indignation of the devout
reader when it assures us that the 'God' or 'Yahweh'—who is the
book's protagonist and victim—is not God or Yahweh at all, but a
psychological image or archetype."[99]
    Despite Jung's earlier protestations that he had no interest
whatsoever in "the metaphysics of the Trinity,"[100] many theologians
were concerned that Jung was advocating the integration of evil in
the Trinity Itself. Such fears regarding Jung's aspirations to theology had, to an extent, been allayed by Jung's prefatory assertion

that *Job* was about God images and not God. But White still found the book problematic psychologically, and he argued that psychologists would be "baffled" by it, "for while they may have learned that the human psyche can project images, and the ego may be more conscious of them, they will find it hardly intelligible that an image should (as does Yahweh in this account) itself project and become conscious—let alone create a world and become incarnate."[101] White's critique is clear: despite Jung's protestations in the preface, the distinction between God image and God remained deeply ambiguous. It seemed as if Jung was saying that the God image becomes God. It appeared that he was describing what is actually happening in the Trinity Itself. But Jung insisted that, on the contrary, he was not talking about God but about human images of God, that is, the contents of the God archetype.[102] As Jung saw it, God is a *phenomenon* of the psyche which is experienced as good and evil. If images of God—such as the Trinity—do not correspond to this archetypal experience, they must die that new God images might evolve.

As I have argued, Jung thought that the Trinity as a God image *had* lost its symbolic meaning, because it had been uprooted from the inner archetypal experience (the process of individuation) of which it was a conscious expression.[103] It is reinvested as a meaningful symbol of wholeness when the psyche transforms the symbol of Trinity into a quaternity, and this archetype of the Self as God image then projects onto the Trinity.

And it is this projection that White found baffling, in part, I think, because the images are personified. The image is not literally "creating the world" nor "becoming incarnate." Rather, Jung was using images which are, as Palmer put it, *"personifications of unconscious contents."*[104] In other words, to talk of God "becoming incarnate" or of God "incarnating" in each human being, is to personify the experience of the archetype of the Self by the conscious ego in which the ego is transformed, i.e., individuation.[105]

Although White remained perplexed and disturbed by *Job*, he was willing to admit in a 1959 review that he was "powerfully moved by its emotional power, its passionate sincerity, its compassion for the spiritual plight of post-Christian man, its brilliant flashes of insight."[106] However, as White saw it, Jung was "wrestling with some religious problem" that was not his, namely, ". . . some memory of a cosy Victorian liberal optimism, masquerading as Christianity, with a kind goody-goody God and a 'gentle Jesus meek and mild' as its insipid hero."[107] As a Catholic, White could not identify with such a God. He acknowledged, however, that if this were his God he would "appreciate the vigour of [Jung's] protest."[108] White's final comment on *Answer to Job* came as an appendix to his *Soul and Psyche*. This 1960 review was, in fact, the damning 1955 review purged of the *ad hominem* remarks which had caused such offense. Jung was thus transformed from the naked emperor reading Job "so blindly" to "the Professor" who gives us "a reading"[109] of Job which no longer leaves his friends concerned for his repute.[110] White's essential critique of *Answer to Job*, however, remained.

Evil with Hindsight

By the late 1950s, and aided by hindsight, White was convinced that he had unraveled the "polemic" with Jung on evil as a *privatio boni*, concluding that it had been a "not very profitable" argument about the meanings of words.[111] Further, White thought that this "rather tedious discussion" could have been dismissed, and "serious misunderstanding" avoided with the acknowledgment that Jung and White use the word *evil* in very different ways.[112] Indeed, in a 1959 review, White described as "troublesome" the "perplexing meaning which Jung attributes to the words *good* and *evil*. He is, of course, entitled to mean what he likes by his own words, but when he imposes his meanings on doctrines and documents which expressly understand them differently, the resultant confusion is more that I can begin to tidy up."[113]

   Long before White, Aquinas had commented on the ambiguity of the word *malum*. In his *De Malo*, he wrote: "In one sense *malum* can be understood as the subject of badness (*mali*), and this is something real; in another sense it can be understood as badness itself (*ipsum malum*) and this is not something real (*aliquid*) but is the privation of some particular Good."[114] As White saw it, this ambiguity of the word *evil* is overlooked by Jung with very serious consequences: "The whole 'polemic' might be dismissed as a triviality arising from a semantic muddle of the use of the word 'evil' (or its equivalents in Latin, Greek or German) as concrete and abstract noun or adjective."[115]

Stated more explicitly, the word *evil* can function in several ways: as a concrete noun (bad thing) and as an abstract noun (badness) or adjective (bad). It is clear that when White talked of *evil* he was talking of *badness*, that is to say, for White *evil* functioned as an abstract noun, implying that evil is not "a quantitative part of reality."[116] If White used *evil* adjectivally—an evil person, for example—he was simply describing the *badness* of that person. For Jung, on the other hand, the word *evil* functioned as a concrete noun. Thus, *evil* signified an evil thing, which further implied that evil has substance. He failed to see that, for White, as for Aquinas, *evil* functions as abstract noun or adjective. Instead, he imposed his understanding of evil as a concrete noun onto his reading of White and Aquinas with the result that White's statements about evil were rendered nonsensical. White wrote: "Each side, not surprisingly, tends to beg the question and assume that 'evil' means to the other what it means to him, from which it is an easy step to show that his statements about it are ridiculous."[117]

Jung, for example, initially assumed that when White used the word *evil* he was using it in the same way that he himself used it—as concrete noun. It is not difficult to see why, therefore, White's statements regarding evil as a *privatio boni* made little or no sense to Jung *as he read them*. How could a (concrete) evil thing be a *privatio boni*? From White's perspective, on the other hand, the very notion of an evil thing was nonsensical, for without some good, the thing would cease to exist. Ever more cognizant that the ambiguity of the word *evil* lay at the heart of their dispute, White wrote: "The English 'badness' or the German '*Schlechtigkeit*' would have rendered their undoubted meaning less ambiguously, and possibly spared us the whole polemic!"[118]

The implications of this semantic misunderstanding, however, are enormous:

> Its consequences could be, and already are, serious. For it can mean that Christians and Jungians can use the word "evil" in two different senses, that one party can read his own sense into the documents of the other and thereby make deplorable and dangerous nonsense of them,

and that the moral aims of each (the "overcoming of evil by good" and the "integration of evil") may appear mutually contradictory, and each may appear quite immoral to the other.[119]

To Jung, for whom evil is a concrete part of reality which must be integrated, the Christian attitude—that evil is a *privatio boni* and that it must be fought, rejected, and overcome by good—sounds immoral, not to mention detrimental to psychological health. To the Christian, Jung's view—that evil is willed, accepted, and added to good—sounds equally appalling, as if the integrated individual becomes partly evil.[120]

The question, however, which White had rightly raised, is whether Christians and Jungians have truly understood each other. White, to use just one example, was far from confident that he had truly understood Jung's talk of "integrating the shadow," charging it as being "wrapped in certain ambiguities."[121] He wrote: "I must confess that for my part I have great difficulty in understanding just what Jung *does* understand by evil, and how, intellectually, he would have us differentiate it from good. And it is not altogether clear what he would have us understand by 'integrating', 'accepting' and even 'becoming conscious' of it."[122]

A brief summary of Jung's understanding of the shadow and its integration is helpful at this juncture. The shadow, according to Jung, is "the 'negative' side of the personality, the sum of all the unpleasant qualities we like to hide, together with the insufficiently developed functions and contents of the personal unconscious."[123] Simply put, the shadow consists of what an individual does not want to reveal and what she refuses to acknowledge, such as "inferior traits of character and other incompatible tendencies."[124] It includes the capacity for evil, along with suppressed and repressed parts of the self (some of which may be good).[125] As an aspect of the psyche, Jung thought that neglect of the shadow not only "impoverished" the personality but was "deleterious" for psychological health.[126] He thought that if the shadow side was ignored it would be further repressed or projected onto others, and this in turn would hinder true self-knowledge. Indeed, in view of its destructive aspect, Jung thought that the shadow needed to be acknowledged and integrated into consciousness where it could be controlled rationally.[127]

Thus, individuation begins with an acknowledgment or a consciousness of the shadow side.

For Jung, "becoming conscious of the shadow" did not mean having objective knowledge of the contents of the shadow, but rather having an emotional experience of its reality.[128] In becoming conscious of the shadow, one experiences the conflict of good and evil, and this is the beginning of the psyche's drive toward wholeness. The ego casts off the shadow which then becomes dissociated and this intensifies the tension between good and evil. The shadow must then be integrated in the interest of wholeness. This is the point at which lack of clarity in the usage of the word *evil* magnifies the potential for misunderstanding. White wrote: ". . . integration of the shadow cannot mean—as Jung too often seems to suggest—the addition of evil to good, but the overcoming of evil *by* good. Integrated evil ceases to be evil, its privations have been supplied; it is, to the extent that it has been integrated, simply good."[129]

If *evil* is a concrete rather than an abstract noun, then it certainly sounds as though evil is added to the good. But from White's perspective, sin could not be integrated but must rather be rejected because it is wholly destructive of good.[130] White thought that this *was* consistent with Jung's view, arguing by way of analogy that if I have a car that malfunctions and I accept this disorder then the car will not be repaired and will continue to malfunction. ". . . it is hard to see how I can 'integrate' the disorder, for it is itself creating disintegration."[131] White argued that if the disorder itself is integrated, then the *badness* of the car and its behavior (which are analogous to the *malum culpae* and the *malum poenae*) remain. In other words, evil is indeed added to the good. If, however, *evil* is understood as the absence of some good which ought to be there, then integration of the Shadow is about supplying privations. To return to the analogy of the car, the car functions properly when the absent good working order is restored.[132] White was therefore convinced that Jung's talk of integration of the shadow *implied* "the supplying of a privation."[133]

Jung did not share White's reading of the phrase "the integration of evil." But, nor do I think that what Jung meant by the "integration of evil" was the "addition" of evil to the good. Jung often drew attention to Origen's idea that even the devil would be redeemed and brought back to the good as a model of integration. A corrective is needed at this point, and one which may serve to further the discussion in a productive manner. It is not evil which is redeemed and brought back to God (as Jung seemed to think Origen thought) but rather the devil as a creature of God—originally created good—who is brought back to God. Origen's model is essentially a privative one. Psychologically, it is a model which, as Sanford has noted, implies that evil (the Shadow) is redeemed "by being freed from a dissociated destructive condition and won back to the whole."[134] It is not "added to" the good but transformed. Practically speaking, this transformation occurs when that which has been suppressed or repressed is integrated into the conscious attitude of the individual. Following this model, therefore, evil (the Shadow) is seen as that which opposes (but which is necessary to achieve) the good of wholeness, and, so, will be overcome.[135]

The Accident

In the meantime, another shadow was hovering over White. On April 17, 1959, he was involved in a serious motorcycling accident, or as he later recalled it, "a gust of wind blew me off my scooter onto my skull—and cracked it."[136] In addition to a fractured skull, White suffered four fractured ribs, a fractured scapula, loss of vision in his left eye and the loss of hearing in his left ear.[137] His injuries left him hospitalized for several months,[138] and, subsequent to his discharge, he was sent to convalesce at St. Benet's in Worcester. Writing to his friend and fellow Jungian, Mrs. Catherine Ginsberg, White gave his own prognosis in characteristic terms: "I am undoubtedly indescribably better. . . . But there are a lot of difficulties ahead, both interior and exterior."[139]

Mother Michael of the Blessed Trinity, the Prioress of a Contemplative Carmelite Order in Presteigne and a mutual friend, wrote to Jung informing him of White's condition and reassuring him that White did not fully disapprove of his work.[140] Although White could not embrace everything Jung said, or found that it "fail[ed] to chime in with [his] own experience," he was grateful "for the vistas [Jung] has opened up," and "the stimulus . . . to further reflection—and even contradiction."[141] Jung deeply appreciated the letter from Mother Michael and requested further information on White's state of health. White himself replied on October 18, and, delighted with the message he had received through Mother Michael, he disclosed to Jung the enormity of the impact of his psychology, noting that his approval of Jung's work had left him "in quite serious trouble (and in Rome itself!)," his future "quite uncertain." He concluded, "I think you will agree that your work will itself be moribund if there is not some disagreement about it, and some *Auseinandersetzung* from those with different backgrounds and experiences—and perhaps different typologies!"[142]

White's embrace of Jung did indeed leave his future uncertain, and this is perhaps most evident in the continuing disagreement regarding White's written publications, which culminated in the proscription of *God and the Unconscious* in 1959. Shortly after his death, the same fate befell White's *Soul and Psyche*.[143] But there was another reason for the uncertainty of his future: he had not fully recovered from the accident, and a number of other health problems began to plague him. In September 1959 he was admitted to Addenbrookes Hospital with severe vomiting,[144] and by January 1960 it was discovered that he was suffering from cancer. Although he underwent a laporotomy on January 24, it was clear that he had an extensive carcinoma of the caecum and secondaries in the liver.[145]

The Last Word: Psychology or Theology?

It was in that same month that White had been invited by the London Society of Analytical Psychology and the Analytical Psychology Club to discuss the relationship between theology and analytical psychology. The topic: "Who shall have the last word: psychologist or theologian?" White objected to the title, patently perturbed that the psychologists may have assumed "anything so dubious" about the claims of theology.[146] From his convalescence in Cambridge he wrote: "It is axiomatic for any theology to which I could subscribe that it has not the last word even about its own subject matter, let alone any other."[147] As it turned out, White was too sick to attend the conference, and so Kenneth Lambert sent

White some questions, and his responses were later published in the *Journal of Analytical Psychology* as "Theological Reflections."[148] The responses indicated something of Jung's continuing impact on the dying Victor White who, in spite of the split with Jung, wrote with some confidence, "I am convinced how important Jung's pioneer work has been, and how greatly some acquaintance at least with analytical psychology is needed."[149]

The first question with which White was faced was "whether theologians have access to a reality not open to analytical psychologists."[150] The question is a highly significant one because this is *exactly* what was presupposed in White's methodology of supplementation in relation to Jung, and perhaps even more so in his post-split stance that Catholicism (which, in White's case, had been duly transformed by an appropriation of aspects of Jung's psychology) is the revelation that has the power to heal. It was no surprise, then, that White affirmed that theologians do have access to such a reality, and he argued that, to a certain extent, this is true of all disciplines. Clearly Jung would agree—his Kant-based empiricism *precluded* access to theological realities.

The function of religion in the psyche was the subject of the second question, and, in particular, whether psychological facts regarding the religious function could be "shown to be irrelevant by theologians." Convinced that soul and psyche are one and the same,[151] White answered emphatically, "No, no, no—on the contrary . . . if I am wrong about this I have been wasting most of the past twenty years of my life. . . . Analytical psychology and theology have much to offer each other, and at least in our Christian and post-Christian culture, neither can well be encapsulated by or ignore the other."[152]

This led to another question, whether analytical psychologists and theologians are in fact "twin investigators into the phenomena of religion."[153] Although a deceptively attractive analogy, because it is often difficult to distinguish between twins, White thought that they are not. White therefore reaffirmed the stance he had outlined prior to his encounter with Jung, a stance much applauded by Jung: "No; I think the task of theology—as I have outlined it, and as it has been traditionally understood—is not the same as that of analytical psychology, however closely related. And I am rather seriously afraid that if one tries to be any substitute for the other, they can only clash and quarrel. And I think that they can help each other [if each is faithful to its own task, subject-matter, disciplines]."[154] The irony of this response lies in the fact that White believed that Jung had not been faithful to his task and discipline, particularly in *Answer to Job*, and this *had* caused clash and quarrel. In the same breath White's comments served as a call to theologians and psychologists in dialogue to respect the boundaries of their respective disciplines.

The final question focused on the Self, and, in particular, whether White thought that the concept of Self and Godhead are "the same entity." In other words, is Jung's archetype—of the Self as God image—God Godself? White responded: ". . . It is hard to see how it is even comparable with any concept of God or the Godhead—let alone identifiable with it."[155] He continued: "Is the Jungian 'self' the one God *I* can believe in or worship—'the Maker of all things visible and invisible'? Is the Jungian 'self' even a God I can rationally acknowledge by natural theology, and prescinding from faith? I must confess that I doubt it . . ."[156]

Although Jung thought that God should be acknowledged and worshipped in the interests of human wholeness, White doubted that he himself could worship Jung's God.[157] But even prior to questioning whether White could worship Jung's God, one must ask whether *Jung* could worship Jung's God. After all, if God is just the God image—and not God Godself—was Jung *really* worshipping God? And was it even *possible* for Jung to make such an acknowledgment given his methodology? I think that White thought not, for as I have argued, Jung's methodology precluded any possibility that God be formulated rationally. Although White was not so restricted methodologically, it is clear that he did not worship Jung's God.

Indeed, he found it difficult to identify Jung's God (be it the "God" of Jung's subjective experience or, scientifically speaking, the "God image" of the human psyche) with the God revealed in the Judaeo-Christian tradition. White wrote:

> To my consciousness, if not to Jung's, the symbols, signs, and concepts associated with each are sharply distinguishable even empirically. One is a dynamic Trinity, the other a static quaternity. One is a balance of opposites, the other beyond the opposites. One contains good and evil, light and darkness, the other is beyond the *opposites* of good and evil,

and (according to St. John) "all light, and in him there is no darkness at all." One seems to be *only* immanent and relative, the other *both* immanent and transcendent, absolute *and* relative. One an archetype of human psychophysical wholeness, the other has been commonly seen, since St. Augustine, as the Creator and Sustainer of All. It is true that both sets of symbols may occasion numinous experiences, which I do not undervalue. But that is not enough for Christians or any rational theist to identify them—nor, I suspect, for most thinking atheists or agnostics either . . . perhaps my doubts are due to the fact that I do not rightly understand analytical-psychology language about "the Self."[158]

As White saw it, therefore, Jung's archetype of the Self as God image (as he understood it) could not be identified with God Godself.

Elsewhere, White had in fact challenged Jung's assertion that he was concerned with the psychic experience which is understood and formulated as God, arguing that that if a psychic experience is finite and observable, then *by definition* it could not be God:

We must bring to his earnest attention that it is simply not a fact (not therefore, in his own language, a "psychological truth") that we hold that an observable human experience is God, or can formulate it to be God. We recognize his acknowledged incompetence to make statements about divine transcendence, but must protest that the psychological fact is that by "God" we *mean* that which transcends everything finite, and that divine immanence itself can only mean for us the immanence of the transcendent. These are psychological facts, the ideas which exist, in us, and which we must ask him, precisely as an empiricist, to observe.[159]

It seems that White was coming to the same conclusion as Martin Buber, who several years before had argued that Jung's God within is no more than the revelation of man to himself.[160] Further, it implied that Jung's hope for the transformation of the Western God image—a hope that he had pinned on White—was, in reality, a hope that God would be remade in the image of man. For White it was a hope untenable.

The *Opus Magnum*

Jung had also realized that the hope was in vain. Having received news from Mother Michael that White's cancer was terminal, he replied, "As there are so few men capable of understanding the deeper implications of our psychology, I had nursed the apparently vain hope that Father Victor would carry on the *opus magnum*."[161] The *opus magnum* is the name given in alchemy to the completion of the alchemical process of transformation, and it is a term which Jung had adopted to describe the process of individuation. In religious terms, individuation was about the transformation of the Self as God image.

Freud had pinned great hopes on Jung as his successor, appointing him "crown prince" of the psychonalytic movement. Similarly, Jung had pinned great hopes on Victor White, his "white raven," who would be instrumental in the transformation of the Western God image. Jung's reference to the *opus magnum* further serves to support my argument that the appellation "white raven" is to be understood as an alchemical reference. Jung had hoped that Victor White would be instrumental in the *opus magnum*, in the transformation of the Western God image. Clearly, then, it speaks to the significance of White that Jung considered him—a theologian and a Catholic priest—to continue his work. However, just as Father Freud suffered the disappointment of the oedipal betrayal by his "son" Jung, so too, Jung was personally grieved by the split with White,[162] and disappointed that his great hope for the transformation of the Western God image could not be fulfilled in him.

The Last Days

As White's health deteriorated, he moved out of the Dominican Community at Cambridge to No. 5 Harrowby Court, London, where his friend Mrs. Ginsberg nursed him until his death. From there he wrote to Jung, telling him of impending surgery for a malignant growth on his intestines.[163] Ten days later, White wrote to Jung again in a defensive but deeply affectionate letter. He began: "I am somehow moved to send you the assurance of my love for you."[164] It was an assurance that responded to Jung's earlier accusation that White had publicly denounced him. White denied any recollection of such a denunciation, ". . . sorely perplexed to understand *when* and *where*" he had done so, and arguing that, on the contrary, he was "eager" for Jung's work to spread because "it is so *needed.*"[165] Furthermore, he suggested that it was he, and not Jung, who should be offended. Jung had accused White of being "bound hand and foot" to the Church's doctrine, defending every syllogism.[166] Irked by such an attack on his sincerity White wrote: "I have not even heard of these 'syllogisms' which bind me hand and foot."[167] The letter concluded: "I do not know just what all the trouble is about at your end. And I hope you may enlighten me . . . Anyway this poor letter wants to convey my love and gratitude, for what it's worth."[168]

Although the two men clearly had a deep affection for each other, the insults continued to fly. On March 25, 1960, Jung wrote to the terminally ill White beginning with the suggestion that White should re-examine *Answer to Job* in the light of his own suffering, that is, as an insight into the dark side of God.[169] Perhaps aware of the insensitivity of his remarks, Jung wrote: "Your aggressive critique has got me in the rear. That's all."[170] Jung's letter concluded fondly: "Don't worry! I think of you in everlasting friendship. *Ultra posse nemo obligatur* [Nobody is obliged to do more than he can]. Thus I ask for your forgiveness, as is incumbent on one who has given cause for scandal and vexation."[171]

The following day, Jung wrote to Mother Michael, "shaken" by "the stroke of fate" that had befallen White.[172] White was in rapid decline, and although he knew that he was dying, a letter in his medical notes, dated April 8, indicates his desire to live: "I think he has a good deal of work to do, which he would like to finish, and I feel that any opportunity which can be given to him to do this, may be worth while."[173]

Three days later, Jung wrote again to Mother Michael expressing his regret at upsetting White and requesting that White no longer be troubled by their differences: "I am very sorry indeed that the news about Victor White is so bad and the end apparently so near. If you have any chance to let him know about myself I should be much obliged if you would tell him that I am quite at peace with him and that he should not worry any more. I am quite convinced of his sincere and human loyalty."[174] Jung was concerned about the insensitivity of the letter he had written about White's Job-like suffering, realizing—as he would later write—that "the moment was ill chosen."[175]

So Jung penned another letter to White on April 30. Beginning, "my dear Victor," Jung assured White of his friendship and, in lieu of a visit, the eighty-four-year-old Jung sent a photo signed "for Victor." It would be his last letter. Jung wrote: "I hope you don't worry about my letter. I want to assure you of my loyal friendship. I shall not forget all the useful things I have learned through our many talks and through your forbearance with me. I was often sorry to be a *petra scandali*. It is my fate however, not my choice, I had to fulfill this unbecoming role. Things had to be moved in the great crisis of our time. New wine needs new skins."[176]

Jung's final sentence stands in contrast to one of the earliest letters he had written to White—in October 1945. Then, he had suggested that new wine needed to be poured into *old* wine skins.[177] As I argued in Chapter Three, White must have questioned whether new wine could be poured into old wine skins, whether Jung's psychology could be integrated into ecclesiastical doctrine. Further, I drew attention to the fact that Jung's quote was, in fact, a misreading of Matthew's gospel—people do *not* put new wine in old wine-skins. Jung's final letter and his shift to the Matthean analogy is therefore highly significant. It expressed Jung's realization—some fifteen years later—that, contrary to his great hopes, his psychology could not be contained within the limits of ecclesiastical doctrine.

Unable to respond by hand, White dictated a response to Jung's "wonderful and comforting" letter from his sick bed in London on May 8.[178] Expressing his gratitude to Jung to the extent that he had indeed been a "*petrus* (sic) *scandali*," White included a letter he had dictated two days before in which he attempted to clarify "some strange misunderstanding—or non-understanding—which has arisen between us."[179] He had been stunned by the letter in which Jung suggested he re-examine Job from the perspective of his new-found suffering, admitting that the letter left him "shaken . . . quite considerably."[180]

Comparing Jung to Job's so-called friends, White wrote: "I had not expected a 'Job's comforters' letter from you."[181] White was further galled by Jung's accusation that he was bound by the syllogisms of the Catholic Church: "However much I have erred, and possibly been unjust to you I think you must allow that I have never questioned your sincerity (publicly or privately) or suggested that you are 'tied hand and foot' by other people's ideas or syllogisms."[182] White's resistance to the publication of *Job* also emerged in this letter, though White reassured Jung of his deep affection for the text and for his friend: "I think and hope you know that when you first showed me '*Antwort auf Hiob*' I loved it and admired it very much. . . . I still do love your picture of Job, because I love you."[183] Attaching this to his letter of May 8, White signed off with his very last words to Jung, "May I add that I pray with all my heart for your well-being, whatever that may be in the eyes of God."[184]

White died on the morning of May 22, 1960, only fifty-seven years old—his last words, "Dear God, take me."[185] As in living, so in dying: the impact of Jung on White was enormous. Mother Michael wrote to Jung that day and informed him of the news: "My dear Jung, Father Victor's beloved soul has returned to God. He died this morning between 11–12 am from a sudden thrombosis. He was fully awake, and praying before he became unconscious, and they say he had no great pain."[186] Mother Michael also wrote to comfort Mrs. Ginsberg, the woman who had nursed him to his death. Affirming that White had lived by the Christian and Jungian principle that living includes dying, she wrote: "Now there begins a share in his new life—And all his teaching of the dying God is in full light of truth, actually happening."[187]

Mrs. Ginsberg in turn wrote to Jung with the news of White's end, and offered to send him a drawing of White on his deathbed.[188] Jung replied on June 3, 1960, declining the drawing but clearly pleased to have this letter as "a valuable supplement" to "the thoughts that moved me from the moment when I saw that we had come to the parting of the ways."[189] Reflecting on their parting, Jung wrote:

> I was at the end of my resources and had to leave him *nolens volens* to the decree of his fate. I saw that his arguments were valid for him and allowed of no other development. I accepted this in silence, for one can only respect such reasons even though one is convinced that—had the circumstances been favorable—one might yet have reached out beyond them. . . . Knowing how much depended on whether Father White could understand my arguments or not, I still tried to point out the difficulties in my second last letter to him, with the feeling

however, that it would not be granted to me to pierce through to his understanding.

It was then that I sinned against my better insight, but at least it served as a pretext for my asking his forgiveness and offering him a touch of human feeling. . . .

As I have so earnestly shared in his life and inner development, his death has become another tragic experience for me.[190]

Upon receiving Jung's letter, Mrs. Ginsberg wrote to a mutual friend, "[It] confirms fears that Victor had about Jung who probably never understood why V. was so aggravated by his attitude towards God as presented in *Job* and so many other passages in his books."[191] Because Jung's ultimate source of authority was the psyche, God images had to be transformed to correspond to archetypal experience. Jung was confident that because White had experienced the shadow to be "emotionally orthodox" he would also embrace the transformation of the Western God image to include evil as well as good. Not only could White not do this—because his ultimate authority was not the psyche but revelation as mediated through the Church—but he was aggravated by Jung's desire to tamper with Christian doctrines about God. Jung simply did not understand this, even to the end. Nor could he, given his restrictive methodology. He did, however, respect White's faith, and had a Mass said for him in Zurich on what would have been White's fifty-eighth birthday, October 21, 1960.[192]

Jung clearly appreciated the theological input he had received from White, but he was no more likely to embrace Catholicism—as the mediator of healing revelation—than White was to embrace analytical psychology as the third dispensation, or a God who was evil as well as good. As White moved from life to death it seemed that, although many of the disputed questions between the two men remained unresolved, the two were at peace with each other—and the ultimate incompatibility of their beliefs was more readily acknowledged. "Both men loved each other," wrote Everson, "but loved Truth more"[193]—and, one might add, each his version of it.

SEVEN
CONCLUSION

Assessing the Impact

Above the door of Jung's house at Küsnacht, an inscription from the oracle at Delphi reads: "Vocatus atque non vocatus Deus aderit" encapsulating Jung's recognition of the religious nature of the human psyche. Ultimately it was this recognition, coupled with his belief that religion played a crucial role in mental health and sickness, which lay at the heart of Jung's impact on Victor White. In the preceding pages I have attempted to show the frequently complex and multifaceted impact of Jung on White's theology, and its inextricable connection to White's life. A brief summary of the impact as it manifested itself during the different stages of White's life, followed by an analysis of the neo-scholastic climate and the basic theological presuppositions of White in relation to Jung, will lead me to some concluding remarks.

White's Naive Embrace?

Some scholars have suggested that, considering his theological presuppositions as a Thomist, and the strong reaction to modernism that was rife in the Catholic Church, White was somewhat naive in his initial embrace of analytical psychology.[1] As I have shown, the initial impact was *primarily* personal and, therefore, it does seem plausible to suggest that White was too intimately involved with Jung and his psychology before he realized its

221

ultimate incompatibility with his theology. His personal *internal* experience of Jung's psychology would and did clash with the *external* authority of the Church as mediator of God's revelation.

This being said, I think it is a mistake to dismiss White's initial embrace of Jung's psychology as naive—he did express his serious reservations about Jung's psychology *from the very beginning*. This can be seen in at least three places in White's writings. First, in his initial letters to his analyst John Layard in 1940, White voiced his concern that Jungians who go beyond empirical data lay the foundation for an "ersatz religion" which, far from complementing Christianity, radically contradicts it. Second, in what could hardly be called a naive embrace, White anticipated and articulated the difficult "rocks ahead"[2] in any prospective encounter between Catholics and Jungians. Third, White showed a deep awareness of the potentially problematic issue of God's transcendence *in his very first lecture* on Jung's ideas, given in 1942.[3] Far from naive, White suspected *very early on* that Jung repudiated divine transcendence. As I showed earlier, Jung clarified in a letter to White that he did not exclude the *possibility* of a transcendent God, though as an empiricist he was not in a position to defend such a notion. In fact, Jung repeatedly insisted that he did not say that God was *only* "an intra psychic potency."[4]

While it is possible that Jung's assurances may have misled White as to the complexity of the problems that lay ahead, there can be little doubt that White was profoundly aware that potential problems existed, particularly in relation to Jung's concept of the Self as God image. However, and despite these problems, he was optimistic that they could be overcome by distinguishing Jung's God image from God Godself. For these reasons I give little credence to criticisms that White failed to see what the possible impact of Jung's psychology would be from the outset. Rather than depicting him as naive, I think he is better portrayed as one who—despite known obstacles—courageously took the risk to pursue a relationship with Jung. Furthermore, this view is completely consistent with that of some of his brethren who, in his obituary, spoke of White as a "theological explorer, a breaker of new ground."[5]

The Collaborative Years

Pursuant to his experience of Jung's psychology, White was forced in the period 1945–55 to re-evaluate his traditional conception of God who reveals Godself through scripture, tradition, and reason to consider the experiential dimension of God's revelation. For Jung, it was essential to mental health that each human being should experience the God image within. The impact of this central Jungian idea on White's theology was significant, influencing a re-evaluation and a *recovery* of a theology of immanence in Aquinas' notion of "affective knowledge." This impact is further manifested in White's biography, for the seeming immanentism of Jung—and its similarities to the condemned modernists—immediately placed White under the suspicions of Rome and the Dominican Order.

As I have shown, White was undeterred, arguing that analytical psychology had an important role to play in articulating the function of religion in the psyche, and his theology of this period sought to illustrate this. In addition, I have tried to show how White's model of supplementation arose in this period in response to the (methodologically induced) deficiencies of Jung's psychology—when seen from a theological perspective.

The Post-Jung Years

By 1955, however, the impact of analytical psychology on White's theology was more collision than influence. Despite the espousal of commitment to the boundaries of their respective disciplines, both White and Jung were guilty of encroachment into each other's territory. Nowhere was this more evident than in the dispute about evil and its transference onto God in *Answer to Job*. The distinction between God and God image seemed increasingly unclear and White's ability to embrace Jung's God impossible.

Nonetheless, the impact of Jung continued to manifest itself in White's life and theology, albeit in a different way. White remained committed to articulating Jung's discoveries regarding the psyche, but had refined his model of supplementation which had been criticized by some as a pointless syncretism,[6] and "a blind synthesis" of taking the old with the right hand and the new with the left and fitting them together.[7] It was in this final stage of his life that White was more assertive in his affirmation that it is *Catholicism* (which in White's case had been reanimated by aspects of Jung's psychology), and not Jung's psychology, which is the true revelation that heals, the answer to the needs disclosed by the psyche.

Appropriating Errors?

Significant to the analysis of Jung's impact on White is the fact that White lived and worked in a neo-scholastic Church climate that was hostile to the Enlightenment and to Catholic modernism, both of which *appeared* to feature in the psychology of Jung. Jung was heavily influenced by Kant,[8] and in particular Kant's distinction between *phenomena* and *noumena*—which formed the basis of Jung's "empirical" approach and precluded any discussion of God Godself. Jung's dependence on Kant would have set him at odds with the predominantly neo-scholastic Dominican tradition of which White was a part because Kant was a figure of the Enlightenment.

The problem with the Enlightenment for neo-scholasticism was that it supported a natural religion and denied supernatural revelation and the claims of particular historical religions.[9] This is significant regarding the impact of Jung on White because it meant that White was rooted in a tradition which countered Kant *explicitly*,[10] thereby putting him at odds with Jung and—to the extent that he appropriated some of the ideas of Jung—putting him at odds with some in his own tradition. In this respect, White is an important figure in the renewal of Catholic theology. For example, White's neo-scholastic contemporaries exalted the rational dimension of knowledge but neglected the affective dimension—a neglect deemed pathological by Jung. Jung's ideas prompted White's recovery of immanence in Aquinas' notion of affective knowledge.

Parallel to the neo-scholastic critique of the Enlightenment is the condemnation of Catholic modernism. The agnosticism of the modernists—according to which knowledge is limited to experience and religion develops from the need for God in the human soul—was greatly feared by the Church, because it made faithfulness to a religion of authority fortuitous. In effect, it meant that one's personal truth stood against the teaching authority of the Church. The very subjectivity of Jung's gnostic (and yet paradoxically agnostic[11]) position, and his concept of the evolution of the Western God image made him look like a modernist. Jung, therefore, was deemed to be a very dubious figure by the neo-scholastics of White's tradition.

In other words, White's appropriation of Jung's ideas at least *suggested* to some the appropriation of the errors of the Enlightenment and of modernism. In this climate, how could White not have anticipated that the impact of Jung's psychology would lead to anything but conflict? It is understandable, therefore, that some scholars have suggested that White's initial embrace of Jung was naive. Understandable, but as I have argued, flawed. For, in spite of this climate, and not forgetting the very different presuppositions from which he and Jung operated, White saw the importance of Jung's psychology and boldly chose to pursue it.

Theological Presuppositions

It is significant that, although White and Jung both harbored great hopes for their relationship, the basic ideas to which each man was committed pointed toward their ultimate incompatibility. Certainly, both men recognized that each operated from a very different set of presuppositions, White stating explicitly, "We move in different circles, and our minds have been formed in different philosophical climates."[12] No less subtle, Jung at one point accused White of being "trapped" by the "syllogisms" of the Church.[13] And, although this overstates White's commitment to the Church and her teachings, it is fair to say that, to a certain extent, White was committed to *a particular tradition*.

A closer look at White's theological presuppositions suggests that although Jung's psychology is, as Dourley put it, "paradoxically attractive," particularly in that it offers an immediate sense of the divine, it is "ultimately threatening" to Catholicism—at least on the level of Christian doctrine about God.[14] As a Thomist, White was theologically committed to certain views about God: God is utterly transcendent; God is self-sufficient; God is perfect and immutable; and God manifests Himself in history in the person of Jesus Christ. On the other hand, Jung's God, the God who is experienced in the psyche, is: intra-psychic (immanent); involved in "mutual redemption"[15] with human beings; good, evil, and evolving; and not limited to one incarnation in history. A brief consideration of these "conflicting opposites"(!) will serve to highlight not only that White operated from very different presuppositions from those of Jung, but that these presuppositions were an important aspect of the impact of Jung on White's theology.

Transcendence and Immanence

White was committed to divine transcendence; Jung to an experience of the God within. The tension between Jung and his father, whose God was "*outside* man," was in many ways replayed with Victor White. For Jung, God was a living mystery experienced *inside* man. For White, as for Jung's father, God was utterly transcendent, revealed through scripture, the tradition of the Church, and reason. Faith in a transcendent God frustrated Jung intensely.[16] He thought that such an espousal of a deity "*outside* man" blinded people to the experience of the God *inside* human beings that he saw as so necessary for mental health.[17] It is clear that Jung was essentially critical of a position to which White was committed from the very beginning.

Certainly, White saw the problem of a theology that was *exclusively* transcendent, and, as I have shown, he was concerned to correct an overemphasis on the transcendent that seemed both to exclude God from the world and from the inner experience of human beings. Thus, in his early work on affective knowledge, White grappled with the gargantuan gulf between the divine and human,[18] and attempted to *recover* from the Thomistic tradition an immanent sense of God.

Jung had, in fact, charged Aquinas with having been a significant force in "the prejudice that the deity is *outside* man."[19] It is clear that, in the *interpretation* of Aquinas by the neo-scholastics, the immanent had to a large degree been neglected, and the transcendent exalted, because of the pervading fear of the modernists. Jung's impact was important in forcing a *re-evaluation* of immanence. It led White to see that, unlike the neo-scholastics, whose response to the immanence of the modernists was an excess of transcendence, what was actually needed was a recovery and an apologetic of immanence which was already there in the Thomistic tradition.

However, although Jung initially presented a challenge for theology to re-evaluate itself, his overemphasis on the immanent ultimately proved threatening to, and incompatible with, White's theology. To restate Jung's "empirical" position: God exists *solely* in the realm of psychological truth. Certainly Jung admitted of a transcendent function, but it is wholly intra-psychic. This *overemphasis* on the immanent *to the exclusion of* the transcendent (at least from an empirical perspective[20]) placed Jung at odds with a Thomist like White.

Several problems in particular are worthy of note. First, Jung's immanentism was (as he himself was aware) ultimately monistic, for it failed to make any real distinctions between God and human beings. Jung was quite aware that the idea of the God within would imply a dormant divinity inseparable from the individual and that this could be "dogmatically difficult" to orthodox Christian belief.[21] In fact, for Jung, there was no difference, empirically, between images of God and images of Self: both are expressed by symbols of wholeness or individuation. The problem with this is that it *seems* to suggest that Jung equated the Self with a purely immanent God and, further, it could be construed from this that Jung was substituting God with the Self.[22]

Jung *firmly* denied the identification of God and the Self but conceded that the *images* which both produced were often indistinguishable.[23] Consequently, White accepted the Self as a symbol of wholeness but rejected the notion that the Self as God image was synonymous with the God revealed in the Bible and tradition. Essentially, this meant that as long as the unconscious God image was distinguished from God Godself (that is, the God of Bible and tradition), White could accept that the Self was "emotionally orthodox."

Jung, however, did not always make this distinction clear, and therefore it often did seem that he was equating the Self with a purely immanent God. This *apparent* reductionism of God to the psyche predominantly stems from the lack of clarity in the distinctions that Jung made between God image and God. Jung insisted that when he spoke of *God* or *God image* he was concerned *only* with the archetypal God image and not God Godself. Thus, what appears to be a rather troubling equation of the Self and God—with all its implications of Self worship[24]—is, in fact, an equation of *images*. Reading Jung, however, this was not always clear, as the following passage illustrates:

> It is impossible for psychology to establish the difference between the image of God (or the Self) and God himself (i.e., in reality, not merely conceptually). For even the concept of the Self indicates something transcendental; and empirical science is incapable of making positive statements about it. So great is the "numinousness" in our experience of the Self, that it is only too easy to experience the manifestation of the Self as a manifestation of God.[25]

Here Jung's distinction between God image and God is riddled with ambiguity, and even prior to that, what he actually means by *God* or *God image* is somewhat elusive. Jung's vagueness in this matter is clearly relevant to the assessment of his impact on Victor White, particularly in attempting to discern the compatibility of their views on immanence and transcendence—or lack thereof.

On one level, it seems that Jung was, as Palmer has noted, distinguishing between the archetypal form (the eternal and primordial God archetype, which is unknowable) and the archetypal contents (the God images by which the psychic experience of "God," or the Self, is represented). In other words, "God"—the God within—can only be known (revealed) by God images.[26] On another level, and taking this a step further, Jung could mean that the God image or the God archetype is to be distinguished from God—an objective reality (external to the psyche). For, while Jung admitted that "an archetype presupposes an imprinter"[27]—which could be taken to imply that the experience of the God image presupposes the objective existence of God—his methodology only permitted him to say that a psychic experience is "understood and formulated"[28] as God

(which of course says nothing whatsoever about the objective existence of God.)

Victor White understood Jung primarily in the second of these two senses, though he, too, doubted whether Jung's distinction between God and God image was clear, especially in *Answer to Job.* In fairness to Jung, it seems that he *genuinely* thought that he had made a careful distinction between God image and God. This is abundantly clear in several passages written to different theologians:

> You seem not to have noticed that I speak of the *God-image and not of God* because it is quite beyond me to say anything about God at all. It is more than astonishing that you have failed to perceive this fundamental distinction, it is shattering. I don't know what you must take me for if you can impute such stupidities to me . . .[29]

> [The God image] has nothing whatever to do with God *per se* . . . at the very most I speak of an *imago Dei,* as I have repeatedly emphasized in countless places, and I am not like the idiot who believes that the image he sees in the mirror is the real and living I.[30]

> I am not a word-magician or word-fetishist who thinks he can posit or call up metaphysical reality with his incantations.[31]

> In *Job* and elsewhere I am always explicitly speaking of the *God-image.* If my theologian critics choose to overlook this, the fault lies with them and not with me. They obviously think that the little word "God" conjures him up in reality. . . . I must repeat, I speak exclusively of the *God-image* in *Job.*[32]

> No empiricist in his senses would believe his models to be the eternal truth itself.[33]

Jung's desire to distinguish between God and God image had in fact originated in response to accusations from theologians that he had made statements about God Godself, a charge Jung deflected with the accusation that that is precisely what *theologians* do when using the word *God.* As Jung saw it, theologians (which presumably included Victor White) did not really make statements about God but God images.[34] Several passages in Jung's letters to Pastor Bernet support this:

> What impresses me most profoundly in discussions with theologians of both camps is that metaphysical statements are made apparently

without the slightest awareness that they are talking in mythic images which pass directly as the "word of God." For this reason it is so often thoughtlessly assumed that I do the same thing, whereas quite to the contrary I am trained by my daily professional work to distinguish scrupulously between idea and reality.[35]

If theologians think that whenever they say "God" then God is, they are deifying anthropomorphisms, psychic structures and myths. This is exactly what I don't do, for, I must repeat, I speak exclusively of the *God image* in *Job*.[36]

The theologian buttonholes me, asseverating that *his* anthropomorphism is God and damning anyone who criticizes any anthropomorphic weaknesses, defects, and contradictions in it as a blasphemer. It is not God who is insulted by the worm, but the theologian, who can't or won't admit that his concept is anthropomorphic.[37]

Jung's God is unknown and unknowable (a point with which White, as a Thomist, could concur) and, therefore, human beings (including theologians!) can only talk about the God image. Committed to such a viewpoint, it is understandable why, in his writing, it is often the case that *God* and *God image* are synonymous. For Jung, a theologian who speaks of *God* is not speaking of God Godself but of *images* of God. In other words, *as a psychologist*, Jung did not believe in the body of knowledge which Christians believe comes from the revelation of a transcendent God.

If Jung spoke of *revelation*, it was that which happens *within* the psyche when the living archetype of the Self as God image "seizes and controls" him.[38] This is highly significant in any assessment of White. Jung thought the Western God image is just that—an *image* of psychic origin. White, on the other hand, believed that God has been revealed from outside of the psyche, transcendent as well as immanent—a potentially pathological belief from Jung's perspective. Further, in relation to Jung's *Answer to Job*, it reinforced the dichotomy of their world views: Jung saw his criticism of God as a criticism of Western *images* of God. From a psychological perspective, it was, as Stein argued, an evaluation of the inadequacy or incompleteness of statements about God.[39] White, on the other hand, suspected that Jung was criticizing the Judaeo-Christian God of revelation.

Self-sufficiency and Mutual Redemption

The second presupposition to which White was committed concerns his Thomistic belief in the self-sufficiency of God, which is ultimately incompatible with what Dourley called the "mutual redemption" of God and human beings, central to Jung's schema. For White, the redemption of humanity comes from a transcendent God who is, as Jung put it, "*outside* man." For Jung on the other hand, consciousness is required "to redeem the hidden God of the unconscious."[40] It is, as Dourley noted, a "redemptive reciprocity"[41] of man in the image of God, and God in the image of man. Superficially, this "mutual redemption" is attractive, for it means that God is involved in human suffering (particularly the suffering of the divine opposites). But the attraction is somewhat specious. Salvation is viewed in a merely gnostic manner, the individual cooperating with the God within (that is, within—but transcendent to the ego). Human beings are saved (or, in Jung's terms, "made whole") by knowledge (and not by faith which, on the contrary, detracts from wholeness, because it puts God "*outside* man," thereby blinding human beings to the possibility of an inner experience of God).[42]

Although it is deceptively attractive, White was deeply aware that this gnostic dimension of Jung's thought was particularly threatening *precisely because it is religious.*[43] From his own experience, White could certainly connect with Jung's idea that human beings must turn inward, but he did not believe human beings should remain inward. Rather he thought that the experience of God as really present should transform human beings to be a sacramental presence in the world.

Perfection and Integration

This brings me to the third point on which the presuppositions of White and Jung differed irredeemably from the outset—their perspectives on good and evil in relation to God. White was committed to a view of God as *Summum Bonum*, and this did not accord with Jung's experience of the shadow and the anima, the evil and the feminine within. Jung required the transformation of the Western God image to include both of these, but White could not change Christian belief to conform to psychology. He could not, for example, transform Trinity to Quaternity. If God is immutable, there could be no transformation. At best, the impact of Jung on White encouraged a reconsideration of *images* of God, particularly in relation to the feminine, but ultimately forced him to defend the *Church's* doctrine of God, and articulate *this* divinely revealed knowledge as the revelation that heals.

Particularity and Universality

Finally, the fourth of the polarized presuppositions of White and Jung concerns the question of the historical Jesus. White was committed to the uniqueness of the historical Jesus (and, as I have shown, also of Mary), whereas Jung separated the Jesus of history from the Christ symbol, Christ being but one expression of the Self. Jung's separation of the Jesus of history and the Christ symbol echoed precisely the categories of Biblical scholarship condemned by the encyclical *Lamentabili*, condemned because they divided Christ's person and reduced Christ to the gnostic "divine essence" of the soul.[44]

Although White could agree with Jung that symbols and dogmas originate from the deep unconscious needs of the human psyche, White was also committed to a distinct revelation in history, to the *particular* actualization of a myth, and to the conscious response of the human person to revelation within an historical context. Further, this deficiency in Jung could not be "healed" by White's method of supplementation because Jung rejected historicism and the particular—as he saw it, they encouraged blindness to and a "turning away from" an experience of the God of the unconscious.

Jung's "White Raven"?

As far as White was concerned, it is clear that these four theological presuppositions were simply not negotiable. Not only were they not negotiable, but White saw no necessity for God to "become" what Jung's psychology suggested the God image should be. Although White saw the emotional necessity of the transformation of the human person (individuation), he was not and could not be the "white raven" Jung hoped for in relation to the transformation of the Western God image. For Jung, Christianity was deficient, and in order to transform the God image, that which had been rejected by orthodoxy—such as the dark side of God—needed to be recovered and brought back to the whole.

But it was exactly this "heresy"—Jung's designation—that White could not incorporate. According to John Dourley: "To make such a transition would have cost White his faith. His failure to make it may have cost him his life."[45] This is an astounding statement, and yet it is clear that Jung himself thought that White's inability to move toward the transformation of the Western God image was connected with his death. In his book *The New God Image*, Edward Edinger confirmed that this was, without a doubt, Jung's view. He quoted a section from Esther Harding's *Journals*, which refer to a person 'X.' Edinger, having edited this material, disclosed that 'X' was, in fact, Victor White.[46]

> X [a mutual acquaintance, a cleric] had never really faced his problem, nor taken up his cross, that is, the opposition that forms the cross (crossing his fingers as he spoke). He need not have been afraid; the Church would not have rejected him. A Jesuit said to X once, "You make a fist in your pocket and go on with the ritual!" But he could not face the fact of evil—just as he denied that Jesus had a shadow, though that is clearly portrayed in the records we have. Not only did he fail on Palm Sunday, allowing himself to be venerated as an imperial savior, and then cursed the fig tree because it did not fall into line, but also he was actually unable to carry his cross, someone else had to carry it for him, a most significant point. And so he had to be fixed on the cross. If we do not carry our own cross, we will surely be crucified. So, X, who had not enough backbone to carry his cross, had an illness and must die of cancer.[47]

For Jung, shocking as this sounds, White's death was connected to his inability to fully embrace Jung's psychology. The image of Christ crucified is a symbol of the crucifixion of the ego as it suffers the "agonizing suspension" of irreconcilable opposites.[48] Just as

Christ was sacrificed to the father, so the ego is sacrificed to the unconscious. After death comes rebirth as Christ is resurrected in the Spirit, a symbol of the individuated Self.[49] This theme of the dying and rising god as a symbol of individuation was prominent in White's writings. In his own life, however, Jung thought that, like Christ, Victor White could not acknowledge the Shadow and could not therefore undergo the crucifixion of the ego that was necessary for wholeness. Subsequently, in Jung's psychic worldview, death was forced upon him and he was crucified.

Victor White: Crucified and Redeemed

In one of his earliest articles on Jung's psychology, published in 1942, Victor White was absolutely emphatic that any dialogue with Jung would be predicated on a clear distinction between psychology and theology.[50] This is highly significant because it indicates White's awareness—from the beginning—of the basic incompatibility with Jung on the issue of Christian doctrines about God, and it further serves to repudiate scholarly criticisms of White's "naive embrace" of Jung. This ultimate incompatibility should not, however, undermine the intrinsic value of the contributions that Victor White made in responding to the impact of Jungian psychology on Catholic theology.[51] In drawing this work to a conclusion, I will focus on four points which highlight White's contributions to the field of Catholic theology and Jungian psychology and establish him as an important Dominican theologian of the twentieth century.

First, Victor White was one of the first Catholic theologians to respond to the challenge of Jung. Jung himself remarked how, after several failed attempts at dialogue, his long-held desire for fruitful collaboration with a Catholic theologian had finally become a reality with White. This he attributed to the fact that White was the "only" theologian to have truly understood him, to respect the boundaries of his empirical method, and to have seen the import and the implications of his work.[52]

Not only was White one of the first Catholic theologians to consider the impact of Jung and his psychology, but (and this is my second point) his work in this field was deemed exceptional. In his day he had a reputation for being the best expositor and interpreter of Jung's psychology in Europe.[53] Eminent scholars of analytical psychology acclaimed White's psychology as not only on a par with scholarly work in the field but as exceeding that of those trained in analytical psychology.[54] Theologians repeatedly affirmed his work as "the best account available of modern thought about the relationship between analytical psychology, anthropology and traditional Christian theology."[55] Even today, White's pioneer work is applauded as "one of the most significant attempts to mend the split between psychology and religion."[56] As the preceding pages indicate, this is seen predominantly in White's stance of a dialectical supplementation in relation to Jung. Although White's attempt to heal Jung's psychology of its deficiencies ultimately failed, one cannot overlook White's significance as a pioneer in the field.

Further, and this brings me to my third point, the lessons to be learned from the doctrinal incompatibility of Jung's psychology and White's theology have proved immensely valuable to subsequent scholarship. For example, the ultimate failure of the Jung–White dialogue is in many ways a failure precipitated by White's commitment to divine transcendence and Jung's to divine immanence. Although some progress was made by White in recovering a theology of immanence in the Thomistic tradition (and any further discussion on Aquinas and Jung could, I believe, develop this),[57] the ultimate failure of discussion on this level is significant in highlighting that compatibility with Jung would be more likely with a more radical conception of God's immanence.

The most significant contribution since White in this area can be seen in the work of Catholic priest and Jungian analyst John Dourley. Critical of theologies of transcendence such as those of White which, he argued, ultimately "uproot" a human being from the "divine vitalities of its depths," he suggested that any compatibility between Jung and Christian theology focus on "theologies of radical immanence" such as Paul Tillich's notion of God as "the ground of Being."[58] In addition, and from a distinctly Thomistic perspective, there are certainly possibilities, as F. X. Charet has suggested, for potentially fruitful discussion between Jung and the transcendental Thomism espoused by the likes of Karl Rahner and Bernard Lonergan.[59]

My fourth point deals with the (unconscious!) influence of White on the subsequent direction of Catholic–Jungian dialogue and Catholic Dominican theology. Since White's death, the impact of Jung on Catholicism both directly and indirectly has been enormous, from scholarly attempts to "heal the split" between Jung and Catholicism to the use of the Myers-Briggs personality type indicators in many seminaries. In recent years there has been a renewed suspicion of such techniques, a series of responses to the threat posed by Jung to Christianity,[60] and a number of vociferous attacks on Jungian psychology as a kind of Trojan horse—an initially attractive yet ultimately insidious infiltration of Jungian heresy into the Catholic Church.[61]

Jung continues to have an impact directly and indirectly on Catholic theology as others continue on the trail opened by White. For some scholars, this entails a total rejection of Jung as incompatible with and threatening to Christianity.[62] For others it entails the reinterpretation of Christianity from a Jungian perspective to bring about a revitalization.[63] And, for still others, it entails the identification of Christianity and Jungian psychology as having the same healing effect on the psyche.[64] It is testimony to White's pioneer work that an element of each of these contemporary approaches (which are by no means exhaustive) was seen in some way in his work.

White's caution that Jung was "no friend" of religion[65] and his ultimate rejection of Jung's transformation of the God image as incompatible with and threatening to traditional Christianity[66] corresponds to the first approach. His personal experience of the revitalization of theology by Jung's psychology corresponds to the second approach. And, his consideration of the identification of the healing effects wrought by dogma and by psychology corresponds to the third approach. Although White finally distanced himself from Jung on the question of God and Christian doctrine, he continued, until his death in 1960, to assimilate Jung's theories of personality and his idea that a reconnection with the religious nature of the psyche is essential to human flourishing.

In addition, White's influence on the direction of the English Province of the Order of Preachers is multiply attested from his role as the "liberator" from dogmatic Thomism to the indebtedness of his most famous student of Aquinas, the late Herbert McCabe, O. P. In many ways, White's encounter with Jung revitalized not only his own theology but that of the whole English Dominican Province. He challenged the overly rational approach of the neo-scholastics and encouraged a return to a Thomistic engagement with secular knowledge, thereby contributing to the renewal of Catholic Dominican theology.

Victor White was truly a remarkable theologian. He saw in Thomism "a vital organism, embryonic, but endowed with an infinite capacity for the assimilation of new truth and for adjustment to new conditions and environments without loss of its substantial identity."[67] Propelled by this vision, White sought to appropriate in his own theology an openness to the ideas and the questions of his day, to engage with secular knowledge, to make a critical yet sympathetic study of the views of those, like Jung, with whom he disagreed, and to bring whatever he found of truth into the unity of his own synthesis.[68]

Whereas scholasticism had failed to truly understand that Thomas' synthesis, centered in God, was "his great gift to mankind,"[69] Victor White did, and it became his great gift. With all of its successes and its failures, White's personal and theological consideration of the impact of Jung is a phenomenal example of this continuing attempt at Thomistic synthesis. Without a doubt, it is Victor White's greatest contribution to twentieth-century Catholic Dominican theology.

Notes

In citing works, letters, etc. in the notes, short titles have generally been used. A few works, frequently cited, have been identified by the following abbreviations:

CW Read, Sir Herbert, Michael Fordham, Gerhard Adler and William McGuire, eds.. *The Collected Works of C.G. Jung.* Trans. R. F. C. Hull. London: Routledge and Kegan Paul, 1953–1979.

Letters I Adler, Gerhard, and Aniela Jaffé, eds. *C. G. Jung: Letters Volume I, 1906–1950.* London: Routledge and Kegan Paul, 1973.

Letters II Adler, Gerhard, and Aniela Jaffé, eds. *C. G. Jung: Letters Volume II, 1951–1961.* London: Routledge and Kegan Paul, 1976.

MDR Jung, C. G. *Memories, Dreams, Reflections.* Aniela Jaffé, ed. New York: Vintage Books Edition, 1965.

As indicated in the bibliography, the *Archives of the English Province of the Order of Preachers* in Edinburgh is referred to in the notes as the *E. P. O. P. Archives.*

Introduction

1. Fordham, "Letter to White," 14 March 1958 (bibliog. 2.3).
2. Jung, "Letter to White," 1 October 1945, in *Letters I*, 387. This source erroneously shows this letter was dated 5 October 1945.
3. This articulation of Thomas' vision is found in Vann, *Saint Thomas Aquinas* (bibliog. 1.1), 177, and seems consistent with White's approach.
4. McKinnon, "Foreword" (bibliog. 1.1), xii.
5. Gilby, "Personae 6. Victor White" (bibliog. 1.1), 284.
6. Cunningham, "The Fateful Encounter" (bibliog. 1.1).
7. Stein, *Jung's Treatment of Christianity* (bibliog. 1.1, 1986), 5–8; and Stein, *Jung on Christianity* (bibliog. 1.1, 1995), 12–20.
8. Arraj, "Jungian Spirituality" (bibliog. 1.1).
9. Charet, "A Dialogue" (bibliog. 1.1).
10. See, for example, Dourley, "Exercises in Futility" (bibliog. 1.1); Dourley, *The Rerooting* (bibliog. 1.1); Dourley, "The Challenge of Jung's Psychology" (bibliog. 1.1); Dourley, "Jung's Conversations with Buber and White" (bibliog. 1.1); Dourley, "Jung's Impact on Religious Studies" (bibliog. 1.1); Dourley, "The

Religious Implications of Jung's Psychology" (bibliog. 1.1); and Dourley, "The
Religious Significance of Jung's Psychology" (bibliog. 1.1).

11. Cunningham, "Victor White, John Layard, and C. G. Jung" (bibliog. 1.1),
44–57.

12. Bair, *Jung: A Biography* (bibliog. 1.1), 544–48.

13. Gaine, "Review of *Dominican Gallery*" (bibliog. 1.1), 159.

14. This adds a multiplicity of perspectives to that of the now deceased ex-
Dominican Camoldese hermit, Aelred Squire, O.S.B., who was interviewed by
Lammers for her work, *In God's Shadow* (bibliog. 1.1). Lammers presented White
as a loner, with Squire his only real friend in the Order (though it should be noted
that Squire was White's student, not his contemporary). Adrian Cunningham, on
the other hand, noted White's close friendships with Gerald Vann, O. P., and
Richard Kehoe, O. P. Evidence in the *E. P. O. P. Archives* and interviews with a
dozen Dominicans who knew White at Oxford lead me to side with Cunningham
on this issue.

15. Gilby, "Personae 6" (bibliog. 1.1), 283.

Chapter One: 1902–1940

1. See *Provincial Actus*, 1962 (bibliog. 1.1) and the *E. P. O. P. Archives*. White
also mentioned this to Jung in a letter (bibliog. 2.2, 10 August 1952).

2. John Henry White, son of Rev. John White and Jane Dawson, was born in
1865. He was educated at Cambridge, and married Beatrice Mary, the daughter of
a merchant, James Phillips, at St. Peter's Croydon on June 4, 1901. They were married by John Henry's father, Rev. John White. From 1902 to 1918, John Henry was
vicar of St. Augustine's Croydon, living at 39 Avondale Road. His next appoint-
ment was as vicar of Barlescombe Somerset (1918–21), and then vicar of St. Mary's
Tyndalls Park Bristol (1921–34). His brother (White's uncle), Rev. Frederick
Ernest White (1853–1929), was also a vicar. He was educated at Merchant Taylor's
School and worked as a clerk in London until 1882, when he matriculated at
Oxford. There he was awarded a Third in Theology in 1885, was ordained, and,
after nine years as a curate, became vicar of St. Stephen's Dulwich 1894–1915. See
Letter from Smith and Letter from D. White (bibliog. 2.5).

Like White's family, Jung's was also dominated by clerics: there were six
uncles and a grandfather who were parsons on his mother's side and two parsons
on his father's side. See *MDR*, 42.

3. Morris, *Religion and Urban Change* (bibliog. 1.1), 53.

4. On November 16, 1951, White gave the final talk in the BBC series, "The
Dying God," from which this quote is taken. See White, "The Dying God: Pagan,
Psychological and Christian: Differences," (bibliog. 1.4, 1952), 114.

5. Ten years Victor's junior, John Francis Christopher was born in January
1912. He received his B.A. from Lampeter before serving in the army as a chaplain.
He was vicar of All Saints Upper Norwood (1950–57), and then Vicar of Ramsgate

(1957–64). His final post was as vicar of Farnborough with Avon Dassett (1964–69). He died in 1971. White's youngest brother, Basil Phillip Dawson, was born in March 1913. He later worked as a commercial clerk. See Letter from Smith and Letter from D. White (bibliog. 2.5).

6. It is clear from Jung's *Letters* that White shared some of his experiences of his time in Valladolid with Jung. See Jung, "Letter to White," 31 December 1949, in *Letters I*, 541.

7. Most notable in his year was Gerald Vann, O. P., who would also be influenced by the work of C. G. Jung, as can be seen particularly in his work, *The Water and the Fire* (bibliog. 1.1), which devotes a large section to the recovery of symbol.

8. White also received training in French, German, Spanish, Italian, and Latin (which he later wrote that he "could read fairly easily"). See White, "Letter to Jung," (bibliog. 2.2, 9 October 1945). He also shared with Jung the thought that it was the training he received at Hawkesyard which led to the need for the help of an analyst in the 1940s. See White, "Letter to Jung," (bibliog. 2.2, 14 October 1945).

9. Pope, "Why Divorce our Teaching?" (bibliog. 1.1). He was informed that he was unsuitable as a teacher at a pontifical college. See Mulvey, *Hugh Pope* (bibliog. 1.1), 45-48.

10. Pius X, "*Contra neo-reformismum religiosum*" (bibliog. 1.1), 266–69.

11. Pius X, "*Lamentabili Sane*" (bibliog. 1.1), 470–78.

12. Pius X, "*Pascendi Domini Gregis*" (bibliog. 1.1), 593–650.

13. See Pius X, "*Doctoris Angelici*" (bibliog. 1.1), 336–41.

14. See Pius X, "*Sacrorum Antistitum*" (bibliog. 1.1), 655–80. White, too, was required to take this oath in order to teach dogmatic theology at Blackfriars Oxford.

15. White, *Soul and Psyche* (bibliog. 1.4, 1960), 274n1. By *modernists* I mean those—such as Loisy, von Hügel, and Tyrrell—who were part of the liberal Catholic movement. The term *modernism* was used in Pius X's encyclical, "*Pascendi Domini Gregis*" (bibliog. 1.1), to condemn those in the Catholic liberal movement whom he saw as part of an inside conspiracy to undermine the Church. This usage of *modernism* is distinct from (though not unrelated to) philosophical modernism—which is characterised by the epistemological primacy of reason, the progressive nature of human history, and the ethical uniqueness of the individual.

16. See Daly, *Transcendence and Immanence* (bibliog. 1.1), 199–200.

17. Leo XIII, "*Aeterni Patris*" (bibliog. 1.1), 97–115.

18. See Pius X, "*Doctoris Angelici*" (bibliog. 1.1), 336–41.

19. Ibid.

20. Ashley, *The Dominicans* (bibliog. 1.1), 219.

21. Interview with Ryan (bibliog. 2.5). See, for example, Mercier, *Manual* (bibliog. 1.1).

22. Pius XI, "*Studiorum Ducem*" (bibliog. 1.1), 309–26.

23. Code of Canon Law, Canons 589.1, 1366.2.

24. Ryan, "Funeral Homily" (bibliog. 1.1), 308–12. Ryan echoed the words of the prophet Daniel, "Of those sleeping in the Land of Dust, many will awaken, some to everlasting life, some to shame and everlasting disgrace." (Dan 12:2).

25. *Provincial Actus*, 1962 (bibliog. 1.1).

26. Lammers indicated that White lived and studied at Louvain in 1931. See Lammers, *In God's Shadow* (bibliog. 1.1), 46. But information in the *E. P. O. P. Archives* suggests that it was, in fact, two years prior to that—in 1929.

27. *Institute of Philosophy for the Study of Scholasticism.*

28. See Livingston, "Moments of Recovery and Conservatism" in Livingston et al., eds., *Modern Christian Thought* (bibliog. 1.1), 1:327–55; and Fiorenza, "The New Theology and Transcendental Thomism" in Livingston et al., *Modern Christian Thought* (bibliog. 1.1), 2:197–232.

29. Strictly speaking, those referred to as neo-scholastics at Blackfriars Oxford were neo-Thomists, although, as Livingston points out, the terms became historically identical from the time of Leo XIII's encyclical "*Aeterni Patris*" (bibliog. 1.1), when Thomas was elevated above the other scholastics. See Livingston et al., *Modern Christian Thought* (bibliog. 1.1), 2:342.

30. Jarrett, "Letter to Alban King," 4 October 1929, in Bailey, Tugwell, and Bellinger, eds., *Letters of Bede Jarrett* (bibliog. 1.1), 234. Stanislas Martin Gillet, O. P. (1875–1951), was Bede Jarrett's professor, and became Master General of the Order in 1929.

31. Ibid. His vision reached fruition in 1994, when Blackfriars Hall became a permanent private hall of the University of Oxford.

32. In the *E. P. O. P. Archives* there is a 70-page (incomplete) dissertation (the final pages are either lost or the work is unfinished), "Platonism of St. Thomas Aquinas" (bibliog. 2.1). In it, White tried to show how Aquinas brought not only Aristotle but also Plato into his synthesis. White presented some of this in abbreviated form in a lecture, "On Thomas and Platonic Ideas" (bibliog. 2.1). He developed this in 1941 in an article, "The Platonic Tradition in St. Thomas Aquinas" (bibliog. 1.4, 1941), also printed in White, *God the Unknown* (bibliog. 1.4, 1956). This is interesting, for Jung's idea of the archetypes of the collective unconscious was deeply neo-Platonic, as White and Jung both realized.

33. Interview with Ryan (bibliog. 2.5).

34. Interview with Rigney (bibliog. 2.5).

35. Ibid.

36. McCabe, "Foreword," in *God Matters* (bibliog. 1.1), v.

37. Letter from Meath (bibliog. 2.5).

38. Letter from Hill (bibliog. 2.5).

39. Interview with Ryan (bibliog. 2.5).

40. Daly, *Transcendence and Immanence* (bibliog. 1.1), 218, 5–6.

41. Interview with Ryan (bibliog. 2.5).

42. *Acta Capituli Provincialis* (bibliog. 1.1), 56.

43. It is worth remembering that, in 1867, under its Prefect Allesandro Cardinal Barnabò (1856–1874), The Sacred Congregation for the Propagation of the Faith (Propaganda Fide), had requested that the bishops explain that it was "next to impossible" for a Catholic to attend a non-Catholic university without "an intrinsic and very serious danger to purity of morals, as well as faith." See Evennett, "Catholics and the Universities" (bibliog. 1.1). The request

of this Congregation was modified in 1895 on the condition that Catholics attended compulsory lectures taught by Catholics in subjects such as philosophy, theology, and history.

44. White, "Scholasticism" (bibliog. 1.4, 1932); and in Messenger, ed., *Studies in Comparative Religion* (bibliog. 1.1, 1934) 4:27.

45. Ibid., 4:24, 19.

46. Ibid., 4:20

47. Ibid., 4:31.

48. Ibid., 4:29.

49. Mackinnon, "Foreword", p. xii, in Cornelius Ernst O. P., *Multiple Echo* (bibliog. 1.1).

50. See, for example, these articles by White: "Leo XIII on Reunion" (bibliog. 1.4, 1934); "A Reunion Movement in Germany" (bibliog. 1.4, 1935); "An Evangelical Approach to Catholicism" (bibliog. 1.4, 1936); "Faith" (bibliog. 1.4, 1937); "The Background to Papal Infallibility" (bibliog. 1.4, 1937); "Doctrine in the Church of England" (bibliog. 1.4, 1938); "Faith in the Church of England" (bibliog. 1.4, 1938); "Christendoms, New or Old" (bibliog. 1.4, 1938); and "Reunion in Catholicity" (bibliog. 1.4, 1939). See also White, trans., Yves Congar's *Chrétiens désunis* (bibliog. 1.4, 1939). See also Nichols, *Dominican Gallery* (bibliog. 1.1), 58–60, 67, 86–92.

51. Congar also became a controversial figure, banned from entering Blackfriars Oxford in the 1950s by Hilary Carpenter. Congar stayed in Blackfriars Cambridge in 1954, but even there his movements were restricted. He was ordered "to restrict contact with Anglicans to a minimum and to remain silent on ecumenical questions." See Nichols, *Yves Congar* (bibliog. 1.1), 7.

52. These letters are not in the Bibliography, but are in the *E. P. O. P. Archives.* See also Nichols, *Dominican Gallery* (bibliog. 1.1), 56–57.

53. See, for example, these articles by White, "The Christian Revolution" (bibliog. 1.4, 1934); "The Case for Italy" (bibliog. 1.4, 1935); "Wars and Rumours of Wars" (bibliog. 1.4, 1939); and "War and the Early Church" (bibliog. 1.4, 1939).

Chapter Two: 1940–1945

1. Cunningham, "The Fateful Encounter" (bibliog. 1.1), 321. See bibliog. 1.4 and bibliog. 2.1 for White's 1930s writings.

2. Interview with Rigney (bibliog. 2.5).

3. Fordham, "Memories and Thoughts" (bibliog. 1.1), 105. Jung's Presidency of the Congress was very controversial and resulted in accusations of anti-Semitism. Initially named the General Medical Society for Psychotherapy, and based in Germany, its president, Ernst Kretschmer, had resigned when the Nazis came to power. Kretschmer feared that the Nazis would impose their ideology on the society and so, in a political move, he persuaded Carl Jung, a Swiss, to take over in June 1933. As president, Jung internationalized the society. However,

Kretschmer's fears were well founded. Three months later, the Germans created a Nazi section of the society in Berlin, and used the international journal of the society, *Zentralblatt,* which was edited by Jung, as a vehicle for Nazi propaganda— producing a supplement supporting Hitler and distributing it internationally without Jung's knowledge. Although Jung did not resign until 1940, a number of Jewish scholars, notably Gershom Scholem and Rabbi Leo Baeck, were convinced of Jung's innocence. Fordham has argued that Jung befriended Jews and helped many escape persecution (Ibid., 105).

4. White, "Letter to Layard" (bibliog. 2.2, 19 September 1940). It is worth noting that White suffered professional disappointment in 1940, when after only a few months as editor of *Blackfriars*, he was replaced by Conrad Pepler, O. P. See interview with Bailey (bibliog. 2.5).

5. White, "Letter to Layard" (bibliog. 2.2, 19 September 1940).

6. Layard had studied anthropology at Cambridge, and difficulties he met in writing *The Stone Men of Malekula* (bibliog. 1.1) led him into analysis with H. G. Baynes. In the 1930s, he moved to Oxford where he was attached to the Anthropology Department. Layard started his own psychotherapeutic practice there, and his analysands included Vera von der Heydt (see "Obituary of Vera von der Heydt" in *The Times*, November 26, 1996; and "Obituary" in *The Daily Telegraph*, November 25, 1996). He also founded the Psychology and Religion Society with which White would be much involved, but this folded when Layard decided to go to Zurich to be analyzed by Jung. See Fordham and Gordon, "Obituary Notices: John Layard" (bibliog. 1.1).

7. Doris and John Layard were both received into the Catholic Church, though Doris much earlier than John. She took instruction from Victor White and White's great friend in the Order, Richard Kehoe, O. P., and later from Ian Hislop, O. P. Before her reception into the Catholic faith, Doris, who was also a Jungian analyst, is said to have had a dream of a black pony coming home to Blackfriars and lying down in the Church. See interview with Bailey (bibliog. 2.5).

8. See White, "St. Albert's Lectures" (bibliog. 2.1).

9. *MDR*, 93.

10. Ibid., 40.

11. Ibid., 94.

12. Ibid., 40; and Jung, "Letter to Pastor Walter Bernet" in *Letters II*, 257. See also *MDR* 52, 55, 93–96.

13. *MDR*, 69.

14. Ryan, "Funeral Homily" (bibliog. 1.1), 308–12. Ryan echoed the words of the prophet Daniel, "Of those sleeping in the Land of Dust, many will awaken, some to everlasting life, some to shame and everlasting disgrace." (Dan 12:2).

15. Jung, *Psychology and Religion* (bibliog. 1.2, 1938), 72.

16. *MDR*, 69.

17. White, "Letter to Jung" (bibliog. 2.2, 14 October 1945).

18. White, "Scholasticism" (bibliog. 1.4, 1934), 30.

19. White, "Letter to Layard" (bibliog. 2.2, 20 November 1940), addressed from Poppetts Hill Cottage near Tatsworth, Oxon. It was Fr. Richard Kehoe, O. P., who

persuaded White, despite his resistance, to "take the plunge" and go back to the Dominicans. See White, "Letter to Layard" (bibliog. 2.2, 22 November 1940). Kehoe was a contemporary of White, and on all accounts, he was White's best friend in the Order—see interviews with Bailey, Lloyd, and Rigney (bibliog. 2.5). They taught in the Studium at Blackfriars Oxford together, and, as a scripture scholar, Kehoe shared White's developing interest in archetypal symbolism. (White was devastated when Kehoe left the order). White spoke to Layard about Kehoe as his "great friend" and Kehoe often featured in White's dreams. See White, "Noctuary" (bibliog. 2.4).

20.   Bernard Delany, O. P., succeeded Bede Jarrett, O. P. (who had refounded Blackfriars Oxford as a House of Studies in 1921) as Provincial, elected at Woodchester on September 5, 1932. He was re-elected in London on May 5, 1936, and his four-year term of office was extended by Rome, on account of the war, until 1942. See Gumbley, *Dominican Obituary Notices* (bibliog. 1.1).

21.   White, "Letter to Layard" (bibliog. 2.2, 22 September 1940).

22.   White, "Letter to Layard" (bibliog. 2.2, 29 December 1940). See also Nichols, *Dominican Gallery* (bibliog. 1.1), 59.

23.   White, "Letter to Layard" (bibliog. 2.2, 10 December 1940).

24.   Fry, "Memoir" (bibliog. 1.1), 9.

25.   Layard, "Letter to White" (bibliog. 2.3, 3 January 1941).

26.   White, "Letter to Layard" (bibliog. 2.2, 12 January 1941).

27.   Interviews with Bailey (bibliog. 2.5), and correspondence with Brogan (bibliog. 2.5). In Fry, "Memoir" (bibliog. 1.1), 9, he argued that the main reason for the collapse of this ecumenical initiative was an inability to attract suitable people.

28.   Conversation with Bailey (bibliog. 2.5). It is interesting to note that Jung also suffered mental turmoil in the period 1913–16. During this time Jung "plunged down into dark depths," where he encountered and talked with imaginary characters, the most significant being Philemon. Philemon was an old man lame in one foot who had the wings of a kingfisher and the horns of a bull and carried four keys. Philemon was experienced by Jung as a real person, and Jung's identification with him is, in itself, very interesting. Philemon and Baucis were a couple who (in mythology) housed the gods who were wandering the earth. In Goethe's *Faust,* Faust caused the murder of this couple, symbolically signifying the end of man's understanding of himself in relation to the gods. In fact, the inscription over Jung's Tower at Bollingen reads "Philemonis Sacrum, Fausti Poenitentia" (shrine of Philemon, repentance of Faust), symbolizing Jung's desire to worship Philemon and atone for Faust's crime. See Giegerich, "Jung's Betrayal of His Truth" (bibliog 1.1), 46–47.

In his controversial book *The Aryan Christ* (bibliog. 1.1), Noll used the original transcript of Jung's exploration of his own unconscious, rather than the later version in Jung, *MDR*, ch. 6, and told how—during an exercise in active imagination—Jung imagined himself to be a lion-headed god. Noll suggested that it was following this experience that Jung was convinced that Freud should have tried to convert psychoanalysis into a religion. Jung himself, therefore, decided to create a new religion purged of its Jewishness in which he would be the Aryan Christ.

Although Jung would deny that his psychology was a new religion—for example in his "Reply to Martin Buber" in *CW*, 18:669—Noll's theory, though highly speculative, is not without interest. This episode happened after the Freud period (1907–13) when Freud thought that he was preparing his "beloved son" as his successor—the man who would take the "Jewish" doctrine of psychoanalysis to the Gentiles. Freud wrote to Jung, on April 16, 1909, of an incident that had occurred a month earlier: "I formally adopted you as eldest son and anointed you—*in patribus infidelium*—as my successor and crown prince." Years later, after White's breakdown at about the same age as Jung (and, without pushing the analogy too far, White seeing himself as the one taking analytical psychology to Catholics, and yet purging it of its "heresies"), it is clear from their correspondence that Jung thought that he was grooming White as his successor—in his own words as the one who would "carry on the *magnum opus*." Like Freud and Jung, Jung and White would also split over ideological differences.

29.   During this period of analysis, White started to write an autobiography—which he also referred to as "the record of healing." Only a small part of it remains, and we shall probably never know whether the rest was lost or the process was aborted. But it does show White's desire to become more aware of himself and his life, and it is deeply revealing about the man. It begins: "It is difficult to know where to begin this story, for I do not yet know where it is going to end. Perhaps I shall never know: perhaps it never does end. And until I know the end, I shall never know its real beginning. For even were I to introduce the story with a wearisome complete autobiography, still I should not begin from the beginning. I should have to go much further back than the limits of my conscious memory will take me; back to infancy; back to my parents; back to their wombs and their parents and so ad infinitum. Back, perhaps, to palaeolithic and anthropoid ancestors, back to Eden, back to primaeval swamps, back to the Mind of God. And that is just what, as yet I cannot do. I cannot know the beginning until I know the end; and when I know the End, I shall know the beginning." See White, "Autobiography" (bibliog. 2.1).

30.   Kehoe was interested in scripture and symbolism, an interest he shared with White, as can be seen in an article that White kept of Kehoe's, "Baptism and Archetypal Rebirth" (now in the *E. P. O. P. Archives*).

31.   White, "Letter to Layard" (bibliog. 2.2, 22 September 1940).

32.   White, "Letter to Layard" (bibliog. 2.2, November 4, 5–6, 7 1940). It is unclear what these "heresies" were, as White offered no explanation of them. It is possible that the words are misspelled, it being a handwritten letter, though there seems to be no close alternative. It is most likely that these words are made up, common only to White and Layard. In any case, my guess is that "symolismus" has something to do with making symbols themselves the ultimate realities, and "immancatismus" relates to immanence—which would make sense for a Jungian who is basically an immanentist and would have little notion of transcendence outside of the psyche.

33.   White, "The Predicament of the Psychologist" (bibliog. 2.1).

34.   White, "Letter to Layard" (bibliog. 2.2, 29 and 30 December 1940). In fact, *Golden Flower*, or in its fuller title *The Secret of the Golden Flower*, was not written

by Jung but is a Taoist text concerned with Chinese yoga and is, moreover, a Chinese alchemy text. Jung had read it in 1928, and, as he recalled, in *MDR*, ch.7, it was this text that stirred in him the desire to become more acquainted with alchemy. Alchemy was important to Jung because he thought that it provided "the historical counterpart" to the processes of the collective unconscious. In 1938, Jung translated it and wrote "Commentary on *The Secret of the Golden Flower*" in *CW*, 13:1–56. Presumably it is this to which White referred.

35.   See, for example, Lammers, *In God's Shadow* (bibliog. 1.1), 245; Dourley, "Exercises in Futility" (bibliog. 1.1), ch. 2; and Dourley, *The Rerooting* (bibliog. 1.1), 230.

36.   White, "Letter to Layard" (bibliog. 2.2, 20 November 1940).

37.   "Christian suspicions of Jung are to be allayed . . . if there is really to be collaboration rather than opposition." White, "Letter to Layard," (bibliog. 2.2, 20 November 1940).

38.   Ibid.

39.   See, for example, Jung, "Why I Am Not a Catholic" in *CW*, 18: 645–47.

40.   Ibid.

41.   Pius X, "*Sacrorum Antistitum*" (bibliog. 1.1), 655–80.

42.   Ibid.

43.   Ibid. This oath was required of teachers of dogmatic theology and was often also taken by clerics upon receiving holy orders. See Denzinger and Schönmetzer, eds. *Enchiridion* (bibliog. 1.1), no.3542.

44.   White, "Letter to Layard" (bibliog. 2.2, 20 November 1940).

45.   Pius X, "*Sacrorum Antistitum*" (bibliog. 1.1).

46.   White, "Plain Talks on Fundamentals: III Revelation" (bibliog. 1.4, 1936), 840.

47.   White, "Letter to Layard" (bibliog. 2.2, 5 December 1940).

48.   See, for example, Jung, *CW*, 10:328.

49.   Jung, *Psychology and Religion* (bibliog. 1.2, 1938), 1, 3.

50.   Jung, "Letter to White," 5 October 1945, in *Letters I*, 384.

51.   White, "Review of R. Scott Frayn's *Revelation and the Unconscious*" (bibliog. 1.4, 1941), 312–15; also cited in Cunningham, "The Fateful Encounter" (bibliog. 1.1), 321.

52.   White, op. cit., 312.

53.   This was published as a pamphlet, "The Frontiers of Theology and Psychology" (bibliog. 1.4, 1942), and was later revised as "Freud, Jung and God" in White, *God and the Unconscious* (bibliog. 1.4, 1982), ch. 4.

54.   Frayn, "Letter to White" (bibliog. 2.3, 29 September 1942); Adler, "Letter to White" (bibliog. 2.2, 12 July 1942); O'Driscoll, "Letter to White" (bibliog. 2.2, 10 September 1942). O'Driscoll was formerly White's Prior in Oxford but was elected Provincial at Woodchester on April 28, 1942. He resigned office on October 27, 1945 and died shortly afterward. See Gumbley, *Dominican Obituary Notices* (bibliog. 1.1). In the letter, O'Driscoll expressed that he thought White's lecture should be published but that it should be "more specifically Catholic," noting that this suggestion came from White's contemporary in the Order, Mark Brocklehurst, O. P.

55. White, "Letter to Layard" (bibliog. 2.2, 20 November 1940).

56. White, "The Frontiers" (bibliog. 1.4, 1942), 17.

57. Ibid., 5.

58. See, for example, Jung, "Letter to White" (bibliog. 1.3, 24 November 1953) in *Letters II*, 135–38.

59. Dourley, *The Rerooting* (bibliog. 1.1), 130.

60. Jung believed that the psyche was naturally driven to this state but that very few, if any, actually achieved individuation.

61. Dourley, *The Rerooting* (bibliog. 1.1), 23, 130–31. See also Dourley, "Religious Implications" (bibliog. 1.1), 187; and Dourley, *Love, Celibacy and Inner Marriage* (bibliog. 1.1), 71.

62. Sometimes also referred to as "metaphysical reductionism."

63. Jung, *CW*, 11:482. Some years later, in 1952, Martin Buber charged Jung with psychologism. For the discussion which ensued between Jung and Buber, see Jung, "Religion and Psychology: A Reply to Martin Buber" in *CW*, 18:663–70.

64. *CW*, 13:50–51.

65. White, "The Frontiers" (bibliog. 1.4, 1942), 16. In fact White would later defend Jung against the charge of "psychologism" made by Raymond Hostie, accusing Hostie of "philosophism." See White, "Critical Notice on Hostie's Religion and the Psychology of Jung" (bibliog. 1.4, 1958).

66. Ibid., 19, 18.

67. *CW*, 12:11 n.6.

68. Dourley, *The Rerooting*, 228.

69. See, for example, Jung's letter to Catholic psychologist Josef Goldbrunner in *CW*, 18:707.

70. White, "Faith" (bibliog. 1.4, 1937), 34–41.

71. Jung, "Religion and Psychology: A Reply to Martin Buber" in *CW*, 18:663–70.

72. White, op. cit., 15.

73. Jung, *Psychology and Religion* (bibliog. 1.2), 73.

74. White, op.cit., 15–16.

75. White, *God and the Unconscious* (bibliog. 1.4, 1961), 88.

76. White, "Psychotherapy and Ethics: A Postscript" (bibliog. 1.4, 1944), 387.

77. Dourley, The Rerooting (bibliog. 1.1), 23, 130–31. See also Dourley, "Religious Implications" (bibliog. 1.1), 187; and Dourley, *Love, Celibacy and Inner Marriage* (bibliog. 1.1), 71.

78. Ibid., 23

79. Dourley, "The Religious Implications" (bibliog. 1.1), 177.

80. White, "The Frontiers" (bibliog. 1.4, 1942), 17.

81. White, *God and the Unconscious* (bibliog. 1.4, 1961), 89.

82. Ibid, 91.

83. White, "Thomism Part I" (bibliog. 1.4, 1943); "Thomism Part II" (bibliog. 1.4, 1943); and "Thomism Part III" (bibliog. 1.4, 1944).

84. See Dourley, *The Rerooting* (bibliog. 1.1), 132.

85. White, "Thomism Part I" (bibliog. 1.4, 1943), 12.

86. Ibid., 14, cf. Aquinas, *Summa Theologiae* (bibliog. 1.1), 1a.66.1. References to the *Summa* in this book cite the part, question, and article. So, 1a.66.1 indicates *prima pars* (part one), question 66, article 1.

87. White, *Holy Teaching* (bibliog. 1.4, 1958), 16. This parallel of Jung's thinking and feeling judgments with Aquinas' knowledge by study and knowledge by affect also appears in an unpublished six-page manuscript entitled "Thomist Psychology" (bibliog. 2.1) and in White's seminar notes on "Kinds of Opposites" (bibliog. 1.4, 1955), delivered in Zurich (1955) and San Francisco (1956).

88. Aquinas, *Summa Theologiae* (bibliog. 1.1), 2a2ae.45.2, cited in White, "Thomism Part I" (bibliog. 1.4, 1943), 12.

89. See Aquinas, *Summa Theologiae* (bibliog. 1.1), 1a2ae.68.1 ad 4., cited in White, "Thomism Part I" (bibliog. 1.4, 1943), 15.

90. See Aquinas, *Summa Theologiae* (bibliog. 1.1), 2a2ae.9.1 ad 1., cited in White, "Thomism Part I" (bibliog. 1.4, 1943), 15.

91. White, "Thomism Part I" (bibliog. 1.4, 1943), 12.

92. White, "Thomism Part III" (bibliog. 1.4, 1944), 321.

93. White, "Thomism Part I" (bibliog. 1.4, 1943), 15.

94. Ibid., 10.

95. Jung, *Psychology and Religion* (bibliog. 1.2), 72.

96. Dourley, *The Rerooting* (bibliog. 1.1), 1; and Dourley, "The Religious Implications" (bibliog. 1.1), 199. In fact, Dourley goes on to argue that Victor White is "a proponent of uprootedness." See Dourley, *The Rerooting* (bibliog. 1.1), 29.

97. *MDR*, 40.

98. White, "Thomism Part I" (bibliog. 1.4, 1943), 8.

99. Ibid. White used the terms "value perception" and "value experience" interchangeably with "affective knowledge" to mean non-sensory cognitive experience.

100. It is perhaps of some significance that White used von Hügel, the great Catholic modernist, who, as a baron of the Holy Roman Empire, did not suffer the same fate as Fr. Tyrrell. In an interview with Fr. Matthew Rigney, O. P. (bibliog. 2.5), White's former student said it was White and Kehoe who encouraged them to read von Hügel despite the fact that von Hügel was under a cloud of suspicion for being an avowed modernist. This would not have been popular with the rear guard of neo-scholastics at Blackfriars Oxford. Of note also is White's article on von Hügel, "An Orthodox Heresiarch" (bibliog. 1.4, 1937). In fact, it is a review essay of Petre's *Von Hügel and Tyrell* (bibliog. 1.1).

101. In "The Undiscovered Self" Jung wrote: "When any natural human function gets lost, i.e., is denied conscious and intentional expression, a general disturbance results. Hence, it is quite natural that with the triumph of the Goddess of Reason a general neuroticizing of modern man should set in, a dissociation of personality. . . . This boundary line bristling with barbed wire runs through the psyche of modern man." See Jung, "The Undiscovered Self" in Storr, *The Essential Jung* (bibliog. 1.1), 380; and in *CW*, 10:247–305.

102. White, *Soul and Psyche* (bibliog. 1.4, 1960), 274n1.

103. White, *Walter Hilton* (bibliog. 1.4, 1944), 5–6.

104. In fact, White distanced himself not just from the modernists but also from the existentialists and phenomenologists. While he could appreciate the fact that existentialists, like Thomists, viewed knowledge "in its *wholeness* as we experience it," in a footnote in "Thomism and Affective Knowledge Part II" (bibliog. 1.4, 1943), 127 n, White wrote: "We do not of course intend to endorse all the developments of Existentialism and Phenomenology, which have tended to degenerate into anti-metaphysical phenomenalism."

105. Ibid., 129.

106. Jung, *Psychology and Religion* (bibliog. 1.2, 1938), 3.

107. White, *Soul and Psyche* (bibliog. 1.4, 1960), 51. White argued that it is a "linguistic idiosyncrasy" to call something a "truth" which is merely a fact and not a judgment.

108. Giegerich, "Jung's Betrayal of His Truth" (bibliog. 1.1), 59, 62. White also found the expression "psychologically true" to be problematic and indicative of Jung's confusion of fact and truth. In *Soul and Psyche* (bibliog. 1.4, 1960), 88–89, for example, he wrote: "No perceptual fact, be it sensory or imaginative, is of itself true or false. The question of truth or error only arises in judgement, in some affirmation or negation about it."

109. The example White gave is of a patient claiming to be Napoleon. This could be "psychologically true" even though it is quite clearly false in any other sense. See White, *Soul and Psyche* (bibliog. 1.4, 1960), 50–51.

110. White, "Thomism Part I" (bibliog. 1.4, 1943), 8.

111. Ibid., 9.

112. Ibid.

113. White, "Tasks For Thomists" (bibliog. 1.4, 1944), 93–94.

114. White, "Thomism Part III" (bibliog. 1.4, 1944), 322.

115. White, "Review of Febrer's *El Concepto*" (bibliog. 1.4, 1952), 219.

116. Aquinas, *Summa Theologiae* (bibliog. 1.1), 1a.1.8., Cf. White, "Thomism Part I" (bibliog. 1.4, 1943), 12.

117. White, op. cit., 12.

118. Ibid., 12–13.

119. White, "Walter Hilton" (bibliog. 1.4, 1944), 5–23.

120. Ibid., 9.

121. Ibid., 16.

122. Ibid., 20.

123. Ibid., 22.

124. Jung's first encounter with the *anima* came in a dream in which a female temptress tried to deceive him to believe that his fantasies were art, and if they were art he did not have to concern himself with their morality. Arguing with the woman in the dream, Jung later believed that he had encountered the negative aspect of his *anima*: the woman who tempts and deceives. In its positive aspect, *anima/animus* appears when people fall in love and unconsciously project onto the beloved.

125. Ibid., 22.

126. Ibid.

127. Jung, "Letter to Kirsch," 5 March 1954 in *Letters II*, 159. Jung made it quite clear that *only* spiritualities which involved this "conscious confrontation" could bring integration. For this reason, he rejected John of the Cross, for example.

128. White, *The Frontiers* (bibliog. 1.4, 1942), 19.

129. In White, "Thomism Part III" (bibliog. 1.4, 1944), 328, he wrote: "We hope that in a later article it will be possible to piece together these disjointed fragments and to indicate the light they throw on St. Thomas's conception of 'affective knowledge' and to suggest that work still needs to be done to develop his thought in this respect."

130. See, for example, Arraj, *Jungian and Catholic?* (bibliog. 1.1); Dourley, "Exercises in Futility" (bibliog. 1.1); and Dourley, *The Rerooting* (bibliog. 1.1).

131. White, "St. Thomas Aquinas and Jung's Psychology" (bibliog. 1.4, 1945).

132. It is worth noting that Fr. Witcutt left the Church— per an interview with Bailey (bibliog. 2.5). In fact, White joked about this in a letter to his friend the novelist, Antonia White, dated Ascension 1946 (in the *E. P. O. P. Archives*).

133. White, "St. Thomas Aquinas and Jung's Psychology" (bibliog. 1.4, 1944), 209. White wrote: "Neither the depths of the unconscious nor the heights of theological and philosophical speculation hold any terrors for him. From one to the other he passes—we might almost say he gambols—with enviable ease and assurance, unintimidated by any excessive concern for the complexities of the problem he has set himself, or any inhibiting regard for pettifogging accuracy."

134. Ibid.

135. Ibid., 209–10.

136. See also White, "The Frontiers" (bibliog. 1.4, 1942), 23, where he wrote: "The idea that psychotherapy and religion can be kept apart is untenable in the light of traditional Christian teaching (if we accept the principle that 'Grace perfects nature') as Jung has shown it to be untenable psychologically."

137. White, "St. Thomas Aquinas and Jung's Psychology" (bibliog. 1.4, 1945), 212.

138. Ibid. On p. 211, White wrote: "It is not primarily a theoria but a praxis, the theory is only incidental to the therapeutic art—the Heilsweg, the method of liberation and healing."

139. White, "St. Thomas Aquinas and Jung's Psychology" (bibliog. 1.4, 1945), 211.

140. Ibid., 212.

141. Ibid.

142. See, for example, Jung, "Archetypes of the Collective Unconscious" in De Laszlo, *The Basic Writings of C. G. Jung* (bibliog. 1.1), 300–01.

143. Irenaeus, *Adversus haereses* (bibliog. 1.1), II, 7, 5, cited in Jung, "Archetypes of the Collective Unconscious" in De Laszlo, *The Basic Writings of C. G. Jung* (bibliog. 1.1), 300.

144. For a good account of Greek ideas of the psyche and modern psychological experience, see Edinger and Wesley, eds., *The Psyche in Antiquity* (bibliog. 1.1).

145.   White, "St. Thomas Aquinas and Jung's Psychology" (bibliog. 1.4, 1945), 212.
146.   Ibid., 213.
147.   Ibid., 214.
148.   Ibid.
149.   Ibid., 215.
150.   Ibid., 216, citing Aristotle, *Nicomachean Ethics* (bibliog. 1.1), I xiii 7.
151.   White, op. cit., 216.
152.   Ibid.
153.   Ibid., 217
154.   Ibid.
155.   White, "Psychotherapy and Ethics" (bibliog. 1.4, 1945). This article would appear in modified form in White, *God and the Unconscious* (bibliog. 1.4, 1952), ch. 8.
156.   Adler, "Letter to White" (bibliog. 2.2, 18 November 1944). White did in fact practice as an analyst. See Conversation with Giannini (bibliog. 2.5).
157.   White, "Psychotherapy and Ethics" (bibliog. 1.4, 1945), 287.
158.   Ibid., 287–88.
159.   Ibid., 296.
160.   Ibid., 295.
161.   White, "Psychotherapy and Ethics: A PostScript" (bibliog. 1.4, 1945), 386.
162.   Ibid.
163.   White, "Psychotherapy and Ethics" (bibliog. 1.4, 1945), 299.
164.   White, "Psychotherapy and Ethics: A Postscript" (bibliog. 1.4, 1945), 386. However, in a heavily annotated version of this article in the *E. P. O. P. Archives*, which looks like the text of a talk given to the Newman Association (1945), White deleted this sentence.
165.   Ibid.
166.   White, "Psychotherapy and Ethics" (bibliog. 1.4, 1945), 298. Jung agreed with White on this. In his *Letters*, in which he responded to this article that White had sent to him (5 October 1945) he wrote: "I sympathise fully with you when you say: 'The task before us is gigantic indeed.' It is enormous and I marvel at the intellectual pachydermia of those who ought to know better and who didn't take notice apparently, or worse—who try to get rid of the octopus by the most futile arguments. I have frequent discussions with Catholic as well as Protestant theologians. As a rule they are astonishingly innocent of actual psychological experience and often seem to have forgotten the wisdom of the Fathers." *Letters I*, 385. Later, in the same letter, he wrote: "It is a gigantic task indeed to create a new approach to an old truth." *Letters I*, 387.

Chapter Three: 1945–1948

1.   See White, "Letter to Jung" (bibliog. 2.2, 3 August 1945). Jung's letters to White were published in a two-volume collection of all Jung's letters by Princeton University Press, though it is clear from editor's comments that some of Jung's

letters were not included because they were of a private nature (see *Letters I*, 450n). A letter from psychologist Gerhard Adler to Kenelm Foster, O. P., (see *E. P. O. P. Archives*) indicates that some of Jung's letters to White may have been disposed of at Adler's discretion. Copies of White's unpublished letters to Jung, which are currently being edited by Adrian Cunningham and Ann Lammers are kept in the *E. P. O. P. Archives* in Edinburgh. Again, not all of the letters are there, it appears that some have been lost.

2. The articles that White sent were those that I considered in Chapter Three, namely, "The Frontiers of Theology and Psychology" (bibliog. 1.4, 1942); "St. Thomas Aquinas and Jung's Psychology" (bibliog. 1.4, 1944); "Psychotherapy and Ethics" (bibliog. 1.4, 1945); and "Psychotherapy and Ethics: A Postscript" (bibliog. 1.4, 1945), which is his response to J. C. Flugel, *Man Morals and Society* (bibliog. 1.1).

3. Note also that Jung had communicated with Professor Hugo Rahner, S. J., a patristic scholar at Innsbrück—with whom he was impressed. Although he appreciated Rahner's hermeneutics expertise, Jung found him too careful and questioned the extent of his psychological understanding. See Jung, "Letter to White," 5 October 1945, in *Letters I*, 386.

4. Jung, "Letter to White," 26 September 1945, in *Letters I*, 382.

5. Jung, *Psychology and Religion* (bibliog. 1.2, 1938), 72–73; Jung, *CW*, 11:482.

6. Jung, "Archetypes of the Collective Unconscious" in De Laszlo, ed., *The Basic Writings of C. G. Jung* (bibliog. 1.1), 309.

7. Jung, *Psychology and Religion* (bibliog. 1.2, 1938), 58.

8. Jung, "Archetypes of the Collective Unconscious" in De Laszlo, ed., *The Basic Writings of C. G. Jung* (bibliog. 1.1), 309.

9. Jung, *Psychology and Religion* (bibliog. 1.2, 1938), 58.

10. Jung, *CW*, 11: 463.

11. Jung, *Psychology and Religion* (bibliog. 1.2, 1938), 58.

12. As I noted in Chapter Two, Jung's father was a clergyman, as were his maternal grandfather and eight of his uncles. See Jung, *MDR*, 13. Jung remained a Protestant in the Swiss Reformed tradition, describing himself as a "left-wing" Protestant in the period following his falling out with Victor White. See Jung, "Letter to Philp" in *CW* 18: 740-44. This might lead one to speculate that his interest in Catholicism was psychological rather than personal, a view supported in Jung's "Why I Am Not a Catholic" in *CW*, 18:645–47. Jung had, in fact, attempted dialogue with the Catholic theologian, H. Irminger, though the attempts ultimately failed. H. Irminger wrote to Jung a year before the White correspondence. He thought that Jung would eventually become a Catholic, clearly a view Jung did not share, for his reply to Irminger later grew into Jung's "Why I Am Not a Catholic" in *CW*, 18:645–47.

13. Jung, *Psychology and Religion* (bibliog. 1.2, 1938), 61.

14. Ibid., 62.

15. Ibid., 57.

16. Jung, "Letter to White," 5 October 1945, in *Letters I*, 384–85.

17. Ibid.

18. Jung, *Psychology and Religion* (bibliog. 1.2, 1938), 6.

19. Ibid., 57, 111.

20. Ibid., 57, 98.

21. Ibid., 41.

22. Ibid., 56.

23. Jung, "Letter to White," 1 October 1945, in *E. P. O. P. Archives*. This letter is incorrectly dated 5 October 1945 in *Letters I*, 387.

24. Jung, "Letter to White," 5 October 1945, in *Letters I*, 383.

25. See 1 Kings 17:2–6.

26. See, for example, Jung, *CW*, 18:677–88. Jung saw Elijah as a living archetype, as one who represents the initial divine thrust for individuation and has a transcendent unifying function. This view of White as an inner guiding figure to Jung is held by Lammers in her book, *In God's Shadow* (bibliog. 1.1) , 310n20.

27. See Job 38:41; Ps. 147:9; and Lk. 12:24.

28. These two interpretations are taken in Lammers, *In God's Shadow* (bibliog. 1.1), 310n20.

29. Richard Wilhelm had sent him the Chinese alchemical text of *The Golden Flower*. See Jung, *MDR*, 204.

30. Jung, *MDR*, 204.

31. White spoke, for example, of "the seeming gibberish of the old alchemists" in *God and the Unconscious* (bibliog. 1.4, 1982), 65. This is not surprising when one considers that the alchemists thought that their knowledge was, as Von der Heydt expressed it, a "holy gnosis." See Von der Heydt, *Prospects for the Soul* (bibliog. 1.1), 66. As such, they chose to express it in what seemed to be nonsense. Furthermore, many Christian alchemists had to protect themselves from being denounced for heresy (and facing the consequences that went with that).

32. Jung, *MDR*, 205.

33. White, *Soul and Psyche* (bibliog. 1.4, 1960), 106; and White, "Letter to Jung" (bibliog. 2.2, 1 April 1946), where he wrote of Jung's book *Psychologie ünd Alchemie* (bibliog. 1.2), "and of course the whole question it raises of the 'process of individuation.'"

34. See *MDR*, 121. Jung wrote: "In *Mysterium Coniunctionis* my psychology was at last given its place in reality and established upon its historical foundations."

35. Jung, *Psychology and Religion* (bibliog. 1.2, 1938), 111.

36. Ibid.

37. Jung, *CW*, 14:165.

38. Jung, *CW*, 14:165n182.

39. Furthermore, as Edinger noted, the image of the black raven becoming white appeared in a gnostic Manichean myth. In this myth, which Edinger indentified as a *sublimatio* image, the light which inhabited the dark level of the Archons was "extracted . . . from the reptilian level of the psyche—and transferred to the upper realms, to the ravens." Most significantly, the effect on the birds who gathered it up was "to transform them from black birds to white birds." Again the

parallel with Jungian analysis is clear. See Edinger, *The Mysterium Lectures* (bibliog. 1.1), 79–80.

40. McGuire and Hull, eds., *C. G. Jung Speaking* (bibliog. 1.1), 228.

41. Edinger has argued that the *prima materia* which is placed in the alchemical vessel to be transformed was often identified as God. See Edinger, *The Mysterium Lectures* (bibliog. 1.1), 137.

42. White, *God and the Unconscious* (bibliog. 1.4, 1982), 65.

43. Unpublished lecture, White, "Religion and Psychology" (bibliog. 2.1).

44. White, "Letter to Jung" (bibliog. 2.2, 1 April 1946). In a letter of 5 October 1945, Jung had inquired as to whether White read German and offered to send him a copy of *Psychology ünd Alchemie*. See *Letters I*, 386. White of course did – along with French, Spanish, Italian and Latin (White, "Letter to Jung" (bibliog. 2.2, 9 October 1945). The English translation of *Psychology ünd Alchemie* did not appear until 1953 (See *Letters I*, 386 fn11).

45. White, "Letter to Jung" (bibliog. 2.2, 23 June 1946). White visited Jung for two weeks starting August 15, 1946.

46. Jung, "Letter to White," 6 November 1946, in *Letters I*, 448. White replied in a series of letters. His first response to the question came in a letter, dated October 23, 1945, where he informed Jung: "It is difficult to find any trace of opposition to alchemy as such on the part of the Church." A year later, on October 13, 1946, White reported to Jung that while perusing the Dominican General Chapters of the thirteenth and fourteenth centuries, he had discovered details of bans on alchemy, which seemed, as a further letter of December 11, 1946, indicated, to have been a response to what had become common practice in the Dominican Order. These could refer to the papal encyclical *Spondet quas non exhibent* of John XXII, in 1317. It seems likely that White sent Jung an extract from Partington's *Albertus Magnus on Alchemy* (bibliog. 1.1) as it is cited by the editors of the Jung letters in *Letters I*, 448n2. Partington stated that "the study and practice of alchemy were forbidden several times to the Franciscans in the period 1272–1323 . . . and to the Dominicans between 1273 and 1313 . . . with penalties increasing from imprisonment to excommunication, the scandal going on, it is said, in spite of severe prohibitions." See *Letters I*, 448n2. White added, in his letter of October 13, 1946 (bibliog. 2.2) that the bans on alchemy were no longer in force.

47. I am very grateful to Ms. Petrina Morris, a Jungian analyst in North Oxford, for taking the time to discuss Jung's ideas on alchemy with me.

48. White, "Letter to Jung" (bibliog. 2.2, 14 October 1945).

49. Stein, Murray, *Jung's Treatment of Christianity* (bibliog. 1.1, 1986), 8.

50. See, for example, Jung, *MDR*, 74, 99, and 101.

51. Jung, *The Zofingia Lectures* (bibliog. 1.2), 34.

52. White, *Soul and Psyche* (bibliog. 1.4, 1960), 53; and White, "An Inquiry into the Philosophical Foundations of C. G. Jung" (bibliog. 2.1).

53. Jung, *CW*, 18: 772.

54. Ibid.

55. Giegerich, "Jung's Betrayal of His Truth" (bibliog. 1.1), 48.

56. Jung, "Letter to Bernhard Lang," June 1957, in *Letters II*, 379.

57. Jung, "Letter to Mr. Robert Smith," 29 June 1960, in *Letters II*, 570–73. Robert Smith was a graduate student at Villanova researching the Jung–Buber dialogue. Jung wrote: "I was sometimes not careful enough to repeat time and again: 'But what I mean is only the psychic image of a *noumenon*' (Kant's thing-in-itself . . .)"

58. Jung, *Psychology and Religion* (bibliog. 1.2, 1938), 2.

59. Jung, "Letter to White," 5 October 1945, in *Letters I*, 384.

60. Jung, *Psychology and Religion* (bibliog. 1.2, 1938), 112.

61. Jung made an analogy using an elephant, writing: "An elephant is true because it exists. The elephant, moreover, is neither a conclusion nor a statement nor a subjective judgment of a creator. It is a phenomenon." See Jung, op.cit., 8.

62. Ibid.

63. Jung, "Letter to White," 5 October 1945, in *Letters I*, 384–85.

64. Jung, *CW*, 10:328n12.

65. See above, Jung's "white raven" quote in which Jung commends White for being "conscientious enough" to consider his opinions "on the basis of a careful study" of his writings; also Jung's preface to White, *God and the Unconscious* (bibliog. 1.4, 1952).

66. White, "Letter to Jung" (bibliog. 2.2, 9 October 1945).

67. Jung, "Letter to White," 5 October 1945, in *Letters I*, 386.

68. White, "Letter to Jung" (bibliog. 2.2, 23 October 1945).

69. Stein, *Jung's Treatment of Christianity* (bibliog. 1.1, 1986), 8.

70. Dourley, *The Rerooting* (bibliog. 1.1), 211. See also Jung, "Letter to Pastor Bernet," 13 June 1955, in *Letters II*, 257.

71. Jung, "Letter to White," 5 October 1945, in *Letters I*, 384–85.

72. Jung, *Psychology and Religion* (bibliog. 1.2, 1938), 2.

73. Stein, *Jung's Treatment of Christianity* (bibliog. 1.1, 1986), 8.

74. When speaking of Jung's empiricism, White would often add, in parentheses, "however much it may have been modified." See, for example, White, "Review of Igor Caruso's *Psychoanalyse ünd Synthese der Existenz*" (bibliog. 1.4, 1953), 225.

75. See White, "The Philosophical Foundations for Jung's Psychology" (bibliog. 2.1).

76. White, "Review of Igor Caruso's *Psychoanalyse ünd Synthese der Existenz*" (bibliog. 1.4, 1953), 225.

77. Jung, *CW*, 18: 683–84.

78. Jung, *CW*, 18: 682–83.

79. Wilson, *C. G. Jung: Lord of the Underworld* (bibliog. 1.1), 121.

80. Ironically, White had earlier complained to his analyst that at Blackfriars he felt like the cured lepers in the gospels must have felt when they were charged to tell no-one what had been done for them. See White, "Letter to Layard" (bibliog. 2.2, 20 November 1940).

81. One example is White, "Letter to Jung" (bibliog. 2.2, 23 October 1945) where White was greatly reassured by Jung's affirmation that he had understood him.

82. See, for example, Jung's "Reply to Martin Buber" in *CW*, 18:669.

83. Jung, "Psychology and Religion" in *CW*, 11:148; and in Storr, ed., *The Essential Jung* (bibliog. 1.1), 248. See also Charet, "A Dialogue between Psychology and Theology: The Correspondence of C.G. Jung and Victor White" (bibliog. 1.1), 439. Here Charet suggested that in his later years Jung believed "he was spreading a newer and better gospel."

84. White, "Letter to Jung" (bibliog. 2.2, 23 October 1945). It is worth recalling that, in "Psychotherapy and Ethics: A Postscript" (bibliog. 1.4, 1945), 386, White had said that he was "unable to give unqualified assent to every word that Jung himself has written."

85. Jung, "Letter to White," 5 October 1945, in *Letters I*, 387.

86. Ibid.

87. Ibid., 386. It is interesting that Jung said he would happily talk to peasants about God because they, unlike the educated people, would know of what he is talking.

88. Ibid., 387.

89. White, "Letter to Jung" (bibliog. 2.2, 14 October 1945). White wrote to Jung, "Hawkesyard is the place where I received the earlier part of my Dominican training, and doubtless developed many of the 'complications' from which analysis from John Layard, T. Sussman—and a good deal of subsequent attempts at self-analysis—have (I hope) pretty thoroughly delivered me."

90. Jung, "Letter to White," 5 October 1945, in *Letters I*, 387.

91. Ibid.

92. Jung, "Archetypes of the Collective Unconscious" in *CW* 9i: 12

93. Jung, "Letter to White," 5 October 1945, in *Letters I*, 385.

94. See, for example, White's initial concerns regarding the issue of God's transcendence in the previous chapter.

95. Matthew 9:17–18.

96. White reported that the lectures were attended by about one hundred people, clearly a sign of the interest in Jungian Catholic studies.

97. White, "Letter to Jung" (bibliog. 2.2, 16 November 1945). White thanked Jung "for the very great deal that I (and so many others) owe to you and your work."

98. White, "Letter to Jung" (bibliog. 2.2, 23 October 1945).

99. Bright, "Review of Victor White's *God and the Unconscious*" (bibliog. 1.1).

100. White, "Letter to Jung" (bibliog. 2.2, 23 October 1945).

101. Kehoe, for example, was particularly interested in scripture and Jung's notion of archetypes, and Vann had drawn heavily on Jung in his book *The Heart of Man* (bibliog. 1.1).

102. White, "Letter to Jung" (bibliog. 2.2, 23 October 1945).

103. Jung, "Letter to White," 13 April 1946, in *Letters I*, 413.

104. Ibid.

105. Jung, "Letter to Sylvester Schoening," 24 March 1955, in *Letters II*, 234.

106. White, "Letter to Jung" (bibliog. 2.2, 1 April 1946).

107. Jung, "Letter to White," 13 April 1946, in *Letters I*, 419.

108.   See, for example, White, "Letter to Jung" (bibliog. 2.2, 23 June 1946). In it, White expressed the hope that they could discuss Jung's *Psychologie ünd Alchemie* (bibliog. 1.2) during his visit in August. See also White, "Letter to Miss Schmid" (bibliog. 2.2, 29 October 1946). Schmid was Jung's secretary. White had written to her to ask her to draw Jung's attention to an article by Louis Bouyer on the problem of evil or the evil one in *Dieu Vivant* no. 6 (1946). White believed this would be of great interest to Jung, indicating that even at this early stage in their relationship, there had been some discussion of the subject that would eventually tear them apart—evil.

109.   White, "Letter to Jung" (bibliog. 2.2, 27 August 1946). White thanked Jung for his hospitality and expressed that he was looking forward to the Eranos meeting on September 2. See also White, "Letter to Jung" (bibliog. 2.2, 31 August 1946). White suggested that Etienne Gilson and Jacques Maritain be invited to Eranos to talk on God and Philosophy.

110.   White, "ERANOS: 1947, 1948" (bibliog. 1.4, 1949), 395.

111.   This was one of several dreams that White would send to Jung. In fact White kept a noctuary (bibliog. 2.1). Unlike Jung, White did believe that his own dreams must come from outside the psyche. See White, "Letter to Layard," (bibliog. 2.2, 12 December 1941).

112.   Jung, "Letter to White," 6 November 1946, in *Letters I*, 448. By *mandala*, Jung meant a circle or square or quaternity figure which symbolizes the self as psychic totality. The "intuitive sector" refers to one of the four functions of the psyche. Jung categorized human personality types by distinguishing two basic "attitudes": extraversion and introversion; and four "functions": thinking, feeling, sensation, and intuition. Intuition is the capacity to apprehend without knowing facts and details, and thus, an intuitive type will tend to be led by the imagination.

113.   Jung, "Letter to Werner Niederer," 23 June 1947, in *Letters I*, 466. Translation.: Go not outside, return into thyself; truth dwells in the inner man.

114.   White, "Letter to Jung" (bibliog. 2.2, 16 June 1947). The lecture was given on June 17, 1947.

115.   The More Clinic was founded in 1954 and was located at 14 Ely Place London EC1. It was staffed by priests, doctors, and analysts, including Fr. Victor White, O. P., Fr. O'Malley, Dr. Elkisch, and Dr. Ruth Sandemann. Victor White's notes from analyses between 1957 and 1959 are contained in the *E. P. O. P. Archives*. The Clinic closed in 1959 due to old age and illness of its founders. See Elkisch, "Letter to Victor White" (bibliog. 2.3, 5 October 1959).

116.   White, "Theology and Psychology" (bibliog. 2.1), clearly given as one of a series of lectures at St. Albert's in Oakland California, 1954.

117.   See footnote to Jung, "Letter to White," 18 December 1946, in *Letters I*, 450.

118.   See Jung, "Preface" to White, *God and the Unconscious* (bibliog. 1.4, 1952). He wrote: "It is now many years since I expressed a desire for cooperation with a theologian, but I little knew—or even dreamt—how or to what extent my wish was to be fulfilled." See also Jung, "Letter to H. Irminger," 22 September 1944, in

Letters I, 350, in which Jung expressed his desire for "a scholarly Catholic collaborator."

119. Jung, "Letter to White," 18 December 1946, in *Letters I*, 450.

120. "St. Thomas' Conception of Revelation." *Dominican Studies* 1, no. 1 (1948): 3–34. This paper was read at the Eranos Tagung, Ascona, Switzerland in 1947 as part II of his paper "Anthropologia Rationalis: The Aristotelian-Thomist Conception of Man" and published in *Eranos Jahrbuch 1947*, Band 15, *Der Mensch* (Zurich, 1948): 315–83. It appeared in French translation in *L'Anée Théologique* and in revised form in White, *God and the Unconscious* (bibliog.1.4, 1982) as "Revelation and the Unconscious" (ch.7).

121. White, "The Aristotelian-Thomist Conception of Man" (bibliog. 1.4, 1948), 318–19.

122. See Jung, "Letter to B. Milt," 8 June 1942," in *Letters I*, 317, in which he wrote of the "turning away from our psychic origins" caused by Aristotle and Aquinas. White tried to recapture the Platonic in Aquinas, as a 70-page unpublished manuscript on exemplarism indicates. See White, "Platonism of St. Thomas Aquinas" (bibliog. 2.1).

123. Jung, "Letter to Rahner," 4 August 1945, in *Letters I*, 374.

124. See, for example, Jung, "Letter to B. Milt," 8 June 1942, in *Letters I*, 317. See also *MDR*, 69 and Jung, *Psychology and Religion* (bibliog. 1.2, 1938), 72.

125. *MDR*, 55.

126. White, "The Aristotelian-Thomist Conception of Man" (bibliog. 1.4, 1948), 349, 351.

127. Ibid., 380.

128. Ibid., 357.

129. Ibid., 356–57.

130. Aquinas, *Summa Theologiae*, (bibliog. 1.1), 2a2ae.171.1 ad 4, cited by White, Ibid., 357.

131. Marie Louise von Franz made an interesting point about this. Citing White's article "St. Thomas' Conception of Revelation," (bibliog. 1.4, 1948) *en passant,* she suggested that, as a feminine figure, *sapientia* has more to do with feeling. Further, she linked this to Jung's idea of synchronicity (the idea that internal and external events are linked by their subjective meaning, or as Jung expressed it "an a-causal connection between psychic states and objective events"), because the experience of meaning is not only a result of thought but is also, in some way, connected with feeling. See Von Franz, *Psyche and Matter* (bibliog. 1.1), 194–95. For more on Jung's synchronicity principle, see Jung, *CW*, 8: 417–531.

132. White, "The Aristotelian-Thomist Conception of Man" (bibliog. 1.4, 1948), 374. White said that, for St. Paul, it is the most important of the spiritual gifts, for on it depends faith (1 Corinthians 14:1).

133. Ibid., 374–75.

134. Ibid., 365.

135. Ibid., 347, 355.

136. Aquinas, *De Veritate* (bibliog. 1.1), xii.7, 81; *Summa Theologiae* (bibliog. 1.1), 1a2ae.173.2, cited in White, op. cit., 348.

137. Aquinas, *Summa Theologiae* (bibliog. 1.1), 1a.1.9, cited in White, op. cit., 365.

138. Aquinas, *De Veritate* (bibliog. 1.1), xii.7, cited in White, op. cit., 364.

139. Aquinas, *De Veritate* (bibliog. 1.1), xii.5; *Summa Theologiae* (bibliog. 1.1), 1a2ae.172.4, cited in White, op. cit., 348–49, 381. It should be noted that, in his context, Aquinas was countering the Albigensians for whom the spiritual corresponded with goodness, and the bodily with sin. Thus, White argued that in the Albigensian worldview, it would be goodness of morals that was the prerequisite for spiritual vision.

140. Aquinas, *De Veritate* (bibliog. 1.1), 7.5 ad 6, cited in White, op. cit., 381–82.

141. Aristotle, *De Divinatione per Somnia* (bibliog. 1.1), 463 b 13. He also questioned whether dreams might be divine in origin, and White suggested that he thought revelation possible. Cited in White, op. cit., 349.

142. Jung, "Letter to White," 8 March 1947, in *Letters I*, 452.

143. Jung would quote this in his paper, "A Psychological Approach to the Dogma of the Trinity" *CW*, 11: 289 n.1, an adaptation of a 1940 Eranos lecture.

144. White, "The Aristotelian-Thomist Conception of Man" (bibliog. 1.4, 1948), 360. In *Summa Theologiae* (bibliog. 1.1), 1a.78.4. Aquinas used *phantasia* in at least two ways: as the inner sense faculty which is identical with imagination; and as a holder of the different faculties of inner sense: the imagination, the *vis cogitativa*, and the sense memory.

145. White, "The Aristotelian-Thomist Conception of Man" (bibliog. 1.4, 1948), 361. From such drawings (and from hypnosis and automatic writing), Jung developed a method that he called "active imagination." Essentially this was a therapeutic process to consciously activate the unconscious and reconnect the patient with the psychic center, the Self. Collections of Victor White's "therapeutic drawings" can be found in the *E. P. O. P. Archives*.

146. White, "The Aristotelian-Thomist Conception of Man" (bibliog. 1.4, 1948), 361.

147. Aristotle, *De Divinatione per Somnia* (bibliog. 1.1), 463 b 13, cited in White, op. cit., 347.

148. Aquinas did not believe that all dreams were divine in origin, offering other causes such as mental activity and external influences.

149. White, "The Aristotelian-Thomist Conception of Man" (bibliog. 1.4, 1948), 360.

150. Ibid., 367.

151. Ibid. The Torah, for example, was mediated by angels. See Acts 7:53, Gal 3:19.

152. White, op. cit., 369.

153. Aquinas, *De Veritate* (bibliog. 1.1), 11. 13, cited in White, op. cit., 370.

154. White, op. cit., 370–71.

155. Ibid., 371

156. White, "Letter to Jung" (bibliog. 2.2, 8 March 1947). The article sent was "St. Thomas' Conception of Revelation" which would form the second part of White's Eranos lecture.

157. Jung, "Letter to White," 27 March 1947, in *Letters I*, 452.
158. Ibid., 450.
159. Jung, "Letter to White," 23 April 1947, in *Letters I*, 457–58.
160. White, "Letter to Jung" (bibliog. 2.2, 31 December 1946).
161. While preparing his paper for Eranos, White also gave some insight into his daily life at Blackfriars. He continued to lecture at Blackfriars on Aquinas (and by all accounts to expound the *Summa* in relation to its psychological implications). See White, "Letter to Jung" (bibliog. 2.2, 23 October 1945). He lectured on Jung outside the community (for example, in early March 1947, he gave a lecture, "The Problem of the Catholic Patient," to the London Club of Analytical Psychology). See White, "Letter to Jung" (bibliog. 2.2, 8 March 1947). He examined D. Phil and B. Litt degrees in religion and psychology, and he met with his three analysants. See White, "Letter to Jung" (bibliog. 2.2, 19 January 1947).
162. White, "The Aristotelian-Thomist Conception of Man" (bibliog. 1.4, 1948); and later revised as Chapter Six and Seven in White, *God and the Unconscious* (bibliog. 1.4, 1982).
163. Jung himself, for example, thought that Aristotle would admit nothing in the intellect except through the senses. See, for example, Jung "Psychological Commentary on *The Tibetan Book of the Dead*" in *CW*, 11:§785, cited in Dourley, *The Illness* (bibliog. 1.1), 32–33, 104n38.
164. Jung, *Psychology and Religion* (bibliog. 1.2, 1938/1940), 72.
165. White, "Scholasticism," (bibliog. 1.4, 1934), 31.
166. White, "The Aristotelian-Thomist Conception of Man" (bibliog. 1.4, 1948), 319.
167. For Jung, compensation is the psychological process wherein unconscious images reveal our conscious one-sidedness. So, for example, a young man who is unaware that he intimidates people might dream of being bullied. In other words the dream "compensates" for his misguided ideas about himself, and allows him to confront his unconscious tendencies.
168. Aquinas, *De Remediis Tristitiae*, "On the Remedies for Depression" (bibliog. 1.1), q38.
169. White, op. cit., 320.
170. An exchange of the two men's dreams can be found in the *E. P. O. P. Archives*.
171. White, "Letter to Jung" (bibliog. 2.2, 3 January 1948).
172. White, "The Aristotelian-Thomist Conception of Man" (bibliog. 1.4, 1948), 322.
173. Ibid., 327.
174. Jung, "Letter to Bernhard Lang," June 1957, in *Letters II*, 376.
175. Giegerich, "Jung's Betrayal of His Truth" (bibliog. 1.1), 59.
176. Ibid.
177. Ibid.
178. Ibid., 58. For a closer examination of his argument, see Giegerich, *The Soul's Logical Life* (bibliog. 1.1).

179. Giegerich, "Jung's Betrayal of His Truth" (bibliog. 1.1), 58.
180. White, op. cit., 322.
181. Jung, *Answer to Job in CW*, 11:558. Here Jung described such an identification of God image and God as that of the "naive minded" person.
182. Giegerich, op.cit., 59.
183. Ibid.
184. White, *God and the Unconscious* (bibliog. 1.4, 1961), 117.
185. White, "Letter to Jung" (bibliog. 2.2, 8 March 1947).
186. White, "Letter to Jung" (bibliog. 2.2, 19 December 1947). White would give the same lectures to the Studium at Blackfriars in 1949. These lectures were substantially revised in 1952 as Chapter 3 of *God and the Unconscious*. See Preface to White, *God and the Unconscious* (bibliog. 1.4, 1982), xxxi. He certainly lectured at the Analytical Psychology Club in New York—he thanked Jung for the "embarrassingly hospitable Open Sesame." See White, "Letter to Jung" (bibliog. 2.2, 19 December 1947).
187. In fact, when *God and the Unconscious* (bibliog. 1.4, 1952) appeared, with the exception of the first two chapters, this original plan, proving far too ambitious, had been abandoned.
188. Antonia White, "Letter to Victor White," 21 November 1947, (bibliog. 2.3). Carl Gustav Carus was a physician, and one fascinated by animal psychology. In his 1846 book *Psyche*, Carus looked at psychology as the science of the soul's development, proceeding from the unconscious to the conscious. He was very much a precursor to and influence upon Jung.
189. The committee who asked White consisted of Jung and four of Jung's pupils: C. A. Meier; Dr. K. Binswanger; Dr. Jolande Jacobi; and Dr. L. Frey-Rohn. They later formed the first Curatorium of the institute in 1948. See *Letters I*, 482n2. Others included Gebhard Frei, Professor of Modern Philosophy at the Collegium Sacerdotale in Schöneck; Professor Pauli, physicist and Nobel prize winner; Professor Gonseth, mathematician; E. T. H. Rob De Traz, French Swiss novelist; and Ad. Vischer of the Curatorium Universitatis Basiliensis. See *Letters I*, 482.
190. Jung, "Letter to White," 27 December 1947, in *Letters I*, 481–482.
191. Cunningham, "The Encounter" (bibliog. 1.1), 321.
192. *Letters I*, 490n.
193. Jung, "Letter to White," 30 January 1948, in *Letters I*, 490.
194. See the obituary of Vera von der Heydt, "Reconciling Jung and Catholicism" in *The Daily Telegraph*, November 25, 1996. Of significance in this context is the comment "She supported the efforts of the English Dominican Province to build bridges between Jung and Rome."
195. Interview with Ryan (bibliog. 2.5).
196. See *Letters I*, 482n7.
197. White would later deliver this lecture to the Guild of Pastoral Psychology London on December 10, 1948. It was published as Guild Lecture No. 59 in April 1949. It would appear in a revised form as "Gnosis, Gnosticism and Faith," Chapter 11 of *God and the Unconscious* (bibliog. 1.4, 1952).

198. Jung, "Letter to White," 19 December 1947, in *Letters I*, 481.

199. Jung, *Modern Man in Search of a Soul* (bibliog. 1.2), 238–39; quoted by White in "Notes on Gnosticism" (bibliog. 1.4, 1949), 4–5.

200. White, "Notes on Gnosticism," (bibliog. 1.4, 1949), 4.

201. See White, unpublished notes in the *E. P. O. P. Archives*, dated 1942. Jung tells of his fascination with the gnostics in his *Memories, Dreams, Reflections* (bibliog. 1.2), 162. Jung first read the gnostic writings in 1909, but found them difficult to understand. But by 1916 he privately published "Septem Sermones ad Mortuos" under the pseudonym of Basilides (a second-century gnostic writer). See MDR, Appendix V. Following this, Jung began an in depth study of gnosticism between 1918-1926 (See *MDR*, 200–06). For further discussion on Jung and Gnosticism, see Hoeller, *The Gnostic Jung and the Seven Sermons to the Dead* (bibliog. 1.1), and Segal, ed., *The Gnostic Jung* (bibliog. 1.1), Part III of which is on Victor White, O. P.

202. White, "Notes on Gnosticism" (bibliog. 1.4, 1949), 4.

203. Jung, "Psychology and Religion" in *CW*, 11:45.

204. It is interesting to note that the "Gospel of Truth," part of the Gnostic Codex, attributed to Valentinus and discovered at Nag Hammadi in 1945, was acquired for the C. G. Jung Institute in 1952. See Jung, "Letter to White," 24 November 1953, in *Letters II*, 138.

205. White, op. cit., 11.

206. White, op.cit., 12.

207. See Jung, *Modern Man in Search of a Soul* (bibliog. 1.2), 238–39, quoted by White in "Notes on Gnosticism" (bibliog. 1.4, 1949), 4–5.

208. White, *God and the Unconscious* (bibliog. 1.4, 1961), 212.

209. Ibid.

210. White, "Notes on Gnosticism" (bibliog. 1.4, 1949), 25.

211. Ibid.

212. Ibid.

213. It is important to note that Aquinas did *not* say that revelation gives us knowledge of the divine essence. According to Aquinas, the divine essence is utterly (*omnio*) unknown to us. We do not know what God is and we cannot know the whatness of God (*non possamus*). See *Summa Theologiae*, 1a.1.7 ad 1. Quoting from the *Summa* White noted: "Neither a Catholic nor a pagan knows the nature of God as it is in itself, but both know it only by the way of some conception of causality, of transcendence or of negation" (1a.13.10 ad 1). Revelation does however "enable us to know [God] more fully . . . and enables us to attribute to God certain things which are beyond the scope of natural reason, such as God is three and one (1a.12.13 ad 1)." See White, "The Unknown God" (bibliog. 1.4, 1952), later published as chapter 2 of White, *God the Unknown* (bibliog. 1.4, 1956), 16, 22.

214. White, "The Scandal of the Assumption" (bibliog. 1.4), 209.

215. White, "The Unconscious and God" (bibliog. 2.1), delivered at Cambridge.

216. "I thank you very much for your excellent lecture on Gnosticism. I much admire your balanced judgement and your just evaluation of a subject that has

been so often represented in a wrong light and misunderstood by all sorts of com-
prehensible and incomprehensible prejudices. Your presentation of the Pistis
Sophia is excellent. Among the patristic writers about Gnosticism I missed
Hippolytus, the most thorough and the most intelligent of all. Epiphanius, who
shares the former's lot does not deserve much praise." Jung, "Letter to White," 21
May 1948, in *Letters I*, 501.

217.   Ibid., 502.

218.   White, "Letter to Jung" (bibliog. 2.2, 1 June 1948).

219.   See, for example, Jung, "Letter to B. Milt," 8 June 1942, in *Letters I*, 317.
See also *MDR*, 69 and Jung, *Psychology and Religion* (bibliog. 1.2, 1938), 72.

220.   Jung, "Letter to White," 21 May 1948, in *Letters I*, 501. See also, White,
"Faith and Creeds" (bibliog. 2.1).

221.   Jung, "Letter to Lang," June 1957, in *Letters II*, 375. This was in response
Martin Buber, who had informed Jung that he was "the happy possessor of a
'receiver' organ by means of which he can know or tune in the Transcendent." This
notion caused Jung "to reflect on myself and ask myself whether I also possess a
like receiver which can make the Transcendent, i.e., something that transcends consciousness and is by definition unknowable, knowable."

222.   Jung, "Letter to Bernet," 13 June 1955, in *Letters II*, 257–58.

223.   Jung, *Psychology and Religion* (bibliog. 1.2, 1938), 4.

224.   Ibid., 52.

225.   The correspondence between Jung and Buber following Buber's accusation
can be found in Jung, "Reply to Martin Buber" in *CW*, 18:663–70.

226.   For a more detailed exploration of the contradiction between Jung's empirical approach and his gnostic assertions, see Dehing, "Jung and Knowledge" (bibliog. 1.1), 377–96.

227.   White, "An Inquiry into the Philosophical Foundations of C. G. Jung"
(bibliog. 2.1), 9.

228.   Ibid.

229.   Jung, "The Symbolic Life" in *CW*, 18:728.

230.   See, for example, Martin, "Jung As Gnostic" (bibliog. 1.1), 70–-79

231.   Somewhat ironically this was Victor White's fifty-seventh birthday.

232.   The interview, broadcast on October 22, 1959, was published in McGuire
and Hull, eds. *C. G. Jung Speaking: Interviews and Encounters* (bibliog. 1.1), 428.

233.   See *The Listener*, 21 January 1960. See also Jung, "Letter to Brooke," 6
November 1959, in *Letters II*, 521; and Jung, "Letter to Leonard," 5 December
1959, in *Letters II*, 525. These personal letters reiterate Jung's clarification.

234.   Jung made this point clearly in Jung, "Letter to Lang," June 1957, in *Letters
II*, 375.

235.   Ibid.

236.   Jung explained what he meant in *Psychology and Religion* (bibliog. 1.2,
1938), 6:
" . . . *pistis*, that is to say, trust or loyalty, faith and confidence in a certain experience of a numinous nature. . . . The conversion of Paul is a striking example of
this." Jung, *CW* 11: 8.

237. Jung, "Letter to Lang," June 1957, in *Letters II*, 379.

238. Ibid.

239. White, *God the Unknown* (bibliog. 1.4, 1956), 7.

240. White, *God and the Unconscious* (bibliog. 1.4, 1961), 223.

241. White, "The Unconscious and God" (bibliog. 2.1).

242. Hibbert, *Man, Culture and Christianity* (bibliog. 1.1), 30. Gerald Vann, O. P., for example, attempted the catholicization of D. H. Laurence, and Richard Kehoe, O. P., researched Jungian archetypes in the scriptures.

243. See *The Times Literary Supplement*, 29 September 1960. The article mentioned Kehoe's article on baptism as archetypal rebirth from water; White's *God and the Unconscious* (bibliog. 1.4, 1952); and the work of Gerald Vann, O. P., who had explored trees of life with archetypal bearings on Eden and Crucifixion. This "quasi-official" endorsement of Jung by some in the Order is at first surprising because the Dominicans were great Aristotelians, whereas the new Jungianism of archetypes looked like neo-Platonism.

244. White, "Notes on Gnosticism" (bibliog. 1.4, 1949), 23–25.

245. For example, Matthew Rigney, O. P., recalled, "[White] was very frowned upon; yes, you see psychology was a dirty word in those days; it was considered to be subjectivism and terribly dangerous. Now Victor fought that. He did, he fought it like a lion. And, of course, he got into a lot of trouble for it." Interview with Rigney (bibliog. 2.5).

246. Dourley, *The Rerooting* (bibliog. 1.1), 33–34.

247. It is clear from the archives that White lectured at the Analytical Psychology Club of San Francisco; St. Albert's House of Studies in Oakland, CA; San Jose State College; and the University of Chicago. See White, "Letter to Jung" (bibliog. 2.2, 1 June 1948).

248. White, "Modern Psychology and the Function of Symbolism" (bibliog. 1.4, 1948). The article was reprinted in *Life of the Spirit* 3, no. 36 (June 1949): 551–59 (1949). Page numbers in this section refer to the latter.

249. Ibid., 554.

250. Ibid., 553–54.

251. Aquinas, *Summa Theologiae* (bibliog. 1.1), 1a2ae.81.7; St. Paul in 1 Corinthians 14:26.

252. White, "Modern Psychology" (bibliog. 1.4, 1949), 552.

253. Ibid., 551.

254. Ibid., 552.

255. Ibid.

256. Ibid., 556.

257. Ibid., 555.

258. Ibid., 553.

259. Ibid., 556.

260. Ibid.

261. See Aquinas, op.cit., q.9. For a fuller exposition of Aquinas' account, see White, *Holy Teaching* (bibliog. 1.4, 1958).

262. White, "Modern Psychology" (bibliog. 1.4, 1949), 558.

263. Ibid.

264. Ibid.

265. See McCabe, *God Matters* (bibliog. 1.1), ch. 18. On the subject of prayer, he seems to have drawn heavily from Aquinas through White, who was his teacher.

266. This article was reprinted in *Life of the Spirit 4* (1949), and revised as Chapter Nine in White, *God and the Unconscious* (bibliog. 1.4, 1952).

267. Victor White has been accused of making such facile comparisons by later commentators, most notably in Hibbert, *Man, Culture and Christianity* (bibliog. 1.1), 28, where he accused White of failing to produce a synthesis but rather taking "the old with the right hand, as it were, and the new with the left" and trying "to fit them together."

268. White, "The Analyst and the Confessor" (bibliog. 1.4, 1949), 20.

269. Ibid., 20–21.

270. Ibid., 21.

271. This further suggests that psychotherapy owes more to religion than to medicine; both psychotherapy and religion use a model—alienation—which suggests man is imperfect. Medicine, on the other hand, presupposes health to be the norm.

272. White, op. cit., 22.

273. Ibid.

274. Ibid.

275. Ibid., 25.

276. See Jung, *Modern Man In Search of a Soul* (bibliog. 1.2), 278.

277. White, op. cit., 24.

278. Ibid.

279. *Letters I*, 506. Reinhold had written an article severely critical of Jung and his school of analytical psychology which Jung had dismissed as an exercise in intellectual irresponsibility on the basis of its ignorance and prejudice.

280. White, "Jung's Psychology" (bibliog. 2.1).

Chapter Four: 1948–1952

1. White, "Letter to Jung" (bibliog. 2.2, 1 June 1948).

2. White, "Letter to Jung" (bibliog. 2.2, 6 August 1948). White confirmed in this letter that he would sail for England on August 21, arriving in Zurich for September 6–14.

3. Although White's letter has not been preserved (see *Letters I*, 517n), it is clear that White felt isolated on his return—from a letter of encouragement, Jung, "Letter to White," 8 January 1949, in *Letters I*, 517. Jung wrote: "If you feel isolated in England, why don't you make one of your *fratres* a real brother in the spirit? When I came to Zurich, the most materialistic city of Switzerland, there was nobody ready-made for my needs. I then shaped some for me. They were meant for this experience. One could see it from their dreams." There is

also evidence in this letter that White was suffering the tension of being both priest and analyst as Jung's advice suggested: "The combination of priest and medicine man is not so impossible as you seem to think. They are based upon a common archetype, which will assert its right provided your inner development will continue as hitherto. It is true, the 'fringe' of new things is always made up of funny figures. I imagine we could have observed very similar lunatics among the early Christian followers, f[or] i[nstance], those people who were cured of possession."

4. Jung, "Letter to White," 16 December 1948, in *Letters I*, 514.

5. Ibid.

6. Ibid.

7. cf. Rev. 3:20.

8. Interesting in this regard are two personalized Christmas cards (in the *E. P. O. P. Archives*) which White sent to his friends—they contain the biblical verses 2 Corinthians 4:6 and 1 Peter 2:9.

9. Jung, "Letter to White," 8 January 1949, in *Letters I*, 517. In a footnote, he wrote: "'Hic Rhodus, hic salta!' (Here is Rhodes, here jump!), from Aesop's *Fables* ("The Braggart"), in which a man boasts of an enormous jump in Rhodes and is challenged to prove his prowess." Ibid., 517n3.

10. White, "Letter to Jung" (bibliog. 2.2, 5 May 1949).

11. Cunningham, "The Fateful Encounter" (bibliog. 1.1), 322.

12. Jung, "Letter to Mother Prioress," 6 February 1960, in *Letters II*, 536.

13. Jung, *MDR*, 181–82.

14. Jung, "Letter to White," 8 January 1949, in *Letters I*, 514.

15. White, "ERANOS: 1947, 1948" (bibliog. 1.4, 1949), 395–400. White was in fact a founding editor of *Dominican Studies*.

16. "On the Self," later Chapter Four of *Aion* in *CW*, 9ii: 23–25. It is apparent from this review that White had access to the manuscript of *Aion* and not just Jung's paper. See also Letters I, 359fn2.

17. White, op. cit., 397.

18. Ibid., 398.

19. Ibid.

20. Ibid.

21. Jung, *Aion* in *CW*, 9ii:41.

22. White, "ERANOS: 1947, 1948" (bibliog. 1.4, 1949), 398.

23. Ibid.

24. Ibid.

25. Ibid., 399.

26. White, op. cit., 399.

27. Ibid., 398.

28. Again, it seems that White must have seen a manuscript for Jung's *Aion*, for discussion of the *privatio boni* does not occur in Jung's "Ueber das Selbst" (Chapter Four) but rather in "Christ, A Symbol of the Self" (Chapter Five). See also Jung, *Letters I*, 539n2.

29. Jung, *CW*, 9ii:41.

30. Note that Jung lambasted the doctrine of the *privatio boni* as if it were the official Christian teaching on evil rather than one particular approach to talking about evil.

31. Although theologically the doctrine of the *privatio boni* first arose in the writings of the Church fathers—and, particularly in Augustine's response to Mani as described in his *Confessions* (bibliog. 1.1), the philosophical background to this idea goes back to Aristotle's *Metaphysics* (bibliog. 1.1). He held that, in pairs of opposites ("contraries"), one is negative in relation to the other. So, for example, evil is an absence of good, poverty is an absence of wealth, untruth is an absence of truth. In these examples, good represents the fullness of being and evil its lack (*privatio*). As Sanford noted in "The Problem of Evil" (bibliog. 1.1), 112, for Aristotle "evil was untruth and existed only in so far as it is a departure from the truth." Thus, in this schema, truth alone is substantial—untruth as a privation could not exist in and of itself.

32. See White, "ERANOS: 1947, 1948" (bibliog. 1.4, 1949), 400n2. He wrote: "The *privatio boni* in St. Augustine and St. Thomas was . . . in answer . . . to the question *What* is evil, i.e., why is this called Bad?"

33. See Aquinas, *Summa Theologiae* (bibliog. 1.1), 1a.48ad3. The Manichees, of course, offered a dualistic alternative: evil exists (substantially) because there are two gods, one who creates ("brings into existence") good, and one who creates ("brings into existence") evil. In defending monotheism, Augustine argued that there are not two gods because evil has no substantial existence but is parasitic on the good. In other words, he accounted for evil (and defended a wholly good God of monotheism) with the doctrine of the *privatio boni.*

34. Some (Christian Scientists, for example) might say that evil is an illusion but, as argued in Geach, *Logic Matters* (bibliog. 1.1), 305: "If my 'mortal mind' thinks I am miserable, then I am miserable, and it is not an illusion that I am miserable." Similarly, in McCabe, *God Matters* (bibliog. 1.1), 27: "When someone says: 'My toothache hurts like mad,' or 'that cow is suffering from a disease,' or 'Charlie is a wicked and depraved man,' he is making quite literal true statements, just as literal and true as the statement that London is in England."

35. Aquinas, *Summa Theologiae* (bibliog. 1.1), Ia.48.2.

36. Ibid., 1a.48.5.

37. Ibid., 1a.48.3.

38. Ibid. The example Aquinas used is of the strength of the lion or the swiftness of a wild goat. It should be noted that a privation need not necessarily represent a lack. I might, for example, find a dead animal under the bonnet of my car which would clearly result in a bad and defective car. Similarly, a human might have an excess of anger which makes that human "evil" (that is, less than God intended of a human).

39. See "Conversations with McCabe" (bibliog. 2.5). See also Cunningham, "Obituary: Herbert McCabe, O. P." (bibliog. 1.1). There Cunningham wrote: "The climate of formation was decidedly arid, and it was only Victor White's lectures on Aquinas that fired him to his lifelong commitment to the Aristotelian roots of Aquinas' philosophy."

40. McCabe, *God Matters* (bibliog. 1.1), 29.

NOTES TO CHAPTER FOUR

41. Sanford, "The Problem of Evil," (bibliog. 1.1), 112.
42. Jung, *CW*, 18:709. Augustine's account of his arguments against the Manichees can be found in his *Confessions* (bibliog. 1.1), especially 3:7 (p. 46), 5:10–14 (pp. 92–98) and 7:16 (p. 143).
43. Jung, *Aion* in *CW*, 9ii:46.
44. Ibid., 9ii:41.
45. Ibid., 9ii:54.
46. Jung, *The Visions Seminars* (bibliog. 1.2), 213.
47. Jung, *Aion* in *CW*, 9ii:54.
48. Jung, *CW*, 9ii:328ff.
49. Jung, *CW*, 9ii: 96.
50. McCabe, *God Matters* (bibliog. 1.1), 35.
51. Ibid.
52. Jung, *Aion* in *CW*, 9ii:41.
53. White, "ERANOS: 1947, 1948" (bibliog. 1.4, 1949), 400.
54. Jung, "Good and Evil in Analytical Psychology" in *CW*, 10:456–68.
55. Jung, *CW*, 11:337.
56. Jung, *CW*, 18:710.
57. Jung, *CW*, 9ii:53.
58. Jung, *CW*, 10:459.
59. Jung, *CW*, 10:459–60.
60. If, for example the mother's life was in danger, to abort the child would still be an intrinsic evil. However, Catholic teaching invokes the principle of double effect which holds that it is permissible to do good (such as save the life of a pregnant mother) with the foreknowledge that there will be bad consequences (the death of the child). But Catholic teaching also holds that it would be wrong to *intentionally* commit evil that good might come.
61. Jung, *CW*, 9ii: 267.
62. Sanford, "The Problem of Evil," (bibliog. 1.1), 115.
63. Jung, *CW* 9ii:47.
64. Jung, *CW* 9ii: 61.
65. Jung "On Psychic Energy" in *CW*, 8:3–66.
66. Palmer, *Freud and Jung on Religion* (bibliog. 1.1), 103. cf. Jung "On Psychic Energy" in *CW*, 8:3–66.
67. Jung, *CW*, 14:183.
68. Jung, *CW*, 8:9, cited in Palmer, *Freud and Jung on Religion* (bibliog. 1.1), 104.
69. Palmer, op. cit., 103. Cf. Jung, "Two Essays on Analytical Psychology" *CW*, 7:216–17.
70. Jung, *Aion* in *CW*, 9ii:45n1.
71. Jung, *CW*, 9i:322.
72. Jung, *CW*, 11:168–69. Jung wrote: "The opposite of seeming evil can only be seeming good, and an evil that lacks substance can only be contrasted with a good that is equally non substantial. Although the opposite of 'existence' is 'non-existence,' the opposite of an existing good can never be a non existing evil, for the latter is a contradiction in terms and opposes an existing good commensurate with

it; the opposite of a nonexisting (negative) evil can only be a nonexisting (negative) good." See also Jung, *CW*, 18:276.

73. Jung, *CW*, 9ii:267.

74. Jung, "Letter to Rychlak," 27 April 1959, in *Letters II*, 501.

75. Jung, *CW*, 18:722.

76. White, "ERANOS: 1947, 1948" (bibliog. 1.4, 1949), 400.

77. Burrell, *Aquinas: God and Action* (bibliog. 1.1), espec. 105, 110–11.

78. White, op. cit., 399.

79. Ibid., 400.

80. Jung used the word *metaphysics* in a peculiar way. It is roughly equated with Kant's *noumenal*, in the same way that Jung equated the *phenomenal* with the "empirical." Thus, according to Jung, *metaphysics* is essentially that which is supra-sensory and is thus precluded by his methodology. This means that "evil as a real force" *could* be a metaphysical statement, but it was not within Jung's capability to make such a statement. Although heavily dependent on Kant, it is doubtful whether Kant would have recognized Jung's usage—when Kant used *metaphysics* he meant necessary and universal truths about reality. To further complicate matters, Victor White followed the neo-scholastic Aristotelian understanding of metaphysics as pertaining to the basic categories of being.

For a good analysis of *Jung's* different uses of the term "metaphysics" see Dourley, "The Religious Implications" (bibliog. 1.1), 182–83.

81. Ibid.

82. Ibid., 399.

83. Dourley, *The Rerooting* (bibliog. 1.1), 33–34.

84. Jung, *Aion* in *CW*, 9ii:109.

85. Jung, *CW*, 18:716. This quotation is taken from Jung's answers to questions posed by the Reverend David Cox.

86. In fact Aquinas thought that evil has no cause. This is well brought out in Augustine's *Confessions* (bibliog. 1.1) and especially his realization that what made his pear theft evil was the senselessness of it (that is, that it had no cause).

87. Jung, *CW*, 11:313.

88. Jung saw his theory of opposites in the gnostic teaching that Christ was born "not without a kind of shadow," (see Irenaeus, *Adversus Haereses* (bibliog. 1.1), I, II, I, cited in Jung *CW*, 9ii:109) but that he "cast off his shadow" from himself (see *Adversus Haereses* (bibliog. 1.1), II, 5, I, cited in Jung, *CW*, 18:716). Jung believed that this gnostic "abscission of the shadow" was grasped by St. Luke when he spoke of Satan falling out of heaven (Lk 10:18).

89. For adherents of the *privatio boni*, God as *Summum Bonum* could not be the cause of evil because that which has existence is good and evil is insubstantial.

90. Jung, *CW*, 9ii:55.

91. Deuteronomy 32:39, cited in Jung, *CW*, 9ii:52.

92. Jung, "Answer to Questions from the Reverend Philp" in *CW*, 18:717–19. Jung's answers arise from Philp's book, *Jung and the Problem of Evil* (bibliog. 1.1). Philp also corresponded with Victor White, as is evident from letters in the *E. P. O. P. Archives*.

93. White, "ERANOS: 1947, 1948" (bibliog. 1.4, 1949), 399.
94. Jung, "Letter to White," 31 December 1949, in *Letters I*, 539.
95. Ibid. Jung did not give his particular objections to Aquinas here, though these can be found in some detail in his work *Aion*. Briefly stated, Jung's objections were as follows: first, he argued that, psychologically speaking, good and evil are logically equivalent opposites and thus saw Aquinas' arguments as illogical (Ibid., 51); second, he disputed Aquinas' idea that all created things strive for a good—using the devil as an example (Ibid., 52); third, he argued that the *privatio boni* is a euphemism to deal with "the unthinkable,"—that is, that the perfect good could ever have created evil (Ibid., 52); and fourth, he thought that Aquinas' adoption of the *privatio boni* contributed to the minimizing of evil in human consciousness which thereby undermined its seriousness.
96. Ibid., 540. Jung has gleaned this from Basil's *Hexaemeron* (bibliog. 1.1). See Jung, *Aion* in *CW*, 9ii:46–47.
97. Basil the Great, "De Spiritu Sancto" in *Hexaemeron* (bibliog. 1.1), cited in Jung, *CW*, 9ii:47.
98. Dykes, "Some Aspects of the Self" (bibliog. 1.1), 51. See also Jung, "The Relations Between the Ego and the Unconscious" in *CW*, 7: 123–87.
99. Jung, *CW*, 5:55.
100. Jung, *MDR*, 51.
101. Ibid.
102. Jung, *CW*, 18:720.
103. Jung, "Letter to White," 31 December 1949, in *Letters I*, 540.
104. Jung, *Aion* in *CW*, 9ii:62.
105. Jung, "Letter to White," 31 December 1949, in *Letters I*, 540. See also Jung, *Aion* in *CW*, 9ii:62.
106. Jung, Aion in *CW*, 9ii:62.
107. Ibid. Here it is a little clearer that Jung did indeed understand that what made the atrocities of Hitler and Stalin "evil" was not the harm done to others but the harm (or, as he put it, the "accidental lack of perfection") it did to them as perpetrators.
108. Ibid.
109. Ibid.
110. White, "ERANOS: 1947, 1948" (bibliog. 1.4, 1949), 400n2.
111. McCabe, *God Matters* (bibliog. 1.1), 29.
112. Davies, "The Problem of Evil" (bibliog. 1.1), 357–75.
113. Jung, "Letter to White," 31 December 1949, in *Letters I*, 541.
114. Ibid.
115. Ibid.
116. Dourley, *The Rerooting* (bibliog. 1.1), 90.
117. Ibid.
118. Jung, "Letter to White," 31 December 1949, in *Letters I*, 540. This section of the letter is also found in Jung, *Aion* in *CW*, 9ii:171n29.
119. Origen's view was, of course, a little more nuanced than Jung realized: he did not think that evil would be redeemed, but rather that the devil *as a creature of*

God would be redeemed. This is potentially interesting in relation to integration. See, for example, Sanford, "The Problem of Evil," (bibliog. 1.1), 122.

120.   Dourley, *The Rerooting* (bibliog. 1.1), 90.

121.   Ibid. Jung in fact liked to be prayed for, especially by White. See White, "Letter to Jung" (bibliog. 2.2, 19 January 1947).

122.   Lammers, *In God's Shadow* (bibliog. 1.1), 98–100, suggested that this was an examination for the STM which was eventually conferred upon White in 1954, but this is unlikely because the STM was and is an honorary degree conferred by the Dominican Order for teaching, research, and writing. The STM had first arisen in the medieval universities of Europe and was awarded to Dominicans who had been recommended by the Province to which they belonged and approved by the General Chapter of the whole Order. In 1310, Pope Benedict XI allowed the Order to grant the degree to Dominican recipients worthy of such an honor—those considered to be excellent theologians and outstanding preachers. Four years after this journey to Rome, White would have the degree of Master of Sacred Theology conferred upon him. White did journey to Rome in 1950 and his correspondence with Jung suggests that the examination related not to the STM but to the anti-modernist oath that was required of all teachers of theology since its promulgation by Pius X in 1910.

123.   White was invited to lecture at the University in Trinity Term of 1950 and 1951; the bones of these lectures can be found in the *E. P. O. P. Archives*. See bibliog. 2.1.

124.   White, "Letter to Jung," (bibliog. 2.2, 4 May 1950).

125.   Ibid.

126.   Ibid.

127.   See Vardy, *The Puzzle of Evil* (bibliog. 1.1), 27.

128.   Indeed, for a Thomist like White, God could not be a moral agent because God is unchanging; and, according to the doctrine of divine simplicity, God's actions are inseparable from God's self.

129.   White, "Letter to Jung," (bibliog. 2.2, 4 May 1950).

130.   Jung, *CW*, 2:291.

131.   Jung, *Aion* in *CW*, 9ii:291.

132.   Ibid., 9ii:266.

133.   Jung, "Letter to White," 12 May 1950, in *Letters I*, 555.

134.   White visited Jung in late August 1950. See White, "Postcard from France to Jung," in the *E. P. O. P. Archives*. See also White, "Letter to Jung," (bibliog. 2.2, 20 June 1950, 7 July 1950, and 17 July 1950).

135.   White, "The Scandal of the Assumption" (bibliog. 1.4, 1950).

136.   Declared, *ex cathedra*, November 1, 1950.

137.   Jung, "Letter to Père Lachat," 27 March 1954, in *CW*, 18: 689.

138.   See for example Jung's 1938 work "Psychological Aspects of the Mother Archetype" in *CW*, 9i: 75–110.

139.   Jung, "Letter to Lewino," 21 April 1948, in *Letters I*, 499.

140.   Jung, *CW*, 9ii:87.

141.   Jung, "Letter to Dr. Hinkle," 17 March 1951, in *Letters II*, 8.

142.   Ibid.

143. Jung, *CW*, 11:461, and 14:186.
144. Jung, *CW*, 11:171n15.
145. Jung, "Letter to Lachat," 27 March 1954, in Jung, *CW*, 18:689.
146. Jung, *CW*, 11:171.
147. Jung, "Answers to Questions from Philp" in *CW,* 18:713. See also Jung, *CW*, 18:731. See also Jung, "Letter to Cox," in *CW* 18: 731, where Jung wrote: "According to what I hear from Catholic theologians, the next step would be co-Redemptrix." Recent (failed) attempts in the Catholic Church to have Mary proclaimed as co-redemptrix and mediator of graces suggest there is some truth to this. See also *CW* 18: 714.
148. Jung, "Letter to Dr. Hinkle," 17 March 1951 , in *Letters II*, 7-8.
149. White, "The Scandal of the Assumption" (bibliog. 1.4, 1950), 208n9.
150. Ibid., 208, 209n9.
151. Jung, *CW*, 18:713–14.
152. Jung, *CW*, 11:399.
153. White, op. cit., 199.
154. Ibid., 200.
155. Jung quoted this point (made by Victor White) in *CW*, 14:186n387. Cf. White, "The Scandal of the Assumption" (bibliog. 1.4, 1950), 200.
156. White gave the example of the *Aurora Consurgens* (at one time thought to have been penned by Aquinas, see White, op. cit., 201) which White thought read as a profound meditation on the Assumption. Indeed, Jung argued in *Mysterium Coniunctionis* that alchemy is the background to the dogma, especially the notion of the marriage of a fatherly spiritual principle and the maternal corporeality— "earthing" the spirit and "spiritualizing" the earth. See Jung, *CW*, 14:244. As a literary example, White cited Faust's mater gloriosa of the Doctor Marianus, she who drew Faust on to his own redemption. See Jung, *CW*, 14:244.
157. White, "The Scandal of the Assumption" (bibliog. 1.4, 1950), 201.
158. Ibid., 202
159. Ibid., 204.
160. Ibid.
161. Ibid., 206.
162. Genesis 3:16–19.
163. White, op. cit., 207.
164. Ibid., 208.
165. Ibid.
166. Ibid.
167. Ibid., 210.
168. Ibid.
169. Jung, *CW*, 8:107–08.
170. Ibid.
171. Ibid.
172. Jung, *CW*, 11:465–66.
173. Jung, *CW*, 18:714. In Jung, "Letter to Dr. Hinkle," 17 March 1951, in *Letters II*, 8, Jung wrote: "I find the arguments advanced by Protestant critics

lamentable because they overlook the prodigious significance of the new dogma. The symbol in the Catholic Church is alive and is nourished by the popular psyche and is actually urged on by it. But in Protestantism it is dead. All that remains is to abolish the Trinity and the homoousia."

174.   Jung, *CW*, 11:463.

175.   Jung, *CW*, 11:464.

176.   Jung, *CW*, 11:465. This was a point which Cardinal Newman had made, that a Mary-less doctrine of Christ imparted an impersonal or merely masculine picture of the Church. He went on to say that Protestantism's Christology without Mary developed into a Christianity without Christ.

177.   Jung, "Letter to Dr. Hinkle," 17 March 1951, in *Letters II*, 8.

178.   Indeed, in a damning review of Jung's *Answer to Job* (bibliog. 1.2), White would admit this difference of rationale in affirming the logical consistency of the Assumption, declaring: "Pius XII and C. G. Jung seem hardly to be talking abut the same thing in their affirmation of the Assumption." See White, "Jung on Job" (bibliog. 1.4, 1955). By 1959, White's criticism would be even stronger: "I hate to dampen his enthusiasm for the papal definition of the Assumption, but I have a horrid suspicion that he and Pius XII are not talking about the same thing." See White, "Review of Jung's Psychology and Religion" (bibliog. 1.4, 1959), 75.

179.   Not surprisingly, Jung was accused of having an anti-Protestant complex by one of his oldest friends, Adolf Keller. See Jung, "Letter to Adolf Keller," 20 March 1951, in *Letters II*, 9–10. In his response, Jung admitted that his strong criticism of Protestantism had intensified since the Catholic Church declared the dogma of the Assumption, perturbed by "the concretism of historicity and the vacuity of the Protestant message which can only be understood today as an historical vestige."

180.   Jung, "Letter to White," 25 November 1950, in *Letters I*, 566.

181.   See Stevens, Dom Gregory, "Review of *God and the Unconscious*" (bibliog. 1.1), 505, where he criticizes White's integration of Marian themes as "weird . . . of very little value." See also the *E. P. O. P. Archives* for a critical review of White's article (which appeared in Hastings and Nicholl, eds., *A Yearbook of Contemporary Thought* (bibliog. 1.1).

182.   In Jung, *Letters I*, 566, he wrote: "It seems to be the heirosgamos motif: the cut-down tree has been brought into the cave of the mother, in this case: the hold of the ship. It takes up so much space that the people living in the cave are forced to leave it and live outside exposed to wind and weather. This motif refers to the night-sea-journey of the hero in the belly of the great fish mother." Jung understood the dream as referring to the dogma of the Assumption. This is seen more clearly in a letter of 10 April 1954 in Jung, *Letters I*, 166–67, and in Jung, *Symbols of Transformation*, in *CW*, 5:639, where Jung wrote of the Attis cult.

183.   Jung, "Letter to White," 25 November 1950, in *Letters I*, 567.

184.   Jung, *CW*, 5:567.

185.   Jung, *CW*, 11:464; and Jung, "Letter to Dr. Hinkle," 17 March 1951, in *Letters II*, 8.

186.   Jung, "Letter to White," 25 November 1950, in *Letters I*, 567.

187. Jung, *CW*, 14:469.

188. In fact, Jung enclosed an article by a Catholic theology professor, Karrer, which insisted on the Christian nature of the idea rather than upon the historicity of the miracle. Although Jung had not yet seen the papal definition (and asked White for a copy) he said, based on Professor Karrer's understanding, that "'the definition' does not insist upon the reality, but rather upon the belief in the reality of the Assumption and thus upon the reality of the idea." Jung, *Letters I*, 567.

189. Jung, "Letter to White," 25 November 1950, in *Letters II*, 568.

190. White, "Letter to Jung" (bibliog. 2.2, 3 December 1950).

191. Ibid.

192. Pius X, "*Sacrorum Antistitum*" (bibliog. 1.1) had introduced the anti-modernist oath in 1910.

193. White, "Letter to Jung," (bibliog. 2.2, 3 December 1950).

194. Ibid.

195. Burns, Charles "Review of Victor White's *God and the Unconscious*" (bibliog. 1.1): 79–83.

196. White, *How to Study* (bibliog. 1.4, 1947), 13 (of the 1993 edition). Cf. Aquinas, *Summa Theologiae* (bibliog. 1.1), 2a2ae.177.1 ad 3.

197. This was published two years later as White, "Easter Sunday" (bibliog. 1.4, 1953).

198. Ibid., 445.

199. Ibid., 446.

200. For a fuller account of the similarities between cultures in the celebration of the idea of passing from life to death, see White, "Easter Sunday" (bibliog. 1.4, 1953), 446–47.

201. Ibid., 447.

202. Ibid.

203. Ibid., 447–48.

204. This appeared a year later as White, "The Dying God: Pagan, Psychological and Christian" (bibliog. 1.4, 1952) and would be incorporated into Chapter Twelve of White, *God and the Unconscious* (bibliog. 1.4, 1952).

205. White, "The Dying God: Pagan, Psychological and Christian" (bibliog. 1.4, 1952), 60.

206. John 11:50.

207. White, "The Dying God: Pagan, Psychological and Christian" (bibliog. 1.4, 1952), 62.

208. Jung *CW*, 8:15b, cf. White, op. cit., 62.

209. White, op. cit., 67.

210. Ibid., 66.

211. Ibid.

212. This is perhaps best seen for Jung in the symbolism of the Mass. The ego (Christ) is sacrificed to the unconscious (God the Father) and is transformed (resurrected in the Spirit). See Jung, "Transformation Symbolism in the Mass" in *CW*, 11: 201–96. For a good account of this, see Dourley, *The Illness* (bibliog. 1.1), 51–69.

213. White, "The Dying God: Pagan, Psychological and Christian: Differences" (bibliog. 1.4, 1952), 122.

214. White, "The Dying God: Pagan, Psychological and Christian" (bibliog. 1.4, 1952), 67.

215. White, "The Dying God: Pagan, Psychological and Christian: Differences" (bibliog. 1.4, 1952), 113–22.

216. Ibid., 116.

217. Ibid., 119.

218. Dourley, *The Illness* (bibliog. 1.1), 53. See also Dourley, *The Rerooting* (bibliog. 1.1), 130–31.

219. White, op. cit., 121.

220. See, for example, Jung "Transformation Symbolism in the Mass" in *CW*, 11: 201–96.

221. White, op. cit., 118.

222. Ibid., 121. White is referring to Jung's "Transformation Symbolism in the Mass" in *CW*, 11: 201–96.

223. Ibid.

224. White, "The Aristotelian Conception of the Psyche" (bibliog. 1.4, 1948), 327.

225. Later published as White, "Four Challenges to Religion" (bibliog. 1.4, 1952).

226. White, "Four Challenges to Religion" (bibliog. 1.4, 1952), 173. Citations refer to the article as it appeared in *Blackfriars*.

227. Ibid., 203.

228. Jung, 1932, quoted by White "Four Challenges to Religion: Jung" (bibliog. 1.4, 1952), 204. cf. Jung, *Modern Man In Search Of A Soul* (bibliog. 1.2, 1932), 234.

229. Jung, *CW*, 13: 38.

230. Ibid., cited by White, op cit., 206.

231. Jung, *CW*, 13: 38.

232. Ibid.

233. See, for example, Giegerich, "Jung's Betrayal of His Truth," (bibliog. 1.1), 60–61.

234. White, "The Aristotelian Conception of the Psyche" (bibliog. 1.4, 1948), 327.

235. White, "Psychiatry and Religion" (bibliog. 2.1).

236. White, "Religion and Psychology" (bibliog. 2.1).

237. White, "Four Challenges to Religion: Jung" (bibliog. 1.4, 1952), 207.

238. White, "The Way of the Cross" (bibliog. 1.4, 1952), 409–15.

239. Ibid., 409.

240. Ibid., 410–12.

241. Ibid., 412.

242. Ibid., 413

243. Ibid.

244. Ibid., 414.

245. Jung, "Letter to White," Spring 1952, in *Letters II*, 50. There is no date but the footnote indicates that it must have been written before April 9.

246. Dourley, *The Illness* (bibliog. 1.1), 58. For a fuller account of this, see Dourley, "Theopathology and Christopathology" in *The Illness* (bibliog. 1.1), 51–69.

247. Edinger, *The Mysterium Lectures* (bibliog. 1.1), 78.

248. Dourley, *The Rerooting* (bibliog. 1.1), 130–31.

249. Edinger, op. cit., 53; and Dourley, *The Rerooting* (bibliog. 1.1), 23, 130–31.

250. White, "Some Recent Contributions to Psychology" (bibliog. 1.4, 1951), 419.

251. Ibid., 421.

252. Jung, *MDR*, 150.

253. White, op. cit., 421. See also Goldbrunner, *Individuation* (bibliog. 1.1). One example is White's criticisms of Jung's "torturous theory of what he calls synchronicity." Synchronicity for Jung is the idea that internal and external events are linked by their subjective meaning.

Chapter Five: 1952–1955

1. Jung, *Aion* in *CW*, 9ii:46. Jung wrote: "The *Summum Bonum* . . . is the effective source of the concept of the *privatio boni* which nullifies the reality of evil."

2. Jung, *CW*, 18:725.

3. White, "Letter to Jung" (bibliog. 2.2, 23 October 1951).

4. White, "Letter to Jung" (bibliog. 2.2, 30 March 1952). White had heard from analytical psychologist Michael Fordham that Jung's *Answer to Job* was in print in Switzerland. White wrote to Jung requesting a copy.

5. See Charet, "A Dialogue" (bibliog. 1.1), 421. Charet, in fact, ascribed the term to an old professor of his: " . . . as one of my former professors put it, [Jung] cornered God the Father, pinned him to the nearest couch and promptly set about psychoanalysing him." In fact Victor White later referred to the work in similar terms, speaking of ". . . [the] subjection of the Divine to psychological exploration." See White, "Review of Jung on Religion" (bibliog. 1.4, 1958), 375.

6. Jung, *CW*, 11:287.

7. Forsyth, *Freud, Jung and Christianity* (bibliog. 1.1), 118, 117–125. See also Jung, "A Psychological Approach to the Dogma of the Trinity," in *CW*, 11:107–200; and *MDR*, 359–60.

8. Jung, *CW*, 11:270. See also *Answer to Job* (bibliog. 1.2, 1973), §574.

9. Jung, *CW*, 11:396–97.

10. Ibid., 11:383.

11. Ibid., 11:391, cf. Proverbs 8.

12. Ibid., 11:397.

13. Ibid., 11:428.

14. Ibid., 11:313. In the book of Job, Job does not see God's unconscious shadow (which is jealous and unjust) but only God's *persona*, the *Summum Bonum*.

15. Ibid., 9ii:213.

16. Jung, *MDR*, 333.

17. Jung, *CW*, 18:710. See also *CW*, 11:369.

18. Ibid., 18:740.

19. Ibid., 18:402. See also *CW*, 11: 394, 377.

20. Ibid., 11:383.

21. Ibid., 5:404.

22. Ibid., 5:391.

23. Ibid., 5:404.

24. Jung, *CW*, 11: 404–05.

25. Ibid., 11:397.

26. Ibid., 11:405; see also *CW*, 18:718, where, in response to a question by H. Philp, Jung suggested that God is more limited than man.

27. See, for example, *CW*, 11:419, where Jung wrote: "All he [God] does, in the shape of his own son, is to rescue mankind from himself."

28. *CW*, 11:405.

29. Ibid., 18:718–19.

30. Ibid., 18:740–41.

31. Ibid., 11:456.

32. Ibid., 11:406.

33. Ibid., 11:397.

34. Jung, "Late Thoughts" in *MDR*, 328.

35. Jung, *CW*, 9ii:103.

36. Ibid., 11:432.

37. Jung, "Letter to Doniger," November 1955, in *Letters II*, 281–82. In *Answer to Job*, Jung went to great lengths to demonstrate the continued work of Satan as seen in the temptation of Christ (Mk3:21), and the inspiring of Judas. See Jung, *CW*, 11:409. But, according to Jung, Satan is now "comparative[ly] ineffective," as if he has been "partial[ly] neutraliz[ed]." See Jung, *CW*, 11:410. Jung suggested that Satan no longer shares the same "confidential relationship" to Yahweh for several reasons: first of all, Yahweh did in fact consult his omniscience this time and "careful preparations" were made for the birth of Christ; and secondly, he pointed to the passage in Lk 10:18, where Christ says he saw Satan fall like lightning from heaven. This, said Jung: ". . . indicates the historic and—so far as we know—final separation of Yahweh from his dark son." See Jung, *CW*, 11:410. Jung's point is essentially that, although God may have become the *Summum Bonum*, Satan is still active in the world because Yahweh's attitude toward him is ambiguous. "Evil is by no means fettered, even though its days are numbered. God still hesitates to use force against Satan. Presumably he still does not know how much his own dark side favours the evil angel." See Jung, *CW*, 11:434.

38. Jung, "Letter to James Kirsch," 16 February 1954, in *Letters II*, 154.

39. Jung, *CW*, 18:734.

40. Ibid., 18:717. Jung in fact made the same point about Mary, arguing that she cannot be whole because she did not conceive in sin like other mothers. See Jung, *CW*, 11:399.

41. Ibid., 18:734.

42. Jung, *CW*, 11: 460.

43. Ibid., 18:710ff; see also Ibid., 11:197.

44. Palmer, "God and Individuation" in Palmer, *Freud and Jung on Religion* (bibliog. 1.1), 155–56.
45. Jung, *CW*, 11:287.
46. White, "Letter to Jung" (bibliog. 2.2, 30 March 1952).
47. White, "Letter to Jung" (bibliog. 2.2, 5 April 1952). See also Jung, "Letter to White," Spring 1952, in *Letters II*, 50–51. The original letter from Jung is undated, and White added " Spring 1952" to the head of the letter.
48. Stein, "The Rôle of Victor White" (bibliog. 1.1), 16–17. This view is further supported by White's own words, writing to Jung in 1955, "I wonder what induced you to publish it: when you gave me the MS to read you were so emphatic that you would not!" See White, "Letter to Jung" (bibliog. 2.2, 17 March 1955).
49. White, "Letter to Jung" (bibliog. 2.2, 5 April 1952).
50. Ibid.
51. Ibid.
52. Ibid.
53. Ibid.
54. An alternative view is offered by Lammers in her pamphlet "The Missing Fourth" (bibliog. 1.1), 18–19. Here she argued that White was following classical Greek in distinguishing μή and οὐ, whereas Jung was not. She argued that this was a mistake on White's part, because ". . . by the time of the New Testament and early Church Fathers, the strict distinction between the participles μή and οὐ had disappeared, and they were virtually interchangeable." This is incorrect, as any introductory text to New Testament Greek would reveal.
55. Jung, "Letter to White," 9–14 April 1952, in *Letters II*, 52.
56. Dourley, *The Rerooting* (bibliog. 1.1), 51.
57. Ibid.
58. White, "Letter to Jung" (bibliog. 2.2, 20 April 1952). See also *Letters II*, 59n2.
59. White, "Letter to Jung" (bibliog. 2.2, 9 April 1952).
60. Jung, "Letter to White," 30 April 1952, in *Letters II*, 59.
61. Ibid.
62. Ibid.
63. Ibid.,60
64. *MDR*, 40.
65. Jung, "Letter to B. Milt," 8 June 1942, in *Letters I*, 317.
66. *MDR*, 94. For an excellent account of Jung's notion of an uprooted humanity that needs re-rooting, see Dourley, *The Rerooting* (bibliog. 1.1).
67. Jung, "Letter to White," 30 April 1952, in *Letters II*, 60.
68. White, "Letter to Jung" (bibliog. 2.2, 9 July 1952).
69. Jung, "Foreword" to White, *God and the Unconscious* (bibliog. 1.4, 1952), xx.
70. Ibid., xviii.
71. Ibid., xvii.
72. Ibid., xviii.
73. Ibid., xxiii.
74. Ibid., xxvii.
75. Ibid., xvii, xxiv.

76. Ibid., xx.
77. Ibid., xx–xi.
78. Ibid., xxi.
79. Ibid., xxii.
80. Jung wrote, "I know of no empirical fact which would come anywhere near such an assertion." Jung continued with a more hesitant restatement of his view that the *privatio boni* may be archetypally motivated. "It is possible that there are—as is the case with other metaphysical statements, particularly dogmas—archetypal factors in the background here, which have existed for an infinitely long time as psychically effective, pre-forming factors; and these would be accessible to empirical research. In other words, there might be a pre-conscious psychic tendency which, independently of time and place, continually causes similar statements, as in the case of mythologems, folklore motifs and the individual production of symbols. But apparently the existing empirical material—at least as far as I am concerned with it—permits no decisive conclusion which would point to an archetypal conditioning of the *privatio boni*." See Ibid., xxii. White, on the other hand, believed that Jung's empirical psychology showed that evil was a privation of the good.
81. Stein, "C. G. Jung: Psychologist and Theologian" in Moore, and Meckel, eds., *Jung and Christianity in Dialogue* (bibliog. 1.1), 10.
82. White, "Letter to Jung," (bibliog. 2.2, 20 April 1952).
83. Jung, "Foreword" to White, God and the Unconscious (bibliog. 1.4, 1952), xxii.
84. Ibid.
85. Ibid., xxiii.
86. Ibid., xxiv.
87. See White, "Lecture to the Guild of Pastoral Psychology" (bibliog. 2.1). Elsewhere White wrote, "I am a visitor, a tourist—an enthusiastic but I must admit a rather perplexed tourist." See White, Zurich Lectures (bibliog. 2.1). See also White "Review of C. G. Jung's Psychology and Religion" (bibliog. 2.1) where White refers to himself as "an eager if dull pupil in psychology"(71) and "a perplexed learner in psychology"(75). A letter from Michael Fordham, editor of *The Journal of Analytical Psychology* further indicated that White was self-deprecating concerning his abilities as a psychologist. "The trouble with you, if I may say so, is that your psychology is so good that pucka psychologists have difficulty competing." See Fordham, "Letter to White" (bibliog. 2.3, 14 March 1958).
88. White, "Preface" to *God and the Unconscious* (bibliog. 1.4, 1952), xxx. White was bilingual in more than one sense of the word, translating Chapters One, Three, and Four of the book into French and German, the manuscripts of which are in the *E. P. O. P. Archives*.
89. Keenan, "Review of Victor White's *Soul and Psyche*" in the *E. P. O. P. Archives*.
90. Fordham, "Letter to White" (bibliog. 2.3, 14 March 1958).
91. Demant, "Review of *God and the Unconscious*" (bibliog. 1.1).
92. Mairet, "God and Therapy" (bibliog. 1.1).

93. Bright, "Review of *God and the Unconscious*" (bibliog. 1.1), 43. Bright was also critical of the "remarkable variations" in White's style, from those articles which are "models of clarity" to others which "give the impression of having been translated into English by someone not well acquainted with the language."

94. Allers, "Mental Trouble and the Moral Life" (bibliog. 1.1). Like Bright, Allers drew attention to "a certain lack of clarity" in some of White's writings.

95. A. E., "Psychotherapy and the Healing of Human Beings" (bibliog. 1.1).

96. Letter from Dowling (bibliog. 2.5).

97. Interview with Ryan (bibliog. 2.5).

98. White, *God and the Unconscious* (bibliog. 1.4, 1952), xxx.

99. Ibid.

100. Ibid.

101. Ibid., xxxiii.

102. Beguin, *L'Art Romantique et Le Rêve* (bibliog. 1.1); Hans Schaer, *Religion and the Cure of Souls in Jung's Psychology* (bibliog. 1.1); and Josef Goldbrunner, *Individuation* (bibliog. 1.1).

103. White, *God and the Unconscious* (bibliog. 1.4, 1952), xxix.

104. Ibid. Chapter Three, "The Unconscious and God," is an amalgamation of notes from lectures given in America in 1948 and in Oxford in 1949; Chapter Four, "Freud Jung and God," is a 1942 lecture to the Guild of Pastoral Psychology, reworked in the light of his BBC broadcasts, "Recent Challenges to Religion"; Chapter Five, "The Frontiers of Theology and Psychology," is a re-written version of his 1942 pamphlet for the Guild of Pastoral Psychology; Chapter Six which focuses on "Aristotle, Aquinas, and Man," and Chapter Seven which focuses on "Revelation and the Unconscious" were published together in the *Eranos Jahrbuch* of 1947; Chapter Eight, "Psychotherapy and Ethics," was first published in *Blackfriars* in 1945; Chapter Nine, "The Analyst and the Confessor," appeared in *Commonweal* in 1948; Chapter Ten, "Devils and Complexes," was a paper presented to the Aquinas Societies of Oxford and London in 1950 and 1952; Chapter Eleven, on Gnosticism, was read to the Analytical Psychology Club of New York in 1948; and the final chapter, "The Dying God," is essentially two talks White gave for the BBC in November 1951.

105. White, *God and the Unconscious* (bibliog. 1.4, 1982), 1.

106. Ibid.

107. Ibid., 2.

108. Ibid.

109. Ibid., 3.

110. Ibid., 8.

111. Ibid., 17. cf. Jung, "Der Geist Der Psychologie," in *Eranos Jahrbuch* 1946, 400.

112. Ibid.

113. Ibid., 21.

114. On March 21, 1953, White gave a lecture for the BBC "London Calling Asia" Service entitled "The Impact of Eastern Wisdom on the West." This was later published in *Blackfriars* (bibliog. 1.4, 1953).

115. White, "Letter to Jung" (bibliog. 2.2, 25 June 1952).

116. White replied that it was not a formal dogma but a "*sententia communis.*" See *Letters II*, 71n1.

117. Jung, "Letter to White," 30 June 1952, in *Letters II*, 72.

118. Ibid., 73

119. Ibid.

120. Ibid.

121. Ibid. This is potentially interesting in relation to the view that annihilation (that is, that pure evil would cease to exist), rather than eternal hell fire, awaits the body and soul after death and the final judgment.

122. Jung, "Letter to White," 30 June 1952, in *Letters II*, 73.

123. Ibid., 72.

124. White, "Letter to Jung" (bibliog. 2.2, 9 July 1952).

125. Ibid.

126. Ibid.

127. Ibid.

128. White, "Good and Evil," (bibliog. 2.1), 9. References in this section refer to the unpublished manuscript from the *E. P. O. P. Archives.*

129. Ibid.

130. Ibid.

131. White, "Letter to Jung" (bibliog. 2.2, 9 July 1952).

132. Ibid.

133. Jung, "Letter to White," 7 August 1952, in *Letters II*, 79.

134. Jung, "Letter to Barbara Robb," 19 November 1952, in *Letters II*, 93.

135. Jung, "Letter to R. J. Zwi Werblosky," 21 May 1953, in *Letters II*, 116. Jung tells Werblsoky, "Fr. White came to Zurich the day before yesterday."

136. White, "Letter to Jung" (bibliog. 2.2, 15 September 1953).

137. White, "Letter to Jung" (bibliog. 2.2, 8 November 1953).

138. Ibid.

139. White, "Good and Evil," (bibliog. 2.1), 9.

140. Ibid.

141. Ibid. The paper was presented again in February 1955 to the Analytical Psychology Club of Los Angeles, and the archival manuscript evinces White's editorial hand. Text in parentheses indicates White's additions to the 1953 manuscript. The paper was published posthumously in *Harvest: Journal for Jungian Studies* 12, in 1966. Citations in this section refer to the original manuscript in *E. P. O. P. Archives.*

142. Ibid., 2.

143. Ibid., 9.

144. Jung, "Letter to White," 7 August 1952, in *Letters II*, 79.

145. White, "Good and Evil" (bibliog. 2.1), 9.

146. Ibid.

147. Ibid.

148. Ibid.

149. Ibid.

150. Ibid., 10. Cf. Aquinas, *Summa Theologiae* (bibliog. 1.1), 1a2ae.36.1.

151. White, "Good and Evil" (bibliog. 2.1), 10.

152. Ibid., 10–11.

153. Ibid., 11.

154. Ibid.

155. Ibid.

156. Ibid., 11–12.

157. Ibid., 12.

158. Ibid.

159. White, "The Aristotelian-Thomist Conception of Man" (bibliog. 1.4, 1948), 322.

160. Ibid., 12.

161. Ibid., 13.

162. Ibid., 9. It is interesting to note that White deleted this sentence in the manuscript, an edit which appears to have been made *after* his presentation to the Analytical Psychology Club of London in November 1953, and prior to his presentation to the Analytical Psychology Club of Los Angeles in February 1955.

163. Ibid., 15–16.

164. Ibid., 3.

165. Ibid., 5.

166. Ibid., 6–7.

167. Ibid., 21.

168. Ibid., 14.

169. Ibid., 15.

170. Ibid., 15a.

171. Ibid., 23.

172. Ibid., 25.

173. Ibid., 25–26.

174. Ibid., 28.

175. Ibid.

176. Jung, "Letter to White," 24 November 1953, in *Letters II*, 136–37.

177. Ibid.

178. Ibid.

179. Ibid.

180. White, "Letter to Jung" (bibliog. 2.2, 20 November 1953); and White, "Letter to Jung" (bibliog. 2.2, 29 November 1953).

181. White, "Letter to Jung" (bibliog. 2.2, 4 March 1954). White noted that on June 5, 1918, the Holy Roman Office had stated that Christ's soul was not ignorant of anything, and that from the beginning he knew everything.

182. Ibid.

183. Ibid.

184. Ibid.

185. Ibid.

186. See Livingston and Fiorenza, eds., *Modern Christian Thought, Volume II* (bibliog. 1.1), 205.

187. White, "Religious Toleration" (bibliog. 1.4, 1953), 533.

188. "Review of Victor White's 'Religious Toleration.'" (bibliog. 1.1, 1953).

189. Jung, "Letter to Aniela Jaffé," 6 April 1954, in *Letters II*, 163. Jung informs Jaffé that he's "writing a long letter to Pater White," that being the letter of 10th April 1954.

190. Jung, "Letter to White," 10 April 1954, in *Letters II*, 169.

191. Ibid., 170.

192. Ibid., 171.

193. Ibid.

194. Ibid., 168 fn. Others have mentioned, though only in passing, the typologies of these two men. See for example, Stein, *Jung on Christianity* (bibliog. 1.1, 1995), 13, where White was identified as an introvert; and Lammers, "The Missing Fourth" (bibliog. 1.1, 2005), 17, where she said "Thinking was not Jung's first function (as it was White's)." But by far the most interesting remarks were made by John Giannini (Conversation with Giannini, bibliog. 2.5) who suggested that the key to understanding the Jung-White relationship lies in the fact that both men were deeply reflective introverts and thus carried each other's shadows (he further speculated that both shared a similar troubled relationship with their fathers).

195. Ibid., 172.

196. White, "Letter to Jung" (bibliog. 2.2, 15 May 1954).

197. See *Directories of the English Province of the Order of Preachers* (bibliog. 1.1).

198. The Dominican House of Studies at Oxford, known as "The Studium," was run by a Regent of Studies who was appointed every four years by the Provincial. Hilary Carpenter, O. P., had been Provincial since 1946, re-elected twice at the General Chapter—at Oxford in 1950 and at Woodchester in 1954. Daniel Callus, O. P., was equally long-serving as Regent of Studies—appointed in 1942 and re-elected in 1946 and 1950.

199. Interview with Ryan (bibliog. 2.5).

200. White, "Letter to Jung" (bibliog. 2.2, 25 September 1954).

201. Interview with Ryan (bibliog. 2.5).

202. Ibid.

203. Ibid.

204. Interview with Bailey (bibliog. 2.5).

205. White, "Letter to Jung" (bibliog. 2.2, 25 September 1954).

206. Ibid.

207. Ibid.

208. It is clear from this letter that White had been sent to California, in October 1954, "without any special assignment," but that he found "a widespread interest in religion and psychiatry" and lectured at many colleges, universities, and seminaries—even on television—on such diverse topics as theology and the psyche, the unconscious, signs and symbols, and trinity and incarnation. See Jung, "Letter to White," 19 January 1955, in *Letters II*, 213n., and Lecture Notes in *E. P. O. P. Archives* (bibliog. 2.1).

209. Aquinas, *Summa Theologiae*, (bibliog. 1.1), 1a2ae.36.1.

210. Jung, "Letter to White," 19 January 1955, in *Letters II*, 213.

211. Ibid.

212. White, "Letter to Jung" (bibliog. 2.2, 8 January 1955). See also *Letters II*, 213n3.

213. Jung, op. cit., 213.

214. "Good and Bad." Zurich (bibliog. 2.1, 1953).

215. White, "Letter to Jung" (bibliog. 2.2, 17 March 1955).

216. Ibid.

217. Ibid. White, in fact, suggested in a postscript to the letter that Jung should include a preface to the work explaining that it was purely personal. Jung clearly took this advice as the November 1955 "Prefatory Note"—written to Simon Doniger, editor of *Pastoral Psychology*—indicates. Jung wrote: "I found myself obliged to deal with the whole problem, and I did so in the form of describing a personal experience, carried by subjective emotions. I deliberately chose this form because I wanted to avoid the impression that I had any idea of announcing an 'eternal truth.' The book does not pretend to be anything but the voice or question of a single individual." See Jung, *Answer to Job* (bibliog. 1.2, 1973), x. In addition, Jung's "Lectori Benevolo" was added as a short preface to the work. Again, Jung clearly expressed that *Answer to Job* was his "own personal view" which resonates with the experiences of many. Jung, op. cit., xv. Subsequent editors have, similarly, taken pains to incorporate White's suggestion. Gerhard Adler, for example, wrote: "Without claiming rigid scientific status [*Answer to Job*] contains the most profound insights born out of an intense feeling of inner obligation." *Job* was, as Adler saw it, "an attempt, from intense personal experience, to make peace with this ambivalent God who would allow his faithful servant Job to become the object of a wager with Satan and permit the untold suffering of millions in Jung's own time."See Adler, "Editorial Note" in Jung, op. cit., v.

218. White, "Letter to Jung" (bibliog. 2.2, 17 March 1955).

219. Ibid.

220. Jung, "Letter to White," 2 April 1955, in *Letters II*, 241. We know from this letter that White would return to England on board the Queen Mary on March 17, 1955. See also White, "Letter to Jung" (bibliog. 2.2, 17 March 1955). After departing from America on the Queen Mary in March 1955, White journeyed to the General Chapter of the Order of Preachers that was held in Rome in April, and then on to Zurich in May. There is, therefore, some doubt as to whether White actually received this letter, a suspicion which is confirmed in Jung, "Letter to White," 6 May 1955, in *Letters II*, 251.

221. Jung, "Letter to White," 2 April 1955, in *Letters II*, 241.

222. Ibid., 242.

223. Ibid.

224. White, "Jung on Job" (bibliog. 1.4, 1955), 55.

225. Ibid.

226. Ibid.

227. Ibid.

228. Ibid. White would remove this passage (and several others) in an edited version of the review that would appear as Appendix V of his book *Soul and Psyche* (bibliog. 1.4, 1960), 233–40.

229. White, "Jung on Job" (bibliog. 1.4, 1955), 57.

230. Ibid.

231. Ibid., 56.

232. Ibid., 57.

233. It is in view of this blunt and public criticism that Laurens van der Post accused White of turning on Jung with "unnecessary violence and reprehensible disregard of what he owed him both as a teacher and friend." See van der Post, *Jung and the Story of Our Time* (bibliog. 1.1) cited in Everson, "Introduction" to White, *God and the Unconscious* (bibliog. 1.4, 1982), xii. Writing in 1982, Everson predicted that the publication of White's letters to Jung would exonerate him of such charges. Having seen copies of the letters in the *E. P. O. P. Archives,* this author can attest to the deep gratitude that White felt toward Jung which is evident in the unpublished letters, many of which have been quoted in this work.

234. Jung, "Letter to White," 6 May 1955, in *Letters II,* 251.

235. Jung, "Letter to Schoening," 24 March 1955, in *Letters II,* 234. Jung recommended White's lectures at the Institute at the beginning of May.

236. *Letters II,* 243n7.

237. White, "Letter to Jung" (bibliog. 2.2, 6 May 1955).

238. White, "Letter to Jung" (bibliog. 2.2, 10 May 1955).

239. White, "Problems Arising From Answer to Job" (bibliog. 2.1).

240. Ibid.

241. Ibid.

242. Ibid.

243. Ibid.

244. Ibid.

245. White, "Critical Notice" (bibliog. 1.4, 1958), 439.

246. Ibid.

247. White, "Letter to Jung" (bibliog. 2.2, 19 May 1955).

248. White, "Letter to Jung" (bibliog. 2.2, 21 May 1955). Jungian analyst John Giannini, who was a student in the House of Studies at St. Albert's at this time, remembers White as "very meditative," a "gentle, quiet man" who attended to prayer and study, and never talked about his private life. Given White's personal turmoil at this time, and his split from Jung, this is striking. White was Giannini's analyst for several months in 1955–56, and Giannini credits White with being a transforming agent in his life. As a teacher, however, Giannini recalls that although the content was interesting, White's style was "very British" (this in contrast to his teaching at Blackfriars, as evidenced in Chapter One of this book). See Conversation with Giannini (bibliog. 2.5).

249. Ibid.

250. Ibid.

251. Ibid. See also *Letters II,* 251 n1.

252. Ibid.

253. Murray Stein, "C. G. Jung: Psychologist and Theologian" in Moore and Meckel, eds., *Jung and Christianity in Dialogue* (bibliog. 1.1), 9.

254. Ibid., 10.

Chapter Six: 1955–1960

1. White, "Charles Gustave Jung" (bibliog. 1.4, 1955).

2. There are, as I have suggested, several striking parallels between the Freud–Jung relationship and the Jung–White relationship that are worthy of note. First, Freud saw Jung as the crown prince of the psychoanalytic movement, and "the Joshua to his Moses." See Palmer, *Freud and Jung on Religion* (bibliog. 1.1), 89. In other words, Freud saw Jung as one who would continue his mission, who could take the pyschoanalytic movement from its Jewish origins to the Gentiles. Similarly, Jung saw White as his "white raven," an image which I have argued points to Jung's great hopes that Victor White would be instrumental in the transformation of the Western God image. Second, as "disciples," Jung championed Freud's theories among the non-Jews, White championed Jung's theories among Catholics. Third, Jung's filial devotion to Freud is mirrored in White's affection for Jung as the master (certainly in the field of analytical psychology). Fourth, the hopes of Freud vis à vis Jung and of Jung vis à vis White were short lived. Fifth, that which precipitated the split with Freud was, as Jung saw it, the fear of risking his authority. Similar issues of authority were evident in the Jung–White split, Jung trusting the authority of the psyche, White the authority of the Church. In addition, when Freud expressed that he wanted to "make a dogma" of his sexual theory, Jung thought that this "struck at the heart of our friendship." See Jung, *MDR*, 167. White was equally concerned by what he saw as Jung's desire to make a dogma of psychological opinions, particularly in *Job*—which also struck at the heart of their friendship. Finally, just as Jung attempted to meet the deficiencies of Freudian theory, so too White attempted to meet the deficiencies of Jung's theory, especially vis à vis God.

3. White, "Two Theologians on Jung's Psychology" (bibliog. 1.4, 1955), 385. This quote is taken from a review essay which essentially focused on two different approaches to the collaboration of theology and psychology. In it, White considered Hostie, *Du Mythe à la Religion* (bibliog. 1.1), decried by White as the work of "an external observer," and Zacharias, *Psyche und Mysterium* (bibliog. 1.1), which White saw as "uncritical and synthetic." See White, op. cit., 383, 386.

4. As I showed in Chapter Five, White had earlier expressed the concern that analytical psychology had a tendency "to make dogmas of metapsychological opinions," a tendency which concerned him greatly. See White, "Some Recent Contributions to Psychology" (bibliog. 1.4, 1951), 421.

5. White, "Two Theologians on Jung's Psychology" (bibliog. 1.4, 1955), 385. It is interesting to note that Jung has indeed been accused of founding a new religion. In his book, *The Aryan Christ* (bibliog. 1.1), Noll accused Jung of creating a purified Freudianism for the Gentiles, and others have suggested that, in his later religious psychology, he did in fact intend to set up a new religion. Even White expressed an awareness of the suspicion that analytical psychology was becoming a new religion, or, at the very least, a substitute for it. See White, "Theological Reflections" (bibliog. 1.4, 1960), 152.

6. For a good account of this, see "Trinity and Quaternity," "The Missing Feminine" and "The Integration of Evil" in White, *Soul and Psyche* (bibliog. 1.4, 1960).

7. White, "Review of Jung's *Two Essays*" (bibliog. 1.4, 1954), 126. See also White, "Two Theologians on Jung's Psychology" (bibliog. 1.4, 1955), 386.

8. White, "Two Theologians on Jung's Psychology" (bibliog. 1.4, 1955), 384.

9. Ibid.

10. White, "Review of C. G. Jung's Psychology and Religion" (bibliog. 1.4, 1959), 78.

11. White, "Critical Notice" (bibliog. 1.4, 1958), 62.

12. White, *Soul and Psyche* (bibliog. 1.4, 1960), 49.

13. Ibid., 53.

14. Ibid., 54.

15. Ibid., 54, 52.

16. Ibid.

17. Ibid., 56.

18. In an article written in 1956, White reiterated the point that although theologians and psychologists use the same language, they are often "bewilderingly at cross purposes." See White, "Guilt: Theological and Psychological" (bibliog. 1.4, 1956), 155. In the final article of his life, White argued that language is *the* greatest barrier to understanding between psychologists and theologians. See White, "Theological Reflections" (bibliog. 1.4, 1960), 148.

19. White, *Soul and Psyche* (bibliog. 1.4, 1960), 61.

20. Ibid. White criticized, for example, Hostie's confrontational approach as "somewhat unhelpful."

21. White, "Two Theologians on Jung's Psychology" (bibliog. 1.4, 1955), 388.

22. Ibid. White was, in fact, quoting a letter that he had received from Jung. See Jung, "Letter to White," 5 October 1945, in *Letters I*, 384–85.

23. White, "Dogma and Mental Health" (bibliog. 1.4, 1958), 441. The manuscript of this paper, written in English and in Spanish, is in the *E. P. O. P. Archives*. White first presented the paper at the seventh Catholic International Congress of Psychotherapists and Clinical Psychology in September of 1957. The article later appeared in *Conducta religiosa y salud mental. VII congresso internacional de psicoterapia y psicologia clinica.* Madrid, 10-15.9.1957. (Barcelona: Antibioticos, S.A., 1959), 99–105.

24. White, "Dogma and Mental Health" (bibliog. 1.4, 1958), 441.

25. White, *Soul and Psyche* (bibliog. 1.4, 1960), 48.

26. Ibid., 215.

27. White, "Dogma and Mental Health" (bibliog. 1.4, 1958), 441. Indeed White says it would be "outrageous" to assert "that empirical psychology could add one jot to faith."

28. White, "Two Theologians on Jung's Psychology" (bibliog. 1.4, 1955), 385.

29. White, "Guilt: Theological and Psychological" (bibliog. 1.4, 1956), 155.

30. Ibid., 173.

31. Ibid., 175.

32. White, "The All Sufficient Sacrifice" (bibliog. 1.4, 1957). Note that this also appeared as an appendix to White, *Soul and Psyche* (bibliog. 1.4, 1960), 248–57, under a different title, "Sidelights on the Theology of the Mass from Psychology and Comparative Religion." The article was well received as "a very helpful bridge" by Jolande Jacobi. See Jacobi "Letter to White" (bibliog. 2.3, 27 July 1957).

33. Dourley, *The Illness* (bibliog. 1.1), 51.

34. Jung, "Transformation Symbolism in the Mass" in *CW*, 11:414. Some, like Vera von der Heydt in *Prospects for the Soul* (bibliog. 1.1), 24 have suggested that Jung was writing about the very conscious experience of his own sacrifice—"by 'betraying' Freud he took upon himself the stigma of disloyalty to a revered father-figure" (it is interesting that this is *exactly* what Laurens van der Post accused White of doing).

35. Dourley, *The Illness* (bibliog. 1.1), 53. See also Jung, *CW*, 11: 265 where Jung talks about the path to wholeness as "the way of the cross."

36. White, "The All Sufficient Sacrifice" (bibliog. 1.4, 1957), 541. This idea was also expressed theologically in, for example, the writings of St. Anselm.

37. White emphasized that the sacrifice of the Cross and the sacrifice of the Mass are one and the same sacrifice. This was stated at the Council of Trent (Session 9 chapter 2). The victim is the same, only the way of offering is different—it is without shedding blood (though this is symbolized in the bread and wine). See White, "The All Sufficient Sacrifice" (bibliog. 1.4, 1957), 539n2.

38. Jung, *Psychology and Religion* (bibliog. 1.2, 1938/40), 72.

39. Jung, "Letter to B. Milt," 8 June 1942," in *Letters I*, 317.

40. Pius XII, "Address to the Fifth International Catholic Congress of Psychotherapy and Clinical Psychology" in *L'Osservatore Romano* (16 April 1953), 1, cited in White, *Soul and Psyche* (bibliog. 1.4, 1960), 21 and 265n23.

41. See, for example, White, *Soul and Psyche* (bibliog. 1.4, 1960), 20–29.

42. Ibid., 12–13, 205–206. Cf. Jung, *Modern Man In Search of A Soul* (bibliog. 1.2), 264.

43. White, "Letter to Jung" (bibliog. 2.2, 25 August 1956). White continued to send the occasional letter to Jung, though Jung did not reply. White's joke regarding the Index is in response to Fr. Gemelli's rebuke of White in the journal *Vita e Pensiero*, where Gemelli accused White of utilizing a model of collaboration based on "mutual aid and enrichment," a model that White flatly rejected. See White, "Dogma and Mental Helath" (bibliog. 1.4), 441.

44. Pizzardo, "Letter to Michael Browne, O. P." (bibliog. 2.4).

45. White, "Letter to Jung" (bibliog. 2.2, 25 August 1956).

46. Browne, "Letter to White" (bibliog. 2.3, 23 July 1957).

47. White, "Religious Toleration" (bibliog. 1.4, 1953), 532.

48. White, "Theological Reflections" (bibliog. 1.4, 1960), 149. For an interesting exposition of White's understanding of the role of the theologian, see White, "The Theologian's Task" in his *God the Unknown* (bibliog. 1.4, 1956), ch.1. For White, theology presupposes faith, thereby following the traditional definition of theology as *intelligere quod credimus*, faith seeking understanding. As such, it is clearly distinguishable from the magisterium.

49. Leonard, "Letter to White" (bibliog. 2.3, 6 May 1958).
50. White, "Letter to Carpenter" (bibliog. 2.2, 11 August 1957).
51. St. John, "Letter to White" (bibliog. 2.3, 15 August 1959).
52. White, "Letter to Jung" (bibliog. 2.2, 1 June 1958).
53. White, "Letter to Jung" (bibliog. 2.2, 26 July 1958). The date of this letter was Jung's birthday, and White celebrated Mass for him. This is their last known meeting. See also *Letters II*, 251n1 which indicates that the two met in June 1958.
54. Jung, "Letter to White," 21 October 1959, in *Letters II*, 518.
55. White, *Soul and Psyche* (bibliog. 1.4, 1960), 92–93.
56. Ibid., 92.
57. Ibid.
58. Jung, *CW*, 11:109.
59. White, *Soul and Psyche* (bibliog. 1.4, 1960), 105.
60. See, for example, White, "Scholasticism" (bibliog. 1.4, 1934), 24.
61. See White, *Soul and Psyche* (bibliog. 1.4, 1960), 92; White, "Holy Teaching" (bibliog. 1.4, 1958), 11–12.
62. White, *Soul and Psyche* (bibliog. 1.4, 1960), 92.
63. White, "Two Theologians on Jung's Psychology" (bibliog. 1.4, 1955), 385.
64. Department of Theology, University of Birmingham, "Letter to White" (bibliog. 2.3, 5 June 1958, 10 December 1958); Lampe, "Letter to White" (bibliog. 2.3, 17 April 1958).
65. Quinn, "Review of Victor White's *Soul and Psyche*" (bibliog. 1.1).
66. Strauss, "Review of Victor White's *Soul and Psyche*" (bibliog. 1.1).
67. For Jung, the quaternity was a symbol of wholeness. For a good account of Jung's fascination with quaternity symbols, see "Trinity and Quaternity" in White, *Soul and Psyche* (bibliog. 1.4, 1960).
68. Forsyth, *Psychological Theories of Religion* (bibliog. 1.1), 76.
69. White, *Soul and Psyche* (bibliog. 1.4, 1960), 115.
70. Ibid.
71. Ibid., 118
72. Ibid., 123.
73. White was clearly influenced not only by Jung but also by his psychoanalyst John Layard who wrote on puberty rites of initiation as overcoming monosexuality: to be a whole, a man had to experience, "the making of Woman in man." Layard compared this with "the Hindu identification with Mother Kali." See Layard, "The Making of Man in Malekula" (bibliog. 1.1), 210–11, cited in White, *Soul and Psyche* (bibliog. 1.4, 1960), 287n33. It is important to note that masculinity and femininity are archetypes, not abstractions of real men and women. See White, *Soul and Psyche* (bibliog. 1.4, 1960), 245.
74. Forsyth, "C. G. Jung: Religion and Archetype" in *Psychological Theories of Religion* (bibliog. 1.1), 79.
75. According to Jung, God is masculine and the anima is projected onto Sophia.
76. White, *Soul and Psyche* (bibliog. 1.4, 1960), 129, 132.
77. Ibid., 131.

78. Aquinas, *Summa Theologiae* (bibliog. 1.1), 1a.4.3, cited in White, *Soul and Psyche* (bibliog. 1.4, 1960), 126.

79. Aquinas, *Summa Theologiae* (bibliog. 1.1), 3a.3.3, cited in White, *Soul and Psyche* (bibliog. 1.4, 1960), 126.

80. White, op. cit., 161.

81. Jung, *CW*, 11:399.

82. Jung, *Essays on the Science of Mythology* (bibliog. 1.2), 239, cited in White *Soul and Psyche* (bibliog. 1.4, 1960), 293n56.

83. White made a very interesting and, I think, insightful point that feminism has meant "a further assimilation of the woman to the male, her equal competitiveness in man-made society, and the further repression of Eros." White, *Soul and Psyche* (bibliog. 1.4, 1960), 136. Jung agreed that this is disastrous psychologically and socially.

84. Ibid.

85. Ibid., 136.

86. White, "Trinity and Incarnation" (bibliog. 2.1).

87. White, *Soul and Psyche* (bibliog. 1.4, 1960), 108.

88. Jung, *MDR*, 53.

89. Jung, "Letter to B. Milt," 8 June 1942, in *Letters I*, 317.

90. Jung, "A Psychological Approach to the Dogma of the Trinity" in *CW*, 11:226.

91. White, *Soul and Psyche* (bibliog. 1.4, 1960), 109.

92. Ibid., 91.

93. Ibid., 109

94. Ibid., 110.

95. See Palmer, *Freud and Jung on Religion* (bibliog. 1.1), 214n63. White does, however, note "the static and the dynamic" Trinity in White, *Soul and Psyche* (bibliog. 1.4, 1960), 110. See also White, "Theological Reflections" (bibliog. 1.4, 1960), 154, where White identifies Trinity as dynamic but quaternity as static.

96. Jung, "A Psychological Approach to the Dogma of the Trinity" in *CW*, 11:182–92.

97. This is an important point. For Jung, images of God and images of the Self both function as symbols of wholeness. If the God image does not include the feminine or shadow side, therefore, it can no longer function as a symbol of wholeness and is, psychologically speaking, incomplete.

98. White, "Review of Jung on Religion" (bibliog. 1.4, 1958), 375, 374.

99. Ibid., 374–75.

100. Jung, *CW*, 11: 110.

101. White, op. cit., 375.

102. Michael Palmer made a useful distinction between the "archetypal God form" (the inherited capacity or mode of psychic thinking to create the image) and the "archetypal God contents" (what is actually created). See Palmer, *Freud and Jung on Religion* (bibliog. 1.1), 123–37.

103. Forsyth, *Psychological Theories of Religion* (bibliog. 1.1), 76.

104. Palmer, op. cit., 159–60.

105. For an interesting account of this "psychological dispensation" which is subsequent to the Old Testament and New Testament dispensations, see Lawrence Jaffé, *Celebrating Soul* (bibliog. 1.1).

106. White, "Review of C. G. Jung's Psychology and Religion" (bibliog. 1.4, 1959), 76.

107. Ibid.

108. Ibid. White's insistence that Jung was "wrestling with some religious problem" that was not his own is interesting in relation to Stein's claim Jung saw White as "a symbol of the western malaise" and that this was the catalyst that led to Jung's *Answer to Job*. See Stein, "The Rôle of Victor White," (bibliog. 1.1), 8, 11–12. Based on this review, it seems that White would not have recognized himself in this way (at least not in 1959) even if that is how Jung perceived him.

109. White, "Appendix V" in *Soul and Psyche* (bibliog. 1.4, 1960), 235.

110. Ibid., 236.

111. White, *Soul and Psyche* (bibliog. 1.4, 1960), 155.

112. Ibid., 155–56.

113. White, "Review of C. G. Jung's Psychology and Religion" (bibliog. 1.4, 1959), 75.

114. Aquinas, *De Malo* (bibliog. 1.1), I.i, cited in White, *Soul and Psyche* (bibliog. 1.4, 1960), 297n52.

115. White, "Review of Jung's *The Archetypes of the Collective Unconscious* and *Aion*; Jacobi's *Complex Archetype*; and Philp's *Jung and the Problem of Evil* " (bibliog. 1.4, 1960), 90n.

116. White, *Soul and Psyche* (bibliog. 1.4, 1960), 152.

117. Ibid.,155.

118. Ibid., 297n52.

119. White, "Review of Jung's *The Archetypes of the Collective Unconscious* and *Aion*; Jacobi's *Complex Archetype*; and Philp's *Jung and the Problem of Evil* " (bibliog. 1.4, 1960), 90n.

120. White, *Soul and Psyche* (bibliog. 1.4, 1960), 156n.

121. Ibid., 157.

122. Ibid., 156–57. Lammers has suggested that White's problem lay in the fact that he failed to distinguish between the personal shadow, which can be integrated, and the archetypal shadow, which cannot. See Lammers *In God's Shadow* (bibliog. 1.1), 219.

123. Jung, *CW*, 7:103.

124. Jung, *CW*, 9i:284–85.

125. See, for example, Jung *CW*, 9ii:267. Jung wrote: "[the shadow] does not consist only of morally reprehensible tendencies, but also displays a number of good qualities, such as normal instincts, appropriate reactions, realistic insights, creative impulses, etc."

126. Jung, *CW*, 7:236.

127. Forsyth, *Psychological Theories of Religion* (bibliog. 1.1), 63.

128. White clarified this point in his chapter, "The Integration of Evil," in White, *Soul and Psyche* (bibliog. 1.4, 1960), 162.

129. White, *Soul and Psyche* (bibliog. 1.4, 1960), 161.

130. Ibid., 163–64.

131. Ibid., 157.

132. Ibid.

133. Ibid., 259.

134. Sanford, "The Problem of Evil," (bibliog. 1.1), 122.

135. Sanford applauded the merits of Origen's approach and, drawing on the work of Allan Anderson, proposed a similar model for critiquing Jung's idea that good and evil are logically equivalent opposites (to be understood in terms of each other), suggesting that, rather, they should be understood in terms of a norm, the norm being wholeness. In other words, "whatever detracts from or destroys wholeness we call evil and whatever supports, furthers or maintains wholeness we call good." See Sanford, "The Problem of Evil" (bibliog. 1.1), 116–17, 126–30. In fact White proposed precisely this model in *Soul and Psyche* (bibliog. 1.4), 184–88.

136. White, "Lecture to Analytical Psychology Club and Society of Analytical Psychologists" (bibliog. 2.1).

137. White's medical notes were discovered by Michael Stratham in 1998 along with some letters from Catherine Ginsberg who nursed him in his dying days. According to the notes, White suffered a serious motorcycling accident on April 17, 1959, which left him severely incapacitated. He could not go anywhere alone, and needed assistance even to cross the street. See "Medical Notes of Victor White," *E. P. O. P. Archives*.

138. White was admitted to Peterboro Hospital on April 17, 1959, and transferred to Addenbrookes on April 24. He was discharged to Hope Nursing Home on May 6, 1959. See the *E. P. O. P. Archives*.

139. White, "Letter to Ginsberg" (bibliog. 2.2, 22 June 1959). Catherine Ginsberg, also a Jungian, was a friend whom White visited when in London at the More Clinic. She would nurse him in his dying days.

140. Jung, "Letter to Mother Prioress," September 1959, in *Letters II*, 516. Provincial Archivist Bede Bailey, O. P., informed me that the Prioress was named Mother Michael of the Blessed Trinity. White and Mother Michael had been friends for almost two decades, and White served as confessor to the sisters. At the request of the Carmelites, several letters and papers from Mother Michael remain sealed in the *E. P. O. P. Archives* (Bailey, bibliog. 2.5).

141. White, "Review of CG Jung's Psychology and Religion" (bibliog. 1.4, 1959), 73.

142. White, "Letter to Jung" (bibliog. 2.2, 18 October 1959).

143. Lewis, "Letter to Mrs. Ginsberg" (bibliog. 2.4, 24 July 1960). Both women were members of a Catholic Analysts Group which met regularly in London and in which Victor White was a participant.

144. White spent September 10–23 in the hospital. See "Medical Notes of Victor White" in the *E. P. O. P. Archives*.

145. See "Medical Notes of Victor White" in the *E. P. O. P. Archives*; and Kay, "Letter to Dr. Anderson" (bibliog. 2.4, 11 March 1960).

146. White, "Theological Reflections" (bibliog. 1.4, 1960), 147. Lambert was to precede White as a speaker at the conference.

147. Ibid.

148. Ibid.

149. Ibid., 148.

150. Ibid., 149.

151. See, for example, Chapter One of White, *Soul and Psyche* (bibliog. 1.4, 1960). The Catholic psychiatrist, E. B. Strauss, disagreed with White on this point, arguing that "the 'soul' is a theological concept . . . whereas 'psyche' is a psychological construct." (White, op.cit.,16). Although White thought that there were "different ways (*cognoscibiles*) in which the subject could be rendered knowable to the human mind," he did not allow for the separation of soul and psyche. See White, *Soul and Psyche* (bibliog. 1.4, 1960), 263 n15.

152. White, "Theological Reflections" (bibliog. 1.4, 1960), 151.

153. Ibid.

154. Ibid.

155. Ibid., 153.

156. Ibid., 154.

157. As I have argued previously, White did, however, think that worship of God Godself was essential to human flourishing.

158. White, op. cit., 154.

159. White, *Soul and Psyche* (bibliog. 1.4, 1960), 51.

160. Palmer, *Freud and Jung on Religion* (bibliog. 1.1, 1997), 187. See Jung, *CW*, 18:663–70 for the Jung's "Reply to Martin Buber."

161. Jung, "Letter to Mother Prioress," 6 February 1960, in *Letters II*, 536.

162. Some have argued—Laurens van der Post, for example—that the Jung–White split signified the ingratitude of White and his betrayal of the master (bibliog. 1.1, 1976). I disagree, and White's words, as quoted in this book, attest to that. In addition, I would argue that, in matters of theology, *White* was the master.

163. White, "Letter to Jung" (bibliog. 2.2, 8 March 1960).

164. White, "Letter to Jung" (bibliog. 2.2, 18 March 1960).

165. Ibid. In this letter White seems clueless as to his public denunciation of Jung, even speculating that it was his "Review of C. G. Jung's *Two Essays on Analytical Psychology* (*CW* v.7), *Psychology and Alchemy* (*CW* v.12), and *Von Den Wurzein des Bewusstseins*; and Progoff's *Jung's Psychology and its Social Meaning*" (bibliog. 1.4, 1954) which caused offence – ironical because this review is actually effusive in its praise of Jung's work.

166. Ibid. White, it seems, thought that the reference to his apparent "syllogisms" came from Howard Philp's book, *Jung and the Problem of Evil* (bibliog. 1.1). See White, "Letter to Jung" (bibliog. 2.2, 18 March 1960). It was, however, a reference to a letter written by Jung to a colleague. See Jung, "Letter to Dr. Tenney," 23 February 1955, in *Letters II*, 228. This letter was *quoted* by Philp. See also Jung, *CW*, 18: 710.

167. White, "Letter to Jung" (bibliog. 2.2, 18 March 1960). Further comment on these apparent syllogisms can be seen in White, *Soul and Psyche* (bibliog. 1.4), 259,

where White wrote, "It is disappointing but not surprising, that discussion conducted in this fashion gets nowhere at all."

168. White, "Letter to Jung" (bibliog. 2.2, 18 March 1960).

169. Jung, "Letter to White," 25 March 1960, in *Letters II*, 544.

170. Ibid.

171. Ibid., 546.

172. Jung, "Letter to Mother Prioress," 26 March 1960, in *Letters II*, 546–47.

173. Anderson, "Letter to Whom it May Concern" (bibliog. 2.4, 8 April 1960).

174. Jung, "Letter to Mother Prioress," 29 April 1960, in *Letters II*, 552.

175. Jung, "Letter to Mother Prioress,"19 October 1960, in *Letters II*, 603–04. Several months after White's death, Jung expressed that he would not have sent the letter had he realized how sick White was.

176. Jung, "Letter to White," 30 April 1960, in *Letters II*, 555.

177. Jung, "Letter to White," 5 October 1945, in *Letters II*, 387.

178. At the request of the Provincial, the tape of White's dictated letters to Jung became the property of Mrs. Ginsberg after White's death. See Weatherhead, "Letter to Ginsberg" (bibliog. 2.4, 16 October 1960). This tape has been lost.

179. White, "Letter to Jung" (bibliog. 2.2, 6 May 1960).

180. Ibid.

181. Ibid.

182. Ibid. In fact, Jung had elsewhere remarked about "the rigidity of scholastic philosophy, through which Father White is wriggling as well as he can." In particular Jung criticized "the untenable concretism" of the Church's beliefs and "the syllogistic character of Thomistic philosophy." See Jung, "Letter to Dr. Tenney," 23 February 1955 in *Letters II*, 228.

183. Ibid.

184. White, "Letter to Jung" (bibliog. 2.2, 8 May 1960).

185. See "Notes Relating to Victor White's Death" in the *E. P. O. P. Archives*.

186. Mother Michael, "Letter to C. G. Jung" (bibliog. 2.4, 22 May 1960). Unaware of White's death, Mother Michael of the Blessed Trinity had in fact given a conference on death that morning to the nuns. Significantly, one of the texts for the conference was Job 12:22 "The recesses of the darkness he discloses, and brings the gloom forth to the light."

187. Ibid.

188. The picture was a sketch done by Mary Rennell at White's death, and it was a picture which Mrs. Ginsberg sent to many of White's friends. Mother Michael of the Blessed Trinity, for example, responded: "At first I thought you were sending me a copy of a crucified Christ. . . . It was a great shock to discover it was the face of Fr. Victor. I could not recognise him. But it was *wonderful*. He was always my image of Christ Our Lord—not his *persona* but his being—it was a living image, and *is so still*. And this *is* the face of my Christ—crucified—and it is one more showing of the truth that Our Lord unites my soul with the soul of Fr. Victor." See Mother Michael, "Letter to Mrs. Ginsberg" (bibliog. 2.4, 31 May 1960).

189. Jung, "Letter to Ginsberg," 3 June 1960, in *Letters II*, 563.

190. Ibid.

191.   Ginsberg, "Letter to Towers" (bibliog. 2.4, 15 August 1960). Towers was from Jesus College Cambridge where his primary academic interest was Teilhard de Chardin. It was a topic he had discussed often with Victor White, particularly as Teilhard's radical theology of immanence offered a theological point of contact with Jung.

192.   Jung, "Letter to Mother Prioress," 19 October 1960, in *Letters II*, 604. The Mass was said by a Jesuit, Fr. Rudin, a mutual friend who was the Director of the *Institutum Apologeticum* in Zurich.

193.   Everson, "Introduction" (January 1981) in White, *God and the Unconscious* (bibliog. 1.4, 1982), xiii.

Chapter Seven: Conclusion

1.   See, for example, Dourley, "Exercises in Futility" (bibliog. 1.1), ch. 2; Dourley, *The Rerooting* (bibliog. 1.1), 230; and Lammers, *In God's Shadow* (bibliog. 1.1), 55, 245. This, it seems to me, is contrary to sources in the *E. P. O. P. Archives* which I have referred to in this book. This being said, in her more recent pamphlet, "The Missing Fourth" (bibliog. 1.1), 21, Lammers seems to acknowledge that, "White knew there were rocks and even knew where they were located, before writing to Jung for the first time." This is based on a dream that White sent to Jung in 1946. See White, "Letter to Jung" (bibliog. 2.2, 13 October 1946).

2.   White, "Letter to Layard" (bibliog. 2.2, 5 December 1940).

3.   White, "The Frontiers" (bibliog. 1.4, 1942), 18–19.

4.   Jung, "Letter to Dorothee Hoch," 28 May 1952, in *Letters II*, 66–67.

5.   Gilby, "Personae: 6" (bibliog. 1.1), 284.

6.   White, "Review of Igor Caruso's *Psychoanlyse*" (bibliog. 1.4, 1953), 223–25.

7.   Hibbert, *Man Culture and Christianity* (bibliog. 1.1), 28–32. Hibbert argued that White's approach reflects an abstract intellectual synthesis rather than an integration of ideas in actual life and living which ultimately exacerbates the situation of modern man.

8.   Jung, *MDR*, 74, 99, 101.   White was also very aware of the influence of Kant on Jung, as can be seen in White, *Soul and Psyche* (bibliog. 1.1), 53, and an unpublished manuscript, White, "An Inquiry into the Philosophical Foundations of C. G. Jung" (bibliog. 2.1).

9.   Livingston and Fiorenza, eds., *Modern Christian Thought: Volume II* (bibliog. 1.1), 199.

10.   This is especially seen in the work of Reginald Garigou-Lagrange and Jacques Maritain.

11.   In Jung, "Reply to Martin Buber" in *CW*, 18: 663–70, Jung joked that he had been accused of being a gnostic and yet his attitude to the transcendent was agnostic.

12.   White, "Letter to Jung" (bibliog. 2.2, 20 April 1952).

13. White was deeply insulted by this, responding: "However much I have erred, and possibly been unjust to you I think you must allow that I have never questioned your sincerity (publicly or privately) or suggested that you are 'tied hand and foot' by other people's ideas or syllogisms." See White, "Letter to Jung" (bibliog. 2.2, 6 May 1960).

14. Dourley, *The Rerooting* (bibliog. 1.1), 72.

15. Dourley, "Religious Implications" (bibliog. 1.1), 187. See also, Dourley, *The Rerooting* (bibliog. 1.1), 23, 130–31; and Dourley, *Love, Celibacy and Inner Marriage* (bibliog. 1.1), 71.

16. Jung, *MDR*, 52, 55, 93–96.

17. Jung, *Psychology and Religion* (bibliog. 1.2), 72.

18. See White, "Thomism and Affective Knowledge, Part 1" (bibliog. 1.4, 1943); "Thomism and Affective Knowledge, Part 2" (bibliog. 1.4, 1943); "Thomism and Affective Knowledge, Part 3" (bibliog. 1.4, 1944).

19. Jung, op. cit., 72.

20. As I have argued throughout this book, Jung insisted that he did not say that God is only intra-psychic, but that, from an empirical standpoint, this is all he could say about God.

21. Jung, op. cit., 73.

22. This concern was expressed in letters written to Jung by a Catholic theologian, Gebhard Frei. Jung, in response, denied it. See Jung, "Letter to Gebhard Frei" 13 January 1948, in *Letters I*, 486–89.

23. Jung, op. cit., 468–69, 190, cited in Jung, "Glossary" in *MDR*, 394–95.

24. For an interesting critique of Jung, see Vitz, *Psychology as Religion* (bibliog. 1.1).

25. Jung, *CW*, 9ii. Jung's equation of the experience of wholeness with the experience of God was most notable in his *Answer to Job*, though it must be reiterated that, empirically, he was not in a position to distinguish what is from the unconscious, and what is from God.

26. The useful distinction between archetypal God *form* and archetypal God *contents* is made in Palmer, *Freud and Jung on Religion* (bibliog. 1.1), espec. 93–96.

27. Jung, "Psychology and Alchemy" in *CW*, 12:14.

28. See White, *Soul and Psyche* (bibliog. 1.4, 1960), 51.

29. Jung, "Letter to Bernet," 13 June 1955, in *Letters II*, 257–65.

30. Jung, "Letter to Gebhard Frei," 13 January 1948, in *Letters I*, 487.

31. Jung, "Letter to Bernet," 13 June 1955, in *Letters II*, 257–65.

32. Ibid.

33. Jung, "Letter to Smith," 29 June 1960, in *Letters II*, 570–73. Smith was, at the time, writing a thesis on "A Critical Analysis of Religious and Philosophical Issues between Buber and Jung" at Villanova, Pennsylvania. See Jung, "Letter to Neumann," 28 February 1952, in *Letters II*, 243 n.9.

34. In fact Jung could well be referring to White when, in a letter to Bernhard Lang, he criticized the emphasis on intellectualism over experience, such as that of "those Oxfordites who think they can call God up on the telephone." See Jung, "Letter to Bernhard Lang," June 1957, in *Letters II*, 378.

35. Jung, "Letter to Bernet," 13 June 1955, in *Letters II*, 257–65.
36. Ibid.
37. Ibid.
38. Jung, *Psychology and Religion* (bibliog. 1.2, 1938), 4.
39. Stein, "C. G. Jung: Psychologist and Theologian" in Moore and Meckel, eds., *Jung and Christianity in Dialogue* (bibliog. 1.1), 9–10.
40. Dourley, *The Rerooting* (bibliog. 1.1), 23.
41. Ibid.
42. Jung, "Psychology and Religion" (bibliog. 1.2, 1938), 72.
43. Jung was no apologist for religion but rather a threat against which Christianity must defend itself. See, for example, White, "Four Challenges to Religion: Jung" (bibliog. 1.4, 1952): 203–7; and White, "Theological Reflections" (bibliog. 1.4, 1960), 147–54.
44. Pius X, "*Lamentabili Sane*" (bibliog. 1.1), 470–78.
45. Dourley, *The Illness* (bibliog. 1.1), 41. See also Cunningham "The Fateful Encounter," (bibliog. 1.1), 324. Here he wrote, "In the opinion of one person who knew them both it was the disagreement with Jung that shortened White's life." Cunningham gives no indication as to who this person was.
46. Edinger, Cordic, and Yates, eds., *The New God Image* (bibliog. 1.1), 59.
47. Ibid., 60.
48. Jung, *Aion* in *CW*, 9ii:79.
49. See Jung *CW*, 11:265. See also Dourley, *The Illness* (bibliog. 1.1), 53.
50. White, "The Frontiers" (bibliog. 1.4, 1942), 5.
51. This contradicts the author of White's obituary who wrote: "Fr. Victor's interest in Jungian psychology . . . was certainly an important factor in contemporary English theology, though there may be some disagreement over the intrinsic value of his own contributions to the problems which this interest raised for him." See Gilby, "Personae: 6" (bibliog. 1.1), 284. Bede Bailey, O. P., informed me that this obituary is from the pen of Thomas Gilby, O. P. Another comment, made by Gilby, is in the translations of the *Summa* by the Fathers of the English Province of the Order of Preachers. Assuming editorship from White, Gilby wrote: "Many will not have read between the lines to perceive that this edition is not so warm to the *mythos* of depth psychology as Fr. Victor was, nor so cool towards the *logos* of the scholasticism of Cajetan and the theologians of Salamanca, the Baroque, and the Leonine Revival." See Gilby, Introduction to Aquinas' *Summa Theologiae* (bibliog. 1.1), I, p. xvii.
52. Jung, "Letter to Victor White," 1 October 1945, in the *E. P. O. P. Archives*; and Jung, "Preface" to White, *God and the Unconscious* (bibliog. 1.4, 19 52), xxvii.
53. Keenan, "Review of Victor White's *Soul and Psyche*" (bibliog. 1.1).
54. Fordham, "Letter to White," (bibliog. 2.3, 14 March 1958).
55. Wicker, *Culture and Liturgy* (bibliog. 1.1), 206. See also Demant, "Review of Victor White's *God and the Unconscious*" (bibliog. 1.1) where Demant described White's work as "the best confrontation" of theology and psychology to date.
56. Arraj, *Jungian and Catholic?* (bibliog. 1.1), ch. 2.

57. Indeed, White himself implied this in his expressed desire to offer a more sustained work on "Affective Knowledge." White, "Thomism and Affective Knowledge, Part III" (bibliog. 1.4, 1944), 328.

58. See Dourley, *The Rerooting* (bibliog. 1.1), 1; and Dourley, *Stategy for a Loss of Faith* (bibliog. 1.1), 30–42, in which he argued that any exchange between Jung's psychology and theologies of transcendence is "an exercise in futility." For an account of Jung's compatibility (albeit problematic) with theologies of radical immanence, such as that of Paul Tillich, see Dourley, *The Psyche as Sacrament* (bibliog. 1.1). It should be noted that, although Tillich's notion of God as "the ground of Being" seems compatible with Jung's sense of the experience of the divine, Tillich would not embrace Jung's quaternity any more than White could, and would find the notion that Job has higher insight than God equally problematic. See Dourley, *The Rerooting* (bibliog. 1.1), "Preface."

59. Charet, "A Dialogue between Psychology and Theology: The Correspondence of C. G. Jung and Victor White." (bibliog. 1.1), 436. In this respect, the work of Robert Doran on Jung and Lonergan is worthy of note. See for example, Doran, Robert, S. J. (bibliog. 1.1).

60. See, for example, Vitz, *Psychology as Religion* (bibliog. 1.1); and, more recently, Noll, *The Aryan Christ* (bibliog. 1.1).

61. See, for example, "Jungian Psychology as Catholic Theology: What is Carl Gustav Jung Doing in the Church?" (bibliog. 1.1); or Benkovic, *The New Age Counterfeit* (bibliog. 1.1), which criticizes the infiltration of Jungian ideas into the Church and its naive but dangerous appropriation.

62. See, for example, Richard Noll *The Aryan Christ* (bibliog. 1.1); and Paul Vitz, *Psychology as Religion* (bibliog. 1.1).

63. See the work of John Dourley, for example, especially *The Illness* (bibliog. 1.1).

64. See for example the work of Edward Edinger (bibliog. 1.1).

65. White, "Four Challenges to Religion: Jung" (bibliog. 1.4, 1952), 203–7.

66. White, "Theological Reflections" (bibliog. 1.4, 1960): 147–54.

67. White, "Scholasticism" (bibliog. 1.4, 1934), 27.

68. Vann, *St. Thomas Aquinas* (bibliog. 1.1), 177. Vann presents a vibrant picture of the vision of Thomas.

69. White, op. cit., 27.

BIBLIOGRAPHY

Published Materials

Unpublished Materials

Published Materials

1.1   Extended List of Secondary Literature

A. E. (otherwise anonymous) "Psychotherapy and the Healing of Human Beings: Review of Victor White's *God and the Unconscious*": 42–46

Acta Capituli Provincialis (Oxford 1932). This is an internal document produced by the Provincial Chapter of the English Province of the Order of Preachers every four years and circulated to the Province and to Rome.

Adams, Marilyn McCord, and Adams, Robert Merrihew, eds. *The Problem of Evil*. Oxford: Oxford University Press, 1990.

Adler, Gerhard, and Aniela Jaffé, eds. *C. G. Jung: Letters Volume I, 1906–1950*. London: Routledge and Kegan Paul, 1973.

———, and Aniela Jaffé, eds. *C. G. Jung: Letters Volume II, 1951–1961*. London: Routledge and Kegan Paul, 1976.

Allers, Rudolf. "Mental Trouble and the Moral Life: Review of Victor White's *God and the Unconscious*." *Books On Trial* (June 1953): 342–43.

Aquinas, Thomas. *De Malo*. Trans. John A. and Jean T. Oesterle. Notre Dame, Indianapolis: University of Notre Dame Press, 1995

———. *De Passionibus*. In Aquinas, *Summa theologiae*, 1a-2ae, q22–48. Trans. Fathers of the English Dominican Province. London: Burns, Oates and Washburne, 1920.

———. *De Remediis Tristitiae*. In Aquinas, *De passionibus* (bibliog. 1.1), q38.

———. *De Veritate*. 3 Volumes, Trans. Robert W. Mulligan S. J., James V. McGlynn S.J., and Robert W. Schmidt, S.J. Indianapolis: Hackett Publishing Co. Inc., 1954.

———. *Summa Theologiae*. Trans. Fathers of the English Dominican Province. London: Burns, Oates and Washburne, 1920.

Aristotle. *De Divinatione per Somnia*. In Richard McKeon, ed. *The Basic Works of Aristotle*. NY: Random House, 1941.

———. *Metaphysics*. In Richard McKeon, ed. *Introduction to Aristotle*. NY: Random House, 1947.

———. *Nicomachean Ethics*. In Richard McKeon, ed. *Introduction to Aristotle*. NY: Random House, 1947.

Arraj, James. *Jungian and Catholic? The Promises and Problems of the Jungian Christian Dialogue*. Chiloquin, OR: Inner Growth Books, 1991.

———. "Jungian Spirituality: The Question of Victor White." *Spirituality Today* 40 (1988): 249–61.

Ashley, Benedict, O. P. *The Dominicans*. Collegeville, MN: The Liturgical Press, 1990.

Augustine. *Confessions*. trans. Rex Warner. New York: Penguin Putnam Inc., 2001.

Aziz, Robert. *C. G. Jung's Psychology of Religion and Synchronicity*. Albany, NY: State University of New York Press, 1990.

Bailey, Bede, O. P.; Simon Tugwell, O. P.; and Aidan Bellinger, eds. *Letters of Bede Jarrett and Other Papers from the Dominican Archives*. London: Blackfriars Publications, 1989.

Bair, Dierdre. *Jung: A Biography*. New York: Little, Brown, 2003.

Barnaby, Karin and Pellegrino d'Acierno, eds. *C. G. Jung and the Humanities: Towards a Hermeneutics of Culture*. Princeton, NJ: Princeton University Press, 1990.

Basil the Great. *Nine Homilies of the Hexaemeron*. In Philip Schaff and Henry Wace, eds. *Nicene and Post-Nicene Fathers* Series II, vol. VIII. Grand Rapids: Eerdmans, 1956.

Beck, G. A., ed. *The English Catholics 1850–1950*. London: Burns and Oates, 1950.

Beguin, Albert. *L'Art Romantique et Le Rêve*: Essai sue le romantisme allemande et la poésie française. Marseilles: Editions des Cahiers du Sud, 1937.

Benkovic, Johnette. *The New Age Counterfeit*. Orlando, FL: LHLA, 2002.

Blacker, Carlos Paton. "Essay on *Answer to Job*." *Harvest: Journal for Jungian Studies* 29 (1983): 105–16.

Bright, Laurence, O. P. "Review of Victor White's *God and the Unconscious*." *The Trident* (1953):40–43.

Brown, Clifford A. *Jung's Hermeneutic of Doctrine*. Atlanta: Scholars Press, 1977.

Bryant, Christopher, S. S. J. E. *Depth Psychology and Religious Belief*. Mirfield, West Yorkshire: Mirfield Publications, 1972.

———. *Jung and the Christian Way*. London: Darton Longman and Todd, 1983.

Buber, Martin. *The Eclipse of God*. New York: Harper and Row, 1952.

Burns, Charles. "Review of Victor White's *God and the Unconscious*." *The Dublin Review* 227 (1953): 79–83.

Burrell, David, C. S. C. "Jung and the *Privatio Boni*." In *Aquinas: God and Action*. Notre Dame, IN: University of Notre Dame Press, 1979.

Carus, Carl Gustav. *Psyche: On The Development of the Soul*. Dallas, TX: Spring Publications, 1989.

Charet, F. X. "A Dialogue between Psychology and Theology: The Correspondence of C.G. Jung and Victor White." *The Journal of Analytical Psychology* 35, no. 4 (October 1990): 421–41.

Chitty, Susan, ed. *Antonia White Diaries 1926–1957, Vol.1*. London: Constable, 1991.

———, ed. *Antonia White Diaries 1958–1979, Vol.2*. London: Constable, 1992.

Clift, Wallace B. *Jung and Christianity: The Challenge of Reconciliation*. New York: Crossroad, 1983.

Corbett, Lionel. *The Religious Function of the Psyche*. London: Routledge, 1996.

Cox, David. *Jung and St. Paul*. London: Longmans, Green, 1959.

Cunningham, Adrian. "Obituary: Herbert McCabe, O. P." *The Guardian*, 16 July 2001.

———. "Victor White and C. G. Jung: The Fateful Encounter of the White Raven and the Gnostic." *New Blackfriars* 62, no. 733/734 (July/August 1981): 320–34.

———. "Victor White, John Layard, and C. G. Jung." *Harvest: Journal for Jungian Studies* 38 (1992) 44–57.

Daly, Gabriel, O.S.A. *Transcendence and Immanence: A Study in Catholic Modernism and Integralism*. Oxford: Clarendon, 1980.

Davies, Brian, O. P. "The Problem of Evil" in *New Blackfriars* 73, no. 862 (July/August 1992): 357–75.

———. *The Thought of Thomas Aquinas*. Oxford: Clarendon, 1992.

De Gruchy, John W. "Jung and Religion: A Theological Assessment." In Papadoulos, and Saayman, eds. *Jung in Modern Perspective* (bibliog. 1.1): 193–203.

Dehing, Jef. "Jung and Knowledge: From Gnosis to Praxis." *Journal of Analytical Psychology* 35, no. 4 (October 1990): 377–96.

De Laszlo, Violet S., ed. *The Basic Writings of C. G. Jung*. trans. R. F. C. Hull. Princeton, NJ: Princeton University Press, 1990.

Demant, V. A. "Review of Victor White's *God and the Unconscious*." *The Oxford Magazine* (10 February 1953).

Denzinger, H., and A. Schönmetzer, eds. *Enchiridion symbolorum definitionum et declarationum de Rebus fidei et morum*. 34th ed. Barcelona: Herder, 1967.

De Voogd, Stephanie. "Fantasy Versus Fiction: Jung's Kantianism Appraised." In Papadoulos and Saayman, eds. *Jung in Modern Perspective* (bibliog. 1.1): 204–28.

Dillistone, F. W. "Review of Victor White's *Soul and Psyche*." *Liverpool Daily Post* (24 February 1960).

Directory of the English Province of the Order of Preachers. Oxford: Blackfriars Publications, 1996.

Doran, Robert, S.J. "Jung and Catholic Theology." In *Catholicism and Jungian Psychology* (bibliog. 1.1): 41–73.

———. "Jungian Psychology and Lonergan's Foundations: A Methodological Proposal." *Journal of the American Academy of Religion* 47:1 Supplement (1979): 23–45.

———. "Jungian Psychology and Christian Spirituality: I, II, III." In *Carl Jung and Christian Spirituality* (bibliog. 1.1): 66–108.

Dourley, John P. "The Challenge of Jung's Psychology for the Study of Religion." *Studies in Religion* 18, no. 3 (Summer 1989): 297–311.

———. *The Goddess Mother of the Trinity: A Jungian Implication*. Lewiston, NY: Edwin Mellen, 1990.

———. *The Illness That We Are: A Jungian Critique of Christianity*. Toronto: Inner City Books, 1984.

———. "In the Shadow of the Monotheisms: Jung's Conversations with Buber and White." In Ryce-Menuhin, Joel, ed. *Jung and the Monotheisms*. London: Routledge, 1994.

———. *Jung and the Religious Alternative: The Rerooting*. Lewiston, NY: Edwin Mellen, 1995.

———. "Jung and the White, Buber Exchanges: Exercises in Futility." In *A Strategy for Loss of Faith: Jung's Proposal* (bibliog. 1.1).

———. "Jung's Impact on Religious Studies." In Barnaby and d'Acierno, eds. *C. G. Jung and the Humanities* (bibliog. 1.1).

———. *The Psyche as Sacrament: A Comparative Study of C. G. Jung and Paul Tillich*. Toronto: Inner City Books, 1981.

———. "The Religious Implications of Jung's Psychology." *Journal of Analytical Psychology* 40, no. 2 (April 1995): 177–203.

———. "The Religious Significance of Jung's Psychology." *International Journal for the Psychology of Religion* 5, no. 2 (1995): 73–90.

———. *A Strategy for a Loss of Faith: Jung's Proposal.* Toronto: Inner City Books, 1991.

———. "Trinitarian Models and Human Integration: Jung and Paul Tillich Compared." *Journal of Analytical Psychology* 19, no. 2 (July 1974): 131–50.

Dry, Avis M. *The Psychology of Jung.* London: Hazell, Watson and Viney, 1961.

Dykes, Andrea. "Some Aspects of the Self." *Harvest: Journal for Jungian Studies* 35 (1989-1990): 41–62.

Edinger, Edward F. *Anatomy of the Psyche: Alchemical Symbolism in Psychotherapy.* La Salle, IL: Open Court, 1985.

———. *Ego and Archetype.* Baltimore, MD: Penguin Books, 1973.

———. *The Creation of Consciousness.* Toronto: Inner City Books, 1984.

———. *The Mysterium Lectures: A Journey through C. G. Jung's* Mysterium Coniunctionis. Toronto: Inner City Books, 1995.

———. *Transformation of the God Image: An Elucidation of Jung's* Answer to Job. Toronto: Inner City Books, 1992.

———, Diana D. Cordic, and Charles Yates, eds. *The New God Image: A Study of Jung's Key Letters Concerning the Evolution of the Western God Image.* Wilmette, IL: Chiron Publications, 1996.

———, and Deborah A. Wesley, eds. *The Psyche In Antiquity: Book One Early Greek Philosophy.* Toronto: Inner City Books, 1999.

Ernst, Cornelius, O. P. *Multiple Echo: Explorations in Theology.* London: Darton Longman and Todd, 1979.

Evennett, H. Outram. "Catholics and the Universities" in G. A. Beck. *The English Catholics 1850–1950.* London: Burns and Oates, 1950.

Flugel, J. C. *Man, Morals and Society.* London: Penguin, 1945.

Fordham, Frieda. *An Introduction to Jung's Psychology.* London: Penguin, 1953.

Fordham, Michael, "Memories and Thoughts about C. G. Jung." *Journal of Analytical Psychology* 20, no. 2 (July 1975): 102–13.

———, and Rosemary Gordon. "Obituary Notices: John Layard." *Journal of Analytical Psychology* 20, no.2 (July 1975): 216–19.

Forsyth, James. *Freud, Jung and Christianity.* Ottawa: University of Ottawa Press, 1989.

———. *Psychological Theories of Religion.* Upper Saddle River, NJ: Prentice Hall, 2003.

Franz, Marie Louise Von. See Von Franz, Marie Louise.

Frayn, R. Scott. *Revelation and the Unconscious.* London: The Epworth Press, 1940.

Frazer, Sir James. *The Golden Bough*. NY: Touchstone, 1995.

Fry, W. B. J. "Memoir of Dom Bede Winslow." In Armstrong, A.H., and W. B. J. Fry, eds. *Rediscovering Eastern Christendom: Essays in Commemoration of Dom Bede Winslow*. London: Darton Longman and Todd, 1963.

Fuller, Michael. "C. G. Jung: Scientist-Theologian?" *Theology* 95 (1992): 270–77.

Gaine, Simon, O. P. "Review of Aidan Nichols' *Dominican Gallery: Portrait of a Culture*." *The Month* (April 1998): 158–59.

Geach, Peter. *Logic Matters*. Oxford: Blackwell, 1972.

Giegerich, Wolfgang. "Jung's Betrayal of his Truth: The Adoption of a Kant-based Empiricism and the Rejection of Hegel's Speculative Thought." *Harvest: Journal for Jungian Studies* 44, no.1 (1998):46–64.

———. *The Soul's Logical Life: Towards a Rigorous Notion of Psychology*. Frankfurt: Peter Lang Verlag, 1998.

Gilby, Thomas, O. P. "Personae 6: Victor White, O. P. († May 22, 1960) *Blackfriars* 41, no. 482/483 (July/August 1960): 283–84.

———. "Review of Victor White's *Soul and Psyche*." *Blackfriars* 41, no. 481 (May 1960): 183–85.

Goldbrunner, Josef. *Cure of Mind and Cure of Soul*. London: Burns and Oates, 1958.

———. *Holiness Is Wholeness*. London: Burns and Oates, 1952.

———. *Individuation: A Study in the Depth Psychology of Carl Gustav Jung*. London: Hollis and Carter, 1956.

Gruchy, John W. De. See De Gruchy, John W.

Gumbley, Walter, O. P. *Dominican Obituary Notices 1555–1952*. London: Aquin Press, 1955.

Gunton, Colin. *The One, The Three and The Many: God Creation and the Culture of Modernity*. Cambridge: Cambridge University Press, 1993.

Hannah, Barbara. *Jung His Life and Work: A Biographical Memoir*. London: Michael Joseph, 1977.

Hastings, Adrian. *A History of English Christianity 1920–1990*. 3rd ed. London: SCM, 1991.

Hastings, Cecily, and Donald Nicholl, eds. *A Yearbook of Contemporary Thought in Anthropology, Biblical Study, Psychology, Philosophy, Theology, Biology*. London: Sheed and Ward, 1953.

Heisig, James W. *Imago Dei: A Study of C. G. Jung's Psychology of Religion*. Cranbury, NJ: Associated University Presses, 1979.

———. "Jung and Theology: A Bibliographic Essay." *Spring: Journal of Archetype and Culture* (1973): 204–55.

Heydt, Vera Von der. See Von der Heydt, Vera

Hibbert, Giles, O. P. *Man, Culture and Christianity*. London: Sheed and Ward, 1967.

Hick, John. *Evil and the God of Love.* San Francisco: Harper San Francisco, 1978.

Hoeller, Stephen A. *The Gnostic Jung and the Seven Sermons to the Dead.* Wheaton, IL: Quest, 1982.

Homans, Peter, ed. *Essays in Divinity, vol. 3: the Dialogue between Theology and Psychology.* Chicago: University of Chicago Press, 1968.

——. *Jung in Context: Modernity and the Making of a Psychology.* Chicago, University of Chicago Press, 1979.

Hostie, Raymond, S. J. *Religion and the Psychology of Jung.* London: Sheed and Ward, 1957.

Hostie, Raymond, S. J. *Du Mythe à la Religion dans la Psychologie analytique de C. G. Jung.* Paris: Desclee de Brouwer, 1968.

Irenaeus, *Adversus Haereses* (Against Heresies). In Roberts and Donaldson, eds. *Ante-Nicene Fathers,* vol. 1. Grand Rapids: Eerdmans, 1951.

Jacobi, Jolande. *The Psychology of C. G. Jung.* 5th ed. London: Routledge and Kegan, 1962.

Jaffé, Aniela. *Was C. G. Jung a Mystic?* Zurich: Daimon Verlag, 1989.

Jaffé, Lawrence. *Celebrating Soul: Preparing for the New Religion.* Toronto: Inner City Books, 1999.

"Jungian Psychology as Catholic Theology: What is Carl Gustav Jung Doing in the Church?" *St. Catherine Review* (May/June 1997): 1–5.

Kahn, Jack H., and Hester Solomon. *Job's Illness: Loss, Grief, and Integration.* New York: Pergamon, 1975.

Kant, Immanuel. *Critique of Pure Reason.* Trans. Smith, Norman Kemp. London: Macmillian, 1978.

Keenan, Alan, O.F.M. "Review of Victor White's *Soul and Psyche.*"

Kelsey, Morton T. *Christopsychology.* London: Darton Longman and Todd, 1982.

——. "Jung as Philosopher and Theologian." In Papadoulos and Saayman, eds. *Jung in Modern Perspective* (bibliog. 1.1).

Kehoe, Richard, O. P. "Review of C. G. Jung's *Antworf auf Hiob.*" *Dominican Studies* 5 (1952): 228–31.

Lambert, Kenneth. "Can Theologians and Psychologists Collaborate?" *Journal of Analytical Psychology* 5 (1960): 126–46.

Lammers, Ann Conrad. *In God's Shadow: The Collaboration of Victor White and Carl Gustav Jung.* New York: Paulist Press, 1994.

——. "'The Missing Fourth' in the Jung-White Letters." *Guild Lecture No. 287.* London: Guild of Pastoral Psychology, 2005.

Laszlo, Violet S. De. See De Laszlo, Violet S.

Layard, John. *The Stone Men of Malekula.* London: Chatto and Windus, 1942.

Leo XIII. "*Aeterni Patris,*" in *Acta Sanctae Sedis* 12 (1879–80): 97–115.

Livingston, James C., et al., eds. *Modern Christian Thought, Volume 2: The Twentieth Century.* Upper Saddle River, NJ: Prentice Hall, 2000.

Mairet, Philip, ed. *Christian Essays in Psychiatry.* London: SCM, 1956. This book was the result of the collaboration of psychiatrists who met regularly with Victor White, O. P., in Edward Wilson House, run by the Guild of Health.

———. "God and Therapy: A New Enquiry Review of Victor White's *Soul and Psyche.*" *Time and Tide* (19 March 1960).

Martin, Luther H., and James Goss, eds. *Essays on Jung and the Study of Religion.* Lanham, MD: University Press of America, 1985.

McCabe, Herbert, O. P. *God Matters.* London: Geoffrey Chapman, 1987.

McGuire, William, and R. F. C. Hull, eds. *C. G. Jung Speaking: Interviews and Encounters.* Bollingen Series 98: Princeton, NJ: Princeton University Press, 1977.

MacKinnon, Donald. "Foreword" In Ernst, Cornelius. *Multiple Echoes* (bibliog. 1.1).

Meier, Levi. "Job, Judaism and Jung." *Harvest: Journal for Jungian Studies* 27 (1981): 7–13.

Mercier, Desiré Joseph. *A Manual of Scholastic Philosophy*, trans. T. Parker and S. Parker. London: Kegan, Paul, Trench, Trubner and Co., 1917.

Messenger, Ernest C., ed., *Studies in Comparative Religion.* London: Catholic Truth Society, 1934.

Moore, Robert, ed. *Carl Jung and Christian Spirituality.* New York: Paulist Press, 1988.

———, and Daniel J. Meckel, eds. *Jung and Christianity in Dialogue: Faith, Feminism and Hermeneutics.* New York: Paulist Press, 1990.

———, and Murray Stein, eds. *Jung's Challenge to Contemporary Religion.* Wilmette, IL: Chiron, 1987.

Moreno, Antonio, O. P. *Jung, Gods and Modern Man.* London: Sheldon, 1970.

Morris, Jeremy. *Religion and Urban Change, Croydon 1840–1914.* London: Royal Historical Society, 1992.

Mulvey, Kieran. *Hugh Pope and the Order of Preachers.* London: Blackfriars Publications, 1954.

Newton, K. "The Weapon and the Wound: The Archetypal and Personal Dimensions in *Answer to Job.*" *Journal of Analytical Psychology* 38, no. 4 (October 1993): 375–96.

Nichols, Aidan, O. P. *Dominican Gallery: Portrait of a Culture.* Leominster: Gracewing, 1997.

———. *Yves Congar.* London: Geoffrey Chapman, 1989.

Noll, Richard. *The Aryan Christ: The Secret Life of Carl Jung.* New York: Macmillan, 1997.

Palmer, Michael. *Freud and Jung on Religion.* London: Routledge, 1997.

Papadopoulos, Renos K., ed. *Carl Gustav Jung: Critical Assessments: Vol. 1 Jung and His Method in Context.* London: Routledge, 1992.

———, ed. *Carl Gustav Jung: Critical Assessments: Vol. 2 The Structure and Dynamics of the Psyche.* London: Routledge, 1992.

————, ed. *Carl Gustav Jung: Critical Assessments: Vol. 3 Psychopathology and Psychotherapy.* London: Routledge, 1992.

————, ed. *Carl Gustav Jung: Critical Assessments: Vol. 4 Implications and Inspirations.* London: Routledge, 1992.

————, and Graham S. Saayman, eds. *Jung in Modern Perspective.* London: Wildwood House, 1984.

Partington, J. R. *Albertus Magnus on Alchemy.* London: Ambix, 1937.

Petre, Maude. *Von Hügel and Tyrell: The Story of a Friendship.*London: Dent, 1937.

Philp, Howard L. *Jung and the Problem of Evil.* London: Rockliff, 1958.

Pius X. "*Contra neo-reformismum religiosum,*" in *Acta Sanctae Sedis* 40 (Rome 1907): 266–69.

————. "*Doctoris Angelici: De Studio doctrine S. Thomae in scholis catholicis promovendo,*" in *Acta Apostolicae Sedis* 4 (1914): 336–41.

————. "*Lamentabili Sane,*" in *Acta Sanctae Sedis* 40 (1907): 470–78.

————. "*Pascendi Domini Gregis,*" in *Acta Sanctae Sedis* 40 (1907): 593–650.

————. "*Sacrorum Antistitum,*" in *Acta Sanctae Sedis* 40 (1910): 655–680.

Pius XI. "*Studiorum Ducem,*" in *Acta Sanctae Sedis* 15 (1923): 309–26.

Pius XII. "*Humani Generis,*" in *Acta Sanctae Sedis* 42 (1950): 561–78.

————. "Address to the Fifth International Catholic Congress of Psychotherapy and Clinical Psychology." *L'Osservatore Romano* (16 April, 1952).

Plaut, A., ed. "Obituary Notices: John Layard." *Journal of Analytical Psychology* 20, no. 1 (January 1975): 71.

Pope, Hugh, O. P. "Why Divorce our Teaching of Theology from our Teaching of the Bible?" *Irish Theological Quarterly* 8, no. 1 (January 1913): 47–64.

Post, Laurens van der. See van der Post, Laurens.

Provincial Actus (1962). This is an internal document produced by the Provincial Chapter of the English Province of the Order of Preachers every four years and circulated to the Province and to Rome.

Quinn, Edward. "Review of Victor White's *Soul and Psyche.*" *Yorkshire Post* (3 March 1960).

Read, Sir Herbert, Michael Fordham, Gerhard Adler and William McGuire, eds.. *The Collected Works of C.G. Jung.* Trans. R. F. C. Hull. London: Routledge and Kegan Paul, 1953-1979.

Reardon, Bernard, M. J. *Roman Catholic Modernism.* Stanford, CA: Stanford University Press, 1970.

"Reconciling Jung and Catholicism" (Obituary of Vera von der Heydt). *The Daily Telegraph.* (25 November 1996).

"Review of Victor White's 'Religious Toleration.'" *The Listener* 49 (30 July 1953).

Ryan, Columba, O. P. "Funeral Homily for Herbert McCabe, O. P." *New Blackfriars* 82, no. 965/966 (July/August 2001): 308–12.

Samuels, Andrew. *Jung and the Post Jungians*. London: Routledge, 1986.

Sanford, John. "The Problem of Evil in Christianity and Analytical Psychology." In Moore, ed. *Carl Jung and Christian Spirituality* (bibliog. 1.1).

Schaer, Hans. *Religion and the Cure of Souls in Jung's Psychology*. Trans. R. F. C. Hull. New York: Pantheon, 1950.

Schwartz-Salant, Nathan, ed. *Jung on Alchemy*. London: Routledge, 1994.

Scott, Rivers. "Healers of the Mind: Review of Victor White's *Soul and Psyche*." *Daily Telegraph* (8 April 1960).

Segal, Robert Alan. "The Allure of Gnosticism." *Harvest: Journal for Jungian Studies* 41 (1995): 78–88.

―――. *The Gnostic Jung*. Princeton, NJ: Princeton University Press, 1992.

"Soul of Man: Review of Victor White's *Soul and Psyche*." *Church Times* (20 May 1960).

Spiegelman, J. Marvin, ed. *Catholicism and Jungian Psychology*. Phoenix, AZ: Falcon, 1988.

Stein, Murray, ed. *Jung on Christianity*. Princeton, NJ: Princeton University Press, 1999.

―――, ed. *Jung on Evil*. London: Routledge, 1995.

―――. *Jung's Treatment of Christianity: The Psychotherapy of a Religious Tradition*. Wilmette, IL: Chiron, 1985.

―――. "The Rôle of Victor White in C. G. Jung's Writings." *Guild Lecture No. 285*. London: Guild of Pastoral Psychology, 2004.

Stern, Karl. "Jung and the Christians: Review of Victor White's *God and the Unconscious*." *Commonweal* 58 (June 5, 1953): 229–31.

Stevens, Anthony. *On Jung*. London: Routledge and Kegan Paul, 1991.

Stevens, Dom Gregory. "Review of Victor White's *God and the Unconscious*." *Theological Studies* 9 (1953): 505–06.

Storr, Antony, ed. *The Essential Jung: Selected Writings*. London: Fontana, 1983.

―――, *Jung*. London: Fontana, 1973.

Strauss, E. B. "Review of Victor White's *Soul and Psyche*." *The Tablet* (19 March 1960).

"The Theologian and Psychiatrist Meet," *The Pulse* (St Mary's Hospital California), 1955.

Toynbee, Philip. "Review of C. G. Jung's *Answer to Job*." *The London Observer* (9 January 1955).

Tredgold, R. F. "Review of Victor White's *Soul and Psyche*." *Mental Health* (Spring 1960).

Ulanov, Barry. *Jung and the Outside World*. Wilmette, IL: Chiron, 1992.

van der Post, Laurens. *Jung and the Story of Our Time*. London: Hogwarth, 1976.

Vann, Gerald, O. P. *The Heart of Man*. New York: Longmans and Green, 1945.

———. *Morals Makyth Man.* London: Catholic Book Club, 1939.

———. *St. Thomas Aquinas.* London: J. M. Dent and Sons, 1940.

———. *The Water and the Fire.* London: Collins, 1953.

Vardy, Peter. *The Puzzle of Evil.* Armonk, NY: M. E. Sharpe, 1997.

Vitz, Paul C. *Psychology as Religion: The Cult of Self Worship.* Grand Rapids, MI: Eerdmans, 1977.

Von der Heydt, Vera. *Prospects for the Soul: Soundings in Jungian Psychology and Religion.* London: Darton Longman and Todd, 1976.

Von Franz, Marie Louise. *Psyche and Matter.* Boston: Shambhala, 2001.

Voogd, Stephanie De. See De Voogd, Stephanie.

Weinandy, Thomas, O. F. M. Cap. "Gnosticism and Contemporary Soteriology: Some Reflections." *New Blackfriars* 76, no. 899 (December 1995): 546–54.

Weisstub, Eli. "Questions to Jung on *Answer to Job*." *Journal of Analytical Psychology* 38, no. 4 (October 1993): 397–418.

Werblosky, R. J. Zwi. "Psychology and Religion." *The Listener* 49, no. 1260 (23 April 1953)

———. "God and the Unconscious." *The Listener* 49, no. 1262 (2 May 1953).

Wicker, Brian. *Culture and Liturgy.* London: Sheed and Ward, 1963.

Wilson, Colin. *C. G. Jung: Lord of the Underworld.* England: Aquarian, 1984.

Young-Eisendrath, Polly, and Terence Dawson, eds. *Cambridge Companion to Jung.* Cambridge: Cambridge University Press, 1997.

Zacharias, Gerhard P. *Psyche und Mysterium: die Bedeutung der Psychologie C. G. Jung fur die Christliche Theologie und Liturgie.* Zurich: Rancher, 1954.

1.2 Works by Carl Gustav Jung

The volume number and page numbers, which follow most of these entries, denote their location in McGuire et al. eds. *The Collected Works of C.G. Jung* (listed in bibliog. 1.1; referred to in the notes as Jung, *CW*). Dates of original publication are given in parentheses, and dates of original composition are given in brackets. Multiple dates indicate revisions.

Jung, C. G. "On the Psychological Diagnosis of Facts." (1905), 1: 219–21.

———. "On the Criticism of Psychoanalysis." (1910), 4: 74–77.

———. "Concerning Psychoanalysis." (1912), 4: 78–81.

———. "The Theory of Psychoanalysis." (1913), 4: 83–87.

———. "General Aspects of Psychoanalysis." (1913), 4: 229–42.

———. "Freud and Jung: Contrasts." (1929), 4: 333–40.

———. *Symbols of Transformation.* (1911-12/1952), 5.

———. *Psychological Types.* (1921), 6.

————. *Two Essays on Analytical Psychology.* (1953; 2nd edn.,1966), 7.

————. "The Transcendent Function."([1916]/1957), 8: 67–91.

————. "The Structure of the Psyche." (1927/1931), 8: 139–58.

————. "On the Nature of the Psyche." (1947/1954), 8: 159–234.

————. "The Soul and Death."(1934), 8: 404–15.

————. "Archetypes of the Collective Unconscious." (1934/1954), 9i: 3–41.

————. "The Concept of the Collective Unconscious." (1936), 9i: 42–53.

————. "Concerning the Archetypes. With Special Reference to the Anima Concept." (1936/ 1954), 9i: 54–72.

————. "Psychological Aspects of the Mother Archetype."(1938/ 1954), 9i: 75–110.

————. "Concerning Rebirth." (1940/1950), 9i: 113–47.

————. "On The Psychology of the Trickster Figure."(1954), 9i: 255–72.

————. "Conscious, Unconscious and Individuation."(1939), 9i: 275–89.

————. "A Study in the Process of Individuation."(1934/1950), 9i: 290–354.

————. *Aion: Researches into the Phenomenology of the Self.* (1951), 9ii.

————. "The Spiritual Problem of Modern Man." (1928/1931), 10: 74–94.

————. "The Meaning of Psychology for Modern Man."(1933/1934), 10: 134–56.

————. "The Fight with the Shadow."(1946), 10: 218–26.

————. "The Undiscovered Self (Present and Future)." (1957), 10: 247–305.

————. "A Psychological View of Conscience."(1958), 10: 437–55.

————. "Good and Evil in Analytical Psychology."(1959), 10: 456–68.

————. *Psychology and Religion.* New Haven and London: Yale University Press, 1938. See also "Psychology and Religion (The Terry Lectures)." (1938/1940), 11: 3–105.

————. "A Psychological Approach to the Dogma of The Trinity."(1942/1948), 11: 107–200.

————. "Transformation Symbolism in the Mass." (1942/1954), 11: 201–96.

————. "Psychotherapists or the Clergy." (1932), 11: 327–47.

————. "Psychoanalysis and the Cure of Souls." (1928), 11: 348–54.

————. *Answer to Job.* trans. R. F. C. Hull, 9th Printing. Princeton, NJ: Princeton University Press, 1973. See also "Answer to Job. Prefatory Note." 11: 355–58; "Answer to Job. Lectori Benevolo" 11: 359–63; and "Answer to Job." (1952), 11: 365–470.

————. "Introduction to the Religious and Psychological Problems of Alchemy."(1944), 12: 1–37.

————. "Religious Ideas in Alchemy." (1937), 12: 225–344.

————. *Mysterium Coniunctionis: An Inquiry Into the Separation and Synthesis of Psychic Opposites in Alchemy.* (1955-56), 14.

————. "What is Psychotherapy?"(1935), 16: 21–28.

————. "Some Aspects of Modern Psychotherapy."(1930), 16: 29–35.

————. "The Aims of Psychotherapy."(1931), 16: 36–52.

————. "Problems of Modern Psychotherapy." (1929), 16: 53–75.

————. "Psychotherapy and a Philosophy of Life."(1943), 16: 76–84

————. "Why I am Not a Catholic." (1954), 18: 645–47.

————. "Concerning Answer to Job." 18: 662.

————. "Religion and Psychology. A Reply to Martin Buber," 18: 663–70.

————. *Memories, Dreams, Reflections.* Aniela Jaffé, ed. New York: Vintage Books Edition, 1965.

————. *Modern Man In Search of a Soul.* New York: Harcourt Brace and World, 1933.

————. *The Zofingia Lectures.* J. Von Heinck, transl; William McGuire, ed. Princeton, NJ: Princeton University Press, 1983. See also *CW* Supplementary Volume A.

1.3   Letters from Carl Gustav Jung

These letters can be found in Adler, Gerhard, and Aniela Jaffé, eds. *Letters I* and *Letters II* (listed in bibliog. 1.1; referred to in the notes as *Letters I* and *Letters II*). Jung's letters to White were published in a two-volume collection of all Jung's letters by Princeton University Press, though it is clear from editor's comments that some of Jung's letters were not included because they were of a private nature. In addition, a letter from psychologist Gerhard Adler to Fr. Kenelm Foster, O. P., (bibliog. 2.4 and *E. P. O. P. Archives*) indicates that some of Jung's letters to White may have been disposed of at Adler's discretion.

Jung, C. G. "Letter to B. Milt," 8 June 1942

————. "Letter to H. Irminger," 22 September 1944.

————. "Letter to Hugo Rahner, S. J.," 4 August 1945.

————. "Letter to Victor White," 26 September 1945.

————. "Letter to Victor White," 5 October 1945.

————. "Letter to Victor White," 13 February 1946.

————. "Letter to Victor White," 13 April 1946.

————. "Letter to Victor White," 6 November 1946.

————. "Letter to Victor White," 18 December 1946.

————. "Letter to Victor White," 8 March 1947.

————. "Letter to Victor White," 27 March 1947.

————. "Letter to Victor White," 23 April 1947.

————. "Letter to Werner Niederer," 23 June 1947.

————. "Letter to Victor White," 19 December 1947.

———. "Letter to Victor White," 27 December 1947.

———. "Letter to Gebhard Frei," 13 January 1948.

———. "Letter to Victor White," 30 January 1948.

———. "Letter to Walter Lewino," 21 April 1948.

———. "Letter to Victor White," 21 May 1948.

———. "Letter to Victor White," 24 September 1948.

———. "Letter to Victor White," 16 December 1948.

———. "Letter to Victor White," 8 January 1949.

———. "Letter to Victor White," 31 December 1949.

———. "Letter to Victor White," 12 May 1950.

———. "Letter to Victor White," 25 November 1950.

———. "Letter to Doctor H.," 17 March 1951.

———. "Letter to Erich Neumann," 28 February 1952.

———. "Letter to Victor White," 21 September 1951.

———. "Letter to Victor White," Spring 1952.

———. "Letter to Victor White," 9–14 April 1952.

———. "Letter to Dorothee Hoch," 28 May 1952

———. "Letter to Victor White," 30 April 1952.

———. "Letter to Victor White," 30 June 1952.

———. "Letter to Victor White," 7 August 1952.

———. "Letter to Barbara Robb," 19 November 1952.

———. "Letter to R. J. Zwi Werblowsky," 21 May 1953.

———. "Letter to Victor White," 24 November 1953.

———. "Letter to James Kirsch," 16 February 1954.

———. "Letter to James Kirsch," 5 March 1954

———. "Letter to Père Lachat," 27 March 1954

———. "Letter to Aniela Jaffé," 6 April 1954.

———. "Letter to Victor White," 10 April 1954.

———. "Letter to Victor White," 19 January 1955.

———. "Letter to Dr. E.V. Tenney," 23 February 1955.

———. "Letter to Sylvester Schoening," 24 March 1955.

———. "Letter to Simon Doniger," November 1955.

———. "Letter to Victor White," 2 April 1955.

———. "Letter to Victor White," 6 May 1955.

———. "Letter to Pastor Walter Bernet," 13 June 1955.

———. "Letter to Bernhard Lang," 8 June 1957.

———. "Letter to Bernhard Lang," 14 June 1957.

———. "Letter to Bernhard Lang," June 1957.

———. "Letter to Joseph F. Rychlak," 27 April 1959.

———. "Letter to Mother Prioress," September 1959.

———. "Letter to Victor White," 21 October 1959.

———. "Letter to Valentine Brooke," 6 November 1959.

———. "Letter to M. Leonard," 5 December 1959.

———. "Letter to Mother Prioress." 6 February 1960.

———. "Letter to Victor White," 25 March 1960

———. "Letter to Mother Prioress," 26 March 1960.

———. "Letter to Mother Prioress," 29 April 1960.

———. "Letter to Victor White," 30 April 1960.

———. "Letter to Robert Smith," 29 June 1960.

———. "Letter to Mrs. Catherine Ginsberg," 3 June 1960.

———. "Letter to Mother Prioress," 12 August 1960.

———. "Letter to Fr. W. P. Wittcutt," 24 August 1960.

———. "Letter to Mother Prioress," 19 October 1960.

1.4 Works of Victor White, O. P.

These published works are listed in chronological order.

White, Victor, O. P. "Review of H. Bremond's Prayer and Poetry." Blackfriars 9, no. 95 (February 1928): 124–26.

———. "Review of Clive Bell's *Civilization.*" *Blackfriars* 9, no. 102 (September 1928): 566–68.

———. "Review of P. Claudel's *Letters to a Doubter.*" *Blackfriars* 10, no. 116 (November 1929): 1457–1458.

———. "Review of John Laird's *The Idea of Value.*" *Blackfriars* 11, no. 118 (January 1930): 55–57.

———. "Review of Jacques Maritain's *Art and Scholasticism.*" *Blackfriars* 11, no. 123 (June 1930): 378–79.

———. "Review of Christopher Dawson's *Christianity and Sex.*" *Blackfriars* 11, no. 123 (June 1930): 379–80.

———. "Review of Leo Richard Ward's *Philosophy of Value.*" *Blackfriars* 11 (June 1930): 382–83.

———. "Review of D. von Hildebrand's *In Defense of Purity.*" *Blackfriars* 12, no. 135 (June 1931): 892–84.

———. "Scholasticism." (Catholic Truth Society Pamphlet, 1932). Also published in Messenger, ed. *Studies in Comparative Religion* (bibliog. 1.1, 1934), 1–32.

———. 'Spengler Views the Machine Age." *Blackfriars* 13, no. 142 (January 1932): 7–22.

———. "Review of Aldous Huxley's *Brave New World*." *Blackfriars* 13, no. 145 (April 1932):251–53.

———. "The Boom of Youth: Review of Wyndham Lewis' *Doom of Youth*." *Blackfriars* 13, no. 150 (September 1932): 523–29.

———. "Review of Aldous Huxley's *Texts and Pretexts: An Anthology with Commentaries*." *Blackfriars* 14, no. 154 (January 1933): 52–53.

———. "Review of A. Goodier, S. J.'s *The Inner Life of the Catholic*." *Blackfriars* 14, no.157 (April 1933):322.

———. "Review of Christopher Dawson's *Enquiries into Religion and Culture*." *Blackfriars* 14, no. 159 (June 1933): 505–06.

———. "A Synthesis of Sexual Ethics: Review of Jacques Leclerq's *La Famille*." *Blackfriars* 14, no. 161 (August 1933): 686-694.

———. "Review of Karl Adam's *Jesus Christus*." *Blackfriars* 14, no. 162 (September 1933): 790–91.

———. "The Case for Italy." *Blackfriars* 14, no. 188 (November 1933): 807–11.

———. "The Christian Revolution." *Blackfriars* 15, no. 167 (February 1934): 138–49.

———. "Leo XIII on Reunion." *Blackfriars* 15, no. 172 (July 1934): 450–55.

———. "The Apostolate of the Laity through Catholic Action." *Blackfriars* 15, no. 174 (September 1934): 575-82.

———. "A Note on Poetry and Intelligibility." *Blackfriars* 15, no. 175 (October 1934): 670–71.

———. "A Reunion Movement in Germany." *Blackfriars* 16, no. 181 (April 1935): 272–77.

———. "An Evangelical Approach to Catholicism." *Blackfriars* 17, no. 200 (November 1936): 827–32.

———. "Faith." *Blackfriars* 18, no. 202 (January 1937): 34–41.

———. "The Background to Papal Infallibility." *Reunion* 2, no. 14 (September 1937): 433–48. This was originally read as a paper to the Oxford University Reunion Society in 1936. Also published in White, *God the Unknown* (bibliog.1.4, 1956), part III, ch. 3.

———."An Orthodox Heresiarch," in *Blackfriars* 18, no. 213 (December 1937): 910–16. This is a review essay of Petre's *Von Hügel and Tyrell* (bibliog. 1.1).

———. "Doctrine in the Church of England." *Blackfriars* 19, no. 216 (March 1938): 163–76.

———. "Faith in the Church of England." *Blackfriars* 19, no. 217 (April 1938): 250–63.

———. "Christendoms, New or Old?" *Blackfriars* 19, no. 224 (November 1938): 795–804.

———. *Divided Christendom*. See White, Victor, O. P., trans. Yves Congar's *Chrétiens Désunis* (bibliog. 1.4, 1939).

————. "Reunion in Catholicity." *Blackfriars* 20, no. 230 (May 1939):370–75.

————. "Wars and Rumours of Wars." *Blackfriars* 20, no. 231 (June 1939): 401–413.

————. "War and the Early Church." *Blackfriars* 20, no. 234 (September 1939): 641–54.

————. "Kierkegaard's Journals." *Blackfriars* 20, no.236 (November 1939): 797–810.

————, trans. Yves Congar's *Chrétiens Désunis. Principes d'un 'œcuménisme' catholique* (Paris, Editions du cerf, 1939); English trans. *Divided Christendom.* London: The Centenary Press, 1939.

————. "The Platonic Tradition in Aquinas." *The Eastern Churches Quarterly* 4, no. 5–6 (January–April 1941): 213–21. Also published in White, *God the Unknown* (bibliog. 1.4, 1956), part III, ch.2, as "The Platonic Tradition in St. Thomas Aquinas."

————. "The Works of Dr. Darwell Stone." *Blackfriars* 22, no. 253 (April 1941): 186–96

————. "Review of R. Scott Frayn's *Revelation and the Unconscious.*" *Blackfriars* 22, no. 255 (June 1941): 312–15.

————. "Membership of the Church." *Blackfriars* 22, no. 258 (September 1941): 455–70. Also published in White, *God the Unknown* (bibliog. 1.1, 1956), part III, ch.2.

————. "Towards a Theology of Politics." *Blackfriars* 22, no. 261 (December 1941): 649–57.

————. "The Effects of Schism." *Blackfriars* 23, no. 263 (February 1942): 49–58.

————. "The Frontiers of Theology and Psychology," *Guild Lecture No.19,* London: Guild of Pastoral Psychology, 1942; and in White, *God and the Unconscious* (bibliog. 1.4, 1952), Ch. 5.

————. "The Meaning of the Church Unity Octave." *Eastern Churches Quarterly* 5, no. 3–4 (1942): 53–65. This article was originally delivered as a lecture during the Church Unity Octave at Blackfriars, Oxford (January 1942). Also published in White, *God the Unknown* (bibliog. 1.4, 1956), part III, ch.1.

————. "The Church of the Body of Christ." *Sobornost* 26 (December 1942): 9–14. This article was originally delivered as a paper read to the Orthodox and Anglican Fellowship of SS. Alban and Sergius in Oxford. Also published in White, *God the Unknown* (bibliog. 1.4, 1956), part II, ch.5, as "Western and Eastern Theology of Grace and Nature."

————. "The Atonement." In *What the Cross Means to Me: A Theological Symposium.* London: James Clarke, 1943.

————. "Thomism and Affective Knowledge Part 1." *Blackfriars* 24, no. 274 (January 1943):8–16

————. "Thomism and Affective Knowledge Part 2." *Blackfriars* 24, no. 277 (April 1943): 126–31.

————. "Christian Life in the Church." *Blackfriars* 24, no. 280 (July 1943): 264–69.

————. "Tasks for Thomists." *Blackfriars* 25, no. 288 (March 1944): 93–117.

————. "St. Thomas Aquinas and Jung's Psychology." *Blackfriars* 25, no. 291 (June 1944): 209–19.

————. "Thomism and Affective Knowledge Part 3." *Blackfriars* 25, no. 294 (September 1944): 321–28.

————. "Walter Hilton: An English Spiritual Guide," *Guild Lecture No. 31*, London: Guild of Pastoral Psychology, 1944; reprinted in 1963.

————. "Psychotherapy and Ethics." *Blackfriars* 26, no. 305 (August 1945): 287–300. This article was originally read as a paper to the Oxford branch of the Newman Association in 1945; also published as *Psychotherapy and Ethics*. London: Newman Association, 1945, and revised in White, *God and the Unconscious* (bibliog. 1.4, 1952), ch. 8.

————. "Psychotherapy and Ethics: A Postscript." *Blackfriars* 26, no. 307 (October 1945): 381–87; also published in revised form in White, *God and the Unconscious* (bibliog. 1.4, 1952), ch. 8.

————. "The Concept of Justice in Summa of St. Thomas Aquinas." *The Presbyter* 5, no. 1 (First Quarter, 1947): 15–22. Also published in White, *God the Unknown* (bibliog. 1.4, 1956), Part II, ch.4 as "The Concept of Justice in Aquinas."

————. *How to Study, being The Letter of St. Thomas Aquinas to Brother John, De Modo Studendi: Latin Text with Translation and Exposition.* This was originally a lecture read at the Inauguration of Studies for the Year 1944–45 in the Dominican Priories of Hawkesyard and Blackfriars Oxford; also published as a booklet by London: Aquin Press, 1947 and Oxford: Blackfriars Publications, 1947; reprinted by Oxford: Blackfriars Publications, 1993.

————. "Anthropologia Rationalis: The Aristotelian-Thomist Conception of Man." *Eranos Jahrbuch 1947*, Band 15, *Der Mensch* (Zurich, 1948): 315–83. This paper was originally read at the Eranos Tagung, Ascona, Switzerland in 1947. Part I of this article is on "The Aristotelian Conception of the Psyche" and is also published in revised form in White, *God and the Unconscious* (bibliog.1.4, 1952) as "Aristotle, Aquinas and Man" (ch.6). Part II is on "St. Thomas' Conception of Revelation" and is also published in revised form in *Dominican Studies* 1, no. 1 (1948): 3–34 and in White, *God and the Unconscious* (bibliog.1.4, 1952) "Revelation and the Unconscious" (ch.7).

————. "St. Thomas' Conception of Revelation." *Dominican Studies* 1, no. 1 (1948): 3–34. This paper was read at the Eranos Tagung, Ascona, Switzerland in 1947 as part II of his paper "Anthropologia Rationalis: The Aristotelian-Thomist Conception of Man" and published in *Eranos Jahrbuch 1947*, Band 15, *Der Mensch* (Zurich, 1948): 315–83. Also published in White, *God and the Unconscious* (bibliog.1.4, 1952) as "Revelation and the Unconscious" (ch.7).

———. "Modern Psychology and the Function of Symbolism." *Orate Fratres* 22, no. 6 (18 April 1948): 247–56; and in *Life of the Spirit* 3, no. 36 (June 1949): 551–59.

———. "Notes on Gnosticism." *Guild Lecture No. 59*. London: Guild of Pastoral Psychology, April 1949; also in *Spring: Journal of Archetype and Culture* (1949): 40–56; and in White, *God and the Unconscious* (bibliog. 1.4, 1952) as "Gnosis, Gnosticism and Faith" (ch. 11).

———. "The Analyst and the Confessor." *The Commonweal* (23 July 1948): 346–49; also published in *Life of the Spirit* 4 (September 1949): 20–27; and in White, *God and the Unconscious* (bibliog.1.4, 1952), ch. 9.

———. "The Supernatural." *Dominican Studies* 2, no. 1 (January 1949): 62–73.

———. "Satan." *Dominican Studies* 2 (April 1949): 193–98.

———. "The Morality of War." *Life of the Spirit* 4, no. 39 (September 1949): 97–104. This article was originally given as a talk to the Oxford University Catholic Chaplaincy, Trinity Sunday 1949.

———. "ERANOS: 1947, 1948." *Dominican Studies* 2 (October 1949): 395–400.

———. "The Scandal of the Assumption." *Life of the Spirit* 5, no. 53 (November/December 1950): 199–212.

———. "The Prolegomena to the Five Ways." *Dominican Studies* 4 (1951): 134–58. Also published in White, *God the Unknown* (bibliog. 1.4, 1956), part I, ch.4, as "Prelude to the Five Ways."

———. "Chief Druid and Chief Bishop: A Parallel in Caesar's *Gallic War* with Irenaeus' *Against the Heresies* III, 3." *Dominican Studies* 4 (1951): 201–03.

———. "Review of Xiberta's *Introductio in Sacram Theologiam*; Febrer's *El Concepto de Persona y la Union Hipostatica*; and Scheeben's *Mysteries of Christianity*" *Dominican Studies* 4 (1951): 217–20.

———. "Some Recent Contributions to Psychology." *Blackfriars* 32, no. 378 (September 1951): 419–27.

———. "Buddhism Comes West." *Blackfriars* 32, no. 381 (December 1951): 585–91.

———. "The Dying God: Pagan, Psychological and Christian." *Blackfriars* 33, no. 383 (February 1952): 60–66. This article was originally broadcast on the BBC in November 1951; also published in White, *God and the Unconscious* (bibliog.1.4, 1952), ch. 12.

———. "The Dying God: Pagan, Psychological and Christian: Differences." *Blackfriars* 33, no. 384 (March 1952): 113–22; also published in White, *God and the Unconscious* (bibliog.1.4, 1952), ch. 12.

———. "The Way of the Cross." *Life of the Spirit* 6, no. 70 (April 1952): 409–15.

———. "Challenges to Religion I: Theology and Sigmund Freud." *Commonweal* 55 (March 7 1952): 537–39. Also published as "Four Challenges to Religion: Freud." *Blackfriars* 33, no. 385 (April 1952): 170–74.

————. "Challenges to Religion II: Jung and the Supernatural." *Commonweal* 55 (March 1952): 561–62. Also published as "Four Challenges to Religion: Jung." *Blackfriars* 33, no. 386 (May 1952): 203–07.

————. "Challenges to Religion III: Frazer and Comparative Religion." *Commonweal* 55 (March 21 1952): 585–87. Also published as "Four Challenges to Religion: Frazer." *Blackfriars* 33, no. 387 (June 1952): 250–53.

————. "Challenges to Religion IV: Karl Marx and Materialism." *Commonweal* 55 (March 28 1952): 611–12. Also published as "Four Challenges to Religion: Marx." *Blackfriars* 33, no. 388/389 (July/August 1952): 317–22.

————. *God and the Unconscious.* With a foreword by C. G. Jung. London: Harvill, 1952. Also see bibliog. 1.4, 1961 and bibliog. 1.4, 1982. (See footnote 104 of Chapter Five for more detailed information about the origins of the chapters of White's book.)

————. "Review of C. G. Jung's *Aion.*" *Dominican Studies* 5 (1952): 240–43.

————. "The Unknown God." *Life of the Spirit* 7, no. 74/75 (August/September 1952): 51–59. Also published in White, *God the Unknown* (bibliog. 1.4, 1956), part I, ch.2.

————. "As I See It: Changes In European Consciousness." European Service General News Talk (22 September 1952).

————. "Easter Sunday." *Life of the Spirit* 7, no. 82 (April 1953): 443–48.

————. "The Impact of Eastern Wisdom on the West." *Blackfriars* 34, no. 400/401 (July/August 1953): 329–33. This was originally broadcast on the BBC Overseas 'London Calling Asia' Service, 21 March 1953.

————. "Religious Toleration." *Commonweal* 58, no. 22 (4 September 1953): 531–34. This was originally given as a talk for the BBC.

————. "Can A Psychologist Be Religious?" *Commonweal* 58, no. 22 (4 September 1953): 531–34. This was originally given as a German broadcast on 8 June 1953. See "Can A Psychologist Be Religious?" English transcript of German broadcast in *E. P. O. P Archives* (bibliog. 2.1)

————. "Review of Igor Caruso's *Psychoanalyse ünd Synthese der Existenz.*" *Dominican Studies* 6 (1953): 223–25

————. "Review of *Eranos Jahrbuch* Band 21, 1952." *Dominican Studies* 6 (1953): 225–27.

————. "Review of *Tolérance et Communauté Hunaine: Chrétiens dans un monde divisé.*" *Dominican Studies* 6 (1953): 227–28.

————. "Review of *The Principal Upanishads* and Jung's *Psychological Reflections.*" *Blackfriars* 35, no. 406 (January 1954): 31–33.

————. "Review of C. G. Jung's *Two Essays on Analytical Psychology* (CW v.7), *Psychology and Alchemy* (CW v.12), and *Von Den Wurzein des Bewusstseins*; and Progoff's *Jung's Psychology and its Social Meaning.*" *Blackfriars* 35, no. 408 (March 1954): 125–27.

————. "Anathema-Maranatha: Love and Wrath in St. Paul." In De Jesus-Marie, B., ed. *Love and Violence*. London: Sheed and Ward, 1954.

————. "Incarnations and the Incarnation: An Essay in the Theological History of Religion." *Dominican Studies* 7 (1954): 1–21. This article was originally delivered as a lecture to the Oxford University Society for the Study of Religion. Also published in White, *God the Unknown* (bibliog. 1.4, 1956), part II, ch.1, as "Incarnations and the Incarnation."

————. "Review of Watts' *Myth and Ritual in Christianity*; R. C. Zaehner's *Foolishness to Greeks*; and Bouquet's *Sacred Books of the World*." *Blackfriars* 35, no. 412/413 (July/August 1954): 331–33.

————. "Jung on Job." *Blackfriars* 36, no. 420 (March 1955): 52–60; also in *La Vie Spirituelle*, Supplement no. 9, 1956. A revised version of this review appeared in Appendix V of White, *Soul and Psyche* (bibliog. 1.4, 1960).

————. "Charles Gustave Jung." *Time and Tide, The Independent Weekly*, Special Issue: Jung at Eighty, 36 (23 July 1955).

————. "Kinds of Opposites." *Studien Zur Analytischen Psychologie C. G. Jungs Fetschrift zum 80. Geburtstag von C. G. Jung. Band 1*: "Beiträge aus Theorie und Praxis." Zurich: Rascher Verlag (1955): 141–50. This was originally delivered as a lecture in Zurich in 1955 and later in San Francisco in 1956. A revised and condensed version of this article is found in the Blackfriars edition of the *Summa Theologiae*, of which White was an editor. See *Summa Theologiae*, Ia. 48. 1.

————. "Two Theologians on Jung's Psychology." *Blackfriars* 36, no. 427 (October 1955): 382–88.

————. *God the Unknown*. London: Harvill, 1956.

————. "Review of Braceland, Francis, ed., *Faith, Reason and Modern Psychiatry: Sources for a Synthesis* (New York 1956)." *Blackfriars* 37, no. 431 (February 1956): 82–83.

————. "Review of C. G. Jung and W. Pauli's *The Interpretation of Nature and the Psyche*." *Blackfriars* 37, no. 431 (February 1956): 83–84.

————. "Guilt: Theological and Psychological." In Mairet, ed. *Christian Essays in Psychiatry* (bibliog. 1.1). An adapted version of this chapter was given as a lecture to the Society for the Study of Theology at Cambridge on April 3, 1957.

————. "Review of Goldbrunner's *Individuation: A Study of the Depth Psychology of Carl Gustav Jung*." *Blackfriars* 37, no. 440 (November 1956): 501–02.

————. "Review of *Eranos Jahrbuch* Band 24, 1955." *Blackfriars* 38, no. 443 (February 1957): 81–83.

————. "Review of Tillich's *Biblical Religion and the Search for Ultimate Reality* and Robinson's *Christ and Conscience*." *Blackfriars* 38, no. 444 (March 1957):137–38.

————. "The All Sufficient Sacrifice: Sidelights from Psychology and Anthropology." *Life of the Spirit* 11, no. 132 (June 1957): 537–48. Also published as an appendix to White, *Soul and Psyche* (bibliog. 1.4) as

"Sidelights on The Theology of the Mass from Psychology and Comparative Religion", 248–57.

———. "Mysticism and Mysticism." *Blackfriars* 38, no. 440/441 (July/August 1957): 301–10.

———. "The Knowledge of God." *The Downside Review* 76, no. 242 (January 1958): 41–53.

———. "Critical Notice on *Religion and the Psychology of Jung* by Raymond Hostie, SJ." *Journal of Analytical Psychology* 3, no. 1 (January 1958): 59–64.

———. "Review of Ryder Smith's *The Bible Doctrine of Grace*; and Pettazzoni's *The All-Knowing God*." *Blackfriars* 39, no. 456 (March 1958): 135–36.

———. "Dogma and Mental Health." *Life of the Spirit* 12, no. 142 (April, 1958): 436–42. The manuscript for this paper, written in English and Spanish is in *E.P.O.P. Archives* (bibliog. 2.1). White first presented this paper at the seventh Catholic International Congress of Psychotherapists and Clinical Psychology in Madrid in September of 1957. The article later appeared in *Conducta religiosa y salud mental.* VII congresso internacional de psicoterapia y psicologia clinica. Madrid, 10-15.9.1957. Barcelona: Antibioticos, S.A. (1959): 99–105.

———. "Holy Teaching: The Idea of Theology According to St. Thomas Aquinas." *Aquinas Paper No.33*, 1958. Oxford: Blackfriars Publications, 1958.

———. "Review of Jung on Religion." *National Review: A Weekly Journal of Opinion* (19 April 1958): 374–75.

———. "The Church Unity Octave." *Life of the Spirit* 13, no. 151 (January 1959): 291–99.

———. "Review of C. G. Jung's Psychology and Religion." *Journal of Analytical Psychology* 4, no. 1 (January 1959): 73–78.

———. "Some Recent Studies in Archetypology." *Blackfriars* 40, no. 470 (May 1959): 216–19.

———. "Review of Jung's *The Archetypes and the Collective Unconscious* and *Aion: Researches into the Phenomenology of the Self*; Jacobi's *Complex, Archetype, Symbol in the Psychology of C. G. Jung*; and Philp's *Jung and the Problem of Evil*." *Blackfriars* 41, no. 478 (January/February 1960): 40–41.

———. *Soul and Psyche: An Enquiry into the Relationship of Psychiatry and Religion*. London: Collins and Harvill, 1960.

———. "Theological Reflections." *Journal of Analytical Psychology* 5, no. 2 (July 1960): 147–54.

———. *God and the Unconscious*. With a foreword by C. G. Jung and an appendix by Gebhard Frei. Cleveland, OH: Meridian Books, 1961. Also see bibliog. 1.4, 1952 and bibliog. 1.4, 1982.

———. "Good and Evil." *Harvest: Journal for Jungian Studies* 12 (1966): 16–34.

―――. *God and the Unconscious*. With a foreword by C. G. Jung and an introduction by William Everson. Dallas, TX: Spring Publications, 1982. Also see bibliog. 1.4, 1952 and bibliog. 1.4, 1961.

1.5   Letters Referring to Victor White, O. P.

Jung, C. G. "Letter to Werner Niederer," 23 June 1947.

―――. "Letter to Gebhard Frei," 13 January 1948.

―――. "Letter to Barbara Robb," 19ᵗʰ November 1952.

―――. "Letter to R. J. Zwi Werblosky," 21 May 1953.

―――. "Letter to Aniela Jaffé," 6 April 1954.

―――. "Letter to Dr. E. V. Tenney," 23 February 1955.

―――. "Letter to Sylvester Schoening," 24 March 1955.

―――. "Letter to Mother Prioress," September 1959.

―――. "Letter to Mother Prioress," 6 February 1960.

―――. "Letter to Mother Prioress," 26 March 1960.

―――. "Letter to Mother Prioress," 29 April 1960.

―――. "Letter to Mrs. Ginsberg," 3 June 1960.

―――. "Letter to Mother Prioress," 12 August 1960.

―――. "Letter to Fr. Witcutt," 24 August 1960.

―――. "Letter to Mother Prioress," 19 October 1960.

Unpublished Works

2.1   Works by Victor White, O. P.

These unpublished works are in the *Archives of the English Province of the Order of Preachers* (referred to in the notes as the *E. P. O. P. Archives*). Since many of the works are impossible to date, they are listed here in alphabetical order by title—dates are given when possible.

White, Victor, O. P. "Analytical Psychology and Religion." Notes to Oxford University lecture (Trinity 1951).

―――. "Autobiography." There are only a couple of pages of what appears to be an aborted autobiography of Victor White.

―――. "Can A Psychologist Be Religious?" English transcript of German broadcast (8 June 1953).

―――. "Catholic Belief and Practice." Manuscript (1947–49?).

―――. "Christian Doctrine and Practice in the Light of Analytical Psychology." Lecture to Oxford University (Trinity 1950).

————. "Christian Life in the World Today." Rugby (15 May 1943).

————. "Christianity and the Unconscious." Leeds University.

————. "Diaries." (1945–59). These diaries contain details of White's day to day appointments, lists of people for whom he prayed, and occasional personal reflections.

————. "Does Praying Get Us Anything?" (February 1942).

————. "Does Praying Get Us Anywhere?" (February 1942).

————. "Dogma and Mental Health" Manuscript of lecture in English and Spanish.

————. "Drawings." A collection of White's drawings and mandalas.

————. "Faith and Creeds."(1952).

————. "Faith, Creeds and Theology." Zurich lectures (1953). See also White. Zurich Lectures (bibliog. 2.1).

————. "The Foundations of the Theology of Prayer." Lecture to the Studium (1929).

————. "Freud, Jung and God." (February 1957).

————. "Freud's Critique of Religion." Leeds University.

————. "Gnosticism and Jung." (1942).

————. "God and the Unconscious." Book manuscript in English. Chapters 1, 3 and 6 are also translated into French and German.

————. "Good and Bad." Zurich (1953).

————. "Good and Evil." Manuscript (1953). Also published posthumously. See bibliog. 1.4, 1966.

————. "Good Friday." Transcript of European Service General News Talk

————. "Guilt." Lecture at Spode Ecumenical Conference (1957–58).

————. "Guilt, Devils and Complexes." Stockholm (16–17 February 1957). Part of this lecture ("Devils and Complexes") was read to the Aquinas Society of Oxford and London in 1950 and 1952. This would later be adapted and written as ch. 10 of *God and the Unconscious* (bibliog. 1.4)

————. "Holy Teaching: The Function of Theology According to St. Thomas Aquinas." 29-page manuscript. Later published by Blackfriars Publications (bibliog. 1.1).

————. "The Impact of Eastern Wisdom on the West." Transcript of BBC Overseas Broadcast (21 March 1953).

————. "The Incarnation: One Person Two Natures." Zurich lectures (1953). See also White. Zurich Lectures (bibliog. 2.1).

————. "An Inquiry into the Philosophical Foundations of C. G. Jung." Manuscript.

————. "An Inquiry into the Relationship between Medical and Pastoral Functions in the Prevention and Treatment of Emotional Maladjustment." Manuscript.

————. "Job Review." Manuscript.

————. "Jung and Religion Seminars." University of Chicago (1956).

————. "Jung on Reductive Analysis." Leeds University.

————. "The Jungian Approach to Religion." Coventry (31 May 1957).

————. "Jung's Psychology." Lecture presented at Oxford (Trinity 1951).

————. "Lecture to the Guild of Pastoral Psychology." Cambridge (1952).

————. "Lecture to Analytical Psychology Club and Society of Analytical Psychologists, London." 21 January 1960. This would later be published as "Theological Reflections." (bibliog. 1.4)

————. "Man's Need for Religion." Vallejo Lecture.

————. *Noctuary: Diary of Dreams* (2 October 1944–1 September 1945; 2 September 1945–22 February 1946; 22 February–24 March 1948; 12 March 1953–2 February 1959; 23 August 1954–20 October 1954; and 30 December 1957–14 January 1959).

————. *Notes from Analyses* (1957–1959). These are White's notes from analyses at the More Clinic. The More Clinic was founded in 1954 and was located at 14 Ely Place London EC 1. It was staffed by priests, doctors and analysts, including Fr. Victor White, O.P.

————. "The Occult." Lecture to London Wiseman Society (1952).

————. "On Searching Into God." Manuscript.

————. "On Thomas and Platonic Ideas." presented to Aquinas Society London (5 April 1938). White developed this article in 1941 in an article, "The Platonic Tradition in St. Thomas Aquinas" (bibliog. 1.4, 1941), also printed in White, *God the Unknown* (bibliog. 1.4, 1956).

————. "Orthodoxy and Humanism." Manuscript.

————. "The Philosophical Foundations for Jung's Psychology."

————. "Platonism of St. Thomas Aquinas: Outline of Thomist Exemplarism." 32,000 words, 70-page unfinished manuscript.

————. "The Predicament."

————. "The Problem of the Catholic Patient." London Club of Analytical Psychology (1947).

————. "Problems Arising From *Answer to Job*." Manuscript (10 May 1955).

————. "Psychiatry and Religion." Leeds, San Jose and St. Bonaventure Colleges, California.

————. "The Psychology of Guilt and Forgiveness." Society for the Study of Theology, Cambridge (3 April 1957).

————. "Religion and Psychology." Lecture to William Temple and Fisher Societies Cambridge (January 1958).

————. "Religious Toleration." Transcript of talk given for the third in a series of talks for the BBC, 1953.

————. "Revelation and Faith." Lecture to the Spode Ecumenical Conference (1957).

———. "St. Albert's Lectures: Theology and Psychology; The Unconscious: Directions and Functions; Signs and Symbols; Trinity and Incarnation." California (1955).

———. "Science and Thomism." Manuscript.

———. "Signs and Symbols." St. Albert's lectures, California (1955). See also White. St. Albert's Lectures (bibliog. 2.1).

———. "Sin Original and Actual." Zurich lectures (1953). See also White. Zurich Lectures (bibliog. 2.1).

———. "Sobornost paper on the Mystical Body" (1942). Lecture to the Orthodox and Anglican Fellowship of SS. Alban and Sergius in Oxford. Later adapted and published as "The Church of the Body of Christ." (bibliog.1.4, 1942) and reprinted in White, *God the Unknown* (bibliog. 1.4, 1956), part II, ch.5, as "Western and Eastern Theology of Grace and Nature."

———. "The Symbol, Archetype, Religion and the god-image." Oxford Lecture 8.

———. "Theological Truth and the Psychology of the Unconscious." Lectures.

———. "Theology and Psychology." St. Albert's lectures, California (1954-55). See also White. St. Albert's Lectures (bibliog. 2.1).

———. "Thomas as Teacher." The London Summa lectures.

———. "Thomism." Manuscript for Chambers Encyclopaedia.

———. "Thomist Psychology." Manuscript.

———. "Transubstatiation." Lecture to Spode Ecumenical Conference (1958).

———. "Trinity and Incarnation." St. Albert's lectures, California (1955). See also White. St. Albert's Lectures (bibliog. 2.1).

———. "Trinity: Three Persons One Nature." Zurich lectures (1953). See also White. Zurich Lectures (bibliog. 2.1).

———. "When is a Christian a Socialist?" (February 1942).

———. "The Unconscious and God." Cambridge. This would be adapted to ch.3 of *God and the Unconscious* (bibliog. 1.4)

———. "The Unconscious: Directions and Functions." St. Albert's lectures, California (1955). See also White. St. Albert's Lectures (bibliog. 2.1).

———. "Zurich Lectures: Faith, Creeds and Theology; Trinity: Three Persons One Nature; The Incarnation: One Person Two Natures; Sin Original and Actual." (1953).

2.2   Letters from Victor White, O. P.

Copies of these letters are in the *Archives of the English Province of the Order of Preachers* (referred to in the notes as the *E. P. O. P. Archives*).

White, Victor, O. P. "Letter to John Layard," 19 September 1940.

———. "Letter to John Layard," 22 September 1940.

———. "Letter to John Layard," 4–7 November 1940.

———. "Letter to John Layard," 20 November 1940.

———. "Letter to John Layard," 5 December 1940.

———. "Letter to John Layard," 10 December 1940.

———. "Letter to John Layard," 29, 30 December 1940.

———. "Letter to John Layard," 3 January 1941.

———. "Letter to John Layard," 12 January 1941.

———. "Letter to Carl Gustav Jung," 3 August 1945.

———. "Letter to Carl Gustav Jung," 9 October 1945.

———. "Letter to Carl Gustav Jung," 14 October 1945.

———. "Letter to Carl Gustav Jung," 23 October 1945.

———. "Letter to Carl Gustav Jung," 16 November 1945.

———. "Letter to Carl Gustav Jung," 7 February 1946.

———. "Letter to Carl Gustav Jung," 1 April 1946.

———. "Letter to Carl Gustav Jung," Easter Sunday 1946.

———. "Letter to Carl Gustav Jung," 23 June 1946.

———. "Letter to Carl Gustav Jung," 27 August 1946.

———. "Letter to Carl Gustav Jung," 31 August 1946.

———. "Letter to Carl Gustav Jung," 13 October 1946

———. "Letter to Miss Schmid (C. G. Jung's secretary)," 29 October 1946.

———. "Letter to Carl Gustav Jung," 11 December 1946.

———. "Letter to Carl Gustav Jung," 31 December 1946.

———. "Letter to Carl Gustav Jung," 19 January 1947.

———. "Letter to Carl Gustav Jung," 4 February 1947.

———. "Letter to Carl Gustav Jung," 8 March 1947.

———. "Letter to Carl Gustav Jung," 2 May 1947.

———. "Letter to Carl Gustav Jung," 2 June 1947.

———. "Letter to Carl Gustav Jung," 16 June 1947.

———. "Letter to Carl Gustav Jung," 14 September 1947.

———. "Letter to Carl Gustav Jung," 23 October 1947.

———. "Letter to Carl Gustav Jung," 27 December 1947.

———. "Letter to Carl Gustav Jung," 3 January 1948.

———. "Letter to Carl Gustav Jung," 1 June 1948.

———. "Letter to Carl Gustav Jung," 6 August 1948.

———. "Letter to Carl Gustav Jung," 5 May 1949.

———. "Postcard to Carl Gustav Jung," May 1949.

———. "Letter to Carl Gustav Jung," 19 May 1949.

———. "Postcard to Carl Gustav Jung," 30 May 1949.

———. "Letter to Carl Gustav Jung," 30 June 1949.

——. "Letter to Carl Gustav Jung," 10 February 1950.

——. "Letter to Carl Gustav Jung," 4 May 1950.

——. "Letter to Carl Gustav Jung," 18 May 1950.

——. "Letter to Carl Gustav Jung," 20 June 1950.

——. "Letter to Carl Gustav Jung," 7 July 1950.

——. "Letter to Carl Gustav Jung," 10 July 1950.

——. "Letter to Carl Gustav Jung," 17 July 1950.

——. "Postcard to Carl Gustav Jung," 20 July 1950.

——. "Letter to Carl Gustav Jung," 3 December 1950.

——. "Letter to Carl Gustav Jung," 6 September 1951.

——. "Postcard to Carl Gustav Jung," 3 October 1951.

——. "Letter to Carl Gustav Jung," 7 October 1951.

——. "Letter to Carl Gustav Jung," 23 October 1951.

——. "Letter to Carl Gustav Jung," 21 February 1952.

——. "Letter to Carl Gustav Jung," 25 March 1952.

——. "Letter to Carl Gustav Jung," 30 March 1952.

——. "Letter to Carl Gustav Jung," 5 April 1952.

——. "Letter to Carl Gustav Jung," 20 April 1952.

——. "Letter to Carl Gustav Jung," 13 May 1952.

——. "Letter to Carl Gustav Jung," 25 June 1952.

——. "Letter to Carl Gustav Jung," 9 July 1952.

——. "Letter to Carl Gustav Jung," 10 August 1952.

——. "Letter to Carl Gustav Jung," 2 April 1953.

——. "Letter to Carl Gustav Jung," 22 June 1953.

——. "Letter to Carl Gustav Jung," 15 September 1953.

——. "Letter to Carl Gustav Jung," 8 November 1953.

——. "Letter to Carl Gustav Jung," 29 November 1953.

——. "Telegram to Carl Gustav Jung," 4 January 1954.

——. "Letter to Carl Gustav Jung," 4 March 1954.

——. "Letter to Carl Gustav Jung," 15 May 1954.

——. "Letter to Carl Gustav Jung," 25 September 1954.

——. "Letter to Carl Gustav Jung," 8 January 1955.

——. "Letter to Carl Gustav Jung," 17 March 1955.

——. "Letter to Carl Gustav Jung," 6 May 1955.

——. "Letter to Carl Gustav Jung," 10 May 1955.

——. "Letter to Carl Gustav Jung," 21 May 1955.

——. "Letter to Carl Gustav Jung," 25 August 1956.

——. "Letter to Hilary Carpenter, O. P.," 11 August 1957.

————. "Letter to Mrs. Ginsberg," 25 September 1957.

————. "Letter to Carl Gustav Jung," 1 June 1958.

————. "Letter to Mrs. Ginsberg," 11 June 1959.

————. "Letter to Mrs. Ginsberg," 22 June 1959.

————. "Letter to Mrs. Ginsberg," 19 July 1959.

————. "Letter to Carl Gustav Jung," 26 July 1958.

————. "Letter to Carl Gustav Jung," 18 October 1959.

————. "Letter to Mrs. Ginsberg," 28 October 1959.

————. "Letter to Mrs. Ginsberg," 8 November 1959.

————. "Letter to Carl Gustav Jung," 18 March 1960.

————. "Letter to Carl Gustav Jung," 28 March 1960.

————. "Letter to Carl Gustav Jung," 6 May 1960.

————. "Letter to Carl Gustav Jung" (dictated to Mrs. Ginsberg), 8 May 1960.

2.3 Letters to Victor White, O. P.

These letters are in the *Archives of the English Province of the Order of Preachers* (referred to in the notes as the *E. P. O. P. Archives*).

Adler, Gerhard. "Letter to Victor White," 12 July 1942.

————. "Letter to Victor White," 18 November 1944.

Atkinson, Aelwin Tindal, O. P. "Letter to Victor White," 12 August 1954.

Browne, Michael, O. P. "Letter to Victor White," 23 July 1957.

De Lubac, Henri. "Letter to Victor White," 5 April 1949.

————. "Letter to Victor White," 22 April 1949.

Department of Theology, University of Birmingham. "Letter to Victor White," 5 June 1958.

————."Letter to Victor White," 10 December 1958.

Elkisch, Dr. "Letter to Victor White," 5 October 1959.

Fordham, Michael. "Letter to Victor White," 14 March 1958.

————. "Letter to Victor White," 22 December 1959.

Frayn, R. Scott. "Letter to Victor White," 29 September 1942.

Jacobi, Jolande. "Letter to Victor White," 27 July 1957.

Lampe, G. H. "Letter to Victor White," 17 April 1958.

Léonard, Augustin, O. P. "Letter to Victor White," 6 May 1958.

Maritain, Jacques. "Letter to Victor White," 10 September 1948.

O'Driscoll, Benet, O. P. "Letter to Victor White," 10 September 1942.

St. John, Henry, O. P. "Letter to Victor White," 15 August 1959.

White, Antonia. "Letter to Victor White," 21 November 1947.

2.4 Letters Referring to Victor White, O. P.

These letters are in the Archives of the English Province of the Order of Preachers (referred to in the notes as the *E. P. O. P. Archives*).

Adler, Gerhard. "Letter to Fr. Kenelm Foster, O. P."

Anderson, Dr. "Letter to Whom it May Concern," 8 April 1960.

Gilby, Thomas, O. P. "Letter to Mrs. Catherine Ginsberg," 14 July 1960.

———. "Letter to Mrs. Catherine Ginsberg," 18 July 1960.

———. "Letter to Mrs. Catherine Ginsberg," 25 July 1960.

Ginsberg, Mrs. Catherine. "Letter to Thomas Gilby, O. P.," 15 July 1960.

———. "Letter to Thomas Gilby, O. P.," 21 July 1960.

———. "Letter to Dr. Bernard Towers," 15 August 1960.

———. "Letter to Thomas Gilby, O. P.," 26 August 1960.

Kay, R. G., Medical Registrar. "Letter to Dr. Anderson," 11 March 1960.

Lewis, Eve. "Letter to Mrs. Catherine Ginsberg," 24 July 1960.

Mother Michael of the Blessed Trinity. "Letter to C. G. Jung," 22 May 1960.

———. "Letter to Catherine Ginsberg," 31 May 1960.

Pizzardo, E. of the *Suprema Sacra Congregazione del Santo Offizio* "Letter to Michael Browne, O. P.," 10 December 1957.

Towers, Bernard. "Letter to Mrs. Catherine Ginsberg," 10 August 1960.

Weatherhead, Benet, O. P. "Letter to Mrs. Catherine Ginsberg," 16 October 1960.

2.5 Interviews and Correspondence

Interviews with Fr. Bede Bailey, O. P., Archivist for the *English Dominican Province*, 29–30 January 1996, 22 August 1996, and 21–24 April 1999.

Private written correspondence from Fr. Dom Cuthbert Brogan, O. S. B., Prior of St Michael's Abbey, Farnborough, July 1996.

Private written correspondence from Fr. Bede Bailey, O. P. (born 6 March 1917, professed 30 September 1936), 2 April 1998, and 27 April 1999.

Private written correspondence from Adrian Cunningham, University of Lancaster, February 1996, May 2003, August 2005.

Private written correspondence from the late Fr. Adrian Dowling, O. P. (born 14 April 1924, professed 29 September 1942), August 1996.

Conversation with John Giannini, formerly of the Order of Preachers, Oakland, CA (now at C. G. Jung Institute, Chicago), 3 November 2005.

Private written correspondence from Fr. Edmund Hill, O. P. (born 23 July 1923, professed 24 September 1949), 16 August 1996.

Interview with the late Br. Kevin Lloyd, O. P. (born 6 April 1913, professed 11 December 1936), 15 July 1996.

Conversations with the late Herbert McCabe, O. P., 1996–99.

Interview with Timothy McDermott, formerly of the Order of Preachers, November 1996.

Private written correspondence from the late Fr. Gerard Meath, O. P. (born 14 May 1914, professed 28 September 1931), 17 September 1996.

Private written correspondence from the late Fr. Stanislaus Parker, O. P. (born 18 April 1918, professed 21 May 1946), 16 August 1996.

Interview with the late Fr. Matthew Rigney, O. P. (born 23 April 1913, professed 28 September 1933), 16 July 1996.

Interview with Fr. Columba Ryan, O. P. (born 13 January 1916, professed 30 September 1936), September 1996.

Private written correspondence from Douglas W. Smith, distant relative of Victor White, O. P., 26 March 1996.

Private written correspondence from David White, Rouge Croix Pursuivant, the College of Arms, and third cousin twice removed of Victor White, O. P., 18 April 1999.

INDEX